THE GENESIS OF MISSOURI

THE GENESIS
OF MISSOURI

From Wilderness Outpost to Statehood

WILLIAM E. FOLEY

UNIVERSITY OF MISSOURI PRESS
Columbia and London

Library of Congress Cataloging-in-Publication Data

Foley, William E., 1938–
    The genesis of Missouri : from wilderness outpost to statehood /
William E. Foley.
        p.   cm.
    Includes bibliographical references.
    ISBN 0-8262-0724-3 (alk. paper)
    ISBN 0-8262-0727-8 (pbk.)
    1. Missouri—History.   I. Title.
F466.F64   1989
977.8—dc20   89–4872
                                                    CIP

Designer: Barbara J. King
Typesetter: Connell-Zeko Type & Graphics
Printer: Thomson-Shore, Inc.
Binder: Thomson-Shore, Inc.
Type face: Palatino

5   4   3   2   1   94   93   92   91   90   89

In Memory of **Lewis Atherton**
and for **Perry McCandless**

CONTENTS

PREFACE

In an essay in the *William and Mary Quarterly*, Francis Jennings chided colonial historians for doing what Frederick Jackson Turner did—landing upon the Atlantic shore and moving west. After reminding his colleagues that the United States has a Gulf shore, a Pacific shore, an Arctic shore, and the shores of the St. Lawrence, the Great Lakes, and the Mississippi, all of which were used by European colonizers, he aptly noted, "St. Louis already had a colonial history when the covered wagons rolled in to start their long journey to Oregon. Detroit and Chicago had long been going concerns when the Yankees descended to remake them in the East's image. What we need is the colonial history of North America."[1]

The colonial and territorial history of Missouri is a part of that larger story. From earliest times, Missouri's abundant natural resources and its location at the confluence of North America's great central river system made it an inviting locale for human habitation. Successive generations of the continent's original inhabitants, the Indians, took advantage of the region's accessibility and its varied animal and plant life. Centuries later, invading Europeans of different nationalities, with assistance from the Africans they brought with them, competed alternately with the territory's Indian occupants and among themselves for the right to control the valuable piece of real estate that is now called Missouri. But more than land and resources were at stake; it was in truth a struggle to determine the region's cultural identity. The story of the mingling and clashing of these diverse cultures—Indian, French, African, Spanish, and Anglo-American—in a virgin land rich in material resources and physical beauty is an extraordinary tale. When Missouri became the twenty-fourth state in the American Union in 1821, it was already, as Jennings suggested, heir to a rich and variegated historical legacy.

Early in the present century, Missouri entrepreneur-turned-historian Louis Houck recognized the importance of Missouri's prestatehood story. His three-volume history of that era remains a storehouse of useful information, but despite its value as a reference work, the long-out-of-print study is dated and reflects many biases of an earlier day. The present volume, which is intended as much for general readers as for specialists in the field, is designed to provide a comprehensive, modern account of Missouri's colonial and territorial periods. I have chosen to omit the prehistoric era from this work; much of that story has already been told in Carl Chapman's two-volume *Archaeology of Missouri*.

Although certain sections of this work draw upon my earlier study published by the University of Missouri Press as Volume 1 of the Sesquicentennial Edition of *A History of Missouri*, this is a different book with a much greater emphasis on people and places, mirroring the newer themes and trends in historical research and writing.[2] It is based upon my own research in the manuscript and printed sources, but it also makes use of the growing body of local, state, and regional scholarship. In addition to Houck's pioneering work, I am especially indebted to studies of Abraham P. Nasatir and John Francis McDermott. Carl Ekberg's prize-winning account of colonial Ste. Genevieve and the important work conducted under the auspices of the University of Missouri's interdisciplinary Ste. Genevieve project and Southwest Missouri State University's Center for Ozarks Studies have been particularly valuable in the preparation of this volume, as have numerous other works cited in the notes.

I appreciate the help provided by the directors and staffs of the various libraries and historical repositories I have visited, and my special thanks go to James W. Goodrich, R. Douglas Hurt, and Fae Sotham of the State Historical Society of Missouri; Robert R. Archibald, Kenneth Winn, Peter Michel, Katherine Corbett, Mary Seematter, and Duane Sneddeker of the Missouri Historical Society; Gary Kremer and his predecessor, Gary Beahan, of the Missouri State Archives; John Neal Hoover of the St. Louis Mercantile Library; Louisa Bowen and John Abbott of the Lovejoy Library at Southern Illinois University at Edwardsville; Nancy Littlejohn, Linda Medaris, and Naomi Williamson of the Ward Edwards Library at Central Missouri State University; and Lucille Mock of the Trails Regional Library in Warrensburg. Andrew Yinger assisted with the compilation of the bibliographic citations, and Ruth Hirner, secretary of the CMSU Department of History and Anthropology, frequently lent a helping hand.

Perry McCandless, Guy Griggs, Jim Goodrich, Lynn Morrow, and Walter Schroeder read the manuscript and provided valuable suggestions. Their perceptive comments and wise counsel helped make this a better book, and for that I am very grateful. Schroeder also designed and drew the maps. James M. Denny of the Missouri Department of Natural Resources, Patsy Luebbert of the Missouri State Archives, Michealle Baird Mitchener of the Jackson County Parks and Recreation Department, and Norbury Wayman all offered their good services in locating illustrative materials. The dedication is an inadequate expression of my indebtedness to two illustrious mentors who taught by example and personified the historical profession at its best. As always, Martha, Laura, and David indulged my preoccupation with the project and provided their ongoing support in untold ways.

I also wish to acknowledge Central Missouri State University for a sabbatical leave that enabled me to complete the early phases of research and writing, and the CMSU College of Arts and Sciences for a Research Professorship that provided released time to see the manuscript through the final stages of publication and a stipend to help underwrite the acquisition of maps and illustrative materials.

THE GENESIS OF MISSOURI

CHAPTER ONE
EXPLORING THE
WILDERNESS

It hardly seemed an auspicious beginning as the small, seven-member French expedition departed from St. Ignace, a remote mission station near the Straits of Mackinac in present-day Michigan. The venture, under the direction of the seasoned Canadian trader Louis Jolliet and his Jesuit partner, Father Jacques Marquette, had set out in mid-May of 1673 in search of the river that the Indians referred to as the *Mississippi*, an Algonquian word meaning "the father of waters." Unbeknownst to the explorers, the stream they were seeking intersected with another great waterway to form a strategic junction in the North American heartland at the place now called Missouri. Marquette and Jolliet were not the first Europeans to reach the Mississippi, but they were the first known to have set foot on Missouri soil.

On the map he drew of the region, Father Marquette penned the word *Missouri*, a French rendition of an Algonquian term that is best translated as "those who have big canoes." He used it to locate a group of Indians residing along the lower reaches of the stream most commonly known as the Pekitanoui—the river of the muddy waters. That was what the Indians called it, but even though the French newcomers frequently mentioned the waterway's thick or muddy appearance, they chose to name it the Missouri.[1]

The French attached the borrowed Indian word *Missouri* to the river and to the Indians who resided along its banks, but they seldom used the word as a general place name. For them and for their Spanish successors, the territory encompassing the present-day state of Missouri was a part of the Illinois Country. During the eighteenth century, the term *Illinois* was applied to the lands on both sides of the Mississippi between the Ohio River and the Great Lakes, and after 1770 the territory on the west side of the Mississippi was commonly referred to as Spanish Illinois. It was also sometimes called Upper Louisiana, following the usage of the French explorer René-Robert Cavelier, sieur de la Salle, who had christened as Louisiana all the lands drained by the Mississippi. When the Americans purchased the immense trans-Mississippi tract from France in 1803, they followed that tradition and named the area north of present-day Arkansas's southern boundary the Territory of Louisiana. The name Missouri was not officially adopted until 1812, when Congress renamed the territory in order

1

to avoid confusion with the new state of Louisiana, formerly known as the Territory of Orleans.

Spanish conquistadores had penetrated portions of North America's interior more than a century before Marquette and Jolliet, but insufficient inducements for further exploration and settlement in the region kept them away from modern-day Missouri. Hernando de Soto explored the lower Mississippi in 1541 while searching for new sources of riches and wealth, but in all likelihood the veteran of Spain's Peruvian conquest never ventured farther north than Arkansas.[2] A similar treasure-hunting expedition, commanded by the youthful and energetic Francisco Vásquez de Coronado in 1541–1542, abandoned its search for the mythical Seven Cities of Cibola and returned to Mexico after reaching an unprosperous Indian village in what is now western Kansas. These and other dismal results confirmed the Spanish decision to concentrate colonial efforts in areas that could promise more immediate returns in the form of gold and silver mines and stable Indian populations to operate them. Mexico and Peru became focal points in the thriving Spanish colonial empire, but a century and a half following Christopher Columbus's entry into the Western Hemisphere, much of the North American continent, including Missouri, remained untraversed by Europeans.[3]

Spain successfully monopolized New World colonization until England, France, and the Netherlands became serious contenders in the race for overseas possessions and planted permanent colonies in North America at the opening of the seventeenth century. The English and Dutch colonizers confined themselves to relatively compact settlements along the Atlantic coast while French settlers, with scarcely a tenth of the numbers of their English counterparts, slowly spread into the great expanses to the west after Samuel de Champlain established France's first permanent North American settlement on the banks of the St. Lawrence at Quebec in 1608.[4]

Although France's Canadian settlements developed very slowly during the early years, French fur traders and missionaries explored the continent's immense interior, seeking contact with the Indians inhabiting those regions. Jean Baptiste Colbert, the renowned mercantilist who took charge of French colonial affairs in 1663, attempted to discourage westward expansion because he believed it would retard development in eastern Canada by draining off badly needed colonists. But Colbert's well-laid plans for controlled settlement could not stay the lure of the West, and a growing number of *coureurs de bois* slipped off into the wilderness to engage in the lucrative fur trade. The term *coureur de bois*, which applied to anyone who ventured into the wilds to traffic in furs, initially carried a pejorative connotation because of the legal sanctions against unauthorized participation in the trade.[5]

Notwithstanding Colbert's disparaging views, the West's attractions seduced some of New France's highest officials. Both the Canadian intendant Jean Talon, who was responsible for the administration of justice, colonial finances, and civil administration within the colony, and Louis de Buade, comte de Frontenac, the provincial governor, who was in charge of military matters and Indian affairs, championed western development. When Frontenac took up his duties as governor in 1672, Talon already had dispatched licensed traders to the far reaches of the Great Lakes, where, in company with Jesuit fathers, they established a string of frontier outposts. Recurring reports about the Mississippi from the interior tribes generated considerable interest among French authorities, who were eager to learn more about the waterway.[6]

Talon commissioned Jolliet to explore the unknown river in 1672, and shortly thereafter Frontenac added his endorsement. The prospect of discovering a water route to the southern or western sea and thereby providing Canada with access to a year-round warm-water port even won over the reluctant Colbert momentarily.[7] Jolliet, a native-born Canadian fluent in several Indian dialects, set out for St. Ignace bearing a commission authorizing that settlement's founder, Father Marquette, to accompany him. The French priest, who had left a teaching post in France to save the souls of North American Indians, had long wanted to move southward into the Illinois Country. As the two men eagerly awaited the beginning of the spring thaw, they solicited information from the local Indians, prepared their equipment, and packed their sparse provisions of Indian corn and smoked meat.[8]

Their journey got underway in mid-May, and by mid-June the expedition had reached the Mississippi by way of the Wisconsin and Fox rivers. As the explorers paddled downstream, they observed flocks of waterfowl and turkey, herds of grazing bison, and fish large enough to tear apart their paper-thin bark canoes. To their surprise they encountered no Indians until they left the river in present-day Iowa and followed a trail that took them to a village where they exchanged presents with a band of Peorias, some of whom were already wearing garments made of French cloth. Once they did make contact, the visiting Frenchmen found the Indians to be generous hosts who willingly shared such favorite tribal foods as boiled corn, fish, wild ox, and dog. The Europeans gladly partook of everything but the dog meat, which they discreetly declined.[9]

After resuming their voyage downriver, the French adventurers were startled to see vivid paintings of monsters staring down at them from the towering bluffs overlooking the Mississippi a short distance above the Missouri junction. The horned, red-eyed, bearded creatures with human-like facial features, scaly bodies, and long, winding fish tails were painted red, green, and black. Father Marquette recorded in his journal that while he and the others were still puzzling over those finely drawn creatures, which they doubted could have been the work of Indians, their party suddenly came upon another wonder, the turbulent Missouri junction: "I have seen nothing more dreadful. An accumulation of large and entire trees, branches, and floating islands was issuing from The mouth of The river pekitanoui, with such impetuosity that we could not without great danger risk passing through it. So great was the agitation that the water was very muddy, and could not become clear."[10]

The thundering river clearly made a lasting impression on the French travelers, who chose not to enter its churning waters.[11] Leaving that challenge for those who would follow them, they proceeded southward along their intended course. By the time the expedition reached Arkansas, it had become clear that the Mississippi did not head toward the Pacific but flowed instead into the Gulf of Mexico. Fearful they might encounter hostile Indians downriver and equally hesitant to encroach upon Spanish domains, Marquette and Jolliet decided against continuing their trip and turned back for Canada on 17 July.[12]

Following their return to the Mission of St. Francis Xavier at Green Bay in September, the trader and the priest briefly compared notes before Jolliet headed for Sault Ste. Marie. When spring arrived, he hurried off to report their findings to the authorities in Quebec. While en route, Jolliet's canoe capsized, destroying his maps and journals. Fortunately Father Marquette had retained his own papers, and they survive. To Jolliet's great disappointment, officials in the Canadian capital rejected his request for a trading concession in the Illinois Country and assigned him instead to a number of minor governmental offices. Jolliet did make trips to Hudson Bay and Labrador before he died in relative obscurity in 1700.[13] Father Marquette resumed his work among the Indians, but the rigor of wilderness living soon took its toll. In the spring of 1675, he returned briefly to the Illinois River to establish a mission, but in May, while on his way back to Mackinac, Marquette died at an isolated campsite on Lake Michigan's eastern shore.[14]

Meanwhile, Governor Frontenac took advantage of his connections at the French court to press ahead with plans for opening the West. He successfully backed a bid by his protégé the Sieur de la Salle to establish trade with Indians south and west of the Great Lakes. In return for a concession to engage in the fur trade along the Mississippi and its tributaries, La Salle promised that within five years he would, at his own expense, descend the great river to its mouth. Louis XIV and Colbert accepted the offer as an economical way of financing further French exploration. La Salle took the time to supervise the construction of several western trading posts before he finally ventured down the Mississippi in 1682. He reached the Gulf of Mexico on 9 April and marked the occasion with formal ceremonies proclaiming the Mississippi and its tributaries to be the possessions of Louis XIV, in whose honor he named the territory Louisiana.[15]

La Salle's return to Canada was anything but a triumph. He discovered that France's old antagonists, the Iroquois, were threatening the Illinois Country and in the process endangering his designs for an inland trading empire. To assist in staving off their assaults, he directed the establishment of Fort St. Louis atop Starved Rock on the Illinois River and placed it under the control of his faithful subordinate Henri de Tonti. More disturbing to La Salle than the reports of the renewed Indian problems was the news that the hostile LeFebvre de La Barre had replaced his friend and ally Frontenac as governor.[16]

With support waning in Canada for his plans to colonize Louisiana, La Salle, who was a nationalist and a dreamer with grand plans, sailed back to France, where the reception was friendlier. A recent outbreak of hostilities between France and Spain heightened interest in his scheme for establishing a French outpost at the mouth of the Mississippi. Once he had garnered the necessary backing, he set out for the New World with a small fleet and headed directly for the Gulf Coast. La Salle missed his intended destination and disembarked instead in Texas in early 1685. After wandering in the wilderness for nearly two years while searching for the Mississippi, he fell victim to a mutiny that cost him his life.[17] Despite the tragic ending to La Salle's enterprise, his discoveries had strengthened France's claim to the Mississippi valley and set the stage for a successful French occupation of the Gulf Coast thirteen years later.

A quest for economic gain through furs, precious metals, and new trade routes and a desire to bring salvation to North American "savages" had propelled France's initial westward advances. But by the dawn of the eighteenth century, the nation's growing rivalry with England increasingly dictated the terms of its American colonial policy. Imperial aims loomed ever larger as the French attempted to keep the Anglo-American colonies confined to the Atlantic seaboard. Having concluded that England's domination of North America would upset the balance of power in Europe, Louis XIV and his ministers endorsed new measures designed to secure French control over the continent's vast central region. The added Spanish threat caused by a dispute over succession rights to that country's throne further underscored the need for action to uphold France's American interests.[18]

To secure the southern flank two brothers, Pierre Le Moyne d'Iberville and Jean-Baptiste Le Moyne de Bienville, established bases on the Gulf Coast at Biloxi in 1699 and at Mobile in 1701. In the latter year Antoine de Lamothe, sieur de Cadillac, also founded Detroit in a corresponding effort to shore up French control in the north. With its limited resources, the French government counted heavily upon the support of Indian allies for holding its North American positions.[19]

That the strategy worked so well was a tribute to the French aptitude for forest diplomacy, trade, and proselytizing. A special talent for winning Indian cooperation and assistance enabled a handful of French soldiers, fur traders, and priests to retain control of large sections of North America for over 150 years. Missionaries were a key component of the successful coalition, and within that group the Jesuits were especially adept in their relations with the Indians. The Black Robes, as the native Americans called them, willingly employed the Indians' own languages and cultural symbols in their preaching.[20]

The frontier missionaries faced enormous challenges. For Europeans unaccustomed to walking long distances through trackless forests and paddling for hours in the cramped quarters of a canoe, the rigors of frontier travel were extremely taxing. Drafty, smoke-filled, and vermin-infested lodges, unpalatable food, and inclement weather often added to their discomfort. Because the acceptance of Christianity required the Indians to reject many parts of their religion and culture, they were ofttimes reluctant converts, hostile and resentful toward those who attempted to spread the message of the Christian gospel. Missouri's first resident Jesuit priest, Father Gabriel Marest, reflected on the difficulties and frustrations of his tasks in a letter to his Canadian superiors: "Our life is passed in threading dense forests, in climbing mountains, in crossing lakes and rivers in canoes, that we may overtake some poor Savage who is fleeing from us, and who we do not know how to render less savage by either our words or our attention."[21]

Father Marquette had passed by Missouri in 1673, but in the fall of 1700 Father Marest accompanied a band of Kaskaskia Indians to the west bank of the Mississippi at the mouth of the River Des Peres, just within the present southern limits of St. Louis. The Kaskaskias had abandoned their village on the Illinois River to escape harassment from westward-moving Iroquois tribes. Encouraged by reports that the Le Moyne brothers had occupied the Gulf Coast, the Kaskaskias anticipated receiving greater French protection and support at the new location.[22] Father Marest had devoted himself to mastering the languages and studying the ways of the Illinois Indians, whom he characterized as intelligent, naturally inquisitive, and able to turn a joke in an ingenious manner.[23]

At the Des Peres location the French priest directed the construction of several cabins covered with rush mats in the Indian fashion, a chapel, and a primitive fort. The following spring a number of French traders and a sizable band of Tamaroa Indians joined Father Marest and the Kaskaskias on the west bank. The influential Kaskaskia chieftain Rouensa had enticed the newcomers to abandon their settlements across the river in favor of the Des Peres site. The departure of the Tamaroas came as a blow to the Seminary Priests of the Foreign Missions, a rival religious order that had established a mission station at Cahokia in 1699 in defiance of Jesuit claims to exclusive ecclesiastical jurisdiction in the Illinois Country. The Jesuits protested the Seminary clergy's entry into the region, but church authorities in Canada dismissed the complaints and in 1702 ordered the Society of Jesus to leave the work at Cahokia in the hands of the competing priests.[24]

The Jesuit settlement known as Des Peres survived only briefly. The Kaskaskias had crossed the Mississippi hoping to escape the Iroquois, but after the move, angry Sioux bands resentful of the Kaskaskia encroachment onto their lands posed a new threat. In 1703 Father Marest and the besieged Indians at Des Peres moved farther down the Mississippi to a site on the east bank where they established the settlement of Kaskaskia. Among other things in its favor, the new village was not far from a tannery that Charles Juchereau de St. Denis had erected near the mouth of the Ohio River.[25] Following the departure of the Kaskaskias from Des Peres, the French settlers also moved away, and Missouri's first European-sponsored settlement disappeared almost as quickly as it had come into existence.

The abandonment of the village at River Des Peres did not diminish the appeal of the unknown lands on the western side of the Mississippi. Unauthorized French explorers periodically ascended the Missouri River hoping to establish commercial ties with the Spaniards in New Mexico, to look for gold and silver mines, or to engage in the lucrative Indian trade. Canadian officials attempted to restrict the traffic in furs to licensed traders known as *marchand voyageurs*, but they could not restrain the unbounded impulses of the lawless *coureurs de bois*, who continued to roam the wilderness. Although these illegal traffickers probably entered the Missouri River as early as the 1680s, their first recorded trip occurred in 1693, when two unidentified traders visited the Missouri and Osage tribes. In 1703 Iberville reported that twenty Canadians had left Cahokia and headed up the Missouri in search of a route to New Mexico, and in the following year Bienville stated that there were as many as 110 Canadians traveling in small bands and trading along the Mississippi and Missouri rivers.[26]

These itinerant traders were the advance agents of French colonization.

Their contacts with the Indians through trade and through marriage made them a connecting link between the two cultures, but many of the earliest *coureurs de bois* remain nameless wanderers who left no written accounts of their activities. Occasionally, however, as in the case of Etienne Véniard de Bourgmont, the first white man known to have explored the Missouri basin systematically, the records are more complete. At the age of nineteen, the well-born Frenchman, who seems to have been prone to youthful excess, fled to North America to avoid punishment for poaching on monastic lands. Following his arrival in Canada, Bourgmont enlisted as an ordinary soldier, rose to the rank of ensign, and eventually found himself in charge of the besieged French outpost at Detroit. When the young commandant was accused of official misconduct in 1706, he deserted his post and headed for the wilds, where he joined his mixed-blood mistress, Madame Elizabeth Techenet, and lived the life of a *coureur de bois*.[27]

Bourgmont and the other early French explorers encountered two Indian tribes residing within Missouri's present limits: the Missouri and the Osage. Father Marquette located both nations on his map, and most subsequent accounts also took note of their presence. The Missouri Indians welcomed the French sojourners to their principal village, which was nestled in a range of low broken hills overlooking the Missouri River in northern Saline County. A semisedentary people who had reached that area sometime before 1673, the Missouris were a part of the Chiwere Sioux linguistic group, along with the Ioways, Otos, and Winnebagos. They combined hunting and fishing with gardening and gathering and inhabited their permanent villages only during the spring planting and fall harvesting seasons. For most of the remainder of the year they pursued deer, buffalo, elk, and other wild game.[28]

In 1712 the Missouris traveled to Detroit to assist the French in defending that outpost against a Fox attack. During that campaign, they encountered Bourgmont, who became a friend and confidant. According to legend, the French adventurer, who had long since parted company with Madame Techenet, took a fancy to the daughter of a Missouri chieftain. Bourgmont's subsequent actions lend a ring of truth to the story. He left the Great Lakes region, went south, and made the Missouri village his base camp. In 1714, a Missouri woman there bore him a son who came to be known as the "Petit Missouri." The preceding year, the wanderlust *coureur de bois* had traveled through Illinois and lower Louisiana, living a "scandalous and criminal life" according to the Jesuit fathers at Kaskaskia. In response to complaints that he was causing trouble among the Indians, the French authorities ordered him arrested, but the directive was never carried out. It seems likely that while in lower Louisiana, Bourgmont struck a deal with Cadillac, his crafty former superior at Detroit. In return for a pardon, Bourgmont apparently volunteered to assist the French in collecting information about the unfamiliar Missouri country.[29]

Whatever the circumstances, Bourgmont was back at the Missouri village in 1714 arranging for an expedition upriver. He traveled up the Missouri at least as far as the mouth of the Platte in eastern Nebraska, and he may have continued as far as the Arikara country in South Dakota. His "Exact Description of Louisiana," a report containing his observations on the region, and a companion geographical log of the lower reaches of the Missouri titled simply "Route to Ascend the Missouri" were both based on that 1714 voyage and provide the earliest detailed information about the river and its people. Bourgmont's precise activities after that trip are unclear, but he seems to have served the French as an intelligence agent and a roving ambassador among the Indian tribes. In 1718, Bienville recommended that the king bestow on him the coveted Cross of St. Louis in recognition of his service to France. Such was the state of affairs in the North American wilds that it was possible to go from deserter to knighthood within the space of a few short years.[30]

In May 1719 the peripatetic Bourgmont joined France's Gulf force during its successful assault on the Spanish post at Pensacola. The following September he escorted a delegation of chieftains from the Illinois Country to Mobile, where all but one fell victim to disease. Bourgmont delayed his planned return to France long enough to accompany the sole surviving chief to his village and to distribute gifts atoning for the deaths of the other tribal leaders. Having made the necessary amends with his Indian friends, he sailed to France, taking along his mixed-blood Missouri son. Bourgmont had left France under a cloud in 1698, but twenty-two years later he returned triumphantly to the applause of the directors of the Company of the Indies, who saluted his discoveries, his work among the Indians, and his military feats. His timing could not have been better. Rapt French audiences caught up in the speculative mania of financier John Law's scheme for developing the Mississippi valley hung on Bourgmont's every word as he related tales of his experiences in the wilderness. The dashing soldier also had the good fortune to marry a wealthy young French widow.[31]

Missouri's other resident Indian tribe in the early eighteenth century, the Osages, played a much more important role than the Missouris in the subsequent history of the region. The Osages, who along with the Quapaws, Kansas, Omahas, and Poncas were members of the Dheghian Sioux language family, had migrated from east of the Mississippi at an unknown date, either while fleeing from Iroquois attacks or while searching for better hunting grounds. Whatever the reason for the Osage migration, the early French traders found them occupying villages adjacent to the Osage River in Vernon County and on the north bank of the Missouri River near the Missouri Indian village in Saline County.[32]

The striking physical appearance of the Osage warriors—tall and muscular, with heads shaved and faces painted—marked them as a tribe to be reckoned with. Indeed the Osages quickly took advantage of their access to firearms and other European trade goods to dominate the region between the Missouri and Arkansas rivers from the Ozark highlands onto the Great Plains. Hunting was the central feature of Osage life, but despite the tribe's preoccupation with the chase, the women cultivated crops and gathered edible wild plants to supplement and vary their diet. Such diversification afforded them a degree of security against undue deprivation in times when drought or some other natural disaster threatened one of their traditional food sources.

Like other Indian tribes, the Osages learned to exploit the seasonal diversity of their environment. For extended periods, all but the oldest residents and a few disabled or infirm individuals left their quasi-permanent villages to participate in hunting expeditions. The first of the three principal Osage hunts began in about February or March, when they searched the nearby Ozark woods and streams for bear and beaver, whose winter coats were then at their finest. In March they returned to their villages so the women could prepare the fields with their wooden-handled stone hoes for planting corn, squash, pumpkins, and beans. They sowed the corn, which was their chief crop, intermingled with the other plants to create a dense ground cover that simultaneously helped hold moisture in the soil and retard weed growth.[33]

After completing the spring planting sometime in May, the Osages abandoned their villages and headed for the plains to the west in search of deer, buffalo, and elk. Prior to the time they acquired horses and firearms, the Osages hunted on foot with bows and arrows. They employed various methods, including driving the herds into confined or restricted areas, setting fire to the prairie grasses to flush the quarry out, or stampeding the game animals off a cliff or riverbank. Deer was the most popular meat, probably because it was the easiest animal to bring down. The fresh meat that could not be consumed was smoked and dried for future use. The animal tallow and bone marrow were also preserved and saved, and the skins and hides were dressed and tanned. In late July the entire entourage again returned to their villages for the fall harvest.[34]

The Osages located their villages on a prairie or in an open clearing not far from a river. The bottomlands were fertile and more easily cultivated with hand tools than the tough prairie sod. When the French first arrived, the Osage villages probably were arranged in an organized camp circle with each clan occupying its proper place according to rank and function. They constructed their rectangular lodges, which were sometimes as much as one hundred feet long, by bending young saplings over a ridgepost to form the roof arch. Woven mats, bark, and animal skins provided the exterior covering for the framework. These dark, smoke-filled long houses accommodated ten or fifteen family members and relatives. During the coldest winter weather and during the spring, summer, and fall hunts, the Osages lived in temporary camps and occupied small and easily trans-ported wigwams covered with rush mats and animal skins.[35]

The men took advantage of the annual fall respite to recuperate from the strenuous exertions of the summer hunt. Their irregular work habits per-mitted them the luxury of this time for resting, planning, and regaling fellow tribesmen with stories of hunting prowess and military feats. It was not a similar time of leisure for the Osage women, whose waking hours were occupied harvesting and preserving crops, gathering nuts, persim-mons, and pawpaws, weaving rush mats, making the family clothing and bedding, and looking after children. In addition to their agricultural and domestic chores, Osage women also had the task of dressing and tanning the animal skins and hides. Their skills as expert skin dressers became especially important to the tribe following the opening of the fur trade with the Europeans. In recognition of their essential contributions to tribal life, Osage women were allowed to participate in the tribe's religious rituals.[36]

In late September or early October, when the fall produce had been harvested and safely stored, the tribe set out on the year's final major hunt. It lasted until November or December, depending on weather conditions and the availability of game. During the coldest months the Osages left the prairies and moved to sheltered, wooded areas where deer, small game, and firewood could be more easily obtained. The advent of the late winter hunt in February or March marked the beginning of yet another annual cycle.

The complex Osage clan structure consisted of twenty-four clans orga-nized into two grand divisions or moieties—the *Tsi-zhu* and the *Hon-ga*. The *Tsi-zhu* division was composed of nine clans and represented sky and peace, while the *Hon-ga* division with its fifteen clans symbolized earth and war. Believing that the world depended upon both earth and sky for its existence, the Osages concluded that their tribe's survival required the unity of its two great divisions. The tribe's political structure was equally compli-cated. In every village, two chieftains, each representing one of the two moieties, governed in association with an influential council, sometimes known as the Little Old Men, that was composed of representatives from each of the clans. Within this intricate structure of limited and shared political power, an Osage leader's authority was carefully circumscribed.[37]

Contact with the invading Europeans brought profound changes to Missouri's Indian peoples. The newcomers and their powerful weapons, unfamiliar animals, attractive trade goods, potent alcoholic beverages, new markets for Indian products, and devastating diseases unleashed a combination of forces destined to affect the Indian way of life for generations to come. The introduction of horses and firearms was particularly momentous. By the time French traders reached their villages, the Missouris and Osages had already acquired horses—or "mystery dogs," as the Osages called them—from tribes in contact with Spanish settlements to the southwest. The two tribes were probably furnished with their first guns by early French traders.

From the outset, relations were good between the French and the Missouri and Osage tribes. Eager to claim them as allies and trading partners, the French saw that they were supplied with firearms and trade goods in exchange for skins, furs, Indian slaves, and occasionally horses. It was a mutually profitable arrangement, but not without costs. Osage raids against Indian nations to the west for the purpose of securing horses and slaves for trading and Osage encroachment on the hunting grounds of neighboring tribes for the purpose of gaining access to new sources of furs intensified intertribal warfare and violence. Emboldened by the success of their more aggressive policies, the Osages capitalized upon their numbers, favorable location, and access to weapons and trade goods to establish themselves as the dominant force on the prairies west and south of their Missouri River villages.[38]

The shift from a subsistence economy geared only to providing essential tribal needs to a market economy capable of securing weapons, ammunition, textiles, metal tools, jewelry, and assorted adornments brought other changes in Osage life as well. The Osages had always been hunters, but their new commercialism resulted in an even greater tribal preoccupation with the chase. They extended the length of their hunting seasons, moved into ever more distant territories, and divided themselves into smaller hunting parties. All of those changes increased their vulnerability to attack. Over time the continued presence of foreign traders in the Osage villages and the growing tribal dependence on the white man's merchandise began to erode traditional Indian cultural patterns and institutions. The emphasis on hunting even altered marriage practices as Osage men began taking additional wives to handle the extra chores of cleaning and preparing the animal hides and skins. At the same time, young warriors whose hunting and raiding skills brought them wealth and prestige occasionally defied tribal elders and challenged the traditional political structure that denied them the influence they considered appropriate to their status. In one regard the Osages were especially fortunate: they escaped the worst ravages of smallpox, typhus, measles, and other diseases carried to the Americas by the Europeans. Those diseases decimated many other tribes, including the neighboring Missouris.[39]

Although *coureurs de bois* ascended the Missouri River to trade with the Indians and an occasional expedition set out in search of treasure-laden mines, French interest in Louisiana was waning. As if the province's problems were not serious enough, in 1710 the French minister of marine, the Comte de Pontchartrain, made the incompetent Lamothe Cadillac governor of Louisiana. The scheming founder of Detroit had been universally disliked in Canada, and his transfer to Louisiana was a classic example of bureaucratic ineptitude. Following his appointment to the Louisiana post, Cadillac returned to France to promote the development of the sparsely settled region he had been assigned to administer. Because it was a financial drain on the royal treasury, court officials were eager to interest private investors in the undertaking.[40]

At Cadillac's urging, Antoine Crozat, a wealthy merchant and financier, agreed in 1712 to underwrite the cost of French activity in the province. Crozat received a fifteen-year monopoly on Louisiana's trade and mining activities in return for his financial support. Crozat's grant, which did not extend to Upper Louisiana, specifically excluded the fur trade. The French entrepreneur regarded the Louisiana venture as a speculative business enterprise. Encouraged by Cadillac's exaggerated assurances, he expected to turn a handsome profit by exploiting the region's mineral resources and opening trade with the Spaniards in Mexico.[41]

Governor Cadillac returned to Louisiana in 1713 determined to make the project succeed. In response to Crozat's plea for the French government's assistance in establishing an outpost at the mouth of the Ohio River, which was aimed to counter English activity in the region, Canadian officials dispatched a small party of troops under the command of Claude-Charles Dutisné. When they found no one at the site of the proposed establishment, the soldiers from Canada proceeded to Cadillac's headquarters at Mobile. Before reaching the mouth of the Ohio, they had stopped briefly at Kaskaskia, where they were given ore samples containing silver, supposedly obtained from nearby mines. After Dutisné showed the samples to Cadillac, the avaricious governor hastily set out to find the mines, dreaming no doubt of discovering riches equal to those the Spanish conquistadores had found in Mexico and Peru. Keeping his intentions secret, the governor departed in February 1715 without bothering to inform his immediate subordinate, Bienville, of his intended destination. In Kaskaskia, Cadillac's party had its hopes dashed by learning that Dutisné's minerals had actually come from Mexico and had been given to him as a joke by the fun-loving Canadian *coureurs de bois* at that post. Whether Dutisné had been a willing accomplice or an innocent dupe in the affair remains unknown, but those involved had correctly gauged the governor's response.[42]

Despite the unhappy news, Cadillac obstinately insisted on visiting the lead mines that the Indians had long worked on the west side of the Mississippi. With a small Tamaroa Indian party guiding them, Cadillac, his son, a few leading Kaskaskians, and a crew of soldiers and laborers, including in all likelihood some black slaves, crossed the river and traveled to the mouth of Saline Creek, located on the Missouri side approximately ten miles below present-day Ste. Genevieve. They encountered several Frenchmen making salt at the Saline, and from there they followed the small stream and clearly marked Indian trails westward to the site of the Indian diggings in northern Madison County. After reaching the mines, Cadillac ordered his men to dig a trench, but when they reached a depth of seven to nine feet a rock ledge made further excavation impossible. The governor collected samples from the ore near the surface and returned to his headquarters on the Gulf. Lamothe Cadillac's quixotic expedition proved to be a bust, but the inept French official left his name as a permanent reminder of the visit. The rich lead mine he examined would ever after be known as Mine La Motte.[43]

After returning to Mobile, members of the expedition circulated reports that they had found a valuable silver mine, but when pressed for details they declined to be specific. Subsequent tests of the ore samples Cadillac brought back with him confirmed that he had been duped. Cadillac's failure to find valuable metals was only one in a series of disappointments for Crozat's venture. Trade with the Spaniards failed to materialize because of opposition from the viceroy of New Spain, and most other operations in Louisiana had proven equally unprofitable. Faced with mounting financial losses and little prospect for recouping them, Crozat ordered Cadillac's recall in October 1716. The next year he petitioned the king for release from his obligations under the charter, warning that "the establishment of a colony is like building a world, so to speak, and it takes time, patience, and enormous expenditures to succeed."[44] The government granted his request, thereby relieving him of any further responsibility for operations in Louisiana. The costly colony had once again fallen on hard times, but hopes persisted that Louisiana and the Mississippi valley would yet bring French colonizers rich returns.[45] For the moment, however, the region remained securely in the hands of its original inhabitants.

CHAPTER TWO
MISSOURI'S FRENCH FOUNDATIONS

The task of reviving France's waning fortunes in the Mississippi valley fell to the unlikely John Law, a Scottish gambler turned financier whose grandiose schemes unleashed a speculative mania subsequently known as the Mississippi Bubble. Antoine Crozat's unhappy experience had made French officials even more wary of undertaking Louisiana's development. Unwilling to commit the royal treasury's resources to the costly project, Louis XV's regency welcomed Law's offer to create a privately financed company to manage the task. In August 1717 the crown approved a charter granting Law's Company of the West a monopoly on Louisiana's trade, ownership of all mines, use of all forts, depots, and garrisons in the province, the right to import French goods into Louisiana duty free, reduced duties on goods shipped to France, control of Louisiana's commercial and Indian policies, and the right to name all officials in the province. In return for these concessions, the company promised to send six thousand white settlers and three thousand black slaves to the sparsely populated province within ten years.[1]

Law, the driving force behind this new enterprise, had fled from London to the Continent after killing a man in a duel. Once in France, the high-stakes player amassed a considerable fortune at the gaming tables and simultaneously gained acceptance in the highest circles at court. Making good use of his new connections, he persuaded the French regent, the Duke of Orleans, to endorse his plan for creating a state bank to ameliorate the nation's chronic financial problems. The bank's initial success boosted Law's standing at court and helped him secure the royal patent for the Company of the West. Shortly thereafter, the new company's directors gained the crown's approval for a measure removing the Illinois Country from the jurisdiction of Canadian officials and placing it under their control. They successfully argued that the union of the agricultural base of Louisiana with the mineral resources of Illinois would significantly enhance the commercial potential of the entire Mississippi valley.[2]

Law's intensive promotional activities generated great interest in the Mississippi project, which became entangled with the Royal Bank, also under his control. In 1719, Law consolidated the Company of the West with several other trading companies to form the Company of the Indies. Under his flashy direction the expanded enterprise attracted even more capital, as

French speculators clamored to acquire stock in the booming business venture. The Company of the West and its successor took advantage of their steadily rising fortunes to press ahead with Louisiana's development. Jean-Baptiste Le Moyne de Bienville, whom the company had designated as the provincial governor, founded New Orleans in 1718; that same year, Pierre Dugué, sieur de Boisbriant, took command in the Illinois Country, and Marc Antoine de la Loëre des Ursins began serving there as his chief clerk. The company charged the two officials with overseeing the development of French Illinois on both sides of the Mississippi, a task for which they were well prepared. Boisbriant, a Canadian who had first come to Louisiana in 1700 with his cousin Pierre Le Moyne d'Iberville, was intimately acquainted with the Illinois Indians, and Des Ursins had traveled with Cadillac from France to Louisiana in 1713 and had served as Crozat's chief agent at the mouth of the Mississippi.

Shortly after his arrival in the Illinois Country, Boisbriant directed the construction of Fort de Chartres, located eighteen miles upriver from Kaskaskia on the east bank of the Mississippi. The original wooden palisaded structure built in 1719 was the first of three forts to bear that name. A second fort was constructed in 1725–1726, and the stone fort whose remains can still be seen replaced it in the 1750s. Fort de Chartres served as governmental headquarters for the region throughout the French period.[3]

Still hoping to find mines comparable to those Spain had discovered, company officials instructed Boisbriant and Des Ursins to initiate mining operations. They led an expedition across the Mississippi and through a broad belt of forested Ozark hills to reach the mining district Cadillac had visited four years earlier. In June, Des Ursins, assisted by a mining engineer named Lochon, supervised the digging of several shafts at Mine La Motte, where they reported finding pieces of ore they erroneously believed to be silver. Because lead and silver ores were frequently found in close proximity, the French continued to hope that their diggings might uncover a rich silver lode. After investigating mining sites on both sides of the river, the Illinois authorities concluded that the mineral-rich belt located thirty or so miles west of the Mississippi in what would later be Washington, Madison, and St. Francois counties held out the greatest promise as a location for their mining and smelting operations.[4]

The Company of the Indies named Philippe Renault, the son of a wealthy French iron master who managed the king's foundries, to take charge of its mining activities. He arrived in New Orleans in 1720 and proceeded immediately upriver to inspect the mines in the Illinois Country. Shortly after reaching Fort de Chartres, Renault went to the Missouri side, where he discovered a rich vein of lead on the Mineral Fork of the Big River in an area now known as Old Mines in Washington County. He supervised diggings there and at Mine La Motte, but since mining was a seasonal activity that was mostly undertaken from April until harvest time in midsummer and again from late August until early December, he resided during the remaining months at the permanent headquarters he maintained across the river at St. Philippe, several miles north of Fort de Chartres. In 1723 Boisbriant formally granted Renault land concessions at Old Mines, Mine La Motte, and St. Philippe.[5]

Mining operations were understandably primitive. The miners found ore by plunging probes four to five feet long into the earth. When they struck a vein, they dug a large hole and extracted ore from it until they encountered rock or water or until the pit became too deep for throwing out the heavy chunks of ore. At that point, they simply moved to a new site and repeated the process.

Digging was only the first phase in mining operations. When a sufficient quantity of ore had been extracted, attention turned to smelting. That required felling trees and dressing large quantities of timber and firewood, followed by the preparation of a small excavation in the ground that was lined with logs. The miners filled the underground wooden box with ore and then covered it with stacks of wood. As soon as that was done, the logs were ignited from underneath and the melted lead was trapped in the pit. Sometimes it required two or three firings to complete the process. The lead was then collected from the bottom of the excavation, remelted, and shaped into bars weighing between sixty and eighty pounds. The lead bars were transported on horseback through the rugged terrain of the mining country to the Mississippi and by river to Kaskaskia.[6] Since work at the mines was seasonal, once the yearly production had been completed, the miners abandoned their temporary camps and rejoined family and friends on the eastern side of the Mississippi.

Because mining was such an arduous occupation, it was little wonder that mine operators found it difficult to recruit an adequate labor force. When Des Ursins traveled to Mine La Motte in the summer of 1719, he advised his superiors: "You can imagine that soldiers do not work at the mines, therefore the sooner we shall get negroes the better it will be. The Frenchmen are unfit for this kind of work, and if they want to work, their wages will in proportion be much higher than the profit from the mines will permit."[7] Des Ursins employed five black slaves at the mines, and Renault brought a small number with him, but the scarcity and cost of slaves in French Illinois forced miners to rely primarily on white laborers. Some whites may even have been compelled by the authorities to work in the mines. Antoine De Gruy reported from the mines in 1743, "Most of the miners, who numbered eighteen or twenty, . . . were wastrels sent to this spot involuntarily for not having been able to support themselves."[8]

Labor shortages were only one of the problems confronting those who sought to profit from the mines. Inclement weather frequently brought operations to a standstill, and on more than one occasion hostile Indians forced miners to flee from their unprotected hinterland diggings. Production at the mines fluctuated significantly from year to year. In good years, the Missouri mines yielded substantial quantities of lead, but even then the costs of operating the mines consumed most of the earnings. Renault persisted until 1742, when he sold his holdings and returned to France with little to show for the two decades he had spent in the North American wilds. After Renault's departure, mining in the region continued sporadically, but it was not until Moses Austin arrived late in the eighteenth century that the Missouri mines returned much of a profit.[9]

The search for precious metals prompted the French to renew their attempts to open trade with the Spaniards in New Mexico. In the spring of 1719 Boisbriant dispatched the seasoned explorer and veteran Indian negotiator Claude-Charles Dutisné on a mission to arrange alliances with two key Plains tribes—the Wichitas and the Padoucas, or Plains Apache. Dutisné, who was traveling under the auspices of the Company of the Indies, also had orders to look out for valuable mines. Ironically, the fraudulent ore samples he had taken to Mobile in 1714 had precipitated Governor Cadillac's futile journey to Mine La Motte in search of silver.[10]

Dutisné made his way up the Missouri in 1719, intending to travel as far as the mouth of the Kansas River before heading south onto the Great Plains. But when his party reached the Missouri Indian village in present-day Saline County, he encountered an unexpected problem. Eager to ensure that the French trade goods and weapons did not fall into the hands of their enemies to the west, the Missouris refused to allow the expedition to proceed upriver. They probably also believed that the rush to do business with enemy tribes suggested that their French friends were taking the obligations of their alliance too lightly. After failing to change the Missouris' minds, Dutisné returned to Kaskaskia, where he persuaded Boisbriant to allow him to make another attempt to reach the western tribes via an overland route. In midsummer he headed west, following the Indian trail leading to the Osage villages in southwest Missouri. While traveling through the Ozarks, Dutisné reported crossing "many mountains of rock, covered with oak groves."[11]

Although numerous unauthorized *coureurs de bois* had preceded him, Dutisné was the first officially sanctioned trader to visit the Osage villages in what is now Vernon County, on the western border of Missouri. The

Indians warmly welcomed the French party and enthusiastically endorsed Dutisné's proposals for forming an alliance and opening regular trade. The reception turned cooler, however, when the Osages learned of Dutisné's plans for conferring with the Wichitas. They joined the neighboring Missouris in registering strong opposition to any such meeting, but this time the French emissary refused to be dissuaded from making the trip. After threatening to retract all promises to trade if he was not permitted to proceed, Dutisné sought to allay the Osage fears by agreeing to take only three guns and a small amount of merchandise with him to the Wichitas. With those assurances, the Osages reluctantly relented and allowed him to continue.[12]

In mid-September he arrived at the Wichita villages, only to discover that the Osages had sent word that the French travelers were seeking slaves. Dutisné drew upon his skills in Indian diplomacy to convince the Wichitas that the French wanted to be their friends, not to enslave them. Once he persuaded them that his intent was not hostile, the Wichitas consented to an alliance with France and consummated the deal with feasting and the planting of a white Bourbon banner emblazoned with fleurs-de-lis in the center of their village. The Wichitas also exchanged two horses and a mule bearing a Spanish brand for the three muskets, assorted knives, and axes Dutisné had brought with him. They made it clear, however, that there were limits to their newfound friendship. Warning that the Padoucas were their bitter enemies, the Wichitas declined to allow the French delegation to seek them out. It was by then a familiar refrain. Self-interest dictated that each tribe attempt to prevent the flow of French guns into the hands of their adversaries.

Unable to continue his journey westward, Dutisné returned to Kaskaskia by way of the Osage villages. Although the Osages sold him some horses they had stolen from the Pawnees, they signaled their irritation over his discussions with the Wichitas by refusing to furnish a guide for his homeward trek. Dutisné had not discovered any gold or silver mines, nor had he reached the Padoucas, but he did bring back a great deal of information about the western tribes and a better understanding of the changes in intertribal relations being wrought by European contact.[13]

The growing French activity among tribes along the Missouri and beyond gave rise to rumors of a pending invasion aimed at Santa Fe. Although Spanish officials there discounted the exaggerated reports, they worried about the steadily rising number of French incursions into their domains. In the early summer of 1720 New Mexico's governor, Antonio de Valverde, sent Lt. Gen. Pedro de Villasur on a reconnaissance mission to learn the extent of French penetration onto the Plains. The expedition, consisting of fewer than fifty Spaniards and a slightly larger number of friendly Indians, traveled northeast from Santa Fe to the Platte River in Nebraska, where they were massacred by a band of Pawnees. This debacle actually weakened Spain's influence in the region, but the appearance of Spanish troops so far east alarmed Bienville and Boisbriant.[14]

Indian reports suggesting that the Spaniards intended to construct a fort on the Kansas River prompted Bienville to consider plans for fortifying French positions along the Missouri.[15] Dutisne's accounts of growing intertribal conflict, exacerbated by the demands of unauthorized traders for furs, slaves, and horses, further underscored the need for a more substantial French presence in the region. News of these unsettling developments came at a bad time for the Company of the Indies, then in the process of reordering its troubled operations. The bursting of the speculative Mississippi Bubble in 1720 had triggered the collapse of John Law's financial empire and sent its cunning architect in retreat to Vienna. Despite the firm's financial problems, company officials took the threats to their North American holdings seriously and resurrected plans for dispatching an expedition into the Missouri country under the Sieur de Bourgmont's command.[16]

Following his return to France in 1720, the highly regarded veteran Missouri traveler had been named commandant of the Missouri and made a Knight of the Order of St. Louis, but no further steps had been taken to install him in his North American post until the disturbing reports of the Spanish Villasur expedition suggested the need for urgent action. With officers of the crown and company directors looking to him for assistance, Bourgmont was in a strong bargaining position. In return for agreeing to undertake the assignment, he elicited a promise that upon the successful completion of the proposed mission, the king would award him letters of nobility. In January 1722 the council of the Company of the Indies drafted Bourgmont's orders. They instructed him to construct a fort on the Missouri River, to negotiate an alliance with the Padoucas, and to select representative Indian chieftains to accompany him to France for a firsthand view of the French nation's great power.[17]

Bourgmont left France in June 1722. When he arrived in New Orleans the following September, he found a colony in shambles. Starvation, disease, and desertion were rampant as Louisiana's hard-pressed officials struggled to make do with their shrinking resources. It was little wonder that the members of the Superior Council were lukewarm to the company's plans for occupying the remote Missouri country and resisted Bourgmont's efforts to draw upon their limited supplies in equipping his proposed venture. Bourgmont managed to depart from New Orleans in February 1723 with an undermanned and poorly provisioned force. Desertions during the voyage upriver further thinned the ranks of his party and compelled him to seek reinforcements from the small Illinois garrison. Assistance unexpectedly came from a band of Missouri Indians, who journeyed to the Mississippi to greet their old friend and escort him to the village where he had once resided. They were especially delighted to see that Bourgmont's nine-year-old mixed-blood Indian son, known as the Petit Missouri, was with him.[18]

Slowly Bourgmont, his forty-member French force, and their Indian confederates propelled the three barges and assorted canoes upriver against the strong Missouri currents. When they finally reached their destination in November 1723, Bourgmont ordered an immediate start on construction of the new outpost at a site in the wilds along the north bank of the Missouri in present-day Carroll County, across the river from the Missouri Indian village. Disagreements between Bourgmont and officers more concerned with personal gain than company interests hampered progress on the fort, but one by one the buildings, constructed of upright logs covered with thatched-grass roofs, began to take shape.[19]

Fort Orleans, as it was called, was a busy place. Construction progressed with the aid of Indian women from nearby villages, who cut and prepared grass for the roofs and excavated an ice cellar. The Indian men who came there to trade pressed their demands on the French for guns and ammunition, while the Indians' dogs roamed the grounds of the partially completed fort, feasting on the unprotected pigs and chickens the French had brought with them. Father Jean Baptiste Mercier of the Society of Foreign Missions mingled among the Indians attempting to win converts, and Bourgmont pressed ahead with efforts aimed at restoring peace among the various tribes on the prairies and plains between Missouri and New Mexico. Toward that end, he attempted to diminish intertribal warfare by prohibiting the Padouca slave traffic. Both Bienville in New Orleans and Boisbriant at Fort de Chartres sought to discourage Bourgmont's plans for visiting the western tribes because they believed the journey would not be worth the expense and effort necessary for its completion. Neither, however, managed to dissuade the commandant, who departed from Fort Orleans in June 1724 on his way to the Padouca villages.[20]

Bourgmont divided his expeditionary force into two groups, sending a small party upriver by canoe while personally leading overland a band that included more than 150 Missouri and Osage warriors and headmen. After rendezvousing at the Kansa village, several members of the two parties came down with a fever. Bourgmont bled five of the ailing Indians, but despite his claims that the treatment and medicines he offered them had good effect, the Osages balked at continuing the trip. Bourgmont himself contracted the malady and was forced to return to Fort Orleans to recuperate. He did send one of his lieutenants on to the Padouca towns. When word reached Fort Orleans in September that the French party had successfully completed its journey and been favorably received, the commandant was sufficiently recovered to set out to join them.

Bourgmont arrived at a Padouca encampment in what is now central Kansas—probably not their main village—on 18 October and promptly arranged an alliance with that tribe, following a round of the customary rites of speechmaking and feasting. The Padoucas solemnly proclaimed the French to be their true friends, after noting that the Spaniards had refused to give them guns. Once the necessary exchange of gifts had been completed, the French commandant and his men headed back to Fort Orleans, where they arrived on 5 November, hailing their new agreement with the Padoucas. They marked the occasion by raising the French flag at the fort to the accompaniment of a volley of muskets, followed by the singing of the *Te Deum* in the fort's chapel.[21]

Having successfully completed his first two assignments, Bourgmont turned his attention to selecting the Indians who would accompany him to France. He chose several representatives from the Osages, the Otos, the Illinois, and the Missouris, including a young woman from the latter tribe who was probably his latest Indian concubine. In New Orleans, cost-conscious members of Louisiana's Superior Council ordered Bourgmont's sizable Indian entourage reduced to five—one chief from each of the four tribes and the Missouri woman. Those who were chosen traveled from New Orleans to Mobile Bay on board the *Bellone*. When that vessel mysteriously sank while resting at anchor, Bourgmont and his companions miraculously escaped with their lives, but the Indians lost the gifts they were planning to exchange with their French hosts. Despite their harrowing experience, the five Indians boarded another ship that carried them to France without further incident.[22]

The North American delegation arrived in Paris on 20 September 1725, and the following week the Indians began a round of audiences with company officials and dignitaries at court during which they dutifully acted out the roles assigned them. On cue, the Native Americans humbled themselves before members of the court and lavishly praised the French for their beneficence, even though they still did not fully understand the purpose of their lengthy journey. Their speeches failed to disclose much about tribal life and customs, but they did convey a simple and direct plea for continued French assistance in coping with the changes forced upon them by the European invasion of their homelands. The French loaded the Indians with impractical presents and treated them to a whirlwind tour of spectacular sights. The Missouri Indian girl wed one of the French soldiers accompanying the delegation in a chapel at Notre Dame after Bourgmont's ardor had cooled when he rejoined his French wife.

Louis XV granted the visiting Indian dignitaries a personal audience, but despite the lavish hospitality bestowed upon them, the Native American travelers remained in the eyes of their French hosts little more than curiosities from some remote and exotic place. The delegates returned to their homes relating to unbelieving tribal brothers and sisters what they had seen and heard—including their observation that French women smelled like alligators. But Bourgmont, who received his promised noble rank, stayed in France and never again visited the American shores.[23]

The Company of the Indies continued to station a garrison at Fort Orleans until officials decided that the limited benefits derived from the fortification did not justify the heavy expenditures required to maintain it. By the time the company abandoned the fort in 1728, Father Mercier reluctantly had given up on his mission work among the Missouris and the Osages and retreated east of the Mississippi. Following the departure of the French, the wilderness gradually reclaimed the once-thriving outpost on the Missouri.[24]

Never a particularly large tribe, the Missouris remained in the same general area until the 1790s, when raiding Sac and Fox war parties inflicted heavy casualties upon them. The hostile invasion, coupled with the scourge of smallpox, so depleted their numbers that they were forced to seek refuge among friendly neighboring tribes. Some joined the Osages, others went to the Kansa tribe, but the largest segment took up residence with their kinfolk the Otos, thus ending the Missouri people's existence as a separate nation.[25]

The evacuation of Fort Orleans was another step in a general policy of retrenchment forced upon the Company of the Indies by the sudden collapse of John Law's Mississippi project. In a desperate attempt to recoup some of their losses, the stockholders continued to operate the company after Law's departure. But French investors became understandably more reluctant to commit additional sums of money to the enterprise. Like Crozat's earlier venture, the company had failed to earn a profit, and its anxious backers sought to reduce their Louisiana expenditures in order to transfer funds to more lucrative opportunities elsewhere. Increasing Indian difficulties in the Illinois Country finally prompted the company to petition the king in 1731 to take Louisiana back, and in that year the area again came under royal control.[26]

The company's demise was a major setback in France's faltering campaign to secure the Mississippi valley, but itinerant wilderness entrepreneurs continued to roam the region seeking profits. One such party, headed by Pierre and Paul Mallet, took advantage of a temporary lull in Indian hostilities on the Plains to travel from the Missouri to Santa Fe in 1739. Their favorable reception in New Mexico rekindled French interest in opening trade with the mineral-rich province, but the dubious Spaniards promptly dashed those hopes and refused to allow subsequent trading expeditions.[27] Indian complaints about unscrupulous *coureurs de bois* caused French officials to take steps to curb illicit trading activities along the Missouri. In 1744 the Chevalier de Bertet, the commandant at Fort de Chartres, granted Canadian trader Joseph Deruisseau exclusive rights to the Missouri River fur trade for a five-year period, with the hope that this action would halt the abusive trading practices and improve relations with the Indians. Deruisseau constructed a small fort on the west bank of the Missouri near a Kansa Indian village not far upriver from where Kansas City would be founded. The French maintained a small garrison at the outpost, subsequently known as Fort Cavagnal, until 1764, but the presence of the French troops did not preclude occasional incidents of violence between Indians and traders along the Missouri.[28]

Although the traffic in furs and the search for precious metals were responsible for drawing most early French adventurers west of the Mississippi, the region had other attractions as well. Long before the first Europeans came to Missouri, Indians had journeyed regularly to the saline springs located a short distance below Ste. Genevieve. By the eighteenth century both French and Indians regularly frequented the site to boil off salt and to hunt the animals attracted by salt residues. When Cadillac crossed the Mississippi in 1715 looking for silver mines, he encountered a small French party making salt at La Saline. Salt was an essential commodity both as a preservative for meat and for use in curing and tanning animal skins. Each year the Missouri saltworks produced sufficient quantities of the valuable product to meet the needs of east-bank communities and to sustain the export of salt meats from the Illinois Country. The early encampments at La Saline were temporary, but in 1766 Jean LaGrange of Kaskaskia sold a house, a slave cabin, a shed, a reverberating furnace with lead and iron kettles, a pump, and other miscellaneous tools and equipment used in making salt at the Saline Creek location.[29]

For most of the French period, the villages east of the Mississippi remained the focal point of French activity in the Illinois Country. The outposts at River Des Peres and Fort Orleans had been maintained only briefly. Traders, miners, and saltmakers regularly crossed the river, but they continued to keep their permanent residences at Kaskaskia, Cahokia, Fort de Chartres, Prairie du Rocher, and St. Philippe on the eastern side. Not until the founding of Ste. Genevieve did the French establish a permanent settlement west of the Mississippi in the Illinois Country. The date of the town's founding has long been hotly debated. The absence of any specific account of Ste. Genevieve's initial settlement makes it impossible to fix a precise year. Carl Ekberg's carefully documented study of Missouri's oldest community, however, provides convincing evidence that it was not established until about 1750, when French habitants (farmers) moved across the river to begin cultivating the rich alluvial soil along the west bank.[30]

The location of the "Old Town" of Ste. Genevieve on the fertile Mississippi floodplain proved to be less than ideal. Because of its frequently damp and muddy condition, the flood-prone settlement earned the unflattering nickname *Misère*, or "misery." The village grew slowly during its earliest years. Most of its original inhabitants were French Canadians like André Deguire *dit* La Rose, who moved across the river from Kaskaskia with his wife, three sons, two daughters, indentured servant, and black slave. The 1752 French census for Ste. Genevieve reported a total population of 23, white and black, free and slave. Twenty years later there were 691 persons residing in the village. Although the proximity of the lead mines and the saline springs may have induced some early settlers to make the move, most who came to Ste. Genevieve were farmers. These French habitants and their black slaves cultivated three principal crops—wheat, corn, and tobacco—on the long, narrow strips of land assigned them in the fenced enclosure known as the Big Field Commons. They grew smaller quantities of cotton, flax, and hemp as cash crops and raised livestock, which they allowed to run at large in the common pasture. Initially, Ste. Genevieve was a west-bank satellite of Kaskaskia that closely resembled its parent community and the other settlements across the river.[31]

The tranquility of those small French villages along the Mississippi belied the intense struggle that engaged France during much of the eighteenth century. A series of intermittent wars pitted France against England in a contest for control of colonial possessions throughout the world. Alliances and loyalties occasionally shifted as one conflict gave way to another, but France and England remained the principal protagonists. Early encounters between the two great powers were inconclusive. In North America the French, with Indian assistance, proved remarkably adept at keeping the numerically superior British confined to the eastern seaboard. The outcome of their struggles remained in doubt until the Seven Years' War, commonly referred to in America as the French and Indian War.

In that decisive contest, the fall of Quebec to English forces in 1759 and the loss of Montreal in the following year seemed to assure that France would be compelled to surrender Canada. Hoping to forestall a total English victory, Spain joined France in the struggle in January 1762, but the Spaniards also were defeated by English forces. Despite the disasters that befell the French and their allies almost everywhere else, France managed to retain firm control in the Illinois Country, where there was little, if any, direct military action. When the outcome of the war became a virtual certainty, France pressed for a speedy end to the conflict on the best terms possible. To persuade the Spanish monarch to sign the preliminaries of peace immediately and to compensate the Spaniards for their losses, France offered to cede Louisiana to Spain. The French had already concluded that without Canada, Louisiana would be difficult to defend. The Spaniards accepted, and the terms were incorporated in the secret Treaty of Fontainebleau, signed in November 1762. Although Louisiana had never been profitable economically, it had served French purposes by keeping the English hemmed in along the Atlantic coast.[32]

With the stroke of a pen Louisiana passed from French to Spanish control. France also surrendered all of Canada and its territories east of the Mississippi to England, but it did manage to retain some key possessions in the Caribbean. The final terms of settlement, incorporated in the Treaty of Paris of 1763, signaled the end of France's North American empire.

Word of the agreement to transfer Louisiana from France to Spain did not reach the province for nearly two years, and in the interim the French had established St. Louis as a second settlement on the western bank of the Mississippi. The founding of St. Louis grew out of an attempt by Louisiana's officials to accelerate postwar economic recovery. During the war the province suffered from disrupted trade, severe shortages, and unstable currency. When Jean Jacques Blaise D'Abbadie became governor in 1763, he sought to revive the lagging fur trade by granting Gilbert Antoine Maxent, a well-known New Orleans merchant, exclusive trading rights with the Indians along the Missouri and the west bank of the Upper Mississippi for a six-year period. Many members of the New Orleans mercantile community strenuously protested the governor's decision to abandon free trade, but Maxent wasted little time before forming a partnership with Pierre de Laclède Liguest to exploit the concession. As junior partner in the new firm known as Maxent, Laclède and Company, Laclède agreed to establish and supervise a trading post in Upper Louisiana.[33]

Like so many other younger sons of well-connected European families, he had taken his inheritance and come to North America in 1755 seeking to build his own fortune. By the time he joined forces with Maxent, the capable and well-educated Frenchman was a successful New Orleans merchant with a personal library of two hundred volumes. In August 1763, Laclède and his thirteen-year-old stepson and clerk, Auguste Chouteau, left New Orleans and headed upriver to initiate trading activities and establish a company headquarters in Upper Louisiana. They reached Ste.

Genevieve on 3 November, but after failing to secure enough storage space there for their supplies and equipment, they proceeded to Kaskaskia. Authorities at nearby Fort de Chartres allowed them to store their supplies there until they could find a more suitable place, and Laclède and his companions set up a temporary trading camp in the adjacent village of Ste. Anne de Fort Chartres. As word of their arrival spread to nearby Indian tribes, delegations eager to exchange furs for goods began arriving at the camp.[34]

Encouraged by his favorable reception, Laclède set out in December with young Chouteau to select a more accessible place for a permanent trading headquarters. Before leaving New Orleans, Laclède had been informed of France's agreement to cede the territory east of the Mississippi to the British, so he confined his search to the west bank. After surveying the land along the Mississippi between Ste. Genevieve and the mouth of the Missouri, he selected the St. Louis site. The location seemed ideal. Its natural elevation afforded protection from flooding, but it also provided convenient access to the Mississippi, Missouri, and Illinois rivers. Laclède and Chouteau notched some trees to mark the spot before returning to Fort de Chartres to await spring. As soon as the late winter thaws made it possible to navigate the Mississippi, Laclède dispatched Chouteau and a party of thirty workers to begin constructing a trading post at the site he had chosen.[35]

Under Chouteau's watchful eye, the laborers cleared the land and erected a storage shed and several cabins. When Laclède visited the site in April, he gave specific instructions for laying out the village and announced his intention to honor Louis XV by naming the new settlement St. Louis after the French sovereign's patron saint, Louis IX, a medieval king who had been canonized for his part in the Crusades. Laclède returned to Fort de Chartres to continue trading and make arrangements for transporting his supplies and equipment across the river.[36]

Laclède had brought word to Upper Louisiana of France's plans to surrender the east bank when he had arrived late in 1763, but Pierre Joseph Neyon de Villiers, the commandant at Fort de Chartres, did not receive official orders to begin preparations for evacuating the area until the following April. Upon receipt of those directives, Captain Villiers summoned all French forces stationed at outlying posts in the Illinois Country to Fort de Chartres. He instructed Capt. Louis St. Ange de Bellerive, the commanding officer at Vincennes on the Wabash River, to abandon that post, and he also called for the withdrawal of the small garrison at Fort Cavagnal on the Missouri. Villiers, who chose not to wait for his English replacement to arrive, departed in June for New Orleans, along with most of his troops and about eighty Illinois residents. The outgoing commandant designated Captain St. Ange to take charge of the small remaining French garrison at Fort de Chartres and to arrange for the post's transfer when the British officials arrived. The task of dismantling French authority must have been disheartening for the veteran St. Ange, who as a young cadet had accompanied Bourgmont to Fort Orleans in 1724.[37]

While waiting for the changeover, the remaining French-speaking inhabitants of the east-bank settlements grew progressively more concerned about their prospects under British rule. Laclède capitalized on the prevailing uncertainty by recruiting them actively for his new establishment. Since word of Louisiana's cession to Spain still had not reached the area, many French settlers accepted the invitation to move to St. Louis. Laclède's promotional activities paid off, for when the west-bank inhabitants did learn of the impending Spanish takeover sometime in November or December of 1764, St. Louis was a well-established village containing between forty and fifty families.

Destined to become a great commercial center, St. Louis continued to attract new settlers, primarily persons of French ancestry who chose Spanish rule over English. It also caught the attention of several hundred Missouri Indians—mostly women and children—who arrived on the scene in October 1764 with plans for taking up residence adjacent to the new trading post. Their declining numbers had increased their vulnerability to enemy raids, and by offering to join Laclède's settlement they hoped to enjoy the mutual benefits of interdependence and intermarriage with their French neighbors. Despite the Indians' friendly intent, the presence of such a large force intimidated some of the outnumbered Creoles, who fled to the less exposed east bank. The youthful and inexperienced Chouteau did not panic, however: he sent to Fort de Chartres for Laclède, and in the meantime took advantage of the situation by hiring the willing Missouri women to dig a cellar for the company trading headquarters he had been directed to build. Once the excavation had been completed, Chouteau put his men to work laying the stones for the impressive structure, situated on what would later become Main Street between Market and Walnut, which stood as a St. Louis landmark for many years.[38]

When Laclède arrived, he conferred with the Missouris, who likened themselves to ducks and geese seeking open water where they could find rest and an easier subsistence. The French trader deftly turned their metaphor to his advantage by suggesting that in open water ducks and geese were more susceptible to eagles and birds of prey than they were in a woody place covered with brush. He cautioned the Missouris that there were six or seven hundred enemy warriors in the vicinity of Fort de

Chartres who would, in all likelihood, pounce upon them if they remained at the exposed new settlement. After listening to Laclède's advice and accepting the gifts he offered them, the Missouris agreed to return to their less exposed mid-Missouri villages. Following their departure, the French settlers who had temporarily moved to Cahokia began coming back to St. Louis.[39]

Capt. Thomas Stirling, the British officer assigned to take possession of the Illinois Country east of the Mississippi, did not reach Fort de Chartres until October 1765. Captain St. Ange promptly surrendered control to him and withdrew across the river to St. Louis, where he established his new headquarters in accordance with instructions from New Orleans. Stirling complained to his superiors about the continuing flight of east-bank residents, noting that some of them had even dismantled their dwellings and taken the building materials with them to the Missouri side. Capt. Harry Gordon, another British officer, warned in 1766 that Laclède's burgeoning river town had become the focal point of fur trading operations on both sides of the Mississippi.[40]

Following his arrival in St. Louis, St. Ange assumed command of the territories west of the Mississippi, exercising both civil and military control until the Spaniards belatedly took charge of the area.[41] In Ste. Genevieve, Philippe François de Rastel, chevalier de Rocheblave, acted as commandant, probably upon orders from St. Ange. The adventurous French aristocrat had moved his family to Ste. Genevieve from Kaskaskia at the time of the British takeover.[42] Louisiana's unsettled situation did not deter disgruntled merchants in Ste. Genevieve and New Orleans from raising strenuous objections to D'Abbadie's suspension of free trade. The Indian trading monopoly he had awarded Maxent, Laclède and Company was especially unpopular among traders long accustomed to a more open system. Jean Datchurut, a prominent Ste. Genevieve trader, attempted to defy the ban by sending a boatload of merchandise up the Missouri in the spring of 1765, but at Laclède's insistence St. Louis officials seized the contraband goods. D'Abbadie justified the monopoly as a measure for controlling Indians and keeping out unauthorized British traders, but officials in the French ministry overruled him and canceled the exclusive grants on grounds that they were detrimental to commerce. The revocation of the trading monopoly was a blow to Maxent and Laclède, who also found themselves compelled to compensate Datchurut for his losses. Laclède elected not to abandon the village he had worked so diligently to found. He bought out Maxent's interests in the company's St. Louis operations and remained an active trader there until his death in 1778.[43]

Even in the waning days of France's North American empire, Missouri remained a primitive and sparsely settled wilderness. With only two small villages along the Mississippi's western bank, the French had failed to make the financial commitment needed to develop the region. To their credit, however, a smattering of French pioneers, with the assistance of their Indian allies, had successfully held their own against more numerous European rivals until the middle of the eighteenth century. They also had established the foundation for a new society in the North American heartland. During the ensuing forty years of Spanish rule, Missouri remained predominantly French in its appearance, language, customs, and outlook. France had left an indelible mark upon early Missouri.

CHAPTER THREE
CREATING A
SPANISH BARRIER

S pain welcomed the acquisition of Louisiana from France as a means
of more effectively safeguarding its valuable possessions in Mexico
against foreign encroachment. During the nearly forty years that the
red and yellow royal Spanish banner flew over Louisiana, officials waged a
continuous struggle to prevent first English and then American penetration
west of the Mississippi. The creation of a strong protective barrier became
the primary object of Spanish policy in Louisiana, but Spain's attempts to
establish a flourishing buffer colony suffered from the same chronic under-
capitalization that had stymied the colonial enterprises of the French.
Spanish officials tried to compensate for the lack of funding by relaxing
immigration policies in order to recruit settlers for the sparsely populated
province. But such tactics were not sufficient to stimulate the economic
growth needed to make Louisiana a profitable colony.

Although France ceded Louisiana to Spain in November 1762, opposition
from some of the Spanish king's advisers, a treasury depleted by heavy
wartime expenditures, and traditional Spanish bureaucratic procrastina-
tion delayed preparations to occupy the province for more than three years.
In the face of Spain's continuing inaction, the French, who were unwilling
to bear administrative costs for a colony that was no longer theirs, pressed
for the transfer. When Louisiana's first Spanish governor, Antonio de Ulloa,
finally did reach New Orleans on 5 March 1766, only ninety soldiers accompanied him. With so few troops at his disposal, Ulloa declined to take
formal possession of Louisiana, pending the arrival of Spanish reinforcements. In the interim, he and the acting French commandant at New
Orleans, Capt. Charles Philippe Aubry, jointly administered the province
under a cumbersome and inefficient arrangement.[1]

At first glance, Ulloa had much to recommend him for the post: previous
colonial administrative experience, a distinguished international reputation as a scientist and author, and fluency in the French language. But the
brusque and overbearing Spanish naval officer received a cool reception in
New Orleans, and his actions during the following months further alienated him from a French populace still resentful over the decision to cede the
province to Spain. From the moment Ulloa arrived in New Orleans, a host
of problems competed for his attention, including increased British activity
along the Gulf Coast and in the Mississippi valley.[2]

The situation was serious in Upper Louisiana, where frequent incursions by British traders threatened to undermine Spanish authority. After reviewing Louisiana's inadequate defenses, the incoming Spanish governor dispatched Capt. Francisco Ríu and a contingent of more than forty soldiers to the Illinois Country in 1767 with orders to construct fortifications at the junction of the Missouri and Mississippi rivers. In sending nearly half of the minuscule Spanish garrison to Upper Louisiana, Ulloa underscored the region's strategic importance.[3]

The Ríu expedition stopped briefly in Ste. Genevieve, where, in marked contrast to Ulloa's New Orleans reception, the welcome was friendly. François Vallé, one of the town's leading citizens, entertained the king's troops and sold them foodstuffs on credit, and Philippe de Rocheblave, the local French commandant, volunteered to accompany the Spanish contingent to St. Louis. By embracing the new regime the Vallés formed a valuable connection that enabled their family to maintain its preeminent position in Ste. Genevieve politics and society throughout the Spanish era. Like their St. Louis counterparts, the Chouteaus, they understood the importance of cordial relations with ranking officials. Despite the auspicious beginning in Ste. Genevieve, though, the incoming Spaniards faced an enormous challenge in laying claim to the remote province.[4]

Ríu's orders stressed keeping the British out of Spanish territory and maintaining cordial relations with the region's Indian tribes. Although Ulloa did not prohibit the trading of guns, he naively suggested that the Indians should be encouraged to forget about muskets. The governor placed Ríu in command of the fort at the mouth of the Missouri, but he made no effort to supersede Captain St. Ange's authority elsewhere. The experienced French officer in St. Louis remained the chief administrative official for that portion of the province south of the Missouri.[5]

When the Spanish expedition arrived in Laclède's town in September 1767, Ríu quickly discovered that his instructions for constructing two forts at the mouth of the Missouri were impractical since floodwaters eight or nine feet deep frequently inundated the location on the north shore that Ulloa had designated for the principal fort. After personally inspecting the site with Capt. Guy de Fossat, the French officer and engineer charged with superintending the project's construction, Ríu proposed moving the main structure to the more suitable south bank and building only a small blockhouse on the opposite side. A hastily convened military tribunal in St. Louis obligingly ratified his recommendation.[6]

As news of Ríu's arrival spread to the surrounding countryside, representatives from nearby Indian tribes came to St. Louis to take stock of their new rulers and participate in the gift-giving rituals that customarily accompanied such occasions. In view of the favorable relationship they had developed with the French, it was hardly surprising that the Indians expressed disappointment over the small amounts of merchandise the tight-fisted Spaniards offered them. The visiting tribal leaders showed themselves to be experienced diplomats and made a point of telling the Spanish agents that their British rivals were more generous. Captain St. Ange, who conducted the meetings for the Spaniards, understood the importance of making a good first impression. But with only a limited supply of gifts to distribute, the veteran negotiator knew that he would need to hold some in reserve for the even larger influx of Indian delegations that would arrive in St. Louis the following spring.[7]

The situation at the nearby Missouri River post, known as Fort Don Carlos, was even worse. Tensions there were so great that an inconsequential disagreement between a Spanish officer and a stonemason over the disposal of a piece of fresh fish provoked Ríu to order the local workman hauled before a St. Louis magistrate in chains. The continual quarreling threatened to halt construction on the fort, and at one point Ríu's own men attempted to bar him from entering the installation he commanded. A short time later, the post's storekeeper and twenty soldiers deserted and went downriver. British officials at Natchez briefly detained the fugitives for questioning before handing them over to Spanish authorities in New Orleans.[8]

St. Ange cooperated with the Spaniards, but he and his French-speaking constituents kept their distance from the disagreements swirling about Ríu until he announced stringent new regulations designed to bring the free-wheeling Indian trade under more direct Spanish supervision. On direct orders from Ulloa, Ríu banned traders from going to the Indian villages, pending the issuance of trading licenses in New Orleans. The St. Louis merchants immediately challenged the restrictive new policies, which promised to curtail severely their trading activities. The Indians did not like the Spanish actions any better, and in one stormy encounter a Kansa chief showed his displeasure by stalking out of a meeting with Ríu. The commandant, who was only following directions from his superiors in New Orleans, wisely agreed to modify the unpopular restrictions when the St. Louis habitants refused to go into their fields for fear of being assaulted by the disgruntled Indians. Ríu's willingness to reconsider his orders improved his standing in St. Louis, but not in time to save him from dismissal. Blaming the embattled Spanish officer for the turmoil in Upper Louisiana, Ulloa dismissed him in August 1768 and designated Capt. Pedro Piernas as his replacement.[9]

Meanwhile, Ulloa faced serious problems of his own. His efforts to

impose Spanish mercantilist regulations limiting Louisiana's trade precipitated an attempt to reinstate French authority in New Orleans. On
29 October 1768, the Superior Council in that city branded Ulloa a usurper
and ordered his removal. Without a sufficient force to resist the rebels, the
Spanish governor fled to Cuba. Before leaving New Orleans, he sent new
orders to Piernas, instructing him to withdraw from Upper Louisiana after
delivering Fort Don Carlos to Captain St. Ange. Inclement weather and ice
floes had impeded Piernas's passage up the Mississippi and delayed his
arrival at the fort on the Missouri until 6 March 1769. He had been there only
thirteen days when he received the directive to evacuate Fort Don Carlos.
He did so immediately, but spent nearly a month in St. Louis attempting to
settle several disputed government accounts with local merchants. Piernas
finally headed downriver in late April and arrived in New Orleans in May.
He and his men sailed for Havana in July, the last Spanish soldiers to leave
the province in the aftermath of the uprising.[10]

Upon learning of Ulloa's ouster, officials in Spain acted quickly to end the
insurgency. They dispatched Lt. Gen. Alejandro O'Reilly to Havana, where
he took charge of preparations for restoring Spanish control in Louisiana.
He assembled a twenty-one-ship flotilla carrying two thousand royal troops
and sailed for New Orleans. Resistance to the Spanish regime collapsed in
the face of this dramatic show of force by O'Reilly, who reoccupied the
capital on 18 August. After ordering the arrest of the anti-Spanish conspir-
ators, he directed all Louisianians to swear allegiance to the Spanish monarchy.[11] O'Reilly's crackdown culminated with the execution of five rebel
leaders before a New Orleans firing squad. There were no arrests or
reprisals in Upper Louisiana—none were needed. The residents of St.
Louis and Ste. Genevieve dutifully acquiesced to the new order, and in
compliance with O'Reilly's instructions they publicly affirmed their loyalty
to their new sovereign, Carlos III. Paradoxically, they did so under the
supervision of the former French commandants St. Ange and Rocheblave.[12]

Following the successful reestablishment of Spanish authority in New
Orleans, O'Reilly carefully assessed the situation in Upper Louisiana after
soliciting information from Piernas about conditions in the upper valley.
Although Piernas had been in Upper Louisiana for only a brief period, his
detailed report was optimistic about the region's potential. He described the
climate as healthy and pleasant; the varied terrain included vast prairies
and cleared, level plains suitable for farming and raising cattle; the fertile
soil produced copious harvests with minimal cultivation; and the abundance of wild game in the territory provided the inhabitants with both food
and profits from the sale of skins.[13]

Upper Louisiana's two settlements, Ste. Genevieve and St. Louis, had experienced substantial increases in population as a consequence of the French exodus from east of the Mississippi following the English occupation of that territory. Ste. Genevieve, with its six hundred inhabitants, appeared larger than it actually was because the houses were separated from each other and scattered along the riverbank over a considerable distance. The town's prosperity derived primarily from agriculture, though some of its residents engaged in hunting, saltmaking, lead mining, and commerce. But as Piernas noted in his report, the settlement's major nemesis remained the Mississippi floodwaters, which periodically inundated the low-lying town.[14]

St. Louis had a slightly smaller population, primarily because it had fewer slaves. Located on a gently sloping ledge sufficiently elevated to spare it from the floods and dampness that plagued Ste. Genevieve, the village quickly developed into a thriving settlement. Its advantageous site, its desirable location, and its designation as the residence for Upper Louisiana's ranking governmental official all contributed to St. Louis's popularity as a center for the growing fur trade. During the peak trading months of May and June, Indians from throughout the Missouri and upper Mississippi valleys flocked there to exchange their furs with local merchants and to receive the presents annually distributed by the government.[15]

The preoccupation with furs in St. Louis encouraged residents to favor the chase over agriculture, much to the chagrin of the town's Spanish administrators. In 1778 the lieutenant governor, Fernando de Leyba, complained that the men of St. Louis were "interested only in trading with the Indians, and neglect their farming. All are or wish to be merchants."[16] The resulting scarcities, which sometimes forced St. Louisans to turn to Ste. Genevieve for flour and other foodstuffs, earned their town the dubious distinction of being known as *Paincourt*, which meant "short of bread." But despite its unflattering sobriquet, St. Louis prospered from its earliest days because of the flourishing traffic in furs.[17]

Even so, life in Upper Louisiana's remote frontier settlements was primitive and rough-hewn at the onset of Spanish rule. St. Louis's first resident parish priest, Father Bernard de Limpach, was unprepared for the conditions he found upon his arrival in 1776. He blamed a combination of too much liquor and a youthful, unmarried, male population "waiting only for the moment of seeing themselves in control of some cash to get away from here" as prime reasons for the unhappy situation. His comments echoed the concerns previously expressed by Captain Piernas regarding the "looseness of conduct, the abandonment of life, [and] the dissoluteness and license" that he encountered in Ste. Genevieve and in St. Louis.[18]

Even the most prominent families lived in a simple style. François Vallé, described by Piernas as the wealthiest man in Ste. Genevieve, had only recently learned to scrawl his last name, and the better-educated founder of St. Louis, Pierre de Laclède, spent much of his time in the wilderness seeking to strike bargains with the Indians. Laclède's stone trading post was a substantial building in the 1770s, but nothing like the fashionable dwelling that it was to become two decades later when Auguste Chouteau remodeled it and added a second story. More typical of the local construction was the "small house of posts in the ground eighteen feet long by fifteen feet wide, roofed with straw, with a clay chimney, bare of floor or ceiling," that Joseph Lefebvre sold in St. Louis in June 1766, or the sturdier one-room "house on joists in a row, boarded top and bottom, roofed with shingles, with a cellar underneath and a stone chimney, and with openings for four windows and two doors" that he replaced it with the next year.[19]

Both Ste. Genevieve and St. Louis were vulnerable to attack, for prior to 1780 neither was fortified. Fort Don Carlos, the region's sole military installation, offered little protection: St. Ange described it as a "poor cabin" situated in the wrong place. As late as 1781 the lieutenant governor at St. Louis felt it necessary to warn persons not to travel outside of their settlements unarmed.[20]

In early 1770 Governor O'Reilly had taken steps to place Upper Louisiana under full Spanish control by appointing a lieutenant governor to supplant St. Ange's authority. He selected Piernas for the newly created post and granted him broad powers for maintaining order, administering justice, regulating trade, and managing Indian affairs, after determining that the distance separating Upper Louisiana from the provincial capital in New Orleans made it necessary to establish a governmental headquarters in the upper valley. Piernas returned to St. Louis, where St. Ange officially transferred power to him on 20 May. Piernas brought thirty-three soldiers with him; nine were posted at Ste. Genevieve, seven at Fort Don Carlos, and the remaining seventeen in St. Louis.[21]

Following his installation as lieutenant governor, Piernas moved quickly to solidify local support behind the Spanish regime. In St. Louis he hired the popular St. Ange as an adviser, and in Ste. Genevieve he retained François Vallé as captain of the militia. With so few forces at his disposal, the incoming Spaniard could not afford to alienate leaders in the close-knit, French-speaking communities. When inexperienced Spanish administrators did attempt to bypass the local power structure, they usually regretted their actions. Antonio de Oro, who served as commandant in Ste. Genevieve briefly during the 1780s, made that mistake. He accused the Vallés of "disobedience and insubordination" following his unsuccessful attempts to reprimand them for allowing their slaves to carry firearms. The local people quickly turned against the outsider, whom they lampooned by posting on the church door an unflattering caricature suggesting that his wife wore the pants in the family. When De Oro's superiors in New Orleans learned of the dispute, they promptly recalled him. His successor, Henri Peyroux de la Coudrenière, fared little better in his efforts to take on the Vallés, even though he was a Frenchman. At one point the high-handed Peyroux jailed François Vallé II following a dispute. With such actions the commandant succeeded in alienating almost everyone in Ste. Genevieve. Peyroux's immediate superior, Lieutenant Governor Zenon Trudeau, described him as presumptuous and self-centered. Eventually the controversial commandant was reassigned to New Madrid; much to his consternation, undoubtedly, the post he vacated was given to his adversary, François Vallé II. With the restoration of the Vallés to their accustomed position, tranquility returned to Ste. Genevieve.[22]

By contrast, Piernas had not shied from working with local French leaders in St. Louis. He took advantage of St. Ange's lengthy experience and solicited his advice for dealing with Indians—a task that the new Spanish commandant quickly discovered commanded a disproportionate share of his time. Piernas, who was temperamentally very different from his French predecessors, had a great deal to learn on the subject. The Indians initially misinterpreted the Spaniard's reserve and dignity as a sign of unfriendliness. In his attempts to win Indian allegiance and trade, Piernas wisely continued the French practices of feasting and giving gifts. In Indian cultures gift exchanges were of paramount importance, implying friendship and promises of something in return. By accepting gifts the Indians obligated themselves to give protection and support to their benefactors. It was assumed that one would be generous with one's friends, but in the absence of those harmonious bonds, it was deemed acceptable to steal from one's enemies. Those meanings made these rituals one of the most effective methods available to the Spaniards for retaining influence among their Indian subjects.[23]

The incoming officials entertained delegations from friendly tribes and showered them with presents, including such items as blankets, cloth, fancy garments, plumed hats, sewing needles, thimbles, ribbons, mirrors, combs, beads, vermilion, thread, awls, hoes, axes, knives, steels, wire, kettles, muskets, gunpowder, and tobacco. The Indian chieftains liked the collars—medals suspended on grosgrain ribbons—that the Spaniards bestowed upon them, but brandy was their favorite gift, even though the authorities repeatedly attempted to outlaw its use in the Indian exchanges. Despite the costs, the Spaniards had no real choice in the matter. According to St. Ange's 1769 report, twenty-three different tribes normally came to St. Louis to receive presents.[24]

For the same reasons, trade was also a crucial instrument in Indian diplomacy. The Spaniards attempted to reward friendly tribes by keeping them well supplied with merchandise and to punish hostile tribes by seeing that they were denied access to trade goods. The negative sanctions were less effective because the Indians simply turned to traders from rival powers to replace the supplies withheld by the Spaniards. Spain's Indian trade policies were more restrictive than those of their French predecessors. The Spaniards outlawed trafficking in Indian slaves and also discouraged trading in horses and mules, most of which the Indians had stolen from Spanish outposts to the southwest. These changes probably helped curb intertribal warfare on the Plains, but they also intensified Indian dependency on hunting and trapping.[25]

In an effort to curtail the unrestrained trading practices of the *coureurs de bois*, the Spanish government required all traders to be licensed. Theoretically the commerce was open to all Spanish subjects, but in practice the licensing requirement limited the actual number of participants to a favored few whom the Spaniards used as quasi-governmental agents. By tradition the lieutenant governor in Upper Louisiana reserved a portion of the trade for himself, and the common practice of granting licenses to the highest bidder permitted a small number of influential traders to monopolize the most lucrative remaining assignments. In 1779 trader Jean Baptiste Martigny angrily protested that the lieutenant governor had granted licenses to those "who could afford to pay" and charged that all of the Missouri posts had gone to the powerful triumvirate of Auguste Chouteau, Sylvestre Labbadie, and Gabriel Cerré "for a considerable sum." Despite periodic attempts to liberalize Spanish trading policies, the closed system generally prevailed.[26]

Spain's initial efforts to close its territories to foreign traders were a miserable failure. Traders in pursuit of profits paid little heed to the ill-defined international boundaries Europe's great powers sought to establish in the wilderness. Following the French and Indian War, British agents regularly crossed the Mississippi to trade with Indians and to incite them against the Spaniards. At the same time, Spanish-licensed traders moved east of the river to woo the Indians there and to invite them to visit St. Louis to receive presents and to transact business. Both European nations protested the actions of their rivals, but neither managed to halt the incursions.[27]

If the territorial limits ordained in Europe meant little to the itinerant traders, they meant nothing to the Indians, who had their own claims to protect against encroachment. In addition to coping with the warring European powers, Upper Louisiana's tribes also had to contend with dislocated eastern Indians moving onto their traditional tribal lands. The angry and frustrated Indians often struck out against the intruders. Hostile actions heightened the tensions and brought demands for satisfaction. An outbreak of Little Osage and Missouri depredations in Upper Louisiana during the summer of 1772 prompted Lieutenant Governor Piernas to ban all trade with those two tribes. Warriors from the two Indian nations had raided Fort Don Carlos, forced the five soldiers stationed there to flee, and seized munitions and provisions from the post's storehouse. Emboldened by its success, the raiding party headed for St. Louis, where its members menaced the townspeople and raised a British flag in a symbolic gesture of defiance. A hastily assembled collection of soldiers and citizens tore down the banner and forced the marauders to withdraw after extracting an apology from them.[28]

Believing that the Spaniards had not properly chastised the errant members of their rival tribes, a party of Potawatomi and Sotaux Indians decided to do it for them. They fell upon the Little Osage marauders and killed two of their leaders. A Little Osage attempt at retaliation succeeded only in bloodying the hapless combatants a second time. Following that fray, the momentarily subdued Little Osages were forced to ask the Spanish authorities in St. Louis to protect them from their attackers. The Spaniards capitalized on the unexpected turn of events by exacting promises of good conduct from the renegades. In the meantime, inhabitants of the Ste. Genevieve district foiled an attempt by the Missouris to steal horses and captured two of the raiding tribesmen, whom they promptly delivered to St. Louis in chains. Although the Indian assaults seldom involved bloodshed on the part of European settlers, they were a constant irritant. Luis de Unzaga, O'Reilly's successor in New Orleans, repeatedly resisted demands for military action against the wayward Indians, stressing that he lacked the personnel, the supplies, and the money necessary for carrying out such a plan.[29]

Instead, both he and Piernas favored trade sanctions for bringing the errant tribes to terms. As previously noted, that strategy had its shortcomings: when Piernas refused to send Spanish-licensed traders to their villages, the Indians simply sought out British replacements. During the winter of 1772, Canadian-born Jean Marie Ducharme and a party of traders secretly crossed the river from British Illinois with two boatloads of merchandise. After managing to slip past Fort Don Carlos under the cover of night, the group traveled up the Missouri, where they exchanged goods with the Little Osages for nearly four months in violation of Spanish regulations.[30]

When he did learn of the British traders' illicit activities, Piernas dispatched forty volunteers, commanded by Pierre de Laclède, to arrest the interlopers. Under an arrangement designed to limit the government's costs, traders Benito Vásquez and Joseph Motard financed the expedition in return for a share of any confiscated furs or merchandise. Laclède and his men captured Ducharme's party and seized his goods, but the elusive British trader escaped his captors and fled to Canada, where he continued trading. After turning over the remaining members of Ducharme's group to Piernas for questioning, the volunteers and their sponsors divided the spoils among themselves.[31]

Despite the problems caused by the Little Osages, the more numerous Big Osages bothered the residents of Spanish Illinois only occasionally during the 1770s. Most of their hostile acts were committed in the vicinity of the Arkansas River, where some members of the faction-ridden tribe had recently taken up residence. For the moment, the pro-British Chickasaws east of the Mississippi proved far more menacing to Upper Louisiana's isolated settlers. In April 1774, a Chickasaw war party killed Joseph Vallé and six members of a mining party at Mine La Motte in one of the bloodiest Indian-white clashes in the history of Upper Louisiana. This was not their first assault. Three years earlier, members of the same tribe had kidnapped several black slaves belonging to two French miners while they were traveling from Ste. Genevieve to Mine La Motte, and the following year they murdered one of the slaveowners. In all likelihood, British agents had a hand in encouraging the Chickasaw raids against the residents of Spanish Illinois, which succeeded in bringing mining operations to a virtual standstill.[32]

Continuing British interference prompted Spain to redouble its efforts to strengthen its hold on Upper Louisiana. As a part of this program, the Spanish government urged officials in the region to recruit additional settlers from among the French Canadians residing in Illinois. Although Francisco Cruzat, who succeeded Piernas as lieutenant governor of Upper Louisiana in 1775, agreed with the plan, he indicated that most of the potential French settlers living in adjacent areas were too poor to make the move without some financial assistance. To overcome this obstacle, the crown in 1778 authorized Spanish authorities to grant land to each family immigrating to Louisiana. As an added inducement it ordered payments from the royal treasury to provide each immigrant family with small quantities of grain, livestock, and essential farming implements during its first year in the province. Spain also extended the offer to French, Spanish, Italian, and German Catholics, whom they invited to settle in Louisiana, but relatively few accepted the terms, and the desired spurt of immigration failed to materialize.[33]

Cruzat, who was less restrained and more outgoing than Piernas, was a good choice to administer a sprawling borderland region. Upper Louisiana's French inhabitants liked him, and under his tutelage they were becoming more comfortable with the ways of the Spanish regime. Although his initial term was short, it came at a crucial moment. The outbreak of the American Revolution threatened to intensify the Anglo-Spanish conflict throughout the Mississippi valley. In New Orleans, Governor Unzaga remained cautious in his dealings with the rebels, but Bernardo de Gálvez, who succeeded him on 1 January 1777, was staunchly pro-American. The new governor actively supported the struggle against the British and made contingency plans for use in the event that Spain formally declared war on England. Mutual animosity toward the British forged this curious alliance between Spanish monarchists and American republicans. In St. Louis, Capt. Fernando de Leyba, who replaced Cruzat as lieutenant governor in June 1778, followed Gálvez's lead. Soon after arriving in Upper Louisiana, he established contact with George Rogers Clark, the leader of the successful American military campaign in British Illinois. When Clark's ragtag band occupied Kaskaskia in July, Leyba hurried off a note congratulating the Americans on their victory and informing them that he was holding a shipment of supplies sent upriver by their New Orleans agent, Oliver Pollock.[34]

A short time later Leyba welcomed the victorious Clark to St. Louis with military salutes and a round of festivities. The two men became fast friends, and Clark, who informed the Continental Congress that he was "proud and pleased at the fine reception he had been given by the Spanish commandant," returned to St. Louis on several occasions to purchase supplies from the local merchants.[35] He received similar support in Ste. Genevieve. Father Pierre Gibault, the popular Kaskaskia priest who unofficially ministered to many Ste. Genevieve parishioners, played a key role in Clark's western campaign. Without such assistance it seems unlikely that the American soldier could have maintained his positions in Illinois.[36]

Leyba faced formidable challenges in defending his exposed domains. Time and the elements had taken their toll on the wooden fortifications originally constructed by Captain Ríu and his men at the mouth of the Missouri. Fort Don Carlos had deteriorated to the point that it was virtually worthless as a defensive establishment. Leyba recommended replacing it with a new stone fortress situated further up the Missouri at Cold Water Creek, where the Americans later built Fort Belle Fontaine, and a smaller second installation on the upper Mississippi River at the mouth of the Des Moines River. He also urged his superiors to station 200 regular troops in Upper Louisiana: 130 at the proposed new headquarters at Cold Water Creek, 20 at the Des Moines River, 25 at St. Louis, and 25 at Ste. Genevieve. Gálvez declined to approve the proposed outlays, noting that he had no authority to authorize such large expenditures from the royal treasury.[37]

The unsettled conditions throughout the Mississippi valley disrupted

Indian trade and destroyed traditional Indian alliances. Leyba reported that the unprecedented numbers of Indians descending upon him seeking advice and assistance had exhausted his supplies of food and merchandise. Following a two-week stay by a large band of Missouri Indians, the lieutenant governor lamented that they were "eating us out of house and home."[38] By requisitioning goods from local merchants, he avoided offending the visiting Indians, but his actions further depleted the already short supply of merchandise available for trading. When Auguste Chouteau was unable to secure Indian trade goods in New Orleans in 1779, he had to settle for a boatload of drinkables, coffee, and sugar. Such goods might find customers in St. Louis and Ste. Genevieve, but in the wilderness—with the exception of the rum, which was outlawed for use in the Indian trade—there would be few buyers. Leyba warned his superiors that the shortage of goods in St. Louis would cause the Indians to turn to the British. Under the circumstances, he permitted five St. Louis merchants to make purchases from suppliers across the Mississippi in contravention of Spanish mercantilist restrictions. Because they had to pay substantially higher prices for the goods that had been imported from Canada, Leyba attempted to compensate them by granting fewer trading licenses and allowing them to trade directly with the Indians. He justified his actions on the grounds that they were necessary for retaining the loyalty of the Missouri River tribes, but the competing traders who found themselves temporarily eliminated from the fur business openly took issue with the lieutenant governor's decisions.[39]

Worsening relations with the British pushed Spain ever closer to open warfare. With an eye toward regaining control of Gibraltar in Europe, recovering Florida in America, and ending illicit British commerce with its colonies, Spain formally declared war on England on 21 June 1779. While the Spaniards planned to attack British positions along the Gulf Coast, British officials in Canada prepared to place the Spanish posts along the Mississippi under siege with a bold scheme for encircling the rebellious American colonies, capturing St. Louis, and securing control of the trans-Mississippi fur trade. The British strategy for winning the war in the west counted heavily upon winning assistance from friendly Indians. Patrick Sinclair, the British lieutenant governor at Michilimackinac, authorized trader Emanuel Hesse to recruit Indians for the attack on St. Louis. At the same time the British instituted patrols along the Mississippi and instructed their Indian allies to seize all enemy vessels attempting to ascend the river.[40]

When Auguste Chouteau returned from New Orleans in February 1780 bearing news that Spain had formally declared war on England, Leyba promptly accelerated his efforts to secure Upper Louisiana's settlements against attack. St. Louis was especially vulnerable. Its strategic location and its use by the American rebels as an unofficial supply base made it a prime target for a British assault, but there were fewer than forty regular Spanish troops in all of Upper Louisiana to assist with its defense. Even before Leyba had learned of the state of war, he had authorized the construction of a public road linking Ste. Genevieve and St. Louis. The road, more accurately a crude trail, was intended for use in the event that one of those communities came under attack during the winter months when ice blocked travel on the Mississippi. The lieutenant governor also had taken steps to reorganize the local militia into a more viable fighting force.[41]

The peril became clear in late March when trader John Conn arrived in St. Louis, warning of an imminent Indian attack from the north. Since Leyba's requests for additional support from New Orleans had been denied, he was forced to secure the funds needed for fortifying St. Louis through a public subscription. The one thousand piastres that Leyba raised included a four hundred piastre contribution from his own pocket. Leyba proceeded with his plans for constructing four stone towers to aid in the city's defense. Work got underway in early April on the tower located at the crest of the hill on the west edge of the village at what is now the intersection of Fourth and Walnut streets. Although it was not fully completed at the time of the subsequent attack upon St. Louis, the tower known as Fort San Carlos played an important role in repelling the enemy assault, thanks in part to the installation of the five cannons Leyba had taken from the abandoned fort on the Missouri. Leyba scaled down the remainder of the project and canceled work on the three additional towers when he ran out of funds. To economize, he ordered the digging of two trenches extending along the northern and southern sides of the village from the nearly completed stone tower to the Mississippi. St. Louisans considered his insistence on using local resources an unreasonable burden. In addition to the monies they had subscribed, the townspeople also contributed more than four hundred uncompensated workdays constructing fortifications and standing guard for the village.[42]

On 9 May 1780, Leyba received word that a large British-Indian war party had begun moving down the Mississippi. To augment his meager forces, he ordered Don Silvio de Cartabona and the six regular soldiers under his command at Ste. Genevieve to report to St. Louis, along with sixty members of the Ste. Genevieve militia. Leyba also summoned all hunters and trappers within seventy-five miles of the capital to return immediately. The Ste. Genevieve contingent under Cartabona's command arrived four days later, but even with their addition, the total defensive force at St. Louis numbered only slightly more than three hundred. On 23 May a reconnaissance party dispatched by Leyba to scout British activity reported that the enemy force was within seventy-five miles of the city.[43]

The actual attack upon St. Louis came three days later. On 26 May, a force consisting of a few British soldiers, several Canadian traders, and a large body of Sac, Fox, Sioux, Menominee, and Winnebago warriors swooped down upon the city from the northwest. Estimates of the attacking party's size vary, but it may have contained as many as one thousand. The screaming band advanced into the unprotected common fields outside the city, catching at least some of the residents unaware. Jean Baptiste Riviere *dit* Baccane recalled that he had been sleeping in a cabin on the Grand Prairie when the attacking Indians took him captive and carried him away to Chicago as a prisoner. He was one of the lucky ones. His companion, Jean Marie Cardinal, was killed as he attempted to flee from the onrushing Indians.[44]

In St. Louis, a guard on duty at Fort San Carlos sounded the alarm. Leyba left his sickbed and rushed to the fort to direct operations. The women and children took refuge in Laclède's original stone trading headquarters, now serving as the lieutenant governor's official residence, while the soldiers and militiamen reported to their assigned stations along the village's perimeters. The cannon volleys fired from atop the still unfinished stone tower surprised the attackers, who had not expected to find the place fortified. Once they realized that St. Louis could not be easily taken, the enemy retreated, but not before exacting a heavy toll among the farmers and their slaves, who had refused to take seriously the rumors of the impending attack and had remained in the undefended areas outside the city. The successful defense of St. Louis and the simultaneous American repulsion of an assault against Cahokia momentarily thwarted the attempted British takeover.[45]

The hastily organized defenses had saved the city, but the costs had been great. Leyba's report of 8 June listed fourteen whites and seven slaves killed, six whites and one slave wounded, and twelve whites and thirteen slaves taken prisoner. He also indicated that an additional forty-six whites had been taken captive farther up the Mississippi. The fifty-three St. Louis casualties represented a substantial loss for a village with only seven hundred inhabitants, so it is not surprising that the unnerved survivors took umbrage with Spanish officials over their handling of the city's defenses.[46]

Two anonymously written letters sent to Governor Gálvez in New Orleans bitterly denounced Leyba's conduct. His requisitions for money and labor had angered the local populace, and their irritation increased when the seriously ill official refused to distribute gifts among a party of Sac and Fox Indians who came to St. Louis to return six captives. In view of their vulnerable situation, the unhappy townspeople believed they could not afford to alienate this sizable band of Indians, who had shown a willingness to make peace with the Spaniards. This dispute with Leyba was merely the latest in a long series of disagreements over trade, Indian relations, and defenses.[47]

Reports of an impending second attack upon St. Louis renewed the sense of despair. The residents warned Spanish authorities that unless Upper Louisiana's defenses were strengthened immediately, their settlements faced almost certain destruction. In their strongly worded letter of 23 June, they called for the construction of a fort and the stationing of at least two hundred regular troops in the area for their protection.[48]

In the midst of the controversy swirling about him, Leyba's health worsened. The burden of his official duties, compounded by the virulent criticism of his conduct, the unexpected death of his wife, and concerns about the fate of his two young daughters stranded in a wilderness so far from their native land, proved too much for Leyba, who died on 28 June. Cartabona, who had resumed his duties as commandant in Ste. Genevieve, was summoned back to St. Louis to take charge of the government. The people there sought his assistance in requisitioning additional aid from Spanish officials in New Orleans. They prepared a new petition stressing the dangers they faced and assigned Auguste Chouteau to deliver their request to authorities in the provincial capital.[49]

Meanwhile Cartabona attempted to meet the challenges with the limited resources at his disposal. He divided the 150 members of the St. Louis militia into two companies and kept them on constant alert. Hoping to forestall further Indian unrest, he met with representatives from various tribes and distributed the few available goods among them. Despite these precautions, local inhabitants remained hesitant to leave the protection of the village. The heavy casualties in the outlying areas during the spring attack made farmers understandably reluctant to venture into the common fields outside the city to harvest their crops. In an effort to alleviate their concerns, Cartabona sent a detachment of thirty men up the Mississippi to gather intelligence regarding British movements and to provide advance warning in case of a renewed assault.[50]

Governor Gálvez responded to the urgent pleas from Upper Louisiana with shipments of supplies from stockpiles already depleted by the recent Florida campaign. His decision to return the well-liked Francisco Cruzat to St. Louis was a popular one. Cruzat, who had previously served as lieutenant governor between 1775 and 1778, took charge from Cartabona on 24 September 1780 after completing the trip from New Orleans in the unheard-of time of fifty-nine days. The journey normally required about three months; Leyba, for example, had taken ninety-three days to travel upriver during the summer of 1778.[51]

Following Cruzat's arrival in St. Louis, a local delegation came to his headquarters demanding compensation for the services they had been compelled to render in constructing fortifications for their town. Cruzat was unable to grant their request, but his actions during the ensuing months enabled the Spaniards to regain the confidence of the French-speaking subjects. He called upon his diplomatic skills to negotiate agreements with several Indian tribes and to persuade members of the Ioway, Oto, and Sac tribes to surrender their British medals and banners in return for promises of Spanish replacements. Cruzat did complain that the chronic scarcity of trade goods limited his effectiveness and compelled him to make purchases from St. Louis merchants at prices considerably above those in New Orleans. Over the years, Spain expended large sums of money to win the allegiance of the Indian tribes, but the amounts were never enough to satisfy the demands. After Spanish rule ended, Pierre Chouteau, a member of the prominent St. Louis merchant clan, estimated that Spain's Indian expenditures in Upper Louisiana had averaged $13,500 per year. In certain critical times, however, they probably spent as much as $30,000 in a single year.[52]

Persistent rumors of a new spring offensive against St. Louis prompted Cruzat to order the construction of a line of fortifications surrounding the city. He decided not to build a fort, dig trenches, or construct additional towers, but chose instead to surround the village with a stockade ten feet tall. Unlike his predecessor Leyba, Cruzat did not hesitate to draw upon the royal treasury for essential supplies and equipment. Workers hurriedly constructed the wooden palisade on all sides of the village except for the naturally fortified sections along the river.[53]

Acting on his own initiative, Cruzat dispatched an expedition up the Illinois River in January 1781 under the command of Eugene Pourée, captain of St. Louis's second militia company. The recruits from St. Louis and Cahokia joined friendly Indian tribes for the surprise attack that destroyed the British fort at St. Joseph, Michigan, on 12 February 1781. Cruzat hoped that the Spanish show of force would forestall another attack on St. Louis and would prevent wavering Indian tribes from reverting to the British. Whatever else it may have accomplished, the successful operation provided the beleaguered residents of Upper Louisiana with a badly needed boost in morale.[54]

Although Cruzat's military preparations prevented further attacks against Spanish Illinois, they failed to check British influence among the tribes in the upper Mississippi valley. Spain's weak industrial capacity, its overextended lines of supply, and its inability to protect its frontier outposts militarily left Spanish officials in no position to reverse the nation's declining fortunes in the fur trade. Items needed for the Indian trade were still in short supply in New Orleans, where a partial British blockade of the Gulf had disrupted trade. Even when the scarce goods could be procured, there was no assurance that the shipments would reach St. Louis. British fugitives driven out of Natchez following the Spanish conquest of that post joined with itinerant traders and Indians to pilfer boats attempting to pass upstream. One of the roving British bands seized Madame Cruzat and the couple's two sons near present-day Memphis, Tennessee, while they were en route to St. Louis in May 1782. The freebooters released the captives but kept the 4,500 pesos in cash intended for governmental expenses and the precious cargo of Indian goods consigned to Upper Louisiana's merchants.[55]

Unable to provide enough merchandise for the Indian trade and reluctant to permit foreigners to provide it for them, the Spaniards in effect forced many Indian tribes to turn to the better-supplied British traders, who operated from northern posts such as Michilimackinac, in the Straits of Mackinac between Lakes Michigan and Huron; Prairie du Chien, on the upper Mississippi; and Detroit, on the Detroit River a short distance above Lake Erie. Those traders took advantage of superior organization, more capital, fewer governmental restraints, lower taxes, better markets for furs, and plentiful supplies of merchandise to seize the initiative from their Spanish competitors, who found themselves confined to an ever-shrinking trading zone along the lower Missouri.

The Spanish-licensed traders also had to look to foreign suppliers for merchandise. When Manuel Pérez succeeded Cruzat as lieutenant governor in 1787, many St. Louis and Ste. Genevieve merchants maintained regular contacts with British firms in Canada, where they could procure better trade goods and higher prices for their furs. The northern trade route had one additional advantage: the cooler temperatures made it easier to preserve the quality of the finer furs. Following the American Revolution, Upper Louisiana's traders routinely shipped their best pelts to Canada and sent mostly deerskins and buffalo hides to New Orleans. Because the Canadian trade benefited Upper Louisiana and because Spain could not adequately supply its own traders, Lieutenant Governor Pérez and his successor Zenon Trudeau generally overlooked the violations of Spanish regulations and permitted the illicit trade to flourish.[56] But while British dominance of the upper Mississippi valley trade continued to bedevil Spanish authorities in Louisiana, they also had to keep a watchful eye on the victorious, land-hungry Americans who now faced them across the Mississippi.

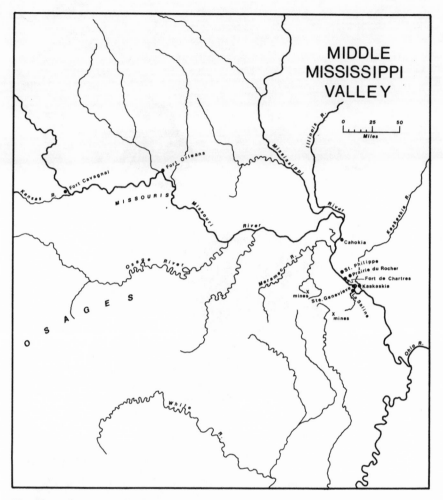

French settlement in the first half of the eighteenth century.

A Kaskaskia brave. Engraving from *A Journey in North America,* by Georges-Victor Collot (Paris, 1826). Courtesy State Historical Society of Missouri.

Osage warriors. Drawing from *Illustrations of the Manners, Customs, and Conditions of the North American Indians,* by George Catlin (London, 1851). Courtesy State Historical Society of Missouri.

René-Robert Cavelier, sieur de la Salle. Courtesy State Historical Society of Missouri.

Antoine de Lamothe, sieur de Cadillac. From etching by Charles A. Barker. Courtesy Burton Historical Collection, Detroit Public Library.

Catholic priest descending the Mississippi. From *The Lance, Cross, and Canoe,* by William Henry Milburn (New York, 1892). Courtesy State Historical Society of Missouri.

Auguste Chouteau. Courtesy Missouri Historical Society.

A facsimile of the first page of text of Auguste Chouteau's fragmentary "Narrative of the Settlement of St. Louis," date unknown, probably between 1810 and 1820. Courtesy the Collections of the St. Louis Mercantile Library Association.

The Chouteau House, St. Louis. Lithograph by J. C. Wild, 1841. Courtesy Missouri Historical Society.

Fort San Carlos, St. Louis, 1780, by Clarence Hoblitzelle. The original is an ink drawing commissioned by Pierre Chouteau in 1897 as support material for his proposal to recreate the village of old St. Louis on the levee. Courtesy Missouri Historical Society.

Francisco Cruzat. Courtesy Missouri Historical Society.

Carlos Dehault Delassus. Courtesy Missouri Historical Society.

Don Francisco Héctor de Carondelet. From *A History of Louisiana,* by Alcée Fortier (1904). Photograph courtesy Historic New Orleans Collection.

CHAPTER FOUR
YOU CANNOT LOCK UP
AN OPEN FIELD

The final two decades of Spanish rule in Upper Louisiana were no less turbulent than the preceding ones. The return of East and West Florida to Spain at the conclusion of the American Revolution in 1783 helped erase the bitter memories of the humiliating debacle that had forced the Spaniards to surrender those territories to England twenty years earlier, but hard-pressed Spanish officials had little time to savor the victory. Even in defeat, the British had managed to solidify their control over the Indian trade on both sides of the upper Mississippi, and in the lower valley the fledgling American republic's vast and restless westward-moving population quickly became a new source of concern. While the Spaniards attempted to fend off the British and American incursions into their domains, they also encountered an unexpected challenge from French revolutionaries, who began to propose the restoration of French rule in Louisiana after the Bourbon dynasty was overthrown.

With England, the United States, and France all threatening the Spanish borderlands, the escalating level of Indian resistance along Louisiana's extended frontiers seemed even more ominous. As the uncertainties born of these rivalries intruded into the daily routines of Missouri's remote frontier settlements, the inhabitants found themselves caught up in a far-ranging international conflict that most understood only vaguely.

The surge of American settlers across the Alleghenies following the American Revolution presented Spanish authorities with a perplexing challenge. For a monarchy grounded in traditional notions of privilege, hierarchy, and order, the hordes of disorderly Americans filling up adjacent territories were alarming. In an effort to block further American expansion, the Spaniards announced the closing of the Mississippi to U.S. commerce in 1784. They hoped this action would destroy the western American settlements by shutting off their only commercial outlet.

The Spanish government also dispatched Diego de Gardoqui to Philadelphia in search of a negotiated settlement with the United States, but his instructions specified that he was not to make any concession on the navigation of the Mississippi. After a year of fruitless discussion, Gardoqui and his American counterpart, John Jay, attempted to break the impasse with an arrangement to trade a commercial treaty for a U.S. agreement sanctioning the closure of the Mississippi for thirty years. The proposal was not popular in either country, and the negotiations broke down. Meanwhile, some free-spirited Americans had responded to Spain's attempts to deny them access to the Mississippi by threatening to open the river forcibly if necessary.[1]

Spain's failure to conclude an agreement with the United States, coupled with a growing recognition that the unsteady young republic might not be able to restrain its rifle-toting settlers from attacking poorly defended Spanish positions, forced officials in Louisiana to consider alternatives for dealing with the American threat. For the first time, the Spaniards seriously discussed the feasibility of inviting Americans residing in the western provinces to abandon U.S. governance and embrace Spanish rule. Proponents of that plan contended that with the proper incentives, the unpredictable Anglos could be changed into loyal subjects, who in turn could transform the isolated border territories into flourishing provinces. Spanish authorities decided to test that hypothesis by agreeing to allow all Anglo-American settlers already residing in their territories to remain, and Governor Esteban Miró began formulating plans for Hispanicizing them by using English-speaking Irish priests to convert them to the king's faith.

Because he had come to believe that the United States was the most promising source of immigrants for populating Louisiana, Miró listened with interest to a proposal for recruiting American settlers from Kentucky put forward by Pierre Wouves d'Argès, a roving Frenchman with firsthand knowledge of the trans-Appalachian wilderness. Following discussions in New Orleans with Miró and the Spanish intendant, Martin Navarro, d'Argès returned to France in 1787. He pressed the Spanish ambassador in Paris to endorse a plan permitting Americans in the western U.S. territories to send their produce down the Mississippi after the payment of a duty and inviting them to settle in Spanish territory. D'Argès's lobbying efforts paid off. Hoping to placate Americans angered by the Mississippi's closing and to capitalize on their disaffection with the U.S. government, officials in Madrid agreed to the d'Argès proposals in mid–1787. Having gained the Spanish court's blessing, the French adventurer returned to North America to spearhead efforts to persuade Americans to move to Louisiana.[2]

In taking the unprecedented step of urging the admission of American Protestants, Miró embraced the notion that many residents of the western U.S. territories were not strongly attached to their government and would, over time, accept Spanish ways and religion. Even before they became the king's faithful servants, he reasoned, the presence of Americans in Louisiana would strengthen the province, and he also predicted that their exodus from the United States would weaken its underpopulated western settlements. To attract them, Spain promised that all immigrants who took a loyalty oath and became bona fide residents of his majesty's domains would be granted free lands, equal commercial privileges with all Spanish subjects, and religious toleration.[3]

At about the same time that Spain announced its new immigration policies, James 'A. Wilkinson, an opportunistic American businessman with a penchant for wheeling and dealing, arrived in New Orleans with a cargo of Kentucky produce and some ambitious schemes of his own for Louisiana. The well-educated Wilkinson was the son of a well-to-do Maryland merchant planter. He had briefly studied medicine, but at the outset of the American Revolution he entered the army, where he quickly won the brevet rank of brigadier general, along with appointment as the U.S. clothier general. Sloppy record keeping subsequently caused the youthful officer to lose the latter position, and at war's end he resigned from the service. Wilkinson moved to the Kentucky frontier, where he dabbled in land speculation, politics, and commerce. His prospects in the business world had not suffered from his marriage to the socially prominent Ann Biddle of Philadelphia. The enterprising American was not above conniving with Spanish officials—or anyone else, for that matter. In an effort to boost his growing trade in western produce, he developed a set of proposals similar to those of d'Argès and urged them upon the Spanish authorities in New Orleans.[4]

Actually, Wilkinson offered two separate strategies for the Spaniards to consider. The first suggested that they use their control over navigation and commerce on the Mississippi to create a pro-Spanish faction in Kentucky sympathetic to separating the province from the United States and making it a part of Louisiana. The alternative proposition called for a liberalized Spanish immigration policy designed to attract American settlers to Louisiana by depopulating Kentucky. Wilkinson contended that the widespread discontent with the Confederation government's ineptitude in handling western problems would make Kentuckians receptive to either plan. Although he personally favored the first approach, he indicated a willingness to work for whichever plan Spanish officials preferred. His presentation impressed Governor Miró, who invited him to return for further discussions, during which the governor suggested he draft a memorial to the Spanish government outlining his recommendations. Wilkinson's second proposal so closely paralleled Miró's own ideas on immigration that the governor may have had a hand in its formulation. He strongly endorsed the American's suggestions and forwarded them to officials in Spain for approval.[5]

Wilkinson's machinations undercut d'Argès's plans. Following his return to the United States, the Frenchman encountered unexpected resistance from both Gardoqui and Miró. His lengthening list of personal demands had put off Gardoqui, and Miró had by then cast his lot with the influential Wilkinson's better and more comprehensive schemes. D'Argès declined an appointment as commandant at L'Anse à la Graisse, a minor outpost on the Mississippi at a place soon to be known as New Madrid, and returned to France in frustration.[6]

Officials in Spain were more cautious than their subordinates in America and took their time in responding to Wilkinson's overtures. The Spanish Council of Ministers worried about the danger of a clash between Wilkinson and d'Argès, but Gardoqui's continuing lack of progress in negotiations with the Confederation government prompted them to act. In naming Wilkinson to supplant d'Argès as Spain's principal immigration agent in Kentucky, the ministers authorized their new collaborator to recruit Americans under terms very similar to those previously approved for d'Argès. At the same time, however, the king's advisers rejected Wilkinson's proposal for encouraging a revolution in Kentucky on the grounds that it was too dangerous. While promising to monitor closely the situation there, they declined to take any direct action as long as Kentucky remained a part of the United States. Secessionist sentiment in Kentucky waned rapidly following the ratification of the new federal constitution, and in a 1789 memorial to the Spanish ministers, Wilkinson agreed to concentrate on promoting immigration.[7]

Meanwhile, from his post in Philadelphia, Gardoqui, the Spanish minister to the United States, was independently pursuing his own schemes for encouraging American settlement in Louisiana. Among those whom Gardoqui interested in his colonization project was Col. George Morgan. Morgan had been at various times a trader, public official, revolutionary soldier, U.S. Indian agent for western tribes, and land speculator. After the Continental Congress disallowed certain of his land dealings, the prospect of receiving a Spanish concession on the Mississippi's west bank caught his attention. Morgan was no stranger to the Illinois Country. Twenty years earlier he had resided at Kaskaskia while serving as a representative of the Philadelphia mercantile firm Baynton, Wharton, and Morgan. With the Spanish minister's encouragement, he prepared a detailed plan for establishing a colony in Upper Louisiana across from the mouth of the Ohio.[8]

Morgan envisioned himself as the commandant of the semiautonomous colony with authority to name all local officials and to make land grants in full title. He also suggested permitting the colonists to pass their own laws through a representative assembly, with the proviso that all such statutes would be subject to a royal veto. Under his plan, the colony would enjoy complete religious freedom, and immigrants would be permitted to bring all of their possessions into the territory duty free. Morgan requested a commission in the Spanish army at the same rank that he had held in the American army, but without pay unless in actual service. In addition, he sought grants of land for himself and his family, along with a regular salary for his services.[9]

Gardoqui wholeheartedly supported Morgan's plan and approved his terms, subject to final authorization from the crown. On the strength of the minister's tentative approbation, the American promoter impetuously forged ahead without waiting for royal confirmation. He circulated hand-bills describing the proposed settlement and inviting interested persons to join him on an exploratory mission to select a site and initiate preliminary surveys. U.S. officials generally looked upon Spain's attempt to recruit American settlers as suicidal. Secretary of State Thomas Jefferson wryly observed in 1791, "I wish a hundred thousand of our inhabitants would accept the invitation. It may be the means of delivering to us peaceably what may otherwise cost a war. In the meantime we may complain of this seduction of our inhabitants just enough to make them believe it very wise policy for them, and confirm them in it."[10]

From the large number who volunteered to accompany him to Spanish Louisiana, Morgan selected seventy men. They departed from Fort Pitt on 3 January 1789 and reached the Mississippi on 14 February. The delegation temporarily joined a Delaware encampment across from the mouth of the Ohio, where Morgan renewed friendships with some of the Indians he had worked with while serving as a U.S. Indian agent. Most of the expedition's members remained at the Delaware camp while Morgan and a small contingent traveled to St. Louis for a conference with Lieutenant Governor Manuel Pérez. Pérez cordially welcomed the Americans and offered them horses, guides, and provisions. Buoyed by his favorable reception, Morgan hurried to rejoin his recruits, who already had begun moving southward in search of a suitable place for the new settlement.[11]

Morgan selected a site about a mile below the place known as L'Anse à la Graisse, where several French traders already had taken up residence. The region, which had long been a favorite spot for hunting camps, was located on the west bank of the Mississippi a short distance below the Ohio junction. With an eye toward future promotion, Morgan replaced the original name, which meant "Greasy Bend," with the more elegant-sounding New Madrid. Befitting the city's new name, he drew up elaborate plans, calling for the construction of carefully laid-out streets with adjoining foot paths, churches of various denominations, schools, and a public park adjacent to the town's natural lake.[12]

In his planning Morgan showed a surprising interest in preserving the local environment. He directed:

The timber, trees, and shrubs, now growing thereon, shall be religiously preserved as sacred; and no part thereof shall be violated or cut down, but by the personal direction and inspection of the chief magistrate for the time being, whose reputation must be answerable for an honorable and generous discharge of this trust, meant to promote the health and pleasure of the citizens.[13]

Morgan exhibited a similar concern for the local fauna, which was by all accounts plentiful: the abundant supply of buffalo and bear meat had given the settlement its original name. Morgan's regulations banned professional white hunters from residing in the colony and permitted the killing of buffalo and deer only for feeding the local populace. "This regulation," he wrote, "is intended for the preservation of these animals, and for the benefit of neighboring Indians, whose dependence is on hunting principally—this settlement being wholly agricultural and commercial . . . . "[14] Such concerns were remarkable for both the time and place, but Morgan's interest in making money was more conventional.

As soon as the ordinances had been drafted, the American entrepreneur ordered a land survey and opened a land office, where he offered 320-acre tracts for $48 apiece, subject to final confirmation by the king. During the spring of 1789 New Madrid was the scene of intense activity. The prospective residents cleared a large field, planted crops, built storehouses, and generally busied themselves in preparation for the expected rush of settlers from the United States.[15]

With the necessary arrangements well underway, Morgan departed for New Orleans to discuss his plans with Governor Miró. To his dismay the Spanish officer was barely civil. Miró considered Morgan's proposals for "a little republic" fatally flawed because they offered no incentives to encourage the Americans to embrace Spanish rule and convert to Catholicism. He also saw no reason for allowing the American promoter to enrich himself by selling lands that the Spaniards gave away. The governor's negative assessment had been bolstered by the arguments of James Wilkinson, who looked upon Morgan's scheme as a threat to his own plans. Despite his misgivings, Miró gradually softened his criticism of Morgan, whose services he still hoped to employ in encouraging American immigration. After rejecting Morgan's original plan outright, the governor offered to let the American promoter bring families to New Madrid under the regulations previously set down by the Spanish government in 1787. Miró further agreed to confirm the land patents that Morgan had already awarded to settlers and promised him a one-thousand acre grant with an equal amount for each of his sons. Finally, the governor offered Morgan the vice commandant's position at New Madrid.[16]

Following his departure from New Orleans, Morgan returned to Philadelphia, where he reported to Gardoqui his conversations with Miró. He
indicated a willingness to continue working for American immigration, but
his dissatisfaction with Miró's required changes had cooled his ardor.
Within a short time he abandoned the project entirely. Morgan never went
back to New Madrid, and most of the individuals who had accompanied
him to the settlement in 1789 also decided against remaining and returned
to the United States. Others did come to New Madrid, particularly French
settlers from Vincennes and the American Illinois settlements. The plans
for building an agricultural colony were slow to materialize as hunters,
traders, and boatmen remained the predominant elements in New Madrid's
populace.[17]

Spain's initial efforts to encourage American immigration failed to attract
the large numbers of settlers that proponents of the plan had envisioned.
Between 1 December 1787 and the end of 1789, only 293 Americans availed
themselves of the opportunity to settle in Spanish Illinois, and that figure
included 106 black slaves who had no choice.[18] Wilkinson's activities in
Kentucky had also foundered after he lost interest when the Spaniards
decided to reopen the Mississippi to American commerce subject to the
payment of duties. Wilkinson had vigorously opposed that move because
he insisted the Americans would pay the duties rather than go to the trouble
and expense of moving to Spanish territory. He therefore considered any
further campaigning to recruit American immigrants to be futile.[19]

Recurring reports that an army of American banditti was poised for a
strike against the Mississippi River settlements forced officials in Spanish
Illinois to keep a watchful eye throughout the 1780s. Sporadic Indian hostilities added to the local unease. In May 1784 a Big Osage party forced two Ste.
Genevieve hunters to strip naked and then left them stranded in the
wilderness, bereft of food, clothing, or supplies. Later that summer, members of the same tribe made away with a number of horses belonging to the
town's residents.[20] Fortunately Upper Louisiana's settlements escaped the
most serious Osage depredations. Governor Miró's 1787 order suspending
all trade with that tribe was intended primarily to combat the assaults
committed by breakaway Osage bands occupying the Arkansas River. But
much to the dismay of St. Louis traders, the ban also applied to them. Miró
clearly had doubts about his proposed course, for after ordering the closing
of the Osage trade he cautioned Lieutenant Governor Cruzat not to make
the powerful Osages Spain's permanent adversaries. Treat them, he advised, as errant and disobedient sons rather than as enemies.[21]

Cruzat's successor, Manuel Pérez, who arrived in St. Louis in November
1787, inherited the thorny problem. Miró's hesitant steps to counter the

Osage depredations brought an angry response from tribal leaders, who descended upon St. Louis to protest the unfairness of the governor's decision to close all trade. Less than a month later a Little Osage party murdered, scalped, and then decapitated Jean La Buche while he was hunting along the Meramec with his two sons. The brutal killing, a rarity in Spanish Illinois, left residents of the region shaken. Pérez demanded that the Little Osages turn over the culprit responsible for this act, but when tribal members reported that the accused warrior had subsequently died from injuries suffered in an accident, the lieutenant governor accepted their word and did not pursue the matter further.[22]

The fear of increased Osage attacks prompted the Spaniards to encourage emigrant Indian tribes from east of the Mississippi to move to Missouri so they could act as a buffer between the hostile Osages and Upper Louisiana's exposed settlements. In 1780 approximately two hundred Peoria warriors and their families took up residence a short distance from Ste. Genevieve, and at about the same time members of the Shawnee and Delaware tribes also began settling in Spanish Illinois farther to the south.[23] For many years the eastern tribes occasionally had crossed the Mississippi to hunt or receive presents from the Spaniards, but the destruction of several Shawnee towns during the American Revolutionary War caused some members of that tribe to take refuge on the west bank. One small Shawnee band settled near St. Louis, and Capt. Alexander McKee reported in June 1784 that some Delawares, often referred to by the French as the Loups, were also leaving the United States and moving permanently to the Spanish side of the river.[24]

Louis Lorimier, a Canadian-born métis (mixed-blood) trader with a Shawnee wife and strong ties to both the Shawnees and Delawares, actively recruited them to join him on the Saline Creek south of Ste. Genevieve following his arrival there in 1786. Lorimier, who wore his black hair in a long queue that he allegedly used as a whip while riding his horse, previously had operated a trading post with his father in Ohio. He cast his lot with the British during the American Revolution, and with the aid of his Shawnee allies he once captured Daniel Boone. Lorimier, who barely escaped with his life when George Rogers Clark attacked and burned his post in 1782, eventually found a safe haven in Spanish Louisiana, where Lieutenant Governor Pérez fully supported his efforts to persuade the eastern Indians to follow him west of the Mississippi. By 1787 a reported twelve hundred Shawnees and six hundred Delawares accepted the Tory trader's invitation and settled along the Saline, Apple, Cinque Hommes, and Flora creeks south of Ste. Genevieve. They came seeking to take advantage of Upper Louisiana's expanding fur markets and its plentiful supply of game. There were occasional incidents between the Indian new-comers and the European settlers. Shortly after their arrival, one of the Delawares assaulted Pierre Morin not far from St. Louis. The Frenchman protested his treatment to Pérez, who then ordered a local militia company under Charles Tayon's command to chastise the errant band. When the militiamen killed five Delawares in retaliation for the attack, critics accused them of having used excessive force. Spanish authorities summoned Tayon to New Orleans to answer for his conduct, but the resulting investigation cleared Tayon, who was subsequently appointed commandant of St. Charles.[25]

Elsewhere, the relations between the emigrant Indians and their white neighbors were friendlier. George Morgan's reconnaissance expedition stayed at a Delaware camp across from the Ohio River in early 1789, and tribal representatives helped acquaint the American promoter and his followers with the region. Sometime around 1792, Lorimier moved from Saline Creek to Cape Girardeau, where he opened a new trading establish-ment, and by all accounts his influence among the emigrant tribes re-mained undiminished. The following year Louisiana's new governor, the Baron de Carondelet, confirmed Lorimier's de facto trading monopoly with the Shawnee, Delaware, and other refugee tribes located between the Missouri and the Arkansas rivers.[26]

The transplanted tribes resided in villages scattered in the eastern Ozarks. A 1797 report indicated the presence of Shawnee, Delaware, Peoria, Illinois, Miami, Ottawa, Mascouten, Kickapoo, and Potawatomi Indian camps in Spanish Illinois. Aside from occasional clashes with the fierce Osages, who resented the intrusions, and sporadic incidents of alleged thievery, animal killing, and drunkenness, the emigrant Indians lived peaceably in close proximity to white settlements. The whites, who came in frequent contact with the nearby tribes and maintained regular commercial ties with them, considered some tribes better neighbors than others. The recurring Osage attacks against Ste. Genevieve and its environs suggest that the emigrant tribes were an ineffective shield, but their presence made them very much a part of everyday life in the region.[27]

Governor Miró's successor in Louisiana, the Baron de Carondelet, who took office in 1792, took a dim view of the various schemes for Anglo-American colonization. The intrepid incoming officer of the crown may not always have acted wisely, but his determination to defend Spain's interests was never in doubt. He clearly feared the ambitious Americans, whom he described as "determined bandits armed with carbines . . . hostile to all subjection."[28] Warning that American promises of independence, self-gov-ernment, taxation by consent, and free trade might eventually persuade the

Anglo inhabitants of Louisiana's underpopulated settlements to turn against their Spanish rulers, Carondelet advised his superiors that "a general revolution in America threatens Spain, if that country does not hasten forcibly and promptly to apply the remedy."[29]

Carondelet's remedy was a more aggressive policy for protecting Spain's New World possessions. He proposed to revert to the earlier policy of recruiting a loyal European Catholic population more compatible with Spanish rule and monarchical government. He organized a buildup of Louisiana's military defenses and negotiated alliances with southern Indian tribes, whom he encouraged to resist further American expansion westward. He also contemplated resurrecting plans to promote a separatist movement in the western territories of the United States.[30] The governor's call to man the bulwarks against revolution came at a time when the forces of change were sweeping across Europe. The revolutionary forces that had just toppled the Bourbon dynasty in France unexpectedly confronted the Spaniards as a potential new foe in Europe and America.

As part of his effort to lure European immigrants to Louisiana, Carondelet dispatched Ste. Genevieve's controversial commandant, Henri Peyroux de la Coudrenière, to Philadelphia in 1792 to initiate contact with French, German, Irish, or Flemish emigres who might be willing to move there. Peyroux's mission was a failure: the altered conditions in Europe following Louis XVI's execution and the outbreak of war between France and Spain had dampened European interest in settling in the Spanish colony.[31] Pierre-Charles Delassus de Luzières, a French aristocrat who had fled his homeland to escape the revolution, was a notable exception. With Carondelet's blessing, De Luzières headed an effort to attract French emigre settlers from Gallipolis on the Ohio River and elsewhere to the settlement he established three miles south of Ste. Genevieve on the hills overlooking the Big Field. The staunch royalist named his new village New Bourbon as a tribute to the late French king.

The transition from the fashionable life at the French court to the primitive ways of frontier America was a traumatic experience for the well-born De Luzières family, but especially so for Madame de Luzières. When Moses Austin visited them in 1797, he admired a large painting in their home depicting a grand festival staged by the people of Paris to honor Queen Marie Antoinette on the occasion of the birth of the Dauphin. Madame de Luzières pointed to the coach in which she had been riding on that happy occasion, and then poignantly remarked, "My situation is now strangely changed." It is hardly surprising that so few of their aristocratic emigre compatriots chose to follow them to the North American hinterlands. Spanish Illinois was a far cry from Paris. The De Luzières' son, Charles

Dehault Delassus, fared better than his parents. He joined the Spanish service in 1782, became commandant of New Madrid in 1796, and served as Upper Louisiana's lieutenant governor between 1799 and 1804.[32]

On other fronts, the energetic Carondelet's ambitious plans for rescuing Louisiana moved ahead with greater dispatch. After pronouncing the province's defenses sadly lacking, he gained approval in January 1792 for the construction of a squadron of naval galleys to patrol the Mississippi River. The freshwater fleet's completion came none too soon.[33] That fall, reports again began circulating that American adventurers were planning to attack Spanish positions along the Mississippi, and New Madrid seemed a likely target. The new settlement was strategically located on the first high ground below the mouth of the Ohio on the west bank. Miró had sent Lt. Pierre Foucher and a detachment of royal troops there in 1789 to construct a fort, which they named Fort Céleste in Señora Miró's honor.[34] The threats against the post in 1792 prompted Carondelet to instruct militia units in all other Upper Louisiana settlements to be prepared to report to New Madrid at first signs of an attack. As an added precaution he dispatched *La Flecha*, one of the new freshwater naval vessels, to the Mississippi River outpost with additional arms and munitions.[35]

As officials in Spanish Illinois watched for a possible invasion during the fall of 1792, a small party of travelers from the west unexpectedly arrived in St. Louis. Pedro Vial, a seasoned wilderness pathfinder, arrived in the capital city on 3 October with two traveling companions following a harrowing eleven-hundred-mile trip from Santa Fe. New Mexico's governor, Fernando de la Concha, had sent them eastward in search of a route linking the two Spanish outposts and in order to gather additional information about tribes in the region. Vial returned to Santa Fe the following year with encouraging news concerning the feasibility of the long-desired connection. But Spanish authorities in the southwestern city had begun to have second thoughts about tying themselves to the besieged eastern province and chose not to follow with another expedition. In fact, Vial's journey, which took him along portions of the later Santa Fe Trail, brought home to the Spaniards the expanding American republic's relative proximity to their valuable Mexican mines.[36]

The outbreak of war between France and Spain in 1793 had revived fears that Louisiana might soon be attacked. When Citizen Edmond Charles Genêt came to the United States as the representative of the French revolutionary government, he sought to convert the United States into a base for operations against England and Spain. Shortly after his arrival, Genêt dispatched representatives to the western U.S. provinces to recruit Americans for an assault against Spanish Louisiana and Florida. George Rogers

Clark, a hero of the American Revolution in the west who had since fallen on hard times, accepted a commission from Genêt, and in January 1794 he issued a call for volunteers to open the Mississippi to duty-free navigation. In return for their services Clark promised all recruits land grants in the Spanish territories.[37]

Rumors of an impending Franco-American invasion spread like wildfire among Louisiana's jittery residents during the early months of 1794. Carondelet instructed Spain's secret agent James Wilkinson to monitor carefully any developments in Kentucky, and in January the governor-general ordered six boats from the naval squadron to transport 150 troops upriver to reinforce the Spanish outpost at New Madrid. Thomas Portell, the panicky commandant there, had become convinced that his post was all but lost. All along the Mississippi, residents of Missouri's river towns took special precautions to defend themselves. In Ste. Genevieve, François Vallé spearheaded efforts to build a wooden fort under the supervision of the young engineer-surveyor Antoine Soulard. Louis Lorimier was equally busy at Cape Girardeau attempting to organize support among his Indian friends.[38] When the invading army failed to materialize, the fears gradually subsided, and by 8 June, Lieutenant Governor Trudeau happily reported from St. Louis that "it has been a long time since the country has enjoyed such a great tranquility. I find the inhabitants truly satisfied with the fact that the French expedition never appeared to have taken place."[39] In fact, the Spaniards needed to thank President George Washington and the U.S. government for their assistance in squelching Genêt's attempts to mount an invasion.

The 1794 crisis also had caused Carondelet to reassess Spain's troubled relations with the powerful Osages. When the baron assumed Louisiana's governorship in 1792, it was all too apparent that Miró's efforts to combat the Osage assaults had been no more successful than his immigration policies. On the contrary, the number of Indian depredations was increasing. In Upper Louisiana, Big and Little Osage raiding parties stole horses and destroyed property in the vicinities of Ste. Genevieve, the Saline, and the Meramec. An especially harsh winter that had decimated the tribe's horse herds undoubtedly accounted for the upsurge in animal thievery.[40] In the midst of the escalating violence, Upper Louisiana's incoming lieutenant governor, Zenon Trudeau, found a Big Osage chieftain waiting to confer with him when he arrived in St. Louis. The tribal leader appeared suitably contrite and apologized for the recent depredations. He attributed most of the atrocities to the Little Osages, over whom he exercised no control. Acting no doubt with encouragement from the St. Louis fur merchants, who had suffered from the suspension of trade, Trudeau agreed to allow traders to return to the Big Osage villages. But in what had become an all-too-familiar refrain, he warned the chief that any future misdeeds would lead to an immediate interdiction of all supplies. The amiable Trudeau's willingness to accommodate local interests launched his administration on a positive note and made him the most popular of the lieutenant governors who served in St. Louis during the Spanish era.[41]

The St. Louis merchants welcomed Trudeau's decision to resume trade with the Osages, but elsewhere the reaction was less favorable. The Shawnee, Delaware, Miami, Ottawa, Potawatomi, and Peoria tribes, who accused the Osages of killing their people and stealing their horses, found it difficult to fathom. Likewise there was considerable grumbling in the Ste. Genevieve district, where the Osage raids continued apace. Amid increasing complaints, Carondelet ordered an extension of the total ban on Osage trade and invited the protesting rival tribes to make war on their Osage adversaries. Trudeau had misgivings about the wisdom of those actions and cautioned the baron not to expect a quick or easy victory over the powerful tribe, which, according to his estimates, could field 1,250 warriors.[42]

Trudeau's fears proved justified. Carondelet's attempts to force the Osages into submission not only failed, but produced the opposite effect, as Osage aggression increased. In January 1793 the Little Osages stole twenty horses in the Ste. Genevieve district. Trudeau had delayed publishing Carondelet's declaration of war against the Osages until 23 June 1793 in order to allow traders in the field to return safely to their homes. Spain's Indian allies declined to attack the Osages without assistance from Spanish forces, and a frustrated Trudeau again admonished his superiors in New Orleans that the Spaniards must either "annihilate the Indians or stop irritating them." Even the residents of Ste. Genevieve, who initially had applauded the governor's course, were having second thoughts in the wake of the mounting number of Osage depredations.[43]

So too was Carondelet, who expected Louisiana to be invaded by a Franco-American force at any moment. In an abrupt policy turnaround, in April 1794 he declared the war on the Osages to be at an end, and by mid-May he had willingly accepted Auguste Chouteau's offer to build, arm, and equip a fort on the Osage River near the principal Osage village. Chouteau promised to maintain a garrison of twenty men under the direction of his brother Pierre at the proposed stockade. In return, the St. Louis trader asked the Spaniards to give him a six-year monopoly of the rich Osage trade and two thousand dollars a year for the salaries of the men stationed at the fort. The terms were incorporated in an agreement signed in New Orleans on 18 May.[44]

These arrangements seemed to please everyone who participated in the discussions in the capital city. Carondelet happily turned the Osage problems over to the St. Louis merchant and his brother. The six Osage chieftains who had accompanied Chouteau to New Orleans to lobby for his plan were delighted at the prospect of having a permanent trading post near their villages, and the ambitious Chouteau brothers had successfully cornered exclusive rights to well over half of St. Louis's dwindling fur supply. The following summer, the Chouteaus built the promised fortification on Halley's Bluff in Vernon County and astutely named it Fort Carondelet in the governor's honor. The isolated fort had little, if any, strategic or military value, for the mighty Osages could have overrun it whenever they wished. Fort Carondelet was fundamentally a trading post whose presence near their villages assured the Osages of a constant supply of trade goods and also enhanced their prestige among neighboring tribes, who envied their good fortune.[45]

Auguste Chouteau's triumph had been marred, however, when a Chickasaw war party attacked the Osage dignitaries while they were en route back to their villages following the deliberations in New Orleans. The marauding Chickasaws killed three of the chieftains, including the influential Jean La Fond. The Chouteaus saw to it that the Osages were compensated for their losses, but the unexpected deaths created a leadership void within the tribe. The Chouteau brothers' subsequent attempts, with Spanish assistance, to influence the selection of successors for the deceased Osage leaders further factionalized the already divided tribe. Despite their meddling in internal Osage affairs, the Chouteaus retained tremendous influence with key elements of the tribe. They took advantage of what Lieutenant Governor Trudeau referred to as their "accredited ascendancy" to lessen Osage tensions with the Spanish Illinois settlements, and simultaneously to augment their personal fortunes through the profitable Osage trade.[46]

The assistance the Osages received from Canadian-based British traders had made it easier for them to sustain their independent course of action against the Spaniards through the years. Therefore, Trudeau, with Carondelet's backing, also embarked upon a more energetic program to curb British incursions in Spanish territory. In 1793 he dispatched a military expedition up the Mississippi, hoping to drive out British agents operating in the vicinity of the Des Moines River. The Spanish force captured several members of a trading party descending the Mississippi and brought two of the principals to St. Louis for questioning. One of the captured merchants, Andrew Todd, protested that the Canadians had traded openly in the region for years.[47] The situation on the upper Missouri was no better. Jacques d'Eglise, the first Spanish-licensed trader to reach the Mandan villages, returned to St. Louis in October 1792 and reported that the tribes he had visited were in regular contact with the British. His firsthand account provided further evidence of the need for action to defend Spanish interests in the upper valley.[48]

Declining profits in the St. Louis–based fur trade bore witness to the truth of these reports. Whereas previously Upper Louisiana's traders could expect to receive a 300 to 400 percent return on their investment, the current rate had dropped to only 25 percent.[49] In an effort to revitalize the sagging Indian trade and expand the shrinking St. Louis trading zone, Carondelet unveiled plans in 1792 for liberalizing Spanish trading policies by allowing any resident of Illinois who purchased a license from the government to engage in the fur trade. In October 1793, Trudeau summoned all of Upper Louisiana's traders to St. Louis to consider a detailed set of proposed regulations designed to make trading operations more efficient and eliminate inequities in the government-controlled system. The assembled traders listened carefully to Carondelet's proposals and suggested a number of modifications, including a recommendation that, whenever traders could not secure the merchandise they needed for the trade locally, they should be permitted to seek additional goods from British and American sources.[50]

The suggestions were forwarded to New Orleans for the governor's consideration, and when he issued his final directives shortly thereafter, he consented to their proposed changes. The merchants reassembled in St. Louis in the spring of 1794 to distribute the trade in accordance with the new regulations. Twenty-eight recognized traders attended the meeting and agreed to divide the trade with nine Missouri River tribes into twenty-nine equal parts, with one share reserved for the lieutenant governor. A drawing was held to determine the specific trading assignments, but Carondelet's attempts to broaden participation in the trade soon gave way to practical necessity. Auguste Chouteau's contract with Carondelet to construct a fort among the Osages had overturned the awards made in St. Louis and had given him exclusive control over sixteen of the twenty-nine shares originally allocated to various Missouri traders.[51]

At the initial St. Louis meeting, some of the traders had urged the formation of a company to extend Spanish trading operations along the upper Missouri. In view of the limited number of shares available for distribution, they continued to press for permission to organize such a company. When Carondelet signaled a willingness to approve the proposed venture, Jacques Clamorgan called a special meeting to draw up a tentative charter. By pooling their resources, the traders hoped to accumulate enough capital to finance the costly undertaking. However, not all merchants in Upper Louisiana desired to participate in the venture. Some considered it too risky; others preferred to concentrate on the trade rights they had already been assigned along the lower Missouri; still others refused to join because of personal rivalries and jealousies. The influential Chouteaus were the most conspicuous dissenters, but their reservations did not deter nine other established traders from seeking permission to proceed with the project. Trudeau lent his unqualified support to the new trading firm, officially known as the Company of Explorers of the Upper Missouri, but commonly called simply the Missouri Company. Not only did Trudeau believe that the new venture would boost the lagging Indian trade, but he also looked upon it as a perfect vehicle for securing additional information about the remote region and for counteracting the growing British presence there. The proposed marriage of private enterprise and public interest was a perfect application of Spanish mercantilist theory.[52]

The organizers pressed ahead with their plans and elected Clamorgan to direct the new company. A slave dealer, fur trader, merchant, financier, and land speculator, Clamorgan served as a prototype of the merchant capitalist who became so much a part of the frontier experience. Since his arrival in Upper Louisiana in late 1783 or early 1784 from the West Indies, the new director had cultivated the friendship of influential individuals throughout the Mississippi valley.[53] Even before Spanish officials had given their final approval for the Missouri Company's charter, Clamorgan dispatched a trading party from St. Louis with instructions to open commerce with the Mandan villages on the upper Missouri. To direct the expedition, Clamorgan selected Jean Baptiste Truteau, St. Louis's part-time schoolmaster, who obviously expected the fur trade to be more lucrative than teaching.

Following its departure in June 1794, Truteau's party managed to advance only as far as the Arikara country because of resistance from hostile tribes. Although Truteau remained in the Indian country until 1796, his trading venture turned out to be financially unprofitable for the Missouri Company, at least in part because of competition from Jacques d'Eglise, who had returned to the upper Missouri as an independent operator in direct competition with the new firm. D'Eglise, described by Trudeau as an ignorant man "who hardly knows how to speak his own French language," had rejected the Missouri Company's repeated requests to join them.[54] In spring 1795, the company sent out a second party with additional supplies and equipment for Truteau, whom they supposed to be trading with the Mandans. But the second group, headed by an inept trader named Lecuyer, did not even advance as far upriver as the first. After losing its goods to a band of pillaging Poncas, the party returned to St. Louis empty-handed.[55]

In view of the poor showing of the first two outings, the Missouri Company hired James Mackay, a Scottish trader from Canada who had recently become a Spanish subject, to replace Truteau as principal explorer and director of the company's operations in the Indian country. Mackay's party left St. Louis in August 1795, hoping to drive the British from the Mandan country and then proceed to the Pacific Ocean via the Missouri River. As a further inducement to their efforts, Carondelet had offered a three-thousand dollar prize to the first person to reach the ocean by that route. Mackay set up his headquarters near the mouth of the Platte River in Nebraska and directed the company's operations from there. He selected his Welsh lieutenant, John T. Evans, to lead an expedition upriver and on to the Pacific and, while en route, to keep an account of the region's natural history. Evans had come to North America three years earlier, searching for the legendary descendants of a mythical Welsh prince named Madoc. The young adventurer failed to find the tribe of Welsh-speaking, white Indians believed by some of his countrymen to be inhabiting the American wilderness, but on the expedition for Mackay he did reach the Mandan villages in west-central North Dakota. Once there, the Missouri Company agent commandeered a small British trading post, but the victory was only temporary. Evans subsequently withdrew, and the British traders soon returned.[56] Although the Mackay-Evans expedition was a financial disappointment, like its predecessors, it did yield unexpected dividends in the form of important new geographic and scientific information about the upper Missouri. Its members failed to reach the Pacific coast, but less than a decade later, a detailed map prepared from information provided by Mackay and Evans helped guide Lewis and Clark on the initial leg of their successful journey across the continent.[57]

Interest in pursuing operations on the upper Missouri declined in St. Louis as a consequence of the Missouri Company's poor showing. Unhappy investors in the venture blamed Clamorgan for their losses, but he successfully fended off his critics and through skillful maneuvering secured complete control of the faltering company. With backing from the powerful Canadian merchant Andrew Todd, who had recently transferred his base of operations to New Orleans, Clamorgan won Carondelet's approval for expanding the company's monopoly to include Indian trade on the upper Mississippi as well as the upper Missouri. In granting the additional concessions, Carondelet ignored vigorous protests from Clamorgan's St. Louis detractors. Clamorgan reorganized the Missouri Company's operations, but Todd's unexpected death in 1796 again brought both the firm and its principal stockholder to the brink of financial ruin.[58] Temporarily rescued by Auguste Chouteau and other St. Louis leaders who feared the adverse effects his bankruptcy might have upon the business community, Clamorgan never fully recovered his losses. By the end of the century his competitors began to secure concessions to the trade rights he formerly had monopolized, but the British grip on the trade in those regions was stronger than ever.[59]

In the meantime, as a part of Carondelet's continuing campaign to fortify Spanish possessions in the Mississippi valley, he dispatched Manuel Gayoso de Lemos, the governor of Natchez, on an inspection tour of Spanish Illinois in 1795. By sending Gayoso and a naval squadron to Upper Louisiana, Carondelet hoped to secure firsthand intelligence on conditions in that district and at the same time to impress Indians and local inhabitants with Spanish power, lest some of them be tempted to join Spain's rivals.[60]

The ultra-revolutionary doctrines of the French Jacobins had not attracted many followers in Upper Louisiana. Lieutenant Governor Trudeau admitted that occasionally an incendiary pamphlet might show up in Spanish Illinois, but he assured his superiors in New Orleans that the local citizens paid little heed to such documents. Trudeau cited the grief exhibited by the old French inhabitants at the time of Louis XVI's execution as evidence of continuing support for monarchy. Despite such reassurances, Spanish officials still openly worried that the region's French-speaking populace might be susceptible to the radical doctrines currently in vogue in their ancestral homeland. Wary as always, Carondelet instructed Gayoso to watch for signs of disloyalty. When he attended a gala reception honoring his arrival in St. Louis, Gayoso carefully scrutinized the assembled guests but found no evidence of revolutionary ardor. There were no tricolored ribbons or similar adornments except for the dress of three colors worn by Madame Joseph Robidoux, wife of a well-known trader, but Gayoso brushed that aside as merely a result of the lady's bad taste since he judged her garment to be older than the French Revolution. At virtually every stop on his itinerary—New Madrid, Cape Girardeau, Ste. Genevieve, St. Louis, and St. Charles—local leaders spared no effort in welcoming the visiting Spanish dignitary.[61]

Gayoso did not spend all of his time inspecting military installations, reviewing troops, attending parties and balls, and exchanging pleasantries with members of local elites. At Carondelet's direction, he took advantage of his reconnaissance trip to rendezvous secretly with secessionist agents from Kentucky. The governor-general had quietly resurrected James Wilkinson's earlier plans aimed at encouraging Americans residing in the western U.S. territories to break away from the American republic and place themselves under Spanish protection. The treacherous Wilkinson had been put on the Spanish payroll in 1792 and was receiving two thousand pesos a year for his services, even though he had returned to active duty in the U.S. army. Following the collapse of the Clark-Genêt mission, Wilkinson reported that the disillusioned Kentuckians would be receptive to renewed Spanish overtures. Gayoso followed up on Wilkinson's reports by conducting clandestine meetings in New Madrid with individuals from the U.S. territory known to be sympathetic to secession, but a sudden shift in Spanish policy caused Carondelet's superiors to squelch all such plans before they had a chance to materialize.[62]

In the unexpected diplomatic move, Manuel de Godoy, Spain's minister of foreign affairs, initiated a drive to secure accommodation with the United States. France's armies had overrun northern Spain, and Godoy had decided to sue for peace. In taking that step, Spain had deserted its recent alliance with Great Britain, and the Spanish foreign minister feared that the British might attempt to retaliate by securing U.S. cooperation for a joint assault against Florida, Louisiana, and other Spanish possessions. Hoping to forestall any such Anglo-American rapprochement, the Spaniards offered to settle all outstanding differences with the United States on the most generous terms possible. The two nations quickly reached an accord and signed the Treaty of San Lorenzo. In that 1795 agreement, commonly called Pinckney's Treaty in the United States after American negotiator Thomas Pinckney, Spain granted the Americans free navigation on the Mississippi and the right of deposit at New Orleans. Moreover, it acceded to U.S. demands by designating the thirty-first parallel as Florida's northern boundary.[63]

The provisions of the treaty dismayed Carondelet, for they canceled the effects of his arduous efforts to check American encroachment along the Mississippi. Believing his policies offered the best hope for safeguarding Spanish interests, he considered the treaty a serious mistake and stalled for as long as possible before implementing its provisions.[64]

Despite the peace treaty with France, the Spaniards remained wary of French intent in North America. A visit to St. Louis in 1796 by Victor Collot, a French general and suspected spy, did nothing to allay those suspicions. Collot, who was in fact attempting to gather information about military fortifications in the region, engaged in an elaborate ploy to keep secret the nature of his mission. He kept two journals, including one filled with praise for Governor Carondelet that he intentionally allowed others to read. In a further effort to gain the confidence of Spanish officials, he craftily passed along to them intelligence he had picked up suggesting that a British invasion of Spanish Illinois from Canada was imminent. When Collot learned that he was about to be arrested, he left St. Louis without advising Lieutenant Governor Trudeau. He failed to elude the Spaniards, who arrested his party and escorted him to New Orleans, where he was temporarily detained. After carefully examining his papers, replete with his laudatory observations about the governor-general, the Spaniards quietly ushered him out of the territory. Following his return to Philadelphia, rumors persisted that during Collot's visit many French-speaking St. Louisans had openly called for Louisiana's retrocession to France. Collot continued to pass himself off as a friend of the Spanish regime by again warning Spain's minister to the U.S., Carlos Martínez de Irujo, of the impending British invasion of Spanish Louisiana from Canada and offering his advice for improving St. Louis's inadequate defenses.[65]

Collot recommended that the Spanish employ Nicolas de Finiels, an expatriate French engineer who had served briefly in the American army, to oversee the project of improving the city's defenses. Without authorization from his superiors, Irujo sent Finiels to St. Louis, where he arrived in 1797. Lt. Col. Carlos Howard, the newly designated Spanish military commander for Upper Louisiana, was hesitant to involve this unknown outsider in the sensitive task of constructing military fortifications. He clearly preferred to leave that responsibility in the hands of Louis Vandenbemden, the Flemish engineer Carondelet had hired to oversee the project. Finiels considered Vandenbemden's plans flawed, but he was powerless to act without explicit authorization from Spanish authorities in New Orleans. With little to do while he waited for their decision, Finiels made an inspection tour of Upper Louisiana's settlements, compiled detailed notes about the region and its people, and put his talents as a skilled draftsman to work. James Mackay employed him to prepare a final draft of the famed Mackay-Evans map of the Missouri, which Lewis and Clark later found so helpful, and Finiels also prepared a wonderfully detailed map of the Mississippi showing each of Upper Louisiana's settlements. When suspicious Spanish officials in Upper Louisiana finally removed Finiels from the payroll and ordered him out of the province, he traveled to New Orleans, where he managed to find favor with Governor General Gayoso. The detailed report entitled "An Account of Upper Louisiana" that he compiled for the French prefect Pierre Clément de Laussat in 1803 is perhaps the richest single source document on Upper Louisiana at the end of the colonial period.[66]

The resumption of war between Great Britain and Spain in 1796 and the suspected French intrigues in Louisiana had prompted Governor Carondelet to assign Lt. Col. Carlos Howard to lead a military expedition to St. Louis and supervise arrangements for the region's defense. Carondelet's instructions called for the deportation to New Orleans of any suspected French agitators, the destruction of any British establishments along the Missouri and Mississippi rivers, the organization of nine militia companies in Upper Louisiana, and the strengthening of the fortifications at St. Louis in accordance with Vandenbemden's plan. With these actions the governor hoped to counter the dual threat of a British attack and a local uprising aimed at restoring French rule.[67]

Howard's arrival in St. Louis in April 1797 with a squadron of five Spanish vessels and a force of 110 Spanish regulars awed the residents of that village. Never had they witnessed a comparable display of Spanish military might. The Spanish officer soon concluded that the rumors of local insurrection had been greatly exaggerated and that the greatest danger to the settlement came from the British in Canada. To augment the dilapidated fortifications of St. Louis, he supervised the construction of four stone towers and a wooden blockhouse. Prior to his departure for New Orleans in August, he dispatched two galiots to the Des Moines River to intercept British traders and show the Spanish colors in that vicinity. Howard also sent spies as far north as Prairie du Chien to gather information concerning British activity along the upper Mississippi.[68]

While Howard labored to augment Upper Louisiana's military defenses, the fretful Carondelet reversed himself and agreed to permit a resumption of immigration from the United States in a vain effort to secure additional manpower for defending Louisiana against the British assault that was expected momentarily. Pinckney's Treaty had doomed Carondelet's plans for encouraging the western American provinces to separate from the United States, so he fell back upon the strategy of recruiting Americans. In 1796 and 1797 the Spanish commandants in Upper Louisiana circulated handbills in the United States outlining the advantages of settling in Spanish territory and offering liberal land grants to those willing to move. Spain's earlier efforts to populate Upper Louisiana through immigration had failed to attract the hoped-for influx. Those who had come were primarily French-speaking inhabitants from Canada and the settlements east of the Mississippi, but in response to this latest appeal the Americans started pouring in as early as the fall of 1796.[69]

The promise of free lands and no taxes at a time when many of the choicer lands in the United States had been occupied provided a powerful inducement. Daniel and Rebecca Boone, already renowned for their pioneering skills, were typical of the Americans who found the lure of free land irresistible. The Boones, who had been embroiled in a land dispute in Kentucky, had followed their son Daniel Morgan Boone to Missouri in 1799 after receiving a letter from Lieutenant Governor Trudeau encouraging them to migrate.[70] Two years earlier Moses Austin, who had come to the Spanish province to examine the lead mines, happily recorded in his journal, "Nature has undoubtedly intended this Country to be not onely the most agreeable and pleaseing in the World, but the Richest also."[71] It did not take long for the word to spread. When Carondelet's successor, Manuel

Gayoso de Lemos, attempted to turn back the American tide by again restricting immigration to Catholics, Zenon Trudeau and James Mackay both extolled the virtues of the American newcomers and warned that the prohibition against Protestants would cut off the only available source of industrious settlers.[72] Although Gayoso's efforts may have momentarily slowed the American onslaught, it was already too late to close the floodgates. Victor Collot's fears that the heavy immigration from the United States "would suffocate the French germs and succeed in changing the manners, taste, and even the language" were soon to be realized.[73] By 1804, when the United States formally took control of Upper Louisiana, more than three-fifths of its ten thousand inhabitants were Americans.[74]

For some time Spanish officials had recognized that, despite all of their efforts, Spain's grip on Louisiana had steadily weakened. Repeated failures and the growing expense of maintaining the vast territory had gradually dissipated the original Spanish eagerness to secure Louisiana and transform it into a protective barrier for Spain's other New World possessions. Consequently, by 1795 key officials in Madrid reluctantly concluded that further attempts to develop Louisiana into a buffer against Anglo-American penetration would be a waste of money and effort. As Godoy candidly observed, "You cannot lock up an open field." For this reason he had been willing to make the extensive concessions to the United States in the Treaty of San Lorenzo.[75]

From that time, high-ranking Spanish officials sought to use Louisiana primarily as a tool in diplomatic negotiations. Although the French had shown little interest in their former province during the quarter century immediately following its cession to Spain, the French Revolution rekindled interest in expanding France's overseas territories, and a growing number of French citizens began to call for Louisiana's return. During the 1790s the two nations discussed the possible retrocession of the territory on numerous occasions, but no final agreement had been reached. The Spaniards were resigned to surrendering the colony, but they wanted to wait for an opportune moment to unload it at a good price.[76]

The right time did not arrive until after the ascendancy of Napoleon Bonaparte in France. Following a temporary setback in the 1798 French campaign in Egypt, the first consul turned his attention to reestablishing a French empire in the western hemisphere. With that scenario in mind, he instructed Foreign Minister Talleyrand to secure Louisiana's return. Aware of the Spanish royal family's concern that the duke of Parma, the husband of a Spanish princess, had no position, the French offered to expand the Italian province of Tuscany into the kingdom of Etruria and give it to the duke and his wife in return for the retrocession of Louisiana. The Spaniards refused to include Florida in the transfer, but otherwise they accepted the terms outlined by the French. They incorporated the preliminary agreement in the Treaty of San Ildefonso, which their representatives signed on 1 October 1800.[77]

The treaty pleased both nations. With Louisiana in his possession, Napoleon could proceed with his plans for building an empire in the New World. On the other hand, Spain believed it had rid itself of an increasingly costly burden and at the same time remedied an embarrassing situation within the royal family. However, Spain did not formally surrender the province for nearly four years. During that time, the unexpected course of events drastically altered the situation in Louisiana, but after 1800 Spanish rule in Louisiana was nearing its end.

Louisiana was a great disappointment for the Spaniards, who barely managed to hold their own against Indian, British, French, and American challengers in the strategically situated borderlands province. Spain's wavering efforts to recruit new settlers had lagged until the regime's waning days. Even when growing numbers of Anglo-Americans crossed the Mississippi in the late 1790s, their scattered presence remained almost undetectable in the sprawling wilderness territory. Service in Upper Louisiana frequently proved to be a trying ordeal for Spain's outmanned and underfunded bureaucrats, who perennially struggled to make do with the limited available resources. Reflecting a sense of frustration born of nearly four decades of unrealized Spanish expectations, Upper Louisiana's departing lieutenant governor, Charles Dehault Delassus, scrawled "The devil take all" as his final entry in a ledger listing the distribution of the Indian trade for the years 1799 to 1804.[78]

CHAPTER FIVE
VILLAGES AND FARMSTEADS, COMMON FIELDS AND CLEARINGS

U pon arriving in Upper Louisiana in 1768, the Spaniards found fewer than one thousand white, black, and red settlers huddled in two small villages on the banks of the Mississippi. These newest Spanish subjects, both slave and free, were primarily persons of French and African ancestry who had come by way of Canada, Illinois, Indiana, lower Louisiana, and the West Indies, but their numbers also included second- and third-generation descendants of French-Indian intermarriages and a few full-blood Indian women.[1] Many had crossed the Mississippi at the close of the French and Indian War to escape English rule. Once the transfer of authority had been accomplished, however, the exodus from the east bank diminished significantly. As previously noted, Spain's initial attempts to recruit new settlers to Spanish Illinois proved disappointing until the late 1790s, when an influx of immigrants from the United States increased the population to about ten thousand.

Upper Louisiana's French inhabitants clustered in riverbank villages that differed markedly from American towns in outward appearance. The dwellings did not adjoin one another; instead, each was surrounded by gardens, orchards, barns, stables, and other outbuildings, all enclosed by a stockade fence made of cedar pickets or, for a more lavish residence, by a stone wall. There was no separate business district with shops, stores, and inns—the French simply conducted business out of their residences. The ample town lots gave the villages an appearance of being larger and more populous than they were.[2]

The middle Mississippi valley French vernacular house was a rectangular, single-story dwelling, built of timber or stone, surrounded by attached galleries (covered porches) raised well above ground level. The hipped or four-sided roofs had a double pitch, with the lower pitch over the galleries. The steeper slope of the roofs over the dwelling area of the house was originally designed to shed water in the days when thatched roofs were used. Builders soon replaced the grass coverings, which were both a fire hazard and a nesting place for vermin, with wooden shingles on all of the more substantial buildings, but they retained the distinctive roof style with its sharp angle of incline. The French relied primarily upon locally available materials such as stone, clay, and wood, especially oak, cedar, and pine. There were a few stone houses in St. Louis and later in St. Charles, but the great majority of middle Mississippi valley residences were constructed of squared logs. In contrast with the American practice of placing the timbers horizontally, the French erected them in an upright position, plastered over the cracks with mud and straw chinking, and whitewashed the exterior. There were two principal patterns of wall construction, the *poteaux en terre*, or post in ground, and the *poteaux sur sole*, or post on sill. In the former the bottoms of the logs were buried directly in the earth, and in the latter they stood on a heavy squared timber, which in turn rested on a stone foundation.[3]

The porches or galleries that surrounded one or more sides of all but the simplest dwellings performed dual functions: they kept the rain and snow off the plaster, preventing dampness, and they shaded the structure in the summer, keeping it considerably cooler. In the better houses glass was used in the casement windows, which swung in and out on hinges, in contrast with the vertical sliding windows preferred by American builders. For those unable to afford glass, oiled skin or cloth had to suffice as a window covering. One or two chimneys made of stone or of "cat and clay," a paste made of mud mixed with cut straw, serviced the fireplaces that provided for heating and cooking.[4]

Creole houses varied in size and elegance. The less prosperous habitants and *engagés* lived in crude one-room cabins or in picket lean-tos with dirt floors. The sturdier vernacular dwellings were remarkably similar in basic style and design. The larger residences belonging to the leading families were simply more spacious and better-built versions of the smaller French houses. By modern standards even the finer homes were relatively small. Most had only one or two multifunctional rooms, used for cooking, eating, sleeping, and socializing. A few had a separate side chamber, lean-to, or detached kitchen for food preparation to keep the heat away from the living quarters in summer and to diminish the danger from fire. Even the more humble dwellings were apt to have an outside oven.[5]

The interior walls were normally plastered and whitewashed. The size of the smaller dwellings limited the interior furnishings to a few rough and misshapen, locally produced pieces of furniture, including a bedstead, bedding, a table, chairs, a cupboard for utensils, and a chest for clothing. In contrast, a few of the more elaborate homes contained handsome mahogany and cherry armoires and cabinets, mirrors in gilded frames, elegant bed draperies, window curtains, and lavishly carved tables, which were often set with costly china and sterling silver, but even the more elegant homes did not contain the array of specialized eighteenth-century furniture types found in the better houses in Europe and the Anglo-American seaboard colonies.[6]

The rutted village streets turned into swampy quagmires during periods of inclement weather, and at those times travel by horseback was the only way to avoid becoming covered with mud when going from one residence to another. As if that were not bad enough, carts and plows carelessly abandoned by their owners sometimes cluttered the narrow roadways. Unattended livestock wandered aimlessly through the villages, and when an occasional animal died unexpectedly, its carcass was frequently left to decompose where it had fallen.[7]

Outside the village proper, the habitants worked in the enclosed common fields, where each resident could claim one or more of the long lots in accordance with their wealth and family size. The elongated strips, normally more than a mile in length, facilitated plowing with a team of yoked oxen since there were fewer corners to turn. Each farmer was responsible for maintaining specific sections of the fence that enclosed the field to ward off stray animals. Locally appointed syndics fined those who failed to keep their section in proper repair, and during planting and harvesting seasons a gatekeeper saw that the gate at the main entrance remained closed. Once the harvest had been completed, the gates were thrown open, and livestock was allowed to forage in the fields until time for spring planting. The villages also provided communal wood lots and grazing areas during the early years.[8]

In contrast with Upper Louisiana's French occupants, Americans who accepted Spain's invitation to take up residence in the region typically dispersed themselves in small settlement clusters or on scattered farmsteads in what they considered to be the healthier uplands away from the rivers. Spanish regulations confining European settlement to the river towns in an effort to simplify local administration and facilitate defense had reinforced the French pattern, but the incoming Yankees disregarded all such strictures and searched the interior regions for tracts with rich soil and low-density forests. The American's peripatetic habits seemed curious to Louisiana's old-time inhabitants, who frequently commented on the Yankee preference for occupying remote and unsettled places.

Armed only with a gun, an ax, and a sack of cornmeal, the American pioneers moved through the wilderness, camping out and living off the land until they found the right spot for their new farmstead. After locating a place to settle, they felled trees and constructed crude cabins. In contrast with the vertical placement of timbers favored by their French neighbors, the Americans laid the logs one on the other horizontally.[9] Sometimes they joined two separate cabins with a connecting roof and created a two-room structure known as a dog-trot dwelling. This popular house design was well suited to the early woodland frontier. It was relatively simple to build and provided a convenient way to enlarge a single-pen structure. The covered breezeway, with its bare earth floor, afforded a welcome refuge from summer heat. The American notched-log construction with mortised corners and mud chinking had numerous advantages: it made use of the most plentiful local building material and did not require nails, and buildings constructed in that fashion could be disassembled and the timbers reused.[10]

The Americans planted corn in the spaces they had cleared. Corn, an Indian crop, was an ideal staple. It grew well and the yields were good. People and animals ate it, although French Creoles insisted that it was better suited for livestock feed than for human consumption. When dried, corn kept indefinitely, and it could be transformed into two other frontier dietary staples—pork and whiskey. Like their Indian neighbors, with whom they frequently interacted, these backwoods American pioneers hunted, fished, gathered wild foods, and turned corn into meal cakes and deer meat into dried venison.

Theirs was largely a classless society with few centralized social institutions. They prized their independence and personal freedom, but they also stood ready to come to the aid of a neighbor needing assistance. Even so, it was an isolated and lonely existence, especially for women. Partial relief sometimes came when relatives and friends from former neighborhoods heeded an invitation to occupy nearby empty tracts. The resulting strings or clusters of contiguous improvements were loosely called settlements, but more often than not on the American frontier landscape one's nearest neighbor remained beyond shouting distance.

There were, of course, any number of localized variations in the common patterns. Some Americans chose to live in organized, compact settlements, and some French resided on irregular properties beyond any immediate village confines. A combination of cultural and environmental factors shaped individual choices on where to settle and contributed to the varied settlement forms that dotted the landscape, but on the whole the French retained their preference for the traditional village and the Americans maintained their predilection for a more random and dispersed settlement pattern.[11] Even though they outnumbered the French in Upper Louisiana near the end of the Spanish period, the isolated and scattered Americans remained a largely silent majority until after the advent of U.S. control. As Nicolas de Finiels, the French engineer who visited the region in 1797, noted in his 1803 memoir, "Since the arrival of the Anglo-Americans, several nations have added nuances of their various traits. They brought different manners, habits, and ideas, but these foreign elements are not yet well enough established to convey to the general mass a character that can be defined as a whole."[12] Upper Louisiana's sizable African population was concentrated primarily in the larger villages, but since most of them were slaves, the blacks had little to say about where they lived.

If at the outset the Americans failed to make an indelible impression in Upper Louisiana, the Spanish imprint was even less perceptible. After governing the province for nearly forty years, the Spaniards left surprisingly few traces of their presence. Except for a maze of unconfirmed land concessions and a few scattered place names, vestiges of Spanish rule quickly disappeared after the American takeover. Most of the few Spaniards who resided in the territory came to occupy civil and military posts and departed immediately following the expiration of their terms in office. The few who did settle permanently in Upper Louisiana—Manuel Lisa, Benito Vasquez, and Martin Miloney Duralde, for example—quickly embraced the French modes that prevailed in the colony until its transfer to the United States in 1804.[13]

The gradual increase in population during the final decades of the Spanish era helped sustain a series of new settlements in Upper Louisiana. To facilitate governance in the widely scattered villages and settlement clusters, the Spaniards divided the region into five administrative districts: St. Louis, St. Charles, Ste. Genevieve, Cape Girardeau, and New Madrid. Governor Carondelet created a sixth, New Bourbon, in 1797, primarily to make a suitable position for that settlement's aristocratic founder and leading citizen, Pierre Charles Delassus de Luzières.[14] Most of the new settlements traced their origins to the efforts of a handful of hardy souls who selected a promising site and attempted to carve a foothold in the surrounding wilderness. Some never advanced beyond that stage, but others joined St. Louis and Ste. Genevieve as thriving frontier villages.

St. Louis, the provincial capital and commercial center, was the most cosmopolitan and prosperous of Upper Louisiana's settlements at the end of the eighteenth century. In addition to its farmers, merchants, traders, and hunters, the city also boasted the most diverse array of artisans and craftsmen in the province.[15] When Moses Austin first visited St. Louis in 1797, he described it as "better built than any Town on the Missisipi . . . [with] a Number of wealthey Merchts. and an Extensive Trade, from the Missouri, Illinois and upper parts of the Missisipi."[16] The growing city with its two hundred houses was, he observed, the wealthiest town on the Mississippi. Seven years later Capt. Amos Stoddard, the American officer assigned to assume command of Upper Louisiana for the United States, was similarly impressed with the village that had once been called Paincourt. This is how he described it for his mother: "The compact part of St. Louis contains upwards of 200 houses, mostly very large, and built of stone;

it is elevated and healthy, and the people are rich and hospitable. They live in a style equal to those in the large sea-port towns, and I find no want of education among them."[17] In a similar vein, Finiels characterized St. Louis as "the center of manners, urbanity, and elegance in the Illinois Country."[18]

Commerce, fueled by the flourishing fur trade, was the engine that drove St. Louis from its earliest days. In contrast with Upper Louisiana's other villages, agriculture had always been relegated to a subordinate role in the capital city. Increased commercial and occupational specialization further diminished subsistence farming within the town's confines during the Spanish regime's final days. Successful merchants and artisans abandoned cultivation entirely in order to devote their undivided attention to their principal occupations. Simultaneously, more and more St. Louis farmers left the city and moved to the villages that were springing up in the outlying district. After selling their properties to commercially oriented neighbors eager to enlarge their real estate holdings in the thriving entrepôt, the departing habitants moved to one of the nearby agricultural settlements, where the daily rhythms seemed more attuned to their traditional ways. The exodus of small farmers from the city to the surrounding countryside was the principal reason for the slight decline in St. Louis's population during the 1790s. In 1800 only 1,039 of the district's 2,477 people lived in the city, but within a matter of two decades St. Louis boasted a population of over 4,500 and was well on its way toward becoming a major regional commercial center and the principal gateway to the American West.[19]

The earliest St. Louis satellite, Carondelet, was established in 1767 when Clément Delor de Treget, a former French naval officer, settled near the mouth of the River Des Peres. The fertile soil soon attracted a number of St. Louis farmers to the new settlement, which was located on the Mississippi three miles south of Laclede's original townsite. Initially called Delor's Village, the predominantly French agricultural outpost was successively known as Louisbourg, Vide Poche (Empty Pocket), and finally Carondelet. As its nickname, Vide Poche, suggested, the settlement was never particularly thriving. According to the 1800 Spanish census, the village's 192 residents owned only three slaves. Most village residents lived in crude wooden cabins located along the single street, which ran parallel to the river, and worked in the village's common field. They produced wheat, corn, and tobacco, along with vegetables, fruit, and milk, which they routinely transported to St. Louis for sale. The settlement's sole industry was a crude horse-driven mill used for grinding flour. A sizable contingent of Carondelet's younger males hired themselves out to St. Louis traders as boatmen to escape the drudgery of the fields. As in the other river communities, many of these predominantly French-Canadian males had Indian and mixed-blood wives. Despite Carondelet's poverty, its accessibility and the beauty of the surrounding countryside made it a popular place among early St. Louisans for pleasure excursions.[20]

Fifteen miles northwest of St. Louis, along the southern bank of the Missouri River near Coldwater Creek, was the settlement known either as St. Ferdinand or Florissant. In 1785 French Creole settlers had occupied the site, first called Fleurissant because the natural wet prairie was covered with flowers instead of timber. By 1800 the flourishing farm community boasted a population of 279, including 18 slaves. Blacks and whites labored side by side in the common fields, where they grew sizable quantities of wheat, corn, tobacco, oats, and hay. By 1803, several Americans had already settled in that vicinity.[21]

A group of hunters led by Robert Owens settled five miles southwest of St. Ferdinand in 1794 at a place known as Marais des Liards. Since the French term *liard* had two meanings—either a poplar tree or a small coin—the settlement's name could be translated either "cottonwood swamp" or "two-bit swamp." The two options may have been intentional, for the fun-loving French settlers would have delighted in such a play on words. The humor was evidently lost on the growing tide of American farmers who began moving into the traditional French village and the nearby bottoms during the closing years of the Spanish regime. Once they outnumbered the original Creole inhabitants, they changed the settlement's name to Owens Station and later to Bridgeton.[22]

The settlement of St. Andrews, located on the Bonhomme bottoms of the Missouri River twenty-four miles west of St. Louis, also proved popular with immigrants from the United States. Governor General Gayoso named James Mackay to serve as the commandant at that post in 1798, following his stint as the Missouri Company's chief agent on the upper Missouri. When Mackay took up his duties at St. Andrews in November, he advised Gayoso that twenty-nine American families, mostly from Kentucky, had in a short time cleared a great deal of land and raised a substantial quantity of grain. Mackay actively recruited additional settlers from the United States and vigorously protested Gayoso's attempts to halt the American influx at the close of the century. The fur trader turned town promoter regarded the governor's change of policy as an invitation for the Indians to plunder St. Andrews and other similarly exposed settlements. It was, however, the shifting river channel rather than the Indians that eventually led to that early Missouri village's demise. Amos Stoddard described St. Andrews as a large, flourishing settlement at the time of the American transfer, but when naturalist John Bradbury passed by in 1811, he reported that the village had been abandoned. The nearby and predominantly French settlement of

Creve Coeur (Broken Heart) also had to battle problems caused by flooding.[23]

In the adjoining district of St. Charles, which encompassed the territory north of the Missouri River, Louis Blanchette, a Canadian trader, moved up the Missouri in 1769 and established the settlement of St. Charles, originally known as Les Petites Cotes (The Little Hills). The village was a genuine frontier outpost, comprised mostly of hunters and traders, characterized as having the "Indians' habits without possessing any of their cruelty."[24] By relying on direct exchanges with the Indians for their subsistence, they freed themselves from what they considered to be the drudgery of agriculture. For them the frontier exchange economy provided a satisfactory existence, but for outsiders the primitive system appeared to be backward and unproductive.[25] Victor Collot's was a typical reaction:

St. Charles contains about 100 or 125 ill-constructed houses: the inhabitants do not till the ground, though it be extremely fertile; the ordinary occupations are hunting and trading with the Indians; a few hire themselves out as rowers, and it would be difficult to find a collection of individuals more ignorant, stupid, ugly, and miserable. Such are the side effects of extreme poverty, with its train of cares and evils, that it destroys not only the beauty of the person but even the intellectual powers, and blunts all those feelings of delicacy and sensibility which belong to a state of ease, and the advantages of a good education.[26]

Although, as Collot observed, the people of St. Charles were hunters and traders first and farmers second, they were raising substantial quantities of wheat, corn, and tobacco in the village common fields by the end of the Spanish era. The settlement, which had a population of 614 in 1800, boasted the first successful windmill in Spanish Illinois.[27]

Concerned by reports of American plans to establish a post across from the mouth of the Missouri, Lieutenant Governor Zenon Trudeau encouraged François Saucier to found a settlement in 1799 on the nearby strip of land between the Mississippi and Missouri rivers known as Portage des Sioux, so named when some Sioux Indians evaded a party of Missouri Indians by portaging across the alluvial lowland instead of going by water to the mouth of the Missouri and then proceeding upriver. The village drew most of its inhabitants from the French establishments on the east side of the Mississippi and became the St. Charles district's second-largest compact settlement. There were also scattered occupants residing along Dardenne Creek, which flows into the Mississippi north of the Missouri.[28] The tiny French settlement of La Charette, located on the Missouri fifty miles upriver from St. Charles and now known as Marthasville, was first settled in 1797.[29]

The St. Charles district attracted its share of the incoming American immigrants. Daniel Morgan Boone, scion of the famed pioneering family, first visited the region while on a hunting and exploring trip in the fall of 1797. At his father's request, he conferred with Lieutenant Governor Trudeau about his family's prospects for securing a land grant. The elder Boone was already renowned for his pioneering skills, and early the following year Trudeau invited Daniel and his family to move to Louisiana and granted them a one-thousand-arpent tract on the Femme Osage twenty miles upstream from St. Charles. As an added incentive, the Spanish lieutenant governor also promised six hundred arpents of land to other American families joining the Boones in their move across the Mississippi.[30]

In 1799, Daniel and Rebecca Boone took up residence with their son Daniel Morgan Boone at the Femme Osage. Other members of the Boone clan also accepted the generous Spanish terms. Two of their married daughters, Susannah Hayes and Jemima Callaway, settled nearby with their husbands and children, as did son Nathan and his new bride, Olive. Within a short time numerous members of the Boone, Bryan (Rebecca Boone was a Bryan), and Callaway families had settled on the banks of the Missouri. The elder Boones, who were by then in their sixties, soon found themselves surrounded by children, grandchildren, nieces, nephews, and close friends. In 1800 Lieutenant Governor Charles Dehault Delassus appointed the family patriarch to the office of syndic in Femme Osage. The Boones and their neighbors were in the vanguard of the growing wave of Americans who abandoned their Kentucky homes for the unsettled spaces of Spanish Illinois. In the St. Charles district the American newcomers had already begun scattering themselves along the lower Missouri, Cuivre, and Salt rivers before the end of the Spanish period.[31]

In the Ste. Genevieve district, the inhabitants of the region's oldest settlement, the village of Ste. Genevieve, faced a losing battle in their ongoing struggle to halt the bank cavings and flooding that perpetually ravaged their town. They drew up plans for constructing levees to shield their village from the Mississippi's rampaging waters, but the forces of nature could not be so easily tamed. Accustomed as the original village's inhabitants were to the periodic flooding, the catastrophic 1785 inundation left them in a state of shock when waters between twelve and fifteen feet deep covered their town and forced rivermen to tie their boats to the tall chimneys of the larger residences.[32] That calamity, along with several lesser floods during the same decade, effectively sealed the Old Town's fate; its residents gradually abandoned their flood-prone settlement in favor of a new site located on higher ground up the Mississippi across the Big Field, between the forks of Gabouri Creek. Unlike its predecessor, the new town had the appearance of a planned settlement, with streets intersecting at right angles. Not everyone vacated the original village at the same time, but by the early 1790s officials moved the parish church and the governmental headquarters to New Ste. Genevieve.[33] When Henry Marie Brackenridge returned to Ste. Genevieve in 1811, all that remained in the Old Town were some ruins and several fruit orchards.[34] In its new location, Ste. Genevieve withstood challenges from nearby communities to maintain its position as the district's principal settlement.

Although Ste. Genevieve's 1,163 inhabitants made it slightly larger than St. Louis in 1800, it still retained the aura of a rural village. A simplicity and neighborliness reminiscent of Upper Louisiana's earlier years increasingly differentiated Ste. Genevieve from its more cosmopolitan neighbor up-river. Agriculture remained the principal occupation in Ste. Genevieve, but its citizens also pursued lead mining, saltmaking, and the Indian trade.[35]

New Bourbon, located three miles south of Ste. Genevieve, was the district's second most populous settlement in 1800, with 630 inhabitants.[36] Established in 1793 under the auspices of the French nobleman Delassus de Luzières, its inhabitants were primarily farmers and included several Americans.[37] South of New Bourbon, there were settlement clusters along Saline Creek, a site long favored by saltmakers, and in the Bois Brule bottoms, situated immediately below the mouth of that stream.[38] A number of Kentuckians also entered the upland prairie or barrens in Perry County prior to the Louisiana Purchase. Although miners had long worked at several locations in the interior regions of the Ste. Genevieve district, notably Mine La Motte in Madison County, Mine à Breton and Old Mines in Washington County, and the Big River mines in St. Francois County, the ever-present danger of Indian attacks kept permanent settlers from venturing into the isolated region until near the end of the eighteenth century.[39]

Eventually it was the Americans who took the lead in establishing permanent, year-round interior settlements. Moses Austin dazzled Spanish officials with his proposals for increasing Upper Louisiana's lead production and persuaded them in 1797 to award him a concession for lands in the heart of mining country at Mine à Breton. He asked for a grant of approximately 70,000 acres, but settled for one-square league (about 4,250 acres), the amount allowable under Spanish law. Austin, who had operated mines in Virginia, immediately dispatched his assistants, Elias Bates and Judather Kendal, to Mine à Breton to launch preparations for his mining operations and for the settlement he intended to establish for the miners. Although the French had operated diggings at that location since shortly after François Azor *dit* Breton accidentally discovered the rich lead deposits while on a 1774 hunting trip, the place had remained a transient community. When

Austin's advance team arrived at the mines in 1798, there were a few substantial buildings along Breton Creek, but most of the structures were ramshackle cabins available for occupancy by the miners in season. According to Bates, "There was allmost always a continual changing of ownership in possession of those cabins and lots."[40]

Bates and Kendall were among the first permanent residents at Mine à Breton, later known as Potosi. Austin had no desire to live in the squalor of a crude frontier mining camp. The furnace house his men constructed was a well-proportioned, gabled building, topped with a cupola and a graceful bird-shaped weather vane, and Durham Hall, the two-and-a-half-story frame residence that he and his family occupied in 1799, resembled a Virginia manor house. The same year that the Austins moved into their new home, which Brackenridge described as "castle-like in appearance," the village also got its first flour mill. Three years later, thirty Osage warriors attempted to drive the American intruders from Mine à Breton, but the outnumbered Bostonians, as the Indians called them, stood their ground and repulsed the attackers. They did so without assistance from their nonchalant French neighbors on the other side of Breton Creek, who chose not to get involved in the fray. The assault dramatized the dangers of living so far inland, but Austin left no doubt that he and his family were there to stay. He subsequently rescued a cannon from the mud in Ste. Genevieve and secured District Commandant François Vallé's permission to install it at Durham Hall. Fortunately Austin never found it necessary to fire the three pounder against the Indians, but he once threatened to use it against his American arch rival, the notorious John Smith T. Missouri's earliest inland settlement was obviously no place for the timid.[41]

A number of other interior settlements, located in the infrequent pockets of good soil found in the eastern Ozarks, were established in quick succession after Mine à Breton. Encouraged by Austin's example, Scotch-Irish Protestants from western North Carolina and eastern Tennessee moved in 1798 into the nearby Bellevue Valley at Caledonia, where they began raising foodstuffs that found a ready market among Mine à Breton's growing population.[42] Another group of American farmers established themselves in 1799 at Murphy's Settlement, subsequently called Farmington.[43]

The American example encouraged the French to venture away from the Mississippi, most likely in an effort to prevent the land-hungry newcomers from seizing all of the good interior lands. Thirteen French families, most of whom were from Ste. Genevieve and New Bourbon, received a concession from Spanish authorities in 1799 for a tract containing the best agricultural land in the vicinity of Mine La Motte. In seeking permission to move inland, they complained that the lands they were currently inhabiting were worn out and inadequate for the needs of their families. At their new location, these farmer-miners established St. Michel, or St. Michaels, a traditional French village that was the precursor of Fredericktown.[44]

Three years later, several poor mining families moved from Mine à Breton to Old Mines, complaining that the creek waters at their former place of residence were polluted by animal wastes and ore washing. Philippe Renault had operated diggings at the Old Mines location as early as the 1720s, but the mines had not been worked for many years. The miners' decision to reoccupy the abandoned site and the growing American presence in the mining district rekindled the interest of several prominent Ste. Genevieve mining entrepreneurs in the Vieille Mine, as they called it. The poor miners joined forces with the savvy businessmen, and in 1803 thirty-one petitioners—including members of the Vallé, Guibord, and Pratte families from Ste. Genevieve and the Boyer, Coleman, and Robert families from Old Mines—asked the departing Spanish authorities to grant them a concession at Old Mines. The establishment of settlements at St. Michel and Old Mines did not, however, presage a major French migration inland. Tradition and a small population base kept most of Upper Louisiana's French inhabitants concentrated in the original river villages.[45]

Cape Girardeau was in many ways unlike any of the other Spanish administrative districts. Louis Lorimier had first settled there sometime around 1792 to be near the Shawnee and Delaware Indians who had established themselves between the Cinque Hommes and Apple creeks. The next year, Governor Carondelet awarded Lorimier exclusive trading rights with those tribes, and in 1795 he approved Lorimier's request for a land concession at Cape Girardeau. In the meantime, the first in what was to become a steady stream of Americans began moving into the district. Andrew Ramsay established a settlement three miles southwest of Lorimier's post following his arrival in the district in 1795. He was soon joined by immigrants from Virginia and Kentucky. Near the turn of the century, Amos Byrd and his four sons moved from Tennessee to an upland area sixteen miles northwest of Cape Girardeau, subsequently known as Byrd's Creek. At about the same time, George Frederick Bollinger and a group of Germans from North Carolina settled in the Whitewater River area.[46]

By the end of the Spanish period, these and other scattered settlement clusters had made Cape Girardeau the most Americanized of the Spanish administrative districts. There was not, however, a single town or village of any size in the entire district. Travelers passing by Cape Girardeau on the Mississippi frequently failed to notice the Anglo-American settlements, obscured from view by their smallness and remoteness. They did see Lorimier's trading post, which served as the administrative headquarters at

Cape Girardeau until after the U.S. takeover. At that time Lorimier, who retained his position as commandant under the new regime, donated land and money for the construction of a suitable seat for the district government. In 1806 he laid out the town of Cape Girardeau and offered lots for sale at one hundred dollars apiece. With only limited access to the market economy, most of Cape Girardeau's early inhabitants were rustic subsistence farmers and, by necessity, jacks of all trades.[47]

Two Canadian traders, François and Joseph Le Sieur, established a trading post on the bend of the Mississippi near the mouth of the Ohio in the 1780s, marking the beginning of settlement in the district of New Madrid. With backing from Gabriel Cerré, a prominent Kaskaskia merchant who recently had moved to St. Louis, the brothers developed a thriving trade, capitalizing upon the arrival west of the Mississippi of sizable Shawnee and Delaware contingents. The site was known as L'Anse à la Graisse (Greasy Bend) because the Indians often boiled down buffalo and bear grease there.[48] As previously noted, Col. George Morgan had chosen this place in 1789 to be the seat for his proposed settlement of New Madrid. Although his plans for developing a community of American farmers failed to materialize, many settlers did settle there in subsequent years, and the name chosen by Morgan remained as a reminder of his efforts. In 1789 the Spaniards constructed a military fortification at New Madrid, where they maintained a small garrison until they surrendered the region to the United States fifteen years later. New Madrid also served as Upper Louisiana's port of entry; all vessels going up or down the Mississippi, to or from New Orleans, had to stop for inspection.

After the collapse of Morgan's scheme, New Madrid remained primarily the haunt of traders, hunters, boatmen, and soldiers. Pierre La Forge, a French emigre serving as a Spanish functionary in New Madrid, observed that with a little powder and lead, some cloth, and a few blankets obtained on credit from the local stores, the town's inhabitants procured meat, grease, and suet for their sustenance and furs to pay off their debts. They supplemented their livelihoods by fishing and used the profits to buy whiskey and flour.[49]

Whiskey was a popular item in the Indian trade at New Madrid. David Trotter met an untimely end there in 1802 when a party of Mascouten Indians murdered him and burned his house after they became intoxicated on the liquor he had sold them. Trotter's death created a great deal of excitement and caused Lieutenant Governor Delassus to take personal charge of militia units dispatched from Ste. Genevieve and elsewhere for the purpose of disciplining the errant Indians. Emotions must have been running high when the Mascoutens surrendered Trotter's killer to the

Spanish authorities, for the Spanish took the unusual step of ordering his execution by firing squad in the presence of the militiamen and representatives of nearby tribes. Even in the most troubled periods, Indian executions were a rarity on the Louisiana frontier.[50]

Gradually more American settlers entered the New Madrid district and began cultivating crops, and when the Indian trade declined, some of the local French hunters and traders reluctantly took to the plow. Even so, La Forge doubted that the Creoles would ever make New Madrid a "flourishing settlement."[51] The village of Little Prairie, near Caruthersville, and the Tawapitty Bottoms across from the mouth of the Ohio River were two of the district's principal lesser settlements. Corn, flax, tobacco, and cotton were the major local crops, but many residents continued to pursue the traffic in furs.[52]

Despite a tenfold increase in Upper Louisiana's population during the Spanish years, the territory remained a remote, sparsely populated frontier region. The few roads were little more than poorly marked trails requiring an experienced backwoods traveler to follow them. There was a road of sorts on the west side of the Mississippi between New Madrid and Ste. Genevieve, but the route linking Ste. Genevieve with St. Louis went virtually unused because of the numerous ravines and rivers one had to cross when traversing it. Most overland travelers crossed the Mississippi north of Ste. Genevieve and made their way on the east bank to Cahokia, where they recrossed the river and returned to the Spanish side via one of two local ferries.[53] Other crude roadways, such as the one between Mine à Breton and Ste. Genevieve, linked satellite settlements with larger neighboring communities in Spanish Illinois. Cross-country travelers alternately had to make their way through thick, tangled forests clogged with vines, pass through marshy swamps and across rugged terrain, or ford an occasional river or stream. Since accommodations along the way were nonexistent, the traveler's usual outfit included food, cooking and eating utensils, a hatchet, and a blanket. Wilderness sojourners took their chances with the weather and slept on the ground at night. Because of the poor road conditions, there were few carriages or chaises to be found in Spanish Illinois, but the French habitants did use two-wheeled wooden carts, known as charettes, drawn by oxen or horses, for transporting produce and implements.[54]

Residents traveled by water whenever possible, with the Mississippi and Missouri rivers providing the most direct access to Upper Louisiana's remote villages. Despite their isolated locations and the difficulties of frontier travel, the river settlements maintained regular contact with one another and with the outside world. The arrival of a boat routinely drew to the riverfront a crowd of persons eager to learn from arriving passengers and crews news of the latest happenings beyond their village. For those who could read, the boats sometimes brought mail or a newspaper.

Although it was the most desirable means of traveling, river transportation was not without its hazards. Swollen streams, rampaging waters, floating debris, and underwater obstructions damaged boats and occasionally caused them to capsize or sink with a resulting loss of life or property. Frozen streams and ice jams temporarily closed the waterways to traffic during the winter months, and the extreme heat and humidity of summertime, along with the ever-present swarms of mosquitoes, added to the discomfort of travel during that season.[55]

Upper Louisiana's residents employed boats of various kinds. The birchbark canoe and the sturdier pirogue, shaped like a canoe but made from a hollowed log, were commonly used to carry smaller loads. Larger cargoes had to be transported in the bateau, a flat-bottomed boat with an enclosed area covered by a roof in the rear section. The trip downstream with one of these vessels was relatively easy, but moving a loaded bateau upstream against the current was arduous.[56]

The more streamlined keelboat gradually replaced the bateau as the vessel most commonly used to transport large cargoes up the rivers. This covered freight boat with a keel could be propelled upstream in a variety of fashions. Sometimes it was poled along the shallow waters close to the shore, but when deep waters or soft bottoms made this impossible, the boat was literally pulled up the river by men walking along the bank tugging at the cordelle, a piece of rope attached to the mast. If neither of these methods proved feasible, the boat had to be rowed. Only occasionally did favorable winds make it possible to hoist the square-rigged sail located on the center mast and temporarily relieve the struggling boatmen, whose backbreaking exertions normally moved the sturdy, merchandise-laden keelboats upstream at a rate of between ten and fifteen miles a day.[57] The trip downstream took considerably less time, with a voyage from St. Louis to New Orleans requiring between twenty-five and thirty days. In addition to the keelboats that regularly made the trip, Upper Louisianans often constructed flatboats to carry their heavy cargoes down the Mississippi. When they reached their destination, they dismantled the boats and sold the lumber.

Agriculture was the principal economic activity in Upper Louisiana, but the sparse population, crude farming techniques, and distance from markets prevented the region from reaching its full potential as a center of agricultural production. In the spring French habitants laboring in the common fields and Americans cultivating outlying acreages turned over the ground and planted crops with only the aid of hand tools and ox-drawn wooden plows. Once the crops were in, the French rarely attempted to cultivate or plow their fields, preferring instead to let nature take its course until harvest time. Despite the primitive and haphazard methods employed by the French habitants, the fertile soil produced surprisingly large yields unless a drought, flood, or other natural disaster intervened. In contrast with their French counterparts, the American farmers generally tried to keep their fields free of weeds and to pay more attention to regular cultivation. As a result, the American harvests yielded even greater returns.[58]

As has been previously noted, a wide variety of crops grew well in Upper Louisiana. Wheat, corn, cotton, flax, hemp, and tobacco were the most important staples, and residents cultivated oats, barley, beans, and a variety of other vegetables for their own consumption. Their orchards and vineyards produced apples, peaches, plums, pears, and grapes, from which they made cider, brandy, and wine. Although they distilled whiskey from some of their grains, liquor remained a major import commodity.

Because livestock could be maintained with a minimum of expense and effort by allowing the larger animals to graze in nearby woodlands and meadows where they fed upon grasses, nuts, roots, and berries, most farmers raised cattle and hogs. In 1800 Israel Dodge petitioned Spanish authorities for a one-league land grant, which he proposed to use as a stock farm. In recommending approval for the request, the commandant at New Bourbon advised his superiors that Dodge needed the land to feed and maintain his sizable cattle herd, which was too numerous for the barren hills already belonging to him. Dr. Richard Jones Waters, an American physician who had followed Col. George Morgan to New Madrid, owned one hundred head of cattle in 1797, and in the adjacent Cape Girardeau district, the 1803 census reported that David Bollinger maintained a herd of over four hundred. Although the census did not provide numbers of hogs, there is ample evidence that pork had become a dietary staple. As the numbers of cattle and hogs increased, so did the beef and pork exports. Farmers carried their rifles, barrels, and salt with them into the wooded grazing areas, where they killed, dressed, salted, and packed the meat for shipment. The few sheep introduced into the region were vulnerable to wolves and other wild animals and required protection. Most households also maintained a small flock of fowl for their own use.[59]

Agricultural production in Upper Louisiana increased steadily during the Spanish period despite the continued prevalence of primitive farming techniques. During the 1790s, wheat production averaged between 38,000 and 45,000 bushels a year, but a bumper crop in 1799 yielded 92,000 bushels. The growing number of farmers and the concomitant increase in the amount of acreage under cultivation was the principal reason for the expanded output. Most of the surplus farm produce was marketed locally, but Upper Louisiana's merchants also took advantage of the growing demand for foodstuffs in the lower Mississippi valley by increasing shipments of flour, grains, salted meats, and dairy products to New Orleans. Lower Louisiana was thriving during the late 1790s and early 1800s, thanks to the introduction of commercial sugar production and an early boom in cotton.[60]

Second only to agriculture in importance, the fur trade played a key role in the settlement and development of Upper Louisiana. After the founding of St. Louis in 1764, it had become a center of growing trade in the Missouri and Mississippi valleys. Operating within the framework of Spain's monopolistic system, a small number of influential traders grew rich from the exclusive rights they garnered. St. Louis's leading merchants engaged in the profitable business of outfitting the expeditions that regularly set out to trade with the Indians. Despite the decreasing profits caused by the growing competition for the trade—especially from British traders—large quantities of furs from tribes along the lower Missouri annually poured into St. Louis warehouses. Although St. Louis merchants dominated the trade in Upper Louisiana, residents in other villages often exchanged goods with local Indians in return for furs and skins. One reliable estimate placed the average annual value of furs and peltries in Upper Louisiana during the last fifteen years of Spanish rule at $203,750.[61]

Lead mining, also vital to Upper Louisiana's economy, changed little until near the end of the Spanish period. Through the years, French miners had continued to dig at Mine La Motte and at the sites along the Meramec and its tributaries, but after the discovery of rich deposits at Mine à Breton in the 1770s, that area became the focal point for mining activity. Moses Austin's innovations contributed to increased lead production there during the 1790s and helped spawn a major resurgence in Missouri's lead industry.[62]

Austin sank the first mining shaft in the district and built a reverberatory furnace that was twice as efficient as the stone and log hearths that it largely supplanted. The American mining entrepreneur also conducted his operations on a year-round basis. The tradition-bound French miners were slow to embrace Austin's methods. Deep mining never won acceptance: it was too expensive, and the richness of the surface ores made it unnecessary. But the new smelting process was another matter. Austin's reverberatory furnace, which worked on the principle of an oven, using hot air and not direct contact with the fire to reduce the ore, obtained 75 percent of the lead from the ore. Soon, the local miners began bringing their ore to Austin for smelting. The increased activity at Austin's mines and at those of his competitors produced a substantial increase in Upper Louisiana's production. By 1800 Missouri's lead producers were shipping about two hundred tons annually to New Orleans. When the United States acquired the territory three years later, Austin estimated that the annual value of lead exports exceeded forty thousand dollars.[63]

A small number of residents engaged in saltmaking, the other important contributor to the local economy. Most of the activity was concentrated along the Saline Creek below Ste. Genevieve, where French and American settlers manufactured enough salt to supply the settlements on both sides of the Mississippi and a growing number of Kentucky's inhabitants. At the turn of the century, they were sending approximately thirty-five hundred barrels to New Orleans each year. Although the district of Ste. Genevieve produced the major portion of Upper Louisiana's supply, Martin Bouvet operated a saltworks north of the Missouri on the Salt River intermittently during the 1790s until he was killed by Indians in 1800.[64]

A select group of French merchants residing in the principal villages flourished under the Spanish regime's mercantilist policies. Because those merchants were favorably disposed to blending public interest and personal profit, the Spaniards gave their blessing to the activities of these resourceful capitalists, whose diverse trading interests often involved them in several of the major local enterprises—fur trading, general merchandising, farming, lead mining, and saltmaking. Their far-flung operations were international in scope. They commonly maintained regular business connections in New Orleans, Canada, the United States, and Europe, as well as in the other provincial towns. They took advantage of their varied sources of supply to import all types of merchandise, which they then offered for sale to local residents from the places they set aside in their homes for conducting business. The risks in these frontier ventures were often great, but so were the potential profits.[65]

The shortage of specie, a common situation in undeveloped areas, did not deter Upper Louisiana's merchant traders from transacting business. Very little money changed hands in the local stores, where almost all exchanges were based on credit. Customers signed promissory notes payable when their crops, furs, or minerals were ready. Just as they extended credit to their customers, the frontier merchants in turn bought their merchandise and goods from their suppliers on credit. Because they routinely dealt with firms in distant places, accounts were seldom settled speedily. The fur markets were especially volatile during periods of international instability. When fur prices were declining, shipments sent in payment for the previous year's merchandise sometimes proved to be insufficient in value to cover the combined costs of merchandise, commissions, and interest charges.

Because of the importance of the fur traffic, the Spaniards attempted to facilitate trade by authorizing the use of peltries as legal tender unless otherwise expressly stated in a contract or agreement. In his attempt to describe how the system worked, Nicolas de Finiels wryly observed that "the Indians are the true bankers of this region," noting that the furs they collected secured the local banking system. While Indians sometimes found themselves becoming enmeshed in the complexities of the market economy, many of the region's inhabitants—red, white, and black—remained beyond the pale of these larger commercial networks and subsisted by trading small quantities of goods within the primitive frontier exchange economy.[66]

In St. Louis and Ste. Genevieve the growing number of artisans and craftsmen—including blacksmiths, masons, carpenters, sawyers, joiners, and grain millers—attempted to meet the increasing demands of the local market. Their handicrafts facilitated economic expansion and especially aided local construction in the preindustrial frontier society.

In line with Upper Louisiana's rudimentary economic system, its government under the Spaniards was equally uncomplicated. The simple political structure, which combined civil and military authority, adequately met the needs of the sparsely settled region. The territory's highest resident official, the lieutenant governor, lived in St. Louis, where he exercised civil, military, judicial, and financial powers. His numerous duties included handing down verdicts in important civil and criminal cases, supervising Indian affairs, licensing traders, directing public work construction, issuing land concessions, authorizing surveys, and commanding military operations. His immediate superior, the governor general of Louisiana, established policy for the entire province at his New Orleans headquarters, subject to instructions from the captain general in Havana.[67]

In each of the larger villages Spanish officials appointed a commandant to oversee local matters. He served as judge in civil matters involving small amounts, commanded the local militia, issued permits to travel in the province, sought to maintain friendly relations with local Indians, recommended individuals for land grants, encouraged the development of the area under his jurisdiction, and kept his superiors informed on all local happenings. In the smaller and more remote settlements, a syndic performed similar duties. Decisions made by these officials could be appealed to the lieutenant governor or to the governor general, but they seldom were. The local barons who held these posts drew upon their influence in the community to settle disputes and secure compliance with their decisions.[68]

The administration of justice was simple, direct, and paternalistic; the right of trial by jury did not exist. The local commandant resolved disputes, quarrels, and lawsuits, often without formal judicial proceedings. There were no elections; all officials were appointed. But neither were there any direct taxes or court costs. Despite its authoritarian framework, in practice the Spanish system functioned in a mildly liberal manner. More often than not, local problems were speedily resolved in a manner satisfactory to the interested parties, and from all indications the vast majority of Upper Louisiana's inhabitants lived peaceably and tranquilly under the benevolent patriarchal system.[69]

Unlike the United States, Spain offered free lands to attract bona fide settlers into Upper Louisiana, but, under Spanish law, the process for acquiring a completed title was so complicated that few residents went through the proper channels to establish a final title. To secure a concession, the settler submitted a petition to the local commandant asking for a grant of land. When the settler desired a particular tract, he or she described it in a petition; if the petitioner had not decided where to settle, as was often the case, he or she asked for a certain amount of land that could be located subsequently in any vacant area. If the commandant approved the request, he endorsed the petition and sent it to the lieutenant governor, who issued a concession. Special concessions described the lands to be granted, while the general or floating concessions merely specified the amount of land conceded. After the delivery of the concession, the lieutenant governor ordered a survey of the actual lands selected, although frequently these surveys were never completed. In fact, the Spanish government had not made any regular provision for surveying lands in Upper Louisiana until 1795, when it named Antoine Soulard as surveyor general for the region. If the survey was made, the approved petition and order of survey, along with the completed report of the surveyor, had to be presented to the proper office at New Orleans for final confirmation of title. The distance from New Orleans, compounded by the hardships and expenses of frontier travel, made this final step prohibitive for the vast majority of Upper Louisiana's residents.[70]

Because of the abundance of land and the smallness of the population, Spanish officials routinely granted concessions to those who requested them, and, during the final days of the Spanish regime, they became increasingly generous and frequently ignored the traditional eight hundred arpent limitation on individual grants. Most concessions in excess of that amount were issued near the end of the Spanish period, and—with a few notable exceptions, such as John and Israel Dodge and Moses Austin—the recipients were prominent French residents of Upper Louisiana. Before he left office in 1799, Lieutenant Governor Zenon Trudeau reportedly signed a series of blank concessions that were distributed after his departure and filled in illegally by those who secured them. Trudeau's successor, Charles

Dehault Delassus, supposedly granted extensive concessions to members of his family and to friends.[71]

Spanish officials made no effort to encourage settlers to secure full titles. As late as 1788 only about 6,400 arpents of land had been surveyed in the entire district of St. Louis. Local commandants regularly accepted the incompleted concessions as authorization to hold the lands and raised no questions when they were sold or inherited. Some of the early French settlers, and even more of the incoming Americans, simply squatted on the lands without bothering to request a formal concession from the Spanish authorities. The unexpected sale of Louisiana to the United States in 1803 drastically altered the situation, and the confused state of the land titles created a tremendous headache for American officials, who suddenly found themselves in control of a territory where the traditional Creole ways of doing things were considerably at variance with their own.

CHAPTER SIX

GALLERIES, GUMBO, AND "LA GUIGNOLÉE"

T he unhurried routines of village life in colonial Missouri created an aura of tranquility and a general ambience in which time often was reckoned according to seasonal activities, such as the month when strawberries ripen, or cataclysmic events, as in the year of the great flood, rather than by specific days, months, and years. The tempo was well suited to the easygoing French Creoles, who were the temperamental opposites of the hard-driving Anglo-Americans. Outsiders frequently misread the slower-paced rhythms of daily life and the seeming inattention to the cultivation of fields as signs of Creole laziness. The oft-told stories of Frenchmen leisurely smoking their pipes and cigars in the idyllic village surroundings seldom mentioned the seasonal fluctuations in work loads. As often as not, the so-called Creole slackers were simply resting from the rigors of their strenuous labors in the wilderness, on the rivers, or at the mines. The stereotypical portrait of French Creole indolence likewise ignored the remarkable achievements of the coterie of resolute French entrepreneurs, whose commercial enterprises made them the envy of their ambitious Yankee competitors.

The outward serenity of the French villages also camouflaged uncertainties and tensions born of the convergence of culturally diverse red, white, and black peoples in a frontier environment where the contradictory impulses of civility and barbarity occasionally manifested themselves in curious, or even bizarre, ways. Jesuit priests sacrificed their lives to bring the Christian gospel to the Indians, but they also introduced slavery in the Illinois Country. Well-educated French Creoles with libraries containing the latest Enlightenment writings brutally chastised slaves who defied their claims to absolute authority. Indians and whites committed atrocities against one another while red and white children innocently played together along peaceful village streets.

Upper Louisiana's French inhabitants were a pleasant and cheerful people who combined the best attributes of Old World charm and New World hospitality in the wilderness setting. In the absence of public accommodations, they graciously opened their doors to visiting strangers. The fun-loving, congenial Creoles delighted in many forms of amusement and recreation. Favorite out-of-doors activities included horse racing, sleighing, excursions into the woods, hunting, and fishing. They enjoyed games of all sorts, especially billiards and cards, and seldom passed up an opportunity to make a small wager. Storytelling was another popular French Creole diversion.[1]

On Sundays and festival days townspeople of all ages and ranks came together. They began the day with religious observances at the local church. Since the French had no qualms about mixing business and pleasure on Sunday, the assembled parishioners took advantage of the time immediately following the services to hold auctions, discuss public matters, negotiate deals, and conclude transactions. In the afternoon, they gathered at the home of the commandant or at the residences of the principal families to join in dancing and playing games—the more humorous the better. The fetes began around three in the afternoon and continued until ten in the evening. Only during the Carnival season and on a few special holidays did the festivities last into the night. Christmas was an especially joyous time for French families. Most attended midnight mass and continued with feasting and merriment throughout the following day. On New Year's Eve the young Creoles traveled from house to house in costume, serenading their neighbors with the traditional folksong "La Guignolée" while soliciting pledges of coffee, sugar, chickens, pies, cakes, and similar foodstuffs for the annual Twelfth Night or King's Night Ball, held on 6 January.[2]

Religion and social life were inextricably connected in Upper Louisiana. From the time of the first settlements there, the Catholic Church had been an important force in community life. During the early years the Jesuits directed most missionary and religious activity, but in 1763 French authorities, fearing the order's growing wealth and power, expelled the society's members from Louisiana and confiscated their property. While Illinois Creoles neither knew nor particularly cared about the religious disputes that precipitated the unexpected departure of the Jesuits, they keenly felt the sudden loss of the Black Robes, who had so long attended to their spiritual needs.[3]

The shortage of priests caused by the Jesuits' expulsion grew worse when Louisiana came under Spanish control and responsibility for directing the spiritual affairs of the upper Mississippi valley passed from the bishop of Quebec to the bishop of Cuba. In an effort to assert their jurisdictional prerogatives, incoming Spanish clerics prohibited French priests under Canadian control from conducting services in Spanish territory. The ban temporarily left most parishes in the remote province without the services of a priest.

Father Louis-Sebastian Meurin, a French priest and former Jesuit who had been allowed to return to Ste. Genevieve on the condition that he acknowledge the head of the Capuchin order in New Orleans as his religious superior, was an early casualty of the crossfire between the conflicting ecclesiastical jurisdictions. Upon learning that Bishop Jean-Olivier Briand of Quebec had designated Meurin, who was the only priest in the Illinois Country at the time, as the grand vicar of Louisiana, the Spaniards ordered him to leave Ste. Genevieve and the west bank. The aging priest moved back to Cahokia and Kaskaskia but steadfastly refused to abandon his former parishioners across the river. In the absence of any cleric in Spanish Illinois, Father Meurin periodically crossed the Mississippi, sometimes clandestinely, to perform baptisms and marriages, conduct funerals, and visit the sick. Looking after the far-flung parishes on both sides of the river was an onerous task for the lone priest.

In 1768, Bishop Briand heeded Meurin's pleas for assistance by sending Father Pierre Gibault to the Illinois Country, and the two men regularly but unofficially continued to serve the parishes in St. Louis and Ste. Genevieve. In 1773 the bishop of Cuba finally dispatched Father Hilaire de Géneveaux to take over the priestly duties in Spanish Illinois, but his long-overdue arrival in Ste. Genevieve proved to be a mixed blessing. The new priest's erratic behavior and his unexplained refusal to perform certain clerical duties quickly placed him at odds with virtually everyone in the community. An outburst during which he declared the Vallés and their friend Father Gibault, who was well-liked, to be "Presbyterian heretics" did not help his cause. Father Hilaire's stormy tenure ended abruptly when he departed in 1777 amid a flurry of charges that in a fit of pique he had directed his slaves to vandalize certain church property. After he left, the people of Ste. Genevieve again found themselves without a resident priest, but they gladly turned to Father Gibault in Kaskaskia to administer the sacraments for them. The preceding year St. Louis had gotten its first parish priest, the German-born Capuchin Father Bernard de Limpach, who adapted to the trials of the frontier priesthood with more aplomb than Father Hilaire. When Lieutenant Governor Cruzat created a scene following a Christmas service by protesting the placement of his pew in the sanctuary, Father Bernard acquiesced and moved it in order to avoid an embarrassing public altercation. Although the priest made his unhappiness over the arrangement known to his superiors in New Orleans, he appeared resigned to live with it until the arrival of Cruzat's successor, who, he prudently acknowledged, would be able to conform to more customary practices without suffering a loss of face.[4]

Securing and keeping a priest was a persistent problem throughout the colonial period, especially for smaller parishes. When the residents of St. Ferdinand and St. Charles built churches for their growing settlements in 1790, Lieutenant Governor Pérez recommended that one priest be assigned to serve both parishes. In the absence of a regular priest, laymen sometimes presided at prayer meetings, weddings, and funerals, but since only a priest could celebrate a mass, the use of lay personnel provided only a partial solution to the problem. Spanish authorities sought to improve the situation by importing Irish priests who had been educated in Spanish seminaries. With Ireland ruled by Protestant England, many young Irishmen went to Spain to secure a Catholic education. Because they spoke English, Spanish officials believed the Irish clergy would be effective in dealing with the growing number of Americans in the territory. Father James Maxwell, who served Ste. Genevieve during the final years of Spanish rule, was a noteworthy example of the Irish connection. Maxwell was in many ways a worldly man, and he stayed after the Spanish departure and adapted to American rule more easily than some of his parishioners. He dabbled in land speculation and politics, briefly served as president of the territorial Legislative Council, and appears to have had more in common with the American newcomers than the French Creoles.[5]

Both the French and the Spaniards established the Catholic faith as the official state religion and granted financial assistance for its maintenance. The Spanish crown furnished land for churches and cemeteries, provided funds for constructing parish buildings, and paid the salaries of the clerics, but the amounts provided were seldom enough. In addition to a salary from the Spanish treasury, the priest normally received small sums for interments, baptisms, and marriages. However, when the disgruntled Father Hilaire found it difficult to live on his government salary, he attempted to collect a tithe from his Ste. Genevieve parishioners in 1774. They vigorously protested the priest's unprecedented actions, and Spanish officials ordered the curate to stop the practice after promising to increase his allowance.[6]

In their 1787 agreement that first allowed American Protestants to settle legally in Spanish Illinois, the provincial authorities had predicated their decision on the expectation that the new immigrants could be transformed into loyal Spanish subjects and converted to the king's faith within a generation. To encourage the process, the Spaniards prohibited non-Catholic religious services and authorized only Catholic clergymen to conduct marriages and baptisms, but in practice they seldom enforced those restrictions. Officials in Upper Louisiana interpreted the laws so broadly that any Christian could be declared a Catholic for legal purposes, and commandants occasionally married non-Catholics in civil ceremonies. Moreover, itinerant Protestant ministers sometimes conducted religious services for Americans in Spanish Louisiana, and, as long as they were private, local authorities usually made no attempt to interfere. The urgent need to populate the province had forced Europe's staunchest defenders of Catholic orthodoxy to accept a de facto form of religious toleration, and in a similar fashion most residents embraced a philosophy of live and let live as far as religious beliefs were concerned. Even in the French villages, all of which remained solidly Catholic, there was a marked predisposition to leave religious matters to the priest.[7]

The libraries of a few wealthy citizens contained volumes by the French philosophes and other freethinkers whose works had been condemned by the Church, but this nonconformity did not keep the individuals who read those works from actively participating in parish affairs. Despite occasional official reports complaining about lax moral standards, the overwhelming majority of Upper Louisiana Creoles appear to have been conventionally devout Catholics who attended mass when it was celebrated, joined the religious processions conducted by the clergy through the village streets on special occasions, and prominently displayed crucifixes over the gateways to their residences as a symbol of their faith. At the same time, however, they rejected the intolerant zeal that produced religious strife elsewhere.

Class lines were only loosely drawn in the frontier communities, but there were clear-cut differences in wealth and social status among the inhabitants, even though those distinctions were not always readily apparent to the outsider. Fernando de Leyba, a class-conscious Spanish official, complained in 1778 that "the classes of people are so mixed up that one cannot tell who is a farmer and who is a merchant."[8] Henry Marie Brackenridge, an American lad whose family sent him to Ste. Genevieve in the 1790s to learn French, observed a similar lack of external class distinctions in that settlement: "They all associated, dressed alike, and frequented the same ball room. They were in fact nearly all connected by the ties of affinity or consanguinity."[9]

However, the absence of outward manifestations of class distinction and the open fraternization that prevailed among persons of all ranks in the close-knit frontier communities did not prevent the first citizens in those societies from exercising their traditional social and political prerogatives. Rank had its privileges, and a small set of well-to-do merchant capitalists with diversified business interests stood at the top of the social scale. Everyone else looked to them for entrepreneurial leadership, capital, and employment. Their standing was based on wealth and achievement, not birthright. They were an upwardly mobile, indigenous elite with few genuine European aristocrats within their ranks. Most traced their origins to French bourgeois or peasant stock. Having accumulated substantial assets in property and slaves, these home-grown aristocrats linked themselves by marriage and by business to form a small network of families that included such familiar names as Chouteau, Gratiot, Cerré, Labbadie, and Papin in St. Louis and Vallé, Deguire, Aubuchon, Pratte, St. Gemme

Beauvais, and Bolduc in Ste. Genevieve. Extended family alliances promoted social stability and cohesiveness, and they were equally good for business. The resulting close-knit commercial dynasties brought added prosperity to individual members and made them a force to be reckoned with, both in their communities and in the larger mercantile world.

Immediately below them were a group of less affluent but still successful merchants, traders, farmers, artisans, craftsmen, and other persons of property. Next came a diverse assortment of boatmen, rowers, hunters, trappers, miners, soldiers, and common laborers, who had to settle for a marginal standard of living dictated by their low wages and seasonal unemployment. Many in this category were *engagés*, men who were hired for fixed terms to work at tasks specified in their contract of engagement. Since most, but not all, were engaged to work as boatmen and canoemen in the fur trade, the term *engagé* was often used interchangeably with *voyageur*. Joining them at the lower end of the social ladder were the free blacks, and at the lowest level were the black and Indian slaves.

The gulf separating the leading families from the lower ranks of society widened over the years in the wake of Upper Louisiana's growth and development. The expanding social and economic disparities were most evident in St. Louis, which became the commercial and political center of the province. City customs increasingly vied with rural traditions in that frontier metropolis. A growing number of its townspeople abandoned the apparel of the woods for more fashionable dress, and in 1789 Auguste Chouteau converted Laclède's dilapidated original trading headquarters into a stately residence befitting St. Louis's most prominent family. The enlarged and refurbished mansion with its polished walnut floors, elegant interior furnishings, and large library served as a visible symbol of a growing fondness for luxury among the affluent elite.[10]

As St. Louis expanded and prospered, family gatherings began to supplant the more all-encompassing community affairs. At the same time, visitors sensed a gradual diminution of the unaffected openness and affability that had prevailed in the earliest days. Ste. Genevieve retained more of its sense of community, but even there inequities in wealth increased significantly during the final decades of the eighteenth century. Notwithstanding the growing economic disparities and the continuing presence of a large itinerant population, abject poverty appears to have been uncommon in Upper Louisiana. Even those at the bottom of the social order managed to obtain a basic subsistence, albeit a sometimes precarious one.[11]

A sizable body of youthful transients, seasonally unemployed *engagés*, off-duty soldiers, and disgruntled slaves did cause local officials to keep a watchful eye for disturbances that might disrupt the local serenity. When

Amable Litoureau publicly ridiculed a series of Spanish regulations outside the village church in St. Louis in August 1770, Lieutenant Governor Pedro Piernas made it clear that he did not intend to tolerate any such defiance of his authority. He found the alleged troublemaker guilty of treating officials with contempt, disturbing the peace, being seditious, and giving a bad impression to the public and ordered him banished from the territory for ten years. The next month, Piernas pronounced a similar sentence upon one Jeanot, a "good-for-nothing" whose crimes included destruction of property, stealing, and illicit sexual relations with slave women. Lieutenant Governor Fernando de Leyba installed a pillory in front of the Government House and instituted nightly patrols in an effort to combat an outbreak of petty thievery in St. Louis in the late 1770s. The combined threat of detection and public humiliation apparently proved sufficient to rein in the minor crime wave.[12]

Violent crimes were rare in Upper Louisiana, but in Ste. Genevieve a Spanish soldier stationed there killed a man in a drunken knife fight in 1775.[13] Members of the Spanish garrison caused more than their share of problems. Leyba repeatedly complained to his superiors about the conduct of one such soldier, Joseph Piernas, whose alleged misdeeds included gambling, brawling, stealing, and drunkenness. When St. Louis citizens charged that the errant soldier's "scandalous conduct and irregular mode of life" threatened to ruin their children, the lieutenant governor sent him packing to Ste. Genevieve. Leyba's protests induced provincial officials to retire the troublesome soldier, who ironically chose to return to St. Louis, where he spent his final years. Spanish officials attempted to combat these and other indiscretions with a spate of local ordinances regulating soldiers, slaves, rumormongers, and various other potentially disruptive elements.[14]

A serious imbalance in Upper Louisiana's male-female ratio caused more than a few of these footloose young males to seek illicit sexual relations with black and mulatto slave women. In the early years when the scarcity of women was most acute, Spanish officials actually encouraged single men to take Indian and mixed-blood Indian wives as a means for increasing the population and discouraging amalgamation between blacks and whites. Some Indian wives were descendants of Catholic proselytes from Jesuit missions, others were slaves and daughters of slave women, and still others were the mixed-blood offspring of prominent fur trade families. They won acceptance in Missouri's frontier Creole communities, and during the first generation their biracial progeny could be found in all social and economic levels, but by the 1790s the status of the Indian mixed bloods was declining, and most opted to reside with their Indian kin.[15]

Since men outnumbered women in colonial Missouri, women generally married in their mid-to-late teens, while males typically waited until their mid-twenties. Spinsterhood was rare and large families the rule. Infant and child mortality rates were high. Marie Carpentier Vallé of Ste. Genevieve bore fourteen children between 1778 and 1801, but only seven lived to age five. One-third of all children in that community died before their first birthday. Conceptions were most frequent during the winter months immediately following the return of the absentee male population from the rivers, forests, and mines. Childbearing exacted a toll on the female population: their average life expectancy was substantially shorter than that of Upper Louisiana's males.[16]

Men were the heads of the household. They planted and cultivated the crops in the common fields, built and maintained the fences around those fields, chopped wood for the fireplaces, and provided meat by hunting or by butchering livestock. Slaveholders supervised black workers in performing those tasks, although in many instances the two races toiled together in the fields. In addition to those chores, a good number of males (black and white) worked as miners, saltmakers, hunters, traders, trappers, craftsmen, and boatmen during a part of the year. In fact, a significant number of younger Creole males appear to have considered working on the rivers, in the woods, or at the mines decidedly preferable to working in the fields. The frequent choice of rowing and hunting over farming was perhaps evidence of the continuing influence of mixed-blood Indian mothers whose cultural roots caused them to encourage their sons to follow those traditional male pursuits. Whatever the reason, the aversion to routine agrarian tasks helped popularize the notion of French Creole indolence.[17]

Women assumed primary responsibilities for the daily operation of their households. It was their task to see that the food was prepared, the clothing was made and cared for, and the house was kept in order. Food preparation included planting and caring for the gardens and farmyards, harvesting and preserving the vegetables and fruit, milking cows, baking bread, and cooking the meals.[18]

Upper Louisiana's women were renowned as good cooks. They favored soups, fricassees, and gumbos over roasted and fried fare. The popularity of gumbos is an indication that the sizable Afro-American community influenced the local French cuisine. The Indian and mixed-blood women also introduced Indian foods into the local diet. The French took advantage of the abundant supply of fish and game—venison, squirrel, bear, waterfowl, and catfish—to put meat on the table. During his brief stay in New Madrid, young Henry Brackenridge was repeatedly served a spicy catfish soup seasoned with pepper and garlic. If given their choice, however, the Creoles were likely to opt for beef, pork, and domestic fowl. Ste. Genevieve became famous for its hams, thanks in part to the abundant salt supply available from the nearby Saline. Wheat bread was a staple of the French diet. The Americans, blacks, and Indians might eat cornbread, but the French avoided it if at all possible. When inclement weather prevented boats from traveling to Ste. Genevieve to procure food supplies in 1797, the commandant at New Madrid lamented that they had been "reduced" to eating cornbread.[19]

The French raised a wide variety of fruits and vegetables in their gardens, including cabbage, peas, beans, carrots, turnips, parsnips, cucumbers, radishes, onions, pumpkins, squash, and melons. Apples and pears from Spanish Illinois were esteemed delicacies in New Orleans and the lower valley. To wash their food down, the French consumed coffee, cider, wine, beer, peach and cherry brandy, whiskey, and rum. Most of the food was produced locally, but Upper Louisianans routinely imported maple sugar from the north and sugar, coffee, and distilled spirits from New Orleans. Near the end of the colonial period, the French in Upper Louisiana acquired stills and began making some of their own liquor.[20]

In seeing that their families were properly clothed, the French women differed in one respect from their Anglo-American sisters. They purchased the cloth from which they made the family garments, complying with a French order prohibiting weaving in homes. The absence of spinning wheels in the household inventories suggests that long after that ban had been lifted, French women still shied away from weaving and continued to import the cloth that they needed.[21] Upper Louisiana's merchants always carried a varied array of dry goods in their stocks, and the Indians supplied tanned deerskin ready to be sewn into garments. Everyday dress for the typical French male consisted of buckskin britches or coarse cotton pantaloons, a checked cotton shirt that covered the rest of the body, a blue handkerchief on the head, and leather moccasins. During cold weather they also wore a heavy, hooded blue cape, known as a *capot*, a fur hat that covered the ears and neck, and fur mittens attached to the ends of a long cord suspended around the neck to prevent them from being lost when not in use. On special occasions those men wealthy enough to afford finer attire donned fancy frock coats, ruffled linen shirts, knee britches, silk stockings, and silver-buckled footwear.[22]

As with the men, the French women favored relatively simple dress for daily wear. They typically wore an ankle-length skirt, frequently made of blue or red cotton, a short cotton jacket in summer or a woolen one in winter, a long cotton cloak, known as a *pelisse*, a white or blue handkerchief knotted on the forehead, and moccasins. The most affluent women also decked themselves out in elegant apparel for special events and celebrations. On those occasions they wore silk, satin, and taffeta dresses and embroidered slippers.[23] Caring for the clothing meant washing it in water carried from nearby streams, using homemade soap, and pressing it with a primitive hand iron.

Women were expected to take the lead in looking after the children. With a large number of children, spaced on an average of two-and-a-half years apart, that was no simple task. Nicolas de Finiels described Upper Louisiana's women as good mothers who took their responsibilities seriously. After crediting them with having better-behaved children than their counterparts in the lower country, he concluded that "while still deserving the title worshipful mothers, which all Creole mothers have acquired, those of the Illinois Country supervise their children more closely."[24]

Because of the sparsity of physicians in colonial Missouri, women also assumed the primary responsibility for nursing the sick. When Perrin du Lac visited Ste. Genevieve in the 1790s, he identified Marie Carpentier Vallé as the resident expert on childhood illnesses, observing that she "never refuses her aid when an aggrieved mother comes to her. Day and night she serves the sick, from whom she does not even ask for thanks." Once the common folk remedies had been exhausted, about all that could be done was to attend the patient while the illness was allowed to run its course. Sore throats, whooping cough, scarlet fever, and pneumonia were common winter ailments. In summer, malaria, which was then known as "the fever," was the chronic complaint. Malaria was seldom fatal, but it left its victims in a weakened condition that made them more susceptible to other diseases. Malaria was a more serious problem in flood-prone areas like Ste. Genevieve. Because of the sickle-cell condition, blacks were less affected by it than whites, but blacks were not so fortunate when it came to the other common ailments. Smallpox did not make its deadly presence felt in the French villages until near the end of the eighteenth century. Hunting accidents, falling from a horse, drowning, and other similar mishaps also took their toll in the frontier colony.[25]

While women in colonial Missouri engaged in domestic chores comparable to those of women in the Anglo-American colonies, the wives of Upper Louisiana's most affluent families appear to have been more active participants in family business affairs than their Anglo counterparts. Trading and mercantile affairs frequently called husbands away from their homes for extended periods of time, and in their absence wives took charge of overseeing business and financial matters for the family. French women participated in public sales, purchased property, and concluded other business transactions for their absent husbands.[26] In St. Louis, Madame Marie Thérèse Chouteau, matriarch of the prominent mercantile family, was an active and respected businesswoman with substantial property holdings of her own. Her status as a widow gave her broad authority in the oversight of her financial affairs and contributed to her economic independence.[27]

French law generally gave women greater protection regarding rights of property ownership. Anglo-American wives normally received no more than one-third of their husband's estate, and sometimes only a child's part. Upon remarriage the American woman frequently forfeited any claim to a previous spouse's property. Thanks to a French legal system that attempted to protect property lineage from one generation to another, a French wife fared much better. She inherited one-half of the community property, in addition to special sums such as the *preciput* and the *douaire* that were sometimes specified in a marriage contract. The *douaire*, for instance, was an amount the husband included to ensure that after his death his wife would be able to maintain the same status she had enjoyed as his wife without being dependent on others. A second husband could not interfere with a wife's inheritance from a previous spouse or from her parents. On occasion the rights of black women were recognized, as in the case of Elizabeth D'atchurut, the common-law wife of Antoine Aubuchon and the mother of his ten illegitimate children. Following Aubuchon's death in 1798, she sued his estate and received a small portion of his crops and a few pieces of personal property.[28]

There were, however, limits to the privileges enjoyed by Upper Louisiana's women. For females in the lower ranks of French colonial society with little or no property, the safeguards protecting their assets were a moot point. Moreover, French law may have protected a woman's property, but it did not accord similar protection against spousal abuse. *The Coutume de Paris* affirmed in Article 225 that "Le Mari est Seigneur"—the husband is lord. Women were subject to their husband's authority, and only in extreme cases could they secure relief. Separations could be granted, but the laws did not sanction divorce. Likewise, women were given no direct role in civic and public affairs.[29] Girls from the more affluent families occasionally were allowed to join their brothers in some local classrooms. Young Henry Brackenridge attended coeducational classes in Ste. Genevieve during the 1790s.

Limited educational opportunities in Upper Louisiana during the Spanish period placed even the most rudimentary education beyond the reach of the average child in the province. Although an occasional priest conducted classes for parish children, the few schools were private and generally in operation for only short periods of time. Jean Baptiste Truteau, who operated a small school in St. Louis intermittently between 1774 and 1827, periodically abandoned the classroom to engage in the more lucrative fur trade. With encouragement from Governor Carondelet, Madame Maria Josepha Pinconneau *dit* Rigauche opened a school for girls in the same village in 1797, but it folded when she failed to receive the monthly stipend promised her by the governor. Government officials did attempt to compensate her with a land grant in 1800.[30]

Ste. Genevieve had a primary school during most of the Spanish period. In 1787 Louis Tonnellier, an educated young Parisian, became Ste. Genevieve's first schoolmaster. Like Truteau in St. Louis, Tonnellier left the classroom to pursue better-paying occupations, in his case lead mining and farming. Three nuns accompanied the Delassus de Luzières family to Ste. Genevieve in 1794 with a plan for educating young girls and caring for the sick, but their stay was cut short when Governor Carondelet decided that in view of the uncertain conditions in Upper Louisiana at the time, the Ursuline Convent in New Orleans would be a more suitable place for them. By 1795 Augustin-Charles Frémon de Laurière, an aristocratic French emigre, had opened a unique school in Ste. Genevieve. Stressing practical education, the school promised to prepare students to earn a living and to teach them proper conduct. Even though the educational venture had closed by 1799 after Frémon failed to secure the governmental stipend promised him by Carondelet, the French schoolmaster's approach to education placed him many years ahead of his American contemporaries in both teaching techniques and curriculum.[31]

In New Madrid, Col. George Morgan had outlined a proposal in his master plan for the colony calling for the operation of English schools that would be supported jointly by local families and the government, but nothing came of it following Morgan's abandonment of the colonization project.[32] In 1796 a local New Madrid priest asked the government to build and help support a school in the district, but there is no evidence that the authorities ever acted on the proposal. There were, however, private schools operating in New Madrid in 1793 and in 1802. The earliest-known English-language school in the territory opened in about 1799 at the Ramsay settlement near Cape Girardeau. Known as the Mount Tabor school, it enrolled only a handful of the district's growing number of American children.[33]

Since the local schools at best provided little more than basic instruction in reading, writing, and ciphering, members of some of the more prominent families elected to send their children away for more suitable schooling. Auguste Chouteau dispatched his eldest son to Canada in 1802 after concluding that it would be impossible for him to get a satisfactory education in Upper Louisiana. The decision to convey the nine-year-old so far away was a difficult one for the father, who wrote at the time, "I must send him away from me, from a country where he can never conform himself to the usage of the world and good society and acquire such talents as would distinguish him in the world or at least make him the equal of all that is called good society."[34] Similarly, François Vallé II sent his son François III to New York City in 1796 to learn English.[35] The expense of sending a child to some distant place for an education confined this practice to only the wealthiest families, however. Although the inadequacy of local educational facilities greatly concerned individuals like Chouteau, the average resident probably remained too preoccupied with the more immediate needs of backwoods living to give much thought to the problem. Indeed, the number of persons who used a mark (X) in lieu of a signature on petitions and legal documents makes it clear that a sizable proportion of Upper Louisiana's people remained illiterate, but in the eighteenth century that was not unusual.

Even with its large number of unschooled citizens and its failure to develop a comprehensive education system, Upper Louisiana could hardly be classified as a wasteland of intellectual activity. A small core of well-educated individuals kept abreast of the latest international literary, scientific, and philosophical currents. Their extensive private libraries provided the most eloquent testimony to the breadth of their wide-ranging interests. A few residents in Ste. Genevieve, New Bourbon, and New Madrid owned personal collections of books, but several St. Louisans had the most substantial holdings. By the time of the transfer of the province to the United States in 1804, the private libraries in that village contained between two thousand and three thousand different titles on a wide variety of topics, including political theory, history, philosophy, theology, science, classical and contemporary literature, drama, economics, law, travel, and geography.[36]

Upper Louisiana could boast a number of literate, well-read individuals, but even they were too preoccupied with the tasks of earning a living to devote much time to serious writing. Aside from a satiric poem criticizing the conduct of Spanish officials during the 1780 attack on St. Louis, attributed by tradition to the schoolmaster Truteau, Upper Louisiana's entire literary output consisted of a few commercial and historical journals. But if the rustic frontier setting was not conducive to creation of a formal body of literature, it was an ideal locale for French storytellers to weave their wondrous tales. Handed down from generation to generation by word of mouth, these French folktales, each preferably more humorous and absurd than the last, were a favorite form of entertainment in Upper Louisiana's Creole communities. In a similar manner the French *voyageurs* added to the repertoire of traditional river songs as they made their way along the western rivers. The rhythmic chants sung in unison with the splash of the paddles in the water afforded the perfect counterpoint to the tedium of rowing the heavily laden boats against the river currents for hour upon hour. These tales and songs embody colonial Missouri's true literary legacy.[37]

Upper Louisiana had a significant black population. According to the 1772 Spanish census, nearly 38 percent of the region's inhabitants were of African ancestry.[38] The proportion of blacks in the population gradually declined, but in 1800 they still accounted for 18 percent of the total. In that year almost one-third of the residents of St. Louis and Ste. Genevieve were black.[39] The French, beginning with the pioneering Jesuit missionaries, had imported African slaves into the Illinois Country early in the eighteenth century to help alleviate the chronic labor shortages. The first blacks to inhabit Missouri were the slaves Philippe Renault brought with him to operate the lead mines. Although they resided on the west bank only temporarily, those black workers represented the vanguard of colonial Missouri's sizable black populace. After the Spaniards assumed control in Upper Louisiana, they authorized the importation of additional slaves to boost agricultural production in the region.[40] Black slaves contributed significantly to Missouri's early development. They mined lead, cleared land, planted and cultivated crops, made salt, hunted and trapped, rowed boats, engaged in domestic service, worked as skilled laborers, and carried out numerous other tasks.

Both French and Spanish authorities enacted black codes regulating slave treatment and conduct. The French *Code Noir* or Black Code established the basic legal framework governing the institution. It authorized the buying and selling of slaves as property and attempted to define slave rights. Among other things, the Black Code called for slaves to be adequately fed, clothed, and housed; permitted whipping and binding as forms of punishment but prohibited imprisonment, mutilation, or death without legal due process; limited slave work hours from sunup to sundown; provided for the care of aged and infirm slaves; banned sexual exploitation of women slaves; prohibited the breakup of conjugal slave families; required slave baptism and instruction in the Catholic faith; prohibited slaves from carrying arms; forbade interracial cohabitation; encouraged slave marriages; and required masters to secure governmental authorization before freeing a slave.[41]

Governor Alejandro O'Reilly continued the French code when he took possession of Louisiana for the Spaniards in 1769 as an interim measure, but in time the slave code was modified to conform with Spanish law. Spanish slave law differed from the *Code Noir* in several important respects. Spanish law recognized the right of slaves to own property and to appear as a party in a lawsuit. Under certain circumstances, slaves could sue their masters for mistreatment or for being held illegally. The Spanish statutes also permitted slaves to purchase their own freedom and prohibited Indian enslavement. In practice, the elaborate slave codes were seldom fully enforced, and slavery was a persistent legal and social problem for provincial authorities.[42]

The actual conditions of slave life in Upper Louisiana are difficult to gauge. In comparison with slaves in other parts of North America and the New World, they were probably relatively well off, but in comparison with nonslaves their situation was decidedly inferior. They were less well fed, clothed, and housed than their owners. Cornmeal and meat appear to have been the primary staples of their diet. The records frequently mention separate living quarters for slaves, but none of those dwellings have survived, and little is known about them. During the severe winter of 1792, Lieutenant Governor Manuel Pérez reported that the extreme cold had taken a heavy toll among people and animals, but his offhand comment that most of the twelve persons who had died in St. Louis were slaves strongly suggests that inferior clothing and housing left them more exposed to the elements.[43] In Ste. Genevieve the life expectancy for blacks at birth was about twenty-five years, as compared with nearly twenty-eight years for whites.[44]

Despite the provisions in the Black Code encouraging slaves to marry within the church, there were relatively few legally sanctioned slave marriages in Upper Louisiana. Slave masters appear to have balked at permitting such unions because the slave code also made it illegal to break up a conjugal slave family by sale.[45] In 1766 a St. Louis magistrate blocked an attempt to sell individual members of a slave family at public auction after noting that "the negro Mecure is married in the eyes of the Church . . . [and] you will be careful to have the families sold together not separating any negress from her husband, and no child from its father or mother, unless the girl be twelve years old and the boy fourteen."[46] The same sanctions did not apply to informal liaisons and any offspring produced by them. Nonetheless, the infrequency of slave marriages blessed by the church does not indicate an absence of sustained conjugal relationships between black men and women in Upper Louisiana.

Slavery was by its very nature brutal and inhumane. Even outwardly affable and congenial French Creoles like Madame Vital St. Gemme Beauvais adopted a different tone in dealing with the family's black slaves. Young Henry Brackenridge, who stayed in the Beauvais home, remembered her as exhibiting "an open, cheerful countenance and an expression of kindness and affection to her numerous offspring, and to all others excepting her colored domestics, toward whom she was rigid and severe."[47] Masters were expected to apply the rod and the rope to recalcitrant slaves, but some, like Lieutenant Governor Francisco Cruzat, had no heart for it. Cruzat sold one of his slaves in the summer of 1777 in the hope of acquiring one that he would not have to "order about and whip all the time, which I absolutely detest."[48] Cruzat's dilemma makes it clear that slaves did not willingly enter into servitude. Nowhere was that more evident than in the testimony offered by a slave named Jacob at an inquest convened in Ste. Genevieve to investigate the circumstances surrounding the death of Jean Datchurut's slave Tacoua. He died from a blow to the head delivered by Datchurut's overseer, following a heated dispute. In giving his account of his friend's death, Jacob testified, "Tacoua fell to the earth where he lay refusing to be intimidated." Jacob's poignant deposition demonstrates that even in death the slave Tacoua's spirit had not been broken.[49]

No formal charges were filed against the overseer as a result of the inquest, but slave deaths at the hands of a master or an overseer were exceedingly rare in Upper Louisiana. For that matter, excessive physical mistreatment of slaves appears to have been the exception rather than the rule. Critics (but not the slaves) frequently complained that Upper Louisiana's slaveowners were too lenient. In 1781 Lieutenant Governor Francisco Cruzat promulgated new ordinances governing slave conduct in response to what he branded as "the abuses which are daily creeping in through the unruly conduct of the slaves at this post of St. Louis, owing to the criminal indulgence of some masters who are too little solicitous for their authority and for the public welfare."[50] Cruzat appeared particularly concerned about unauthorized slave gatherings and directed the owners to pay greater attention to those nocturnal slave assemblies. He also sought to prevent blacks from disguising themselves as Indians in order to meet in the woods. There is little direct information to indicate what transpired at the surreptitious assemblages, but in all likelihood they were for the most part harmless social gatherings, not unlike the Creole fetes.[51] Nonetheless, the commandant in Ste. Genevieve clashed with the Vallés over their custom of allowing their slaves to carry firearms in violation of the Black Code, and during his 1797 visit Nicholas de Finiels found evidence of slave unruliness, which he attributed to Spain's lax policies governing slavery.[52] There were no slave rebellions in colonial Missouri, but the persistent concern about slave conduct offers abundant testimony that blacks did not tacitly accept their inferior status.

Not all blacks in Upper Louisiana were slaves, however; there was always a small number of free blacks during the colonial period. The 1800 Spanish census enumerated seventy-seven free blacks, seventy of whom lived in St. Louis.[53] Some had been freed by masters as a reward for faithful service, but others had managed to earn enough money to purchase their own freedom by hiring themselves out during the few spare hours they could call their own. Still others were mulatto children whose white parent arranged to buy their freedom.[54] Despite legal prohibitions against cohabitation between whites and blacks, in numerous instances members of the two races chose to sustain an intimate relationship over an extended number of years.[55]

Relatively little is known about the activities of free blacks in this early period. The men labored as hunters, oarsmen, skippers, traders, and craftsmen. The women in all likelihood were employed as domestics.[56] Free blacks owned property and went to court to collect money owed them. Jeanette Fourchet, a free black woman in St. Louis, already owned a house on Second Street, a piece of land on the Grand Prairie commons, a variety of livestock, and numerous household and personal possessions in 1773 when she married Valentin, a free black gunsmith and trapper. Since she owned more property than her new husband, she requested an inventory to ensure that she would retain control of her possessions in the event of Valentin's death. As a hunter, Valentin frequently roamed the woods in search of game with the government's authorization, and during one of those hunting expeditions in 1789 he unexpectedly died in the Big Osage village. Jeanette, who lived until 1803, provided funds in her will to pay for a Catholic funeral service and additional masses for the repose of her soul and bequeathed the remainder of her estate to her children by her first husband, Gregory. Two children had preceded her in death, but her son Augustin resided in New Orleans and her daughter Susana lived in St. Louis, as did a grandson, Jean Baptiste, whose mother was deceased.[57]

In addition to black slaves, the inhabitants of Upper Louisiana also held a few Indian slaves in spite of repeated Spanish efforts to eliminate the practice. Indian servitude was common in the Mississippi valley during the French regime, but shortly after Spain took possession of Louisiana, Governor O'Reilly decreed the abolition of Indian enslavement in accordance with long-standing Spanish policy. While O'Reilly intended his 1769 proclamation to improve relations with the region's numerous Indian tribes, it stirred up a storm of protests from owners of enslaved Indians. In St. Louis, Lieutenant Governor Piernas reported widespread resistance when he posted the ordinance on the church door in 1770.[58]

Spanish authorities relented under pressure and agreed to allow residents to retain their current Indian slaves pending a review of the policy by the Spanish crown. At the same time, however, they refused to permit the further sale or transfer of Indian slaves. O'Reilly's decree did require all owners of Indian slaves to appear before a local magistrate and declare the number, age, sex, tribe of origin, and value of all such slaves. The 1770–1771 reports from St. Louis and Ste. Genevieve enumerated a total of ninety-eight Indian slaves in those settlements.[59] Although the decision by Spanish officials not to insist on a total ban momentarily eased the slaveholders' worst fears, the action created a great deal of confusion about the legal status of Indian slavery in Upper Louisiana.[60] A dispute that developed between Madame Marie Thérèse Chouteau and her son-in-law Joseph Marie Papin over the methods he employed in apprehending some fugitive Indian slaves apparently prompted Governor Esteban Miró in 1787 to direct officials in St. Louis to republish O'Reilly's original ordinance governing Indian slavery.[61] Because of the prohibition against further Indian enslavement, full-blood Indian slaves gradually became a rarity in Upper Louisiana. Since most Indian slaves were women and most male slaves were black, the children of Indian slaves frequently were part black, and this further complicated their legal status.

Marie Jean Scypion, an Afro-Indian slave woman who originally belonged to the Joseph Tayon family in St. Louis, attempted with assistance from two of Tayon's daughters to press her claims for freedom before the local Spanish magistrate on grounds that Spanish ordinances prohibited Indian enslavement. The dispute divided the Tayon family and the St. Louis community. At one point in the fray, Auguste Chouteau advised Madame Marie Louise Tayon Chauvin that the matter should be kept out of the public eye in order to avoid great injury to all who owned slaves with Indian ancestry. Despite Chouteau's subsequent denials, Madame Chauvin testified under oath that he had advised her that when some of his Indian slaves had been disobedient and claimed their liberty, he had ordered them tied and whipped. After that, Chouteau boasted, they had talked no more about freedom. Marie Scypion died in 1802 without gaining her freedom, but her daughters persisted with the struggle, and thirty-two years after their mother's death the Missouri courts finally freed them.[62]

Spanish concerns over Indian slavery were understandable. The Spaniards placed a high priority on the maintenance of peaceful relations with neighboring Indian tribes because they viewed Indian opposition as a major impediment to Louisiana's settlement and development. The fear of Indian attack was omnipresent in Upper Louisiana. Few deaths resulted from the Indian assaults, but the property losses from thievery were a nuisance. The most persistent threat came from the powerful Osages, but by the late eighteenth century a gradual diminution in the number of Osage raids brought a welcome respite.

The occasional clashes between Indians and whites represent only one part of the larger story of Indian-white relations in colonial Missouri. For every hostile encounter there were dozens of more amicable associations. Meetings to swap furs, food, moccasins, and other items were far more commonplace than raids to steal horses. The commercial ties that developed between the two peoples became essential elements in their respective economies and fostered mutual dependencies. The Indians opened their lodges to the white hunters and to the traders who came to exchange merchandise for furs. The fur trade was big business in St. Louis, but it also became a vital component of the Indian livelihood. In living and working together, the traders and the Indians learned in varying degrees one another's languages and customs.

Few of the traders viewed the Indians as their equals, but neither did they look upon them as murderous vermin whose destruction was essential for the advancement of civilization. Their attitudes could best be described as paternalistic. Good business dictated that they deal with their Indian companions candidly and fairly. The Indians' assessment of their white trading partners is more difficult to ascertain, but the Osages' relationship with Pierre Chouteau, for example, suggests that those associations sometimes forged bonds of mutual friendship and respect. Many traders took Indian wives; it was good business to do so. The marriages enabled them to strengthen their ties with individual tribes and to count on the assistance and protection of their wife's people. These relationships could be equally beneficial to the Indians. Clan leaders frequently pressed traders to marry one of their daughters as a means of helping ensure the maintenance of traditional lines of authority. It was no accident that in so many cases the Indian wives of prominent traders were referred to as Indian princesses.[63]

Some traders openly acknowledged those relationships and their mixed-blood progeny. Andre Roy, who had a French Creole wife, made provisions in his will for the children he fathered by his Indian wives, and Louis Lorimier's Shawnee wife acted as his official hostess, performing the honors of the table with much circumspection, according to Meriwether Lewis, who dined with them. For others, these liaisons were merely transient affairs conveniently forgotten when they returned to the city.[64]

The practice of keeping an Indian wife in the wilderness and a white one in St. Louis was manifested in its most tragic and dramatic form in Manuel Lisa's marriage to Mitain of the Omahas. She bore the Spanish trader two children, but when he traveled up the Missouri with his new wife Mary Hempstead Keeney, Lisa had Mitain sent into the wilderness to avoid an embarrassing encounter. The couple's only subsequent meeting was a brief one, during which Lisa unsuccessfully attempted to force Mitain to surrender their son to his custody. Lisa previously had brought their mixed-blood daughter to St. Louis. In fairness to Lisa, it should be noted that he had been pressured by the Omahas to take the chieftain's daughter as his wife.[65]

The contacts between the two peoples were not confined to Indian villages far up the Missouri. Tribal delegations often visited Upper Louisiana's riverine settlements to parley with officials or to transact business. Occasionally they were menacing, especially when under the influence of alcohol, but usually the Indians came in peace. The presence of the nearby emigrant Indians from east of the Mississippi, relocated by the Spaniards to provide protection against warlike western tribes, also put the two peoples in regular contact. Stephen Austin recalled that the Indians frequently came to his father's store at Mine à Breton to do business. According to his recollection, "My father has had hundreds of them at his home at the Lead mines. He traded with the Shawnees and Delawares and was their friend[.] I was then a little boy and have often played with the Shawnee children."[66]

Indian and white children likewise played together in nearby Ste. Genevieve, much to the dismay of some visitors to that community. Those childhood games do not seem to have bothered young Henry Brackenridge, who remembered being tutored by his redskinned playmates in the art of shooting a bow and arrow.[67] Auguste Chouteau's eldest son, Auguste Aristide, apparently missed the Indian play when he went to Canada for schooling, for shortly after he arrived in Montreal, the nine-year-old lad asked his father to send him his bow, quiver of arrows, and quilled moccasins so that he could exercise.[68] Church records for the Ste. Genevieve parish show that a number of Peorias were baptized, and in 1796 Abbé Paul de St. Pierre included 119 Indians in the census of his parishioners. At Carondelet, 236 Indians were baptized between 1766 and 1818, and 130 were interred in the church cemetery.[69]

Some tribes appear to have fared better than others as a result of their prolonged contacts with whites. By far the most approving comments regarding Upper Louisiana's Indian settlers were directed toward the Shawnee. Their settled ways and devotion to farming drew unstinting praise from the whites who visited their villages located between Cape Girardeau and Ste. Genevieve and near St. Louis. The Shawnee regularly impressed outsiders with their peaceful demeanor and warm hospitality and with their sturdy and well-constructed log dwellings and their fenced fields.[70]

Relations between the Delawares and their white neighbors were another matter. François Vallé complained in 1792 that a drunken band of Delawares had menaced residents at the Saline, where they had killed a calf and several pigs, and Nicolas de Finiels labeled them as savages in every sense of the term, who would do well to emulate the example of their Shawnee friends.[71] In part the oft-noted distinctions between Missouri's early Shawnee and Delaware emigrants may have been a result of the individuals from those tribes who chose to migrate. The Shawnee settlers appear to have been established bands with influential tribal leaders, whereas the first

Delawares were mostly dissident and renegade factions led by persons of lesser standing.

Most tragic of all was the fate of the once-mighty Peorias. In 1802 the inhabitants of New Bourbon petitioned the local commandant to prohibit members of that tribe from establishing themselves within three miles of their settlement. This was to prevent problems arising from their drunken behavior or from their thefts of fruit and grain. That same year Perrin du Lac described the small remnant of that tribe residing in the village of Ste. Genevieve as "entirely destroyed by war, smallpox, and especially by strong liquor."[72] In fact, their numbers were by then so depleted that they seldom dared venture far from settled areas to hunt for fear that they might be attacked by their enemies.

Although the Europeans considered their ways superior to those of their "savage" neighbors, they did borrow from the Indians from time to time. Those who roamed the wilds in pursuit of furs and skins were especially prone to adopt the Indian ways, but the Indian influences were not confined to the woods. Louis Lorimier, the commandant at Cape Girardeau, embraced a lifestyle that was a mixture of Indian and European customs, and even in cosmopolitan St. Louis, Indian culture remained very much in evidence throughout the colonial period. Leather britches and moccasins were more common than knee britches and European footwear. The whites cultivated Indian crops—corn, squash, pumpkins, and beans, among others—and made them a part of their fare. Upper Louisianians also used expressive Indian words and idioms in their daily speech, and some showed a marked interest in Indian decorative arts.[73]

But as the nineteenth century dawned, an aura of change was in the air. While the onslaught of American settlers crossing the Mississippi threatened to overwhelm both the close-knit French Creole communities and their Indian neighbors, diplomats in faraway European capitals pondered the region's future. Spain's decision to retrocede Louisiana to France caught many by surprise, but it was Napoleon Bonaparte's even more stunning agreement to sell the entire territory to the United States that cast the final die. With the stroke of a pen in Paris, all hopes for stemming the American tide had ended, and a new chapter in Missouri's history was about to begin.

Settlement as of about 1800, at the end of the Spanish period.

A Shawnee brave. Engraving from *A Journey in North America*, by Georges-Victor Collot (Paris, 1826). Courtesy State Historical Society of Missouri.

SEVERAL Gentlemen, who propose to make Settlements in the Weftern Country, mean to reconnoitre and furvey the fame the enfuing Winter. All Farmers, Tradefmen, &c. of good Characters, who wifh to unite in this Scheme, and to vifit the Country under my Direction, fhall be provided with Boats and Provifions for the Purpofe, free of Expence, on figning an Agreement, which may be feen by applying to me at Profpect, near Princeton, on or before the 8th Day of October ; or at Fort Pitt, by the 20th Day of November next. The Boats which will be employed on this Expedition, are propofed to be from 40 to 60 Feet long, to row with twenty Oars each, and to carry a Number of Swivels. Each Man to provide himfelf with a good Firelock, or Rifle, Ammunition, and one Blanket, or more if he pleafes— Such as choofe Tents, or other Conveniences, muft provide them for themfelves. Every Perfon who accompanies me in this Undertaking, fhall be entitled to 320 Acres of Land, at one eighth of a Dollar per Acre. Thofe who firft engage to have the Preference of Surveys; which, however, each Perfon may make in fuch Part of the whole Tract as he pleafes, taking none but his Choice of the beft Lands ; provided each Survey is either a Square or Oblong, whofe Sides are Eaft, Weft, North and South : 640 Acres, or more, being firft referved for a Town, which I propofe to divide into Lots of One Acre each, and give 600 of them, in Fee, to fuch Merchants, Tradefmen, &c. as may apply on the Spot, and 40 of them to fuch Public Ufes as the Inhabitants fhall, from Time to Time, recommend: together with one Out Lot of 10 Acres to each of the firft 600 Families who fhall build and fettle in the Town.

All Perfons who fettle with me at New-Madrid, and their Pofterity, will have the free Navigation of the Miffifippi, and a Market at New-Orleans, free from Duties, for all the Produce of their Lands, where they may receive Payment in Mexican Dollars for their Flour, Tobacco, &c.

It is propofed, after fixing on the Spot, to clear and fence in 100 Acres, in a convenient Situation, to plant it with Corn—to hire fuitable Hands to tend it through the Summer; and in the next Fall, Winter and Spring, to diftribute it to all New Settlers at one eighth of a Dollar per Bufhel, that they may have no Dependance fo far as this will go: and as Buffaloes and other Game are very plenty in the Neighbourhood, there can be no Want of Provifions, Contractors being ready to engage to deliver frefh Beef and Venifon throughout the Year, at One Penny per Pound.

Credit will be given to thofe who defire it, as well for the Land as for Provifions, and Payment received in future Produce. All Perfons will be affifted in building a Houfe, clearing a Spot of Ground, and in getting in their firft Crops. Horned Cattle, Horfes, and Swine, will be delivered to the Settlers at New-Madrid in fuch Quantities as they ftand in Need of at firft, at very reafonable Rates, for Cafh or future Produce.

Thofe who fettle at New-Madrid in this or the enfuing Year, fhall have Plough-Irons or other Iron-Work, and farming Utenfils tranfported down the Ohio gratis; alfo their Cloathing, Bedding, kitchen Furniture, and certain other Articles which may not be too bulky.

Schoolmafters will be engaged immediately for the Inftruction of Youth.— Minifters of the Gofpel will meet with Encouragement ; and Grants of Land made in Fee to each of every Denomination, who may agree with a Congregation before the Year 1790: befide particular Grants of Tracts of Land to each Society.

This new City is propofed to be built on a high Bank of the Miffifippi River, near the Mouth of the Ohio, in the richeft and moft healthieft Part of the Weftern Country, about the Latitude of 37°.

Thofe who wifh for further Information, will be pleafed to apply to me in Perfon as above-mentioned, or at the New-City of Madrid, after the firft Day of next December, where Surveyors will attend to lay out the Lands.

GEORGE MORGAN.

October 3, 1788.

George Morgan's 1788 handbill advertising proposed settlement of New Madrid. Courtesy State Historical Society of Missouri.

This map of the New Madrid area appeared in *A Journey in North America,* by Georges-Victor Collot (Paris, 1826). Courtesy State Historical Society of Missouri.

Interior of the Bolduc House, Ste. Genevieve. Photograph by Jack E. Boucher for the Historic American Buildings Survey, Washington, D.C.

Bequette-Ribault House, Ste. Genevieve. Photograph by Jack E. Boucher for the Historic American Buildings Survey, Washington, D.C.

The dogtrot log house was a common type in early Missouri. From *Marion County Atlas* (1875). Courtesy State Historical Society of Missouri.

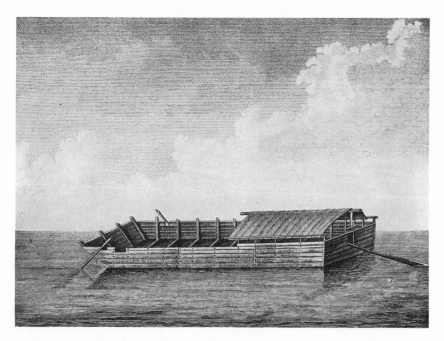

Flat-bottomed boats were used on the Missouri and Mississippi rivers before steamboats became common. Engraving from *A Journey in North America*, by Georges-Victor Collot (Paris, 1826). Courtesy State Historical Society of Missouri.

This engraving by James Otto Lewis of a portrait of Daniel Boone by Chester Harding is the only known representation of Boone done from life. Courtesy Missouri Historical Society.

Madame Marie Thérèse Chouteau. Courtesy Missouri Historical Society.

CHAPTER SEVEN
WE ARE ALL
NOW AMERICANS

T he first unconfirmed reports of the secret transfer of Louisiana from Spain to France reached Washington in 1801. Surprised American officials realized that if the rumors were correct, the unexpected shift would create serious problems for the United States. A warning to the French minister of the grave possible consequences to Franco-American relations should France occupy New Orleans produced only a vague response. To obtain more precise information, President Thomas Jefferson dispatched Robert Livingston to France in the fall of 1801. The president instructed the new American minister to France to attempt to prevent the retrocession if at all possible. If it were too late for that, he directed Livingston to secure the cession of West Florida to the United States. When the French repeatedly evaded his persistent inquiries, the American minister decided the transfer probably had been concluded, and he communicated his suspicions to Jefferson.[1]

Believing the French might soon take control of Louisiana, the United States intensified its behind-the-scenes diplomatic maneuvering early in 1802. The Americans quietly urged France to recognize America's rights to navigate the Mississippi and to deposit goods at New Orleans. Furthermore, Jefferson made it clear that if the French refused to acknowledge American rights, the United States might have to seek an alliance with Great Britain. Jefferson understood that without access to the mouth of the Mississippi and New Orleans, the United States stood to lose everything beyond the Appalachians.[2]

Rumors of the pending transfer had an equally unsettling impact on residents of the affected region. Despite their French heritage, the conservative, tradition-bound, Upper Louisiana Creoles liked the benevolent Spanish regime and had doubts about living under the authority of a military dictator who ruled a nation committed to revolutionary action. The unhappy tales of the French emigre expatriates who had fled to the Louisiana frontier undoubtedly heightened their concerns. But once Louisiana's reversion to France had been confirmed, the pragmatic Creole leaders did not allow any such misgivings to dissuade them from courting the incoming French officials. Shortly after Pierre Clément Laussat arrived in New Orleans in early 1803 to arrange the transfer, Pierre Chouteau, who was then in the port city on business, conferred with him at length about conditions in

Upper Louisiana. On the basis of those conversations, the influential St. Louis merchant returned upriver bearing the new French prefect's assurances that residents of Upper Louisiana had nothing to fear and much to gain from the pending change in governments.[3] The French Creoles were not the only ones to consider courting the incoming regime. Moses Austin saw it as an opportune moment for the Americans to organize and make their growing presence felt. A congratulatory notice to the new French officials would, he believed, "have a good effect . . . and bring the Americans into notice." But before they had time to act, the Yankee settlers received word that the French had abandoned the colony and sold it to the United States.[4]

Dreams of reviving France's colonial empire in the western hemisphere had been the primary reason for Napoleon Bonaparte's decision to press for the retrocession of Louisiana. As a part of his master plan for the New World, the French leader sent a large force under the command of his brother-in-law, Gen. Victor Emmanuel Leclerc, to St. Domingue in February 1802 to reestablish French authority and restore slavery. A bloody slave rebellion there in the 1790s had placed a former slave, Toussaint L'Ouverture, in control of the island. Since pressing problems at home had prevented the French Directory from moving immediately against the rebel black leader, they had commissioned him captain general of the island in an attempt to give an appearance of continuing French control. Napoleon's military campaign in St. Domingue was simply the first step in a larger plan for returning France to the New World. When General Leclerc's forces appeared to be gaining the upper hand, Toussaint accepted an invitation to parley, only to be chained and sent to France, where he died the following year. Yellow fever and the continued resistance of the former slaves, however, slowly turned the tide against the French forces on the island.[5]

While Napoleon's troops were sustaining heavy losses in the Caribbean, Spanish authorities made a dramatic move in Louisiana, which, despite the Treaty of San Ildefonso, they still controlled. In October 1802 the Spanish intendant at New Orleans announced the closing of the port of New Orleans to all foreigners. This action greatly aroused the western American frontier dwellers, who had been apprehensive since first learning of the retrocession. They demanded that immediate steps be taken by the United States to reopen the right of deposit on the banks of that vital artery. Although Spain had the right to close the port of New Orleans, it violated the Treaty of San Lorenzo by refusing to grant the United States an alternate site for unloading American goods. Orders to close the port came from Spain, but Spanish authorities led American officials to believe that the intendant at New Orleans was solely responsible for the action. The reasons for Spain's decision to close the port remain in doubt, but the government's unhappiness with Americans who used the right of deposit as a means to smuggle goods into Spanish territory appears to have been a major factor.[6]

Concluding that the action had been initiated by Spanish officials in New Orleans, the United States moved to resolve the problem through diplomatic channels. The president decided to send James Monroe as an *envoi extraordinaire* to negotiate with France—and, if necessary, with Spain—to find a solution to the situation. Monroe departed in March with instructions to attempt to purchase the island of New Orleans, along with as much of the Floridas as possible. Jefferson's Federalist opponents openly criticized his actions and urged the use of force to gain an outlet on the Gulf. Many in the opposition party also expressed regret over the president's decision to withdraw consular recognition of the Haitian blacks. But overall, Jefferson remained popular, especially in the South and West.[7]

Events soon vindicated the president's decision to seek a diplomatic solution. On the day before Monroe arrived in Paris to join Livingston, France's foreign minister, Talleyrand, asked Livingston if the United States would be interested in purchasing all of Louisiana. Leclerc's death in Saint Domingue and France's futile attempts to regain control of that island had caused Napoleon to lose interest in colonial activity in the New World and turn his attention to other, more promising spheres. The need for additional funds to help finance an expected renewal of warfare with Great Britain was another factor in the first consul's sudden decision to offer the province to the United States. In taking the step, however, the astute French leader also sensed that it might forestall the growing possibility of an Anglo-American rapprochement. Napoleon believed that retaining America's friendship was vital to France's national interest.[8]

Although they had not been authorized to negotiate for the purchase of the entire province, Livingston and Monroe worked out an agreement to that effect with the French minister of finance, François Barbé-Marbois. Since they believed that if they failed to act quickly the offer might be withdrawn, the American ministers had decided to proceed without waiting for final authorization from their superiors in Washington. The terms of the agreement drawn up by the representatives of the two nations were incorporated in a treaty of cession, and the United States agreed to pay fifteen million dollars for the territory. The treaty also stipulated that for a period of fifteen years duties charged French and Spanish vessels in all ports of the ceded province would not exceed those paid by American ships. Finally, Article III of the proposed treaty specified that Louisiana's residents were to enjoy all rights and privileges given to American citizens and were to be speedily incorporated within the United States. On 2 May 1803, officials observed the signing of the Treaty of Cession in formal ceremonies in Paris.[9]

Word that Livingston and Monroe had arranged to purchase all of Louisiana first reached the United States in July 1803. The great majority of Americans enthusiastically welcomed the stunning announcement. Only a few die-hard Federalists found anything to criticize. Timothy Pickering protested the gratuitous enrichment of the tyrant Napoleon, and Rufus King called Louisiana "a great waste, a wilderness unpeopled with any beings except wolves and wandering Indians."[10] King and a small core of ardent Federalists believed that the United States was already too large and feared that the addition of this vast territory would destroy the balance of the Union.

While the Republicans celebrated the agreement to buy Louisiana, they worried about the constitutional issues that it raised. The president, whose strict constructionist views were well known, doubted that he had the constitutional authority to add new territory to the United States or to grant citizenship to Louisiana's inhabitants. Hoping to neutralize the Federalist criticism and to remove any constitutional obstacles to completing the purchase, Jefferson framed a lengthy and involved constitutional amendment designed to facilitate the acquisition of the new territory. The suggested amendment opened with a simple and direct statement: "The province of Louisiana is incorporated with the U.S. and made a part thereof."[11]

In the remainder of the proposed amendment, the president attempted to put in place a framework that would encourage the gradual creation of a peaceful republican civilization in the Louisiana Territory. Following a provision intended to safeguard Indian rights to tribal lands and self-governance, the president's proposal outlined a detailed plan for administering the newly acquired territory. It called for the division of Louisiana along the thirty-first parallel, north latitude. For the more populous portion of Louisiana south of that line, later named the Territory of Orleans, Congress was authorized to erect promptly a territorial government that would guarantee for its inhabitants all rights possessed by other territorial citizens of the United States. Because Jefferson agreed that it would be preferable to postpone any immediate large-scale expansion of the Union, his amendment closed Upper Louisiana to additional settlement by whites for the foreseeable future. To ensure this, Congress was barred from disposing of any of the lands north of the thirty-first parallel without further authorization in the form of a new constitutional amendment.[12]

In order to open additional lands east of the Mississippi River to white settlement and facilitate the relocation of eastern tribes west of the Mississippi, the president's proposed amendment authorized the exchange of the remaining Indian lands in the east for tracts in the closed portion of the Louisiana Territory. In addition, Congress was empowered to encourage the resettlement of Upper Louisiana's white inhabitants on the east side of the Mississippi by offering to exchange their lands on the west bank for comparable tracts in other parts of the United States.[13]

Imbued with the Enlightenment's ideals and a passion for system, Jefferson saw Louisiana as a laboratory for republican institutions and a place where some of the nation's most perplexing problems might be resolved successfully. In particular, the president believed the vast lands of Louisiana would provide a perfect refuge for the depleted and endangered Indian tribes of the eastern United States. He had concluded that their survival depended upon their gradual assimilation into expanding American society. By persuading the Indians to abandon their traditional ways in favor of agriculture, limited ownership of land, and peaceful coexistence, he hoped to transform them from nomadic hunters and gatherers into settled farmers. Despite the disappointing experiences of the eastern Indians, the philanthropic-minded president still hoped to save them through the slow process of acculturation in the Louisiana Territory's immense empty spaces.[14]

By closing Upper Louisiana to further white settlement in the immediate future, Jefferson also wanted to establish a more orderly and controlled settlement process. The relocation of the Indians living east of the Mississippi in lands situated on the western bank provided an opportunity to fill up the eastern side and to prevent a possible drain on the population already located in those areas. Only after those regions of the United States already opened to settlement had been fully occupied would it be necessary to consider expansion into the trans-Mississippi West. When that seemingly distant time arrived, Jefferson believed the government could then "layoff a range of states on the Western bank from the head to the mouth & so, range after range advanc[e] compactly as we multiply."[15] The president considered his scheme far more practical and efficient than the helter-skelter rush he feared would otherwise occur, but his vision of the Louisiana Territory's future stood in stark contrast to the views of frontier settlers with eyes fixed on the "Great Spec."

Jefferson's proposals actually failed to generate much enthusiasm from any quarter. His advisers gave them only a lukewarm reception; the Federalist opposition was openly critical. When the president submitted his proposed amendment to the members of his cabinet for their opinions, Secretary of the Treasury Albert Gallatin indicated that he considered it unnecessary. While he agreed with the ideas in the amendment, Secretary of the Navy Robert Smith warned the president against adding such detailed restrictions to the Constitution. Both he and Secretary of State Madison suggested briefer versions to Jefferson. Senator John Breckinridge of Kentucky, who also expressed sympathy for the plan, cautioned Jefferson that if the existing bona fide land grants in Upper Louisiana were extensive, it would be virtually impossible to keep additional Americans from settling in the region. Even more skeptical was Rufus King, who advised a friend that despite the president's avowed intentions to keep the area closed, "Nothing but a cordon of troops will restrain our people from going over the River and settling themselves down upon the western bank."[16]

Failure to secure general support for his proposed amendment, coupled with a growing concern that the unpredictable Bonaparte might have a change of heart and renege on the deal, forced Jefferson to revise his plans. While he remained uncertain concerning the constitutional authority for incorporating the territory into the Union, he conceded as a matter of practical necessity the need to proceed with the ratification of the transaction, confident that the people subsequently would approve the action. The president even wrote to some of his friends suggesting they not openly discuss the constitutional problems in order to avoid any possible adverse effects on the treaty's final success. By the time the special session of Congress called by the president to consider the Louisiana question opened on 17 October 1803, Jefferson had abandoned the idea of pressing for his constitutional amendment. Instead, he had determined to let members of Congress resolve the matter in whatever fashion they deemed best.[17]

Fear that France might retract the offer to sell prompted the large Republican majority in the Senate to confirm the treaty speedily, with some Federalist support. Alexander Hamilton, John Adams, and John Marshall had all come out in favor of ratification. Nevertheless, in a subsequent, extended congressional debate over measures for implementing the treaty, a core group of New England Federalists from both houses took issue with Jefferson's handling of the Louisiana question and questioned his authority to make the commitment required by Article III in the Treaty of Cession:

The inhabitants of the ceded territory shall be incorporated in the Union of the United States, and admitted as soon as possible, according to the principles of the Federal constitution, to the enjoyment of all the rights, advantages, and immunities of citizens of the United States; and in the mean time they shall be maintained and protected in the free enjoyment of their liberty, property, and religion which they profess.[18]

Although they conceded the right of the United States to acquire new territory, either by purchase or conquest, and to govern it as a dependent province, the Federalist critics insisted that neither the president nor Congress could incorporate the inhabitants into the Union of the United States. The Republicans insisted that Article III did not make statehood mandatory. According to Virginia's John Taylor, the congressional act incorporating the inhabitants into the Union as a territory was all that was needed to fulfill the treaty requirements.[19] That interpretation may have been useful in turning aside the congressional opposition, but it contrasted sharply with the understanding held by those citizens of Louisiana who in subsequent years routinely cited the provisions of Article III in their petitions to Congress demanding increased rights.

The Federalist complaints fell largely on deaf ears. The purchase was popular almost everywhere in the country, and so was the president. Kentucky's John Breckinridge, one of the president's staunchest supporters on Louisiana, accused the Federalists of inconsistency, observing that they once had been willing to risk war to acquire the province but now seemed unwilling to buy it by means of a simple business transaction.[20]

Congress wasted little time in passing a bill authorizing the president to take possession of Louisiana. The measure empowered the chief executive to designate whatever officials he considered necessary to govern the territory and to protect the fundamental rights of territorial inhabitants. Many members of Congress objected to granting the president such extensive authority over the territory, but they reluctantly had agreed to support the controversial measure once it was stipulated that the questionable provisions would remain in effect only until the end of the present term of Congress.

With the passage of this temporary presidential authorization, the administration took immediate steps to complete the transfer of Louisiana to the United States and to establish a temporary government for the territory. President Jefferson appointed William C. C. Claiborne, Mississippi's territorial governor, and James A. Wilkinson, the commanding general of the United States, to supervise the formal transfer for the United States and to take charge of the new territory. If Jefferson had heard allegations of the double-dealing Wilkinson's intrigues with Louisiana's Spanish authorities, he chose to ignore them.[21]

A last-minute hitch unexpectedly threatened to derail U.S. preparations for occupying Louisiana. Despite the Treaty of San Ildefonso, Spain had never transferred Louisiana to French officials, and because of their unhappiness over what they considered to be France's betrayal in selling the province to the United States, the Spaniards hesitated to relinquish their control over it. Much to the relief of worried American officials, Spain belatedly retroceded Louisiana to French representatives on 30 November 1803, and at ceremonies held in New Orleans on the following 20 December, the territory officially came under American control.[22]

Even though the exchange at New Orleans included the transfer of Upper Louisiana as well, the administration planned a separate ceremony for St. Louis to mark the transaction in that region. The task of directing the activities in Upper Louisiana and governing it during the interim period went to Capt. Amos Stoddard. As acting commandant of Upper Louisiana, Stoddard, an artillery captain in the U.S. army and a Revolutionary War veteran who had interrupted his military career for several years to practice law in Maine, received his instructions from General Wilkinson and Governor Claiborne.[23]

By the time Stoddard arrived in St. Louis on 24 February 1804, the residents there had begun to recover from the initial shock of discovering that they were about to become U.S. citizens. The unexpected news had first reached them the previous August when Lieutenant Governor Delassus received a letter from Indiana's territorial governor, William Henry Harrison, informing him of the transaction.[24] The immediate reaction had been one of disbelief. Having scarcely had time to reconcile themselves to the prospect of returning to French rule when they learned of this even more stunning development, Upper Louisianans resented their use as pawns in an international chess game. For the French Creoles, the thought of being governed by the rambunctious Americans, who had already begun to overrun their region, was understandably unsettling. Indeed, it seemed a sign of the times when a defiant mob of Yankee settlers, shouting "Viva Gifferson," forcibly prevented outgoing Spanish authorities from surveying Ste. Genevieve entrepreneur Pascal Detchemendy's six-thousand-arpent concession in the Bellevue Valley. The grant, made by Lieutenant Governor Delassus, threatened to displace ten or twelve American families. Ste. Genevieve's commandant, Jean Baptiste Vallé, summoned the recalcitrant Scotch-Irish Americans to appear before him, but they curtly informed him that they could not respond to "any mandate derived through the authority of the King of Spain without willful violation of our duty to the United States."[25]

When Captain Stoddard declined to intervene in the case, Vallé quietly let the matter drop. He and the other members of Upper Louisiana's pragmatic Creole elite prudently chose instead to safeguard their interests by accommodating the incoming U.S. officials. Despite misgivings about their futures under an American administration, they demonstrated remarkable adaptability in adjusting to the new regime. Vallé, whom the Americans retained as commandant in Ste. Genevieve, put it quite succinctly: "We are all now Americans, and as such I will devote myself to my country's service and to the welfare of my fellow citizens as I have done under all other governments."[26]

Actually, for all their sentimental attachments to the old order, powerful trading families like the Vallés and the Chouteaus stood to gain much from the change in governments. Rising land prices, lucrative government-supply contracts, improved prospects for expanded fur-trading operations, and a growing local retail trade seemed likely to follow the expected American influx. Ironically, some of the strongest initial opposition to the transfer came from American farmers who had migrated to the Spanish province to take advantage of that government's free land policy and to avoid U.S. taxation. Since many had never bothered to claim legally the lands they occupied, their thoughts undoubtedly turned to how they would fare under the more stringent U.S. land laws.[27]

Stoddard's reception in St. Louis was cordial, but the tardy arrival of his troops due to ice on the river, along with the unexpected illness of Lieutenant Governor Delassus, forced a postponement of the official transfer ceremonies until 9 and 10 March 1804. Stoddard represented both France and the United States during the proceedings. Laussat, the French commissioner in New Orleans, had designated him to act as the French government's agent in order to eliminate the expense of sending a representative to the distant post. Stoddard's instructions authorized him to receive Upper Louisiana from the Spaniards and then to deliver the territory to the United States.[28]

On 9 March the members of the Spanish garrison in St. Louis stood at attention before the government house in full dress uniforms as the royal Spanish standard was lowered for the last time, to the accompaniment of drum rolls and cannon fire. Stoddard, acting as a French representative, signed the necessary documents in the presence of Lieutenant Governor Delassus and the small crowd that had gathered to observe the proceedings. On the next day Captain Stoddard returned with his company of American soldiers to assume control of the government in the name of the United States. With appropriate ceremony, the Stars and Stripes were raised and a salute was fired. Stoddard reported that there were tears in the eyes of the assembled natives as he addressed them, but he denied that they were tears of regret—a conclusion that was probably more patriotic than accurate.[29] Most would undoubtedly have preferred to remain under the paternalistic Spanish system with its simple government and its immunity from direct taxation, but since they could do little to alter the situation, they had become resigned to their fate. Elsewhere things were much the same. In the only other formal observance of the transfer in Upper Louisiana, Capt. Daniel Bissell took charge of the small Spanish post at New Madrid for the United States on 18 March. The outgoing commandant reported that during those ceremonies the local citizens had "expressed the greatest grief."[30]

The U.S. government took every possible precaution to minimize resentment against the American takeover. U.S. officials cautioned their representatives in Louisiana to treat the inhabitants with politeness and cordiality and to see that their religious and property rights were protected. On the day he assumed control for the United States, Stoddard issued an address designed to reassure the local residents. Reminding them that the Treaty of Cession had pledged that they were to be incorporated into the Union and admitted as soon as possible to full rights and privileges of U.S. citizenship, the new commandant promised that they could expect fair and equitable treatment from their new government. On the subject of the greatest immediate interest to most inhabitants of the territory—the confirmation of land claims—Stoddard indicated that the American government would confirm their titles speedily.[31]

Most of St. Louis's leading citizens did turn out for the lavish celebrations organized to mark the transfer of the territory to the United States. In accordance with local custom, Delassus entertained the newly arrived Stoddard and his party with a dinner and ball. The American commandant felt obliged to repay the generous hospitality by hosting a gala affair at his residence. Sparing no expense to ensure a successful evening, the commandant spent $622.75 on the elaborate event and then worried whether his cost-conscious superiors would reimburse him.[32]

Meriwether Lewis and William Clark managed to take time away from last-minute preparations for their forthcoming journey to the Pacific to participate in the St. Louis festivities. Lewis, Jefferson's trusted protégé and former private secretary, had in fact been called upon to sign the formal transfer documents as an official witness for the United States. Since December 1803, the two leaders had been assembling the necessary men and equipment at their camp located on the Rivière à Dubois (Wood River), a small stream opposite the mouth of the Missouri. President Jefferson had selected them to lead the exploratory expedition with two purposes in mind: to gather geographic, scientific, and military information and to foster trade and friendship with trans-Mississippi Indians. The president instructed Captain Lewis to convey his good wishes to the western tribes and to invite selected influential chiefs to visit him in the nation's capital.[33]

Jefferson's interest in the American West and its exploration had begun long before anyone seriously pondered the acquisition of Louisiana by the United States. As early as 1783 he had invited George Rogers Clark to consider an exploratory mission across the continent, and a decade later he was actively involved in the American Philosophical Society's plan for sending French botanist André Michaux on an expedition to the Pacific. None of those projects materialized, but Jefferson remained committed to the idea of western exploration. Even the initial preparations for the Lewis and Clark mission began two years before U.S. officials learned that Louisiana was to be theirs, but France's agreement to sell the vast western territory to the United States greatly enhanced the mission's importance and increased the need for cultivating friendly relations with western Indians.[34]

During their stay at Camp Dubois, which lasted from December until May, both Lewis and Clark often traveled to St. Louis, where they became fast friends with the city's leading traders, the Chouteau brothers. The many hours they passed in the comfortable Chouteau homes provided a welcome diversion from camp life, but the pleasant gatherings also allowed them to confer with the persons who knew most about the country the American expedition was preparing to traverse. The Chouteaus, James Mackay, Jean Baptiste Truteau, and various other prominent local traders were intimately acquainted with the Missouri River and its Indian inhabitants, and their firsthand accounts proved invaluable. Lewis and Clark also gained access to various maps and journals from previous Missouri River expeditions, including the important Evans-Mackay materials. Lewis made every effort to build upon the good will fostered by these exchanges with the Creole leaders. Prior to his departure, the army captain had arranged for sons of five leading territorial families—Chouteau, Gratiot, Brouis, Lorimier, and Vallé—to attend the U.S. Military Academy at West Point.[35]

The Creole merchants also took advantage of their new friendships with the American explorers to press their personal views on local issues and to strike bargains for the sale of merchandise to outfit the expedition. When Pierre Chouteau learned from Lewis of Jefferson's desire to confer with Indian leaders, he promptly volunteered to escort a delegation of Osage chieftains to the federal capital. Well aware of Pierre's long experience with the Osages and his influence in their camps, Lewis did not hesitate to accept the offer. The astute Frenchman made the best of the opportunity and returned to St. Louis five months later bearing a commission as the first U.S. Indian agent for Upper Louisiana's tribes.[36]

While Lewis was still in St. Louis completing arrangements for Chouteau's trip to Washington, D.C., and seeing to the last-minute details for his own journey, the remaining members of the Corps of Discovery broke camp on 14 May and headed up the Missouri under Clark's guidance. The expeditionary force stopped at St. Charles to await Lewis's arrival.[37] Lewis reached the Missouri River settlement on 20 May, accompanied by Amos Stoddard, Auguste Chouteau, Charles Gratiot, and several other prominent territorial residents who had escorted him from St. Louis. On the following day, the forty-odd members of the Lewis and Clark expedition began their historic journey amid the rousing cheers of well-wishers who had gathered along the riverbank to see them off.[38]

Following the expedition's departure, Captain Stoddard returned to St. Louis to continue his administrative duties. The president had installed him as commandant of Upper Louisiana until Congress provided a permanent government for the newly acquired province. During that interim he retained the basic Spanish governmental structure. The new American commandant assumed all functions, both civil and military, previously exercised by Spanish officials; but the republican aversion to military rule prompted his superiors to direct him to keep civil and military functions carefully separated.[39]

The U.S. government went to great lengths to maintain this division. Governor Claiborne issued Stoddard's instructions on civil matters, while General Wilkinson provided assistance on military affairs. When Captain Stoddard's military superior, Maj. James Bruff, arrived in St. Louis some time in the summer of 1804, Stoddard retained authority in civil matters, and Bruff assumed control of military activities. Bruff did not get along as well with the local Creoles as his more accommodating subordinate Stoddard, and the major's actions occasionally stirred up controversy. Bruff and Stoddard remained in charge in Upper Louisiana until 1 October 1804, when the territory came under the jurisdiction of the officials of the Indiana Territory.[40]

Stoddard enjoyed wide discretion in handling civil functions. In most instances he reappointed the former commandants to direct civil affairs in their particular districts. Before taking that step, he had conferred with Delassus concerning their qualifications and abilities. Governor Claiborne agreed with the wisdom of this practice but warned Stoddard to monitor the commandants' conduct to guard against any abuse of authority on their part. Although Stoddard retained the commandants to help smooth the transition, he complained to Claiborne that they rendered him little assistance, noting that most cases still came to him for final decision on appeal. Stoddard's attempts to unravel the practices and procedures of his predecessors proved exasperating.[41]

His American legal training left him ill-prepared for handling judicial matters in accordance with established custom and Spanish law. In one troublesome case, Joseph Tayon petitioned Stoddard for permission to sell his biracial, black-Indian slaves, but family members opposed to the sale countered that the individuals in question were free persons under Spanish statutes. The perplexed officer ordered that none of the slaves were to be sold until the territorial court scheduled to sit in October 1804 had an opportunity to sort out the complex issues raised by the case. In taking that action, Stoddard followed Claiborne's advice that he refer all doubtful cases to the incoming territorial judges.[42]

Spanish land claims posed an even more serious problem for the interim administration; the cession of Louisiana had produced a wave of speculative activity within the territory. Confident that a new flood of immigrants would send land values in Upper Louisiana soaring, speculators had begun to accumulate as many private land claims as possible, even before the United States had taken formal control of the region. They knew from recent experience in other American territories that the settlement of private claims would probably delay the sale of public lands for several years. Consequently, land jobbers recognized the importance of the existing private claims, most of which they assumed the U.S. government would eventually confirm.[43]

Private claims in Upper Louisiana were extensive, blanketing the lands along the Mississippi from New Madrid to 150 miles above the mouth of the Missouri, and stretching inland between 60 and 120 miles. Since private claims encompassed virtually all of the most desirable areas for settlement, newcomers found it necessary to purchase a concession or a permit to settle before they could take up residence in the territory.[44]

Americans like Rufus Easton and John Rice Jones, who had come from the United States following the announcement of the cession, joined local residents including Jacques St. Vrain, Louis Labeaume, Charles Gratiot, Auguste and Pierre Chouteau, Jacques Clamorgan, and James Mackay in the race to acquire titles. The competition for the claims sent prices upward as the value of real property in Upper Louisiana rapidly appreciated.

The quest for lands also encouraged fraud. Taking advantage of the incomplete state of most land titles in Upper Louisiana, some individuals obtained, through influence or bribery, antedated petitions from Spanish officials confirming large land grants to them. The holders of these counterfeit titles believed the U.S. government would be unable or unwilling to separate the bona fide from the fraudulent grants since neither had been registered and recorded in New Orleans and since records in Upper Louisiana were incomplete and unreliable.[45]

Shortly after his arrival in Upper Louisiana, Stoddard had reported to his superiors in Washington that he suspected widespread attempts were being made to defraud the United States of extensive tracts of land. As Stoddard became more familiar with the complexity of the problem, he developed a more favorable attitude toward the claimants and their problems. He repeatedly indicated that he believed all bona fide land grants would be confirmed by the U.S. government, but local residents, particularly those with extensive claims, remained apprehensive.[46]

As one of his first official acts, Stoddard had ordered the inhabitants of the territory to surrender all public records, especially those related to land claims, to the American authorities for safekeeping. He promised that each claimant would be provided with an attested copy of original documents. In issuing these instructions Stoddard sought to ascertain the nature of the various land titles and to provide a safe deposit for all original papers relative to such claims, but his action disturbed claimants, who objected to giving up the original copies.[47] Their concern over the commandant's order was quickly overshadowed by reports of a far more menacing threat. Rumors reached the territory that the United States had decided to validate only those titles issued in accordance with Spanish regulations prior to 1 October 1800, the date of the Treaty of San Ildefonso. Under pressure from his constituents, Stoddard informed the administration in Washington of the multiple problems facing bona fide claimants in establishing their titles. Meanwhile the uneasy residents, aroused by the latest statements attributed to high-ranking government officials, began organizing to protect their vital interests.[48]

Other problems competed for Stoddard's attention, with Indian affairs heading the list. Shortly after the transfer of Louisiana to the United States, hundreds of Indians descended upon St. Louis expecting to receive gifts from their new leader. Since both the French and Spanish had employed Indian gift-giving rituals as an important element in their diplomacy, the Indians naturally looked for the Americans to continue the practice. Stoddard found himself at a decided disadvantage in dealing with the visiting delegations. Captain Lewis supplied him with small amounts of tobacco and liquor, but otherwise he had no provisions to give them. The American reluctance to provide the traditional presents signaled an important change in Indian-white relations in Upper Louisiana. In Indian cultures, the ritualized gift exchanges symbolized broader commitments of friendship and loyalty between the participants, and the Indians interpreted the American government's stinginess as a sign of underlying hostility. It was not an auspicious beginning for the U.S. government in its dealings with the trans-Mississippi tribes. Among other things, the decline of gift giving forced the Indians to rely more on commercial exchanges to secure European merchandise. Jefferson clearly viewed trade as the most effective mechanism for controlling the Indians. At the same time that their dependency on their white neighbors was deepening, the western tribes found the land-hungry newcomers much more preoccupied with laying claim to historic tribal territories than either their French or Spanish predecessors. It was little wonder that Stoddard found the Indians increasingly restless.[49]

The U.S. commandant fully recognized the irreconcilable differences that divided Indians and frontier settlers. In April 1804, he issued a proclamation ordering the execution or seizure of a party of vagabond Creek Indians who had recently killed several settlers, but he cautioned against harming members of peaceful tribes residing in the territory. The fair-minded official admitted that the Indians often had just grounds for complaint against the incoming whites, and he cited as an example a case in which a grand jury had refused to return a bill of indictment against a white man who had killed an Indian, apparently for no justifiable reason.[50]

The Sacs and Foxes were in a particularly defiant mood. Not long after Stoddard's arrival, a party of young Sacs had tied a U.S. flag to a horse's tail and dragged it in the dirt. When the tribe declared war on their long-time rivals the Osages in a dispute over hunting grounds, a Sac raiding party attacked, captured, and killed a number of Osages on their way to St. Louis in a boat belonging to a local fur company. Stoddard condemned the assault, and in a council held with the Sacs and their allies the Foxes, he demanded the immediate return of the Osage prisoners. Responding in what Stoddard described as "a pretty elevated tone," the Indians protested the white seizure of their hunting grounds in the Louisiana Territory. Envious of what they believed to be preferred treatment accorded by the United States to the Osages, the Sac and Fox representatives requested the establishment of an American trading factory for their use. To underscore their demands, they also told the commandant that the British, with whom they were on good terms, had invited them to a meeting in Canada.[51]

Relations with the Sacs further deteriorated when five young braves attacked an exposed white settlement on the Cuivre River a few miles north of St. Louis. This was in retaliation for the U.S. decision to invite Osage leaders to Washington to confer with President Jefferson and to receive gifts. Believing the Americans had given their rivals this favored treatment because the Americans feared the Osages, the Sac warriors murdered and scalped three settlers, assuming that their actions would strengthen their bargaining position with the United States.[52]

Fearing that a war was imminent, some of the Cuivre River settlers abandoned their homes, while others began preparing to defend themselves against further Indian depredations by constructing a stockade fort on a prairie three miles upriver from the Mississippi. They appealed to

Major Bruff for provisions, munitions, and funds for guarding the fort and deploying spies to patrol the area. Bruff, who promised to provide assistance if the hostilities continued, summoned Sac leaders and demanded that they surrender the culprits responsible for the killings. With only fifty-one soldiers in his command, many of whom were ill, there was little else that he or Stoddard could do for the moment. Citizens in other parts of the territory were equally apprehensive. Residents of New Madrid proclaimed themselves defenseless against menacing Creek and Mascouten bands and vigorously protested the reduction of the garrison at that post to a meager ten men. Bruff did advise his superiors of the territory's exposed situation and recommended they establish military posts on the upper Missouri at the mouth of the Platte, the upper Mississippi at Prairie du Chien, and the St. Francis River between New Madrid and Cape Girardeau. The cost-conscious Jefferson administration turned a deaf ear to all such suggestions, and the military situation remained essentially unchanged in Upper Louisiana until the eve of the War of 1812.[53]

Early in his administration, Captain Stoddard had attempted to improve the local defenses by creating a territorial militia. Although the U.S. militia system was organized much like the Spanish system, the American republic's newest citizens were slow to respond to their new commandant's summons to arms. The American officer experienced difficulty in obtaining an accurate count of the number of male citizens in the territory capable of bearing arms, and three months later, his successor, Major Bruff, reported that the militia remained unorganized and poorly armed, with units varying in size from twenty to two hundred.[54]

On the whole, however, Stoddard dealt ably with Upper Louisiana's people and its problems. During his brief command— only seven months— he presided over the orderly transfer of authority from Spain to France, and then to the United States; established an acceptable interim government; successfully minimized discord within the territory; and persuaded, at least temporarily, a majority of the territory's white citizenry that they stood to benefit from the American acquisition of Louisiana. In fact, not until they learned of the terms of the act creating a government to replace Stoddard's rule did the local residents openly display dissatisfaction with the newly established American regime.

The Louisiana Purchase was undeniably one of Thomas Jefferson's greatest presidential achievements. The U.S. acquisition of the immense piece of real estate doubled the nation's size and made the future state of Missouri, whose capital appropriately would one day bear Jefferson's name, a part of the expanding republic. It was a change destined to alter the course of American history and to affect profoundly the futures of the territory's culturally diverse inhabitants.

CHAPTER EIGHT

THE BEGINNINGS OF REPUBLICAN GOVERNMENT

Thomas Jefferson's concerns about incorporating Louisiana into the United States were well founded. The territory's French and Spanish inhabitants exhibited little desire to embrace the unfamiliar republican institutions. To attempt to impose a system of representative government seemed unwise, even foolhardy. But when the president, whose republican principles were well known, attempted to create a transitional government more in line with their previous experiences, he opened himself to charges of seeking to perpetuate military despotism.

The problems in Upper Louisiana seemed especially perplexing by late spring in 1804 as disquieting rumors continued to emanate from the banks of the Potomac. Reports of U.S. plans for closing the region to further settlement, relocating eastern Indians west of the Mississippi, and confirming only those land titles fully completed under the provisions of Spanish law prior to 1 October 1800 threatened to undermine Capt. Amos Stoddard's careful efforts to ensure an orderly transition to American control in St. Louis. From the moment they first learned of the Louisiana Purchase, federal officials had carried on a lively exchange concerning the territory and its future. The president actively participated in those discussions, and his views did much to shape the course of the ensuing debate. Jefferson's desire to create a vast Indian sanctuary in the trans-Mississippi region understandably alarmed Upper Louisiana's Euro-American inhabitants, and his doubts concerning the readiness of those inhabitants to assume the responsibilities of republican government placed him at odds with members of his own party in Congress.

Even before the formal transfer ceremonies had taken place in St. Louis, the president advised Kentucky senator John Breckinridge that he favored the retention of an authoritarian administrative system for Louisiana's northern district. Jefferson went so far as to draw up a proposed bill dividing Louisiana into two territories with separate governments. Breckinridge, who had been assigned the task of drafting legislation for Louisiana's governance, welcomed the chief executive's suggestions and introduced his measure—or at least a close facsimile—in the upper chamber on 30 December 1803.[1]

Breckinridge did not identify the president as the bill's author for fear that the disclosure would muddy the legislative waters. Section 8 of the Breckinridge bill, as the measure was called, placed the responsibility for administering Upper Louisiana in the hands of an appointed governor with assistance from military commandants designated for each of the local subdistricts. It also authorized the president to negotiate an exchange of Indian lands east of the Mississippi for comparable tracts on the west bank.[2]

During the lengthy Senate deliberations on the Breckinridge bill, most of the discussion centered on the controversial provisions contained in Section 8. Some Republican senators charged that Upper Louisiana's proposed government smacked of military rule, and even those who were willing to concede that the territory's residents might not be fully prepared for self-government were reluctant to approve the establishment of such an authoritarian framework. Critics of the bill also argued that the efforts to restrict future settlement in Upper Louisiana would infringe upon the rights of persons already residing there.[3]

Georgia senator James Jackson attempted to circumvent those objections by suggesting that Section 8 be deleted and that Upper Louisiana be annexed to the Indiana Territory for administration. Jackson's proposal was favorably received, but a number of senators feared that the consolidation of the two territories might necessitate a drastic revision in Upper Louisiana's existing statutes. As an alternative, they recommended assigning Indiana's territorial officials to govern the two territories as separate administrative units. This arrangement offered the added advantage of permitting Congress to sidestep the potentially divisive decision on the status of slavery in Upper Louisiana that would have been required if the laws of Indiana had been applied to the trans-Mississippi region.[4]

The Senate speedily approved a substitute motion striking out Section 8 of the original bill and authorizing the officers of the Indiana Territory to govern the District of Upper Louisiana.[5] When the bill went to the House of Representatives, members of that body turned their attention to the problem of French and Spanish land titles in Louisiana. Reports of widespread fraud and speculation in Louisiana land claims prompted John Rhea of Tennessee to introduce a resolution nullifying all land grants made by Spanish officials after 1 October 1800, the date of the Treaty of San Ildefonso, by which Spain had retroceded Louisiana to France.[6]

Rhea's attempts to attach his resolution to the pending Louisiana bill elicited objections from House members who feared that the proposal might jeopardize legitimate grants in the new American territory. But despite their insistence that the settlement of land titles was a judicial rather than a legislative matter, a majority of House members agreed with Congressman Rhea's contention that decisive action was needed to check the fraudulent concessions and voted to include the proviso in the Louisiana measure.[7]

A conference committee resolved the differences between the House and Senate versions. The committee reported out a bill dividing Louisiana into the Territory of Orleans, the area south of the thirty-third parallel, and the District of Louisiana, the region north of that line. Congress placed the District of Louisiana under the control of officials in the Indiana Territory. Indiana's territorial government followed the specifications established by the Northwest Ordinance of 1787 for first-class territories. A governor, a secretary, and three superior court judges, all appointed by the president, administered the territory, with the governor and judges empowered to adopt any necessary statutes. To assist the Indiana authorities in governing the trans-Mississippi region, the measure authorized the president to divide Upper Louisiana into subdistricts and to assign commandants for each, subject only to the superintendence of Indiana's territorial governor. The commandants, who were to be primarily responsible for local administration, were granted both civil and military authority.[8]

To ensure an orderly transition, the measure stipulated that the District of Louisiana's existing laws would continue in effect until they were altered or repealed by Indiana's territorial governor and judges. The Louisiana law did nullify all land grants in the territory made subsequent to 1 October 1800, and it sanctioned the use of force in removing unauthorized persons from settling on the public domains of the United States. In accordance with the president's wishes, Congress empowered him to enter into agreements providing for the resettlement in Upper Louisiana of eastern Indian tribes. Both houses agreed to the terms outlined in the committee's report, and President Jefferson affixed his signature to the bill on 26 March 1804.[9]

Word of the bill's final passage had not reached St. Louis when an inner circle of the city's leading citizens met at the home of David Delaunay on 2 April 1804 to discuss the provisions of the distasteful measure. After concluding that the proposed legislation endangered the interests of Louisiana's inhabitants, the small group of self-appointed community representatives designated Auguste Chouteau, Bernard Pratte, Charles Gratiot, Pierre Provenchere, and Louis Labeaume as a committee of five to advise U.S. authorities of the strong local opposition to the Louisiana bill. Those at the 2 April gathering also authorized the committee to convene a general meeting of citizens from throughout the St. Louis district to apprise them of the situation and secure their endorsement for registering the community's distaste for the proposed new law. They ordered the publication of an account of their deliberations in French and English and notified Captain Stoddard of their actions.[10]

The committee invited residents from throughout the district to a follow-up meeting at Auguste Chouteau's St. Louis mansion on 15 April. After selecting their host to preside, those present endorsed the positions taken at the earlier session and added the names of Charles Sanguinet and James Rankin to the original five-member panel as they prepared to enter the lists against the bill.[11]

News that the unpopular bill had already become law merely intensified the local opposition. Upper Louisiana's Creole leaders found much to criticize in the measure that was finally adopted, but the sources of their concerns were distinctly different from those that had caused members of Congress to insist on changes in the proposed bill. In fact, many features of Jefferson's original bill would have been more palatable to them than the final version approved by Congress. The Creole elite found the president's plan for combining civil and military authority reassuring. It was congenial to their well-established habits and seemed conducive to the maintenance of order and stability in the rapidly changing territory. Pierre Chouteau made that perfectly clear during his trip to Washington with the Osage delegation. Following a conversation with the St. Louis merchant, Albert Gallatin advised the president that "as to the Government of Upper Louisiana, he is decidedly in favour of a military one & appears much afraid of civil law and lawyers."[12]

The authoritarian framework that members of Congress had considered so distasteful actually appealed to Upper Louisiana's Creoles. What bothered the Creoles was the prospect of being subject to the authority of absentee officials unfamiliar with their problems and too far away to be easily influenced. Still more alarming were the provisions calling for the relocation of eastern Indian tribes in their midst and the congressionally imposed restrictions limiting the confirmation of Spanish land titles.[13]

As soon as it was affirmed that the legislation had been enacted into law, the St. Louis committee redirected its efforts toward securing the measure's repeal. Its members prepared a circular letter summoning representatives from all parts of the territory to meet in St. Louis on 1 September 1804 to chart a course of action. The authors of the circular suggested that the delegates could meet with Indiana's territorial governor, William Henry Harrison, who was expected to visit Upper Louisiana sometime after 1 October. In attempting to assemble delegates from all parts of the territory, the St. Louis committee stressed that the proposed general meeting would provide a forum for acquainting the new governor with their views concerning the new legislation, but the representational scheme they devised ensured that the St. Louis delegation would be able to dominate the proceedings.[14]

In the midst of the turmoil generated by these latest developments, rumors began circulating in St. Louis that the institution of slavery might also be in jeopardy in Upper Louisiana. During the Louisiana debates in

Congress, Federalist James Hillhouse of Connecticut had proposed to exclude slavery from all of the Louisiana Territory. The members of Congress turned back that attempt, but in legislating for lower Louisiana they did enact Jefferson's proposal for closing Louisiana to the international slave trade, while affirming Afro-American slavery and opening the territory to the interstate slave trade. This produced the effect of creating a market for the surplus slaves of the old upper South, while depriving the people of lower Louisiana of their traditional access to African and Caribbean slaves. Jefferson contended that this arrangement would actually ameliorate the conditions of the slaves by creating a safety valve. In fact, the decision to open the Louisiana Territory to slavery in 1804 set the stage for the Missouri controversy that erupted fifteen years later. For the present, however, there was still room for slavery in Freedom's Empire.[15]

Though largely unfounded, the fears about the future of slavery in Upper Louisiana surfaced when it was discovered that although Congress had specifically sanctioned the institution in the Territory of Orleans, it had omitted any mention of it with regard to the remainder of Louisiana. Complaining that the prevailing uncertainty had encouraged a growing restiveness among the territory's nearly two thousand slaves, a group of anxious St. Louis slaveholders created yet another committee for the purpose of petitioning Stoddard to enforce the black codes that the French and Spanish regimes had employed for controlling the slave population. Although Stoddard, a New Englander, found slavery repugnant, he agreed to establish whatever regulations the local slaveholders considered necessary to maintain order.[16]

Meanwhile, the call from St. Louis for delegates to meet with Governor Harrison brought into the open the widening division between the older French and newer American settlers. In Ste. Genevieve, an American-dominated assembly decided against participating in the convention after charging that the proposed scheme was an unpatriotic attempt by a small coterie of French Creoles determined to maintain the favored position they had enjoyed under Spanish auspices. The Americans, led by Ste. Genevieve physician Dr. Walter Fenwick and mining entrepreneur Moses Austin, urged genuine efforts to eliminate the "jealousy which at this time so apparently exists between the two descriptions of people."[17]

Austin, already at odds with his French neighbors over their claims to mining rights on his Mine à Breton concession, still smarted over their failure to render assistance when the Osages attacked his residence in 1802. Another participant in the Ste. Genevieve meeting, Rufus Easton, a well-connected New York attorney who had just arrived in Louisiana, warned President Jefferson in a confidential letter to be wary of the French clique in

St. Louis. He charged that in spite of their public avowals urging the two groups to cooperate, they had effectively excluded Americans from their recent proceedings. Their true motive, he informed the president, was to secure confirmation of their land claims, many of which were undeniably fraudulent.[18]

Under Chouteau's leadership the St. Louis committee ignored their critics and pressed ahead with plans for convening a territorial assembly. Twelve of the seventeen Upper Louisiana delegates met in St. Louis on 14 September and, in a move to counter the charges against them, elected the pro-American Creole merchant Charles Gratiot as their presiding officer. To further blunt the allegations of disloyalty, the predominantly French delegates invited Captain Stoddard, in his capacity as Upper Louisiana's acting commandant, to administer an oath to the officers and members of the convention, in which they pledged loyalty to the United States and adherence to its Constitution and laws.[19]

Gratiot immediately set about to chart a moderate course for the convention. He attributed the passage of the unpopular congressional legislation to a lack of accurate information on conditions in the District of Louisiana. Gratiot called for a concerted effort to counter what he considered the erroneous reports that had pictured Louisiana's inhabitants as land-hungry schemers bent on gobbling up vacant lands. To ensure a favorable hearing for their proposals, Gratiot urged members of the assembly to set a good example by showing respect for all territorial laws, including the ones they were seeking to have repealed. He also encouraged the disgruntled deputies to give Governor Harrison and his party a respectful and cordial welcome when they arrived in the territory.[20]

A small dissident element favoring a more radical approach unsuccessfully attempted to secure the convention's endorsement for a proposal requesting the French and Spanish governments to intervene in the event that the United States failed to honor its commitments in the Treaty of Cession. The delegates vetoed that proposition and decided instead to petition Congress to repeal the unpopular new law. They also rejected a proposal submitted by residents of the Territory of Orleans calling for the reunification of upper and lower Louisiana, and after conferring with Captain Stoddard, they decided not to request a military government, though that is clearly what most of them would have preferred.[21]

Despite their antirepublican bias, the French Creole landholders went as far as they could in accommodating themselves to the incoming regime. At the urging of Auguste Chouteau, the deputies in the St. Louis convention insisted on toning down the wording of their petition to Congress. They feared that the unusually strong language contained in the original draft might defeat its purpose. In consultation with Stoddard, the delegates made the necessary revisions, but even with those changes the petition left no doubt about their unhappiness with the current state of affairs. In it they complained that the Americans had fashioned a political system for them whose principal features included "the dictates of a foreign government! an incalculable accession of savage hords to be vomited on our borders! an entire privation of some of the dearest rights enjoyed by freemen!"[22]

Citing the provision of Article 3 of the Treaty of Cession promising their speedy incorporation into full rights and privileges of citizenship, the petitioners called upon Congress to repeal the recent act creating a government for Louisiana; to take steps to provide for the permanent division of Louisiana; to grant Upper Louisiana its own governor and judges, along with an elected legislative council; to provide the district with a delegate to Congress; to acknowledge the right to hold slaves and to import them into the territory; and to recognize all contracts engaged in, conformable to the laws of Spain, during the time that Spain ruled Louisiana. The latter provision sought to protect all Spanish land titles, including those issued after 1 October 1800.[23] Convention members signed the final petition in St. Louis on 29 September. On the following day they unanimously elected Auguste Chouteau and Eligius Fromentin, a French emigre and former Catholic priest who had recently come to Louisiana seeking new opportunities, to take the resolution to Washington and speak on its behalf.[24]

This flurry of activity came too late to stay the implementation of Upper Louisiana's new government. Immediately after being advised of his additional duties, Indiana's territorial governor, William Henry Harrison, began making preparations to take charge of affairs in the trans-Mississippi territory.[25] By then, officials of the Jefferson administration had learned of the strong opposition to the changes, and they wisely counseled Harrison to proceed with caution. Secretary of State Madison urged the governor and the judges to move slowly in making legislative changes, and officials in the War Department advised him not to make any agreements for the relocation of Indians in Upper Louisiana until more exact information could be obtained concerning the existing land claims in the territory.[26]

Jefferson gave his personal attention to the matter of appointing Upper Louisiana's commandants. Since they were charged with directing both civil and military affairs in their respective districts, the president sought individuals whom he believed could be depended upon to exercise prudence in the combination of these powers. Nevertheless, some Republicans so opposed the consolidation of civil and military authority that they refused to be mollified by the chief executive's careful scrutiny of all prospective candidates. Secretary of Treasury Gallatin refused even to discuss the appointments with him.[27]

Despite the controversy over the wisdom of employing military commandants as civilian officials, the president was able to find well-qualified individuals to fill the positions. He selected Samuel Hammond to serve in St. Louis, Return J. Meigs, Jr., in St. Charles, Richard Kennon in Cape Girardeau, and Seth Hunt in Ste. Genevieve. All except Hunt, who was given the rank of major, received commissions as colonels.[28] The subsequent decision by Governor Harrison and the Indiana territorial judges to create a separate set of civilian offices in each of Upper Louisiana's administrative districts effectively confined the local commandant's duties to military affairs and thereby removed the primary objection to employing his services.

Upper Louisiana's new government was inaugurated without fanfare on 1 October 1804. Indiana's governor and judges met in Vincennes on that day and enacted fifteen statutes for the District of Louisiana on subjects ranging from local government, criminal punishment, and territorial courts to the regulation of boatmen and the control of slavery. There were no significant innovations in the territory's new law code. Most of the statutes were modeled after existing laws in other territories and states.[29] The slave code, for example, was taken largely from the Virginia and Kentucky codes. It was in many ways less protective of slave rights than the French and Spanish black codes. Not only did it prohibit blacks from testifying against whites in court and from administering medicine of any kind, but it also failed to include provisions concerning food and clothing for slaves, free time on Sundays and holidays, care of aged slaves, and safeguards designed to prevent excessive physical abuse.[30] Although the new 1804 slave code did not significantly alter slave life in Upper Louisiana, it dashed any hopes among blacks that slavery was on its way out.

A significant number of the new laws dealt with local government and administration. Governor Harrison heeded the president's advice and retained the existing administrative districts of St. Charles, St. Louis, Ste. Genevieve, Cape Girardeau, and New Madrid. He did eliminate the district of New Bourbon, which Carondelet had created largely as a favor for the French nobleman who founded that settlement. Each of the five districts or counties had a court of common pleas, a court of quarter sessions of peace, a probate court, and individual justices of the peace.[31]

The American administrative and judicial structure was considerably more complex than its Spanish predecessor, but Harrison's decision to include members of influential Creole families in his list of appointments facilitated the transition to the new system. By announcing his choices prior to his arrival in the territory, the incoming governor helped pave the way for a favorable reception.[32] When Harrison and his entourage arrived in St. Louis on 12 October 1804, accompanied by an escort of mounted regulars, the welcome could not have been more cordial. Auguste Chouteau hosted a lavish gala for the American officials and took an immediate liking to Harrison. The French merchant and his brother Pierre, who had just returned from Washington, D.C., bearing a commission as Upper Louisiana's first U.S. Indian agent, wasted little time in courting the affable American. Harrison discreetly declined Auguste's invitation to join him in a business partnership, but he did not hesitate to call upon the influential brothers for assistance during his stay in Upper Louisiana.[33] In fact, Pierre subsequently accompanied Harrison to Ste. Genevieve, where they encountered Charles Dehault Delassus. The outgoing Spanish lieutenant governor was still attempting to collect the final pieces of Spanish property for shipment to New Orleans.[34]

Harrison's popularity in Upper Louisiana had not suffered from his decision to waive the fees usually charged for trading licenses. By restricting the issuance of trade permits to residents of the territory, he earned further plaudits in the local trading community. As one anonymous observer noted at the time, "The inhabitants are much pleased with Govr. Harrison now here."[35] Despite his relative youthfulness—only thirty-one years old—the governor was already an old hand at conducting Indian negotiations. The unsettled conditions along the northern frontier required his attention. Residents of the scattered settlements above St. Louis lived in constant fear of a renewed attack from the Sac and Fox warriors whose recent assaults had visited death and destruction in their region. Tribal leaders had acknowledged that four of their members had been responsible for the carnage, but they thus far had ignored demands to turn over the culprits to U.S. authorities.

Harrison, under orders to negotiate a land deal with the Sac and Foxes, sent word to tribal officials via Pierre Chouteau that they should come to St. Louis with the alleged murderers for a conference. No mention about arranging a land cession appeared in the initial summons. In little more than a week, a delegation of lesser chieftains arrived in the capital with one of the accused warriors, whom they immediately surrendered to Maj. James Bruff. In accordance with the protocol that prevailed on such occasions, the visiting leaders were treated to several rounds of whiskey, even though official policy frowned upon giving liquor to Indians. When Harrison met with the leaders, he agreed to pardon the other accused murderers in return for their testimony against the lone Sac prisoner, who had been jailed in the military guardhouse at the old Spanish fort on the hill. Bruff, who adamantly insisted that all of the culprits should be tried, exhibited little patience with the arrangement, but the bargain was struck over his heated objections. Only Bruff's vigorous exception prevented Harrison from releasing the Sac prisoner on a legal technicality. Harrison did, however, promise the visiting tribal dignitaries that he would seek a pardon for the imprisoned Sac brave from their Great Father in Washington.[36]

With the matter of the Cuivre murders conveniently out of the way, Harrison turned to the business at hand: an agreement ceding Sac and Fox lands to the United States. Prior to their discussions, Harrison had arranged with the Chouteau brothers to distribute more than $2,000 worth of goods among the visiting Indian delegates. The presents, along with liberal samplings of whiskey, put the Indian negotiators in a receptive mood for considering the governor's proposals. Harrison adroitly held out promises of American protection against the Osages, a tribe most of his hearers considered to be protégés of the United States.[37]

The negotiations proceeded smoothly, and the Sac and Fox representatives assented to an agreement promising them U.S. protection, $1,000 in yearly annuities, and the establishment of government trading factories for their use, in return for their agreement to relinquish fifteen million acres of land in present-day Wisconsin, Illinois, and Missouri. Under the terms of the treaty the Indians could live and hunt on the ceded lands until the United States government disposed of them. The agreement also called for a cessation of all hostilities between the Sacs and Foxes and the Osages. At the insistence of the Chouteaus, who helped with the deliberations, the treaty included a proviso stipulating that the cessions would not invalidate Spanish land grants in the region.[38]

Although members of the Indian delegation who negotiated the treaty had been authorized to make payments as compensation for the Cuivre River murders, they had not been empowered to grant the vast concessions embodied in the final agreement they signed. Once they learned of the terms embodied in the 1804 treaty, Sac and Fox leaders vigorously protested what they considered to have been a bad bargain, and the resulting ill will poisoned U.S. relations with the two tribes for nearly thirty years. Harrison's attempts to resolve the Indian problem also provoked a serious rift between civil and military authorities in Upper Louisiana. The obstreperous Major Bruff continued to express his unhappiness over the leniency shown by Harrison in dealing with the Indians. His rigid views frequently put him at odds with other officials in St. Louis and contributed to a seemingly unending chain of local jurisdictional disputes. Bruff especially objected to Harrison's claim to have supreme control over the military in Louisiana, and on this issue Secretary of War Dearborn agreed with Bruff that the governor had overextended his authority.[39]

Louisiana's new government had barely taken effect when the second session of the Eighth Congress convened in the fall of 1804, but word of the widespread territorial dissatisfaction with the provisions of the Louisiana measures had already reached Washington. Jefferson did not mention the mounting criticism in the annual message he submitted to Congress in November, but he did include a report about Louisiana's lead mines in which Moses Austin recommended that Congress should institute an immediate inquiry into the occupation and titles of all lead mines in the territory. Austin's report created a considerable stir according to Simeon Baldwin of Connecticut, who caustically observed that "the attention of the Democrats gazing at the wonders of Louisiana is turned from the splendour of the mountain of salt to streams of Lead pouring from Austin's mines."[40]

Despite the president's failure to call for any changes in Upper Louisiana's government, members of Congress found it impossible to ignore the barrage of strongly worded protests regarding the controversial measures they had enacted during the preceding session. Eligius Fromentin had presented the petition drafted by the inhabitants of the District of Louisiana in St. Louis the preceding September to Jefferson's son-in-law, Virginia congressman John W. Eppes. The St. Louis convention had designated both Fromentin and Auguste Chouteau to deliver the petition and to represent the territory in the national capital, but a case of the gout forced Chouteau to return to St. Louis after traveling only a short distance.[41]

The efforts by Upper Louisianans to secure changes in the provisions governing their territory received an added boost from Governor Harrison's endorsement of their actions. In a letter written to accompany the St. Louis petition, Harrison stressed their strong attachment to the United States, and he attributed the harsh language contained in their document to an understandable resentment produced by the insulting misrepresentations that had been made about them. Harrison informed Auguste Chouteau of his exertions in their behalf, relating that he had sought to discredit the erroneous notion that the French were disdainful toward the American government.[42]

Members of Congress listened courteously to Fromentin, but they proceeded cautiously after receiving letters from the territory disparaging the recent proceedings in St. Louis. Rufus Easton's letter to the president charging that the entire affair was nothing more than a carefully disguised ploy by a small group of persons seeking confirmation of their specious land titles proved especially damaging.[43] Many of the legislators also had been put off by the allegations in the petition charging that the congressional law had violated the provisions of the Treaty of Cession. They suggested that the Louisianans would have made a much stronger case for their requests had they based their petition upon an appeal to the rights guaranteed by the general principles underlying the American system of government, rather than on the provisions of the treaty with France.[44]

Despite those misgivings, Congress eventually did approve two important new pieces of legislation for Upper Louisiana.

The federal legislature responded favorably to the District of Louisiana's request for a separate government, and the original Senate bill granted them an elected territorial assembly. Lingering doubts concerning their readiness for republican government caused members of the upper chamber to delete that provision in favor of the pattern outlined in the Northwest Ordinance for the first grade of territorial government. It was virtually identical to the one in the Indiana Territory. The new statute, signed into law on 3 March 1805, also changed the name from the District of Louisiana to the Territory of Louisiana.[45]

While willing to grant Upper Louisiana's inhabitants a separate territorial government, most members of Congress remained committed to checking speculation and fraud in land titles. An act for ascertaining and adjusting land titles, approved on 2 March 1805, sought to establish regular procedures for the confirmation of land claims in Louisiana. Although it repealed the unpopular law of 26 March 1804, the new law retained extremely rigid guidelines for approving titles and created a board of land commissioners authorized to validate land titles in Upper Louisiana. The presidentially appointed board, consisting of a recorder of land titles and two additional commissioners, was empowered to consider and rule upon grants presented for confirmation, in accordance with the provisions spelled out in this act and subject to the approval of Congress.[46]

In outlining the conditions for confirmation, Congress sought to ensure the approval of all legitimate claims made by bona fide settlers on small tracts of land. The act, however, did not provide for the wholesale confirmation of all land grants sought by local residents. Consequently, these measures failed to eliminate discord in Upper Louisiana. The claimants of large tracts redoubled their efforts to secure approval for their grants, and under the leadership of the new governor, James Wilkinson, the territory entered a period of factionalism and bitterness seldom seen even in unstable frontier communities.

The attempts to extend republican government beyond the Mississippi had raised serious problems for Jefferson and his supporters. In the end they chose to employ the basic governmental framework outlined in the Northwest Ordinance of 1787, but they omitted its strictures against extending slavery. The decision to perpetuate slavery in the region made early Missouri a favorite choice among emigrants from the Old South and thereby gave a decidedly southern flavor to its emerging social and cultural patterns. Beyond that, these initial decisions affecting slavery in the trans-Mississippi territory raised broader national issues that future generations of Americans would have to resolve.

CHAPTER NINE
PETTIFOGGERS, RENEGADOES, AND IMPATIENT NATIVES

J
ames Wilkinson's journey to St. Louis in the early summer of 1805 to assume his duties as governor of the Louisiana Territory was a trying experience. While the incoming official struggled to cope with the unpleasant effects of summer heat and swarming mosquitoes, he found himself bombarded by feuding constituents seeking his support. During a brief stopover at Kaskaskia, Maj. Seth Hunt, the loquacious military commandant of Ste. Genevieve, filled Wilkinson's ear with tales of intriguing French Creoles eager to plunder the American public domain, and a short time later Pierre Chouteau boarded his boat to present the case for the other side.[1] Chouteau, the new U.S. Indian agent, had joined the governor's party below St. Louis on the pretext of conferring about urgent Indian business, but his main object was to make a favorable impression on the new American official before he heard from the anti-French faction in the territorial capital.[2] By the time the weary governor reached St. Louis on 1 July, it was obvious to him that personal animosities were raging almost everywhere in the frontier territory, exacerbated in his judgment by small cliques of "pettifoggers, renegadoes, and impatient natives."[3]

The volatile conditions that greeted Wilkinson had been building since the Louisiana Purchase, fueled by ill-defined U.S. policies and a steady stream of ambitious newcomers eager to capitalize on the American acquisition. The merchants, lawyers, and land speculators who entered the territory after 1804 were a different breed from the pioneer farmers who had crossed into Spanish Louisiana in the late eighteenth century. A commitment to republican principles and an eagerness to assume active roles in shaping the territory's political destinies distinguished the new American settlers from their apolitical backwoods antecedents who, in Wilkinson's words, "wore their political morality as loosely as they do their cloaths."[4] The rapidly changing territorial demographics threatened French power and influence and understandably alarmed the outnumbered Creoles, who were already disturbed by the American government's hesitancy to confirm their land titles. The stakes were high as the contesting factions maneuvered to win the new governor's confidence.

Wilkinson, an intriguer and opportunist who had served simultaneously as a Spanish secret agent and the commanding general of the U.S. army, was a curious choice to undertake the difficult task of bringing stability to the strife-torn territory. His quest for personal advancement frequently led him down strange and contradictory paths. The enigmatic Wilkinson was a Federalist-turned-Republican with influential friends: Vice-President Aaron Burr, Secretary of the Navy Robert Smith, and Senators Samuel Smith, Joseph Anderson, and James Jackson, to name a few.[5] In choosing to place the controversial general in the territory's top post, the president ignored the rumors of his alleged double-dealing already whispered in the halls of the Capitol. Jefferson justified Wilkinson's nomination on the grounds that his military background would equip him to handle the distinctive problems of the frontier outpost, whose location at the center of western operations affecting the Spaniards, English, and Indians was too important to be "placed in nerveless hands."[6] Jefferson may, of course, also have been mindful that the appointment would set well with Burr, who was slated to preside over the upcoming impeachment trial of Supreme Court justice Samuel Chase, a judicial arch-enemy targeted by the Republicans for removal. Importantly, Jefferson had no inkling that during the preceding year the duplicitous general had suggested that the Spaniards cut off and arrest Lewis and Clark.[7]

Wilkinson, disappointed in his earlier efforts to secure a territorial governorship, welcomed the new assignment and the $2,000 annual salary that went with it. The added stipend promised to augment his $225-a-month salary as brigadier general and help alleviate his chronic financial difficulties. Territorial officials frequently complained about the high cost of living on the frontier. For instance, John B. C. Lucas, one of Louisiana's new territorial superior court justices, estimated that his expenses in St. Louis were double what he had incurred in Pittsburgh.[8]

Other appointees besides Wilkinson also enjoyed Burr's backing. The vice-president's brother-in-law, Joseph Browne, had been given the post of territorial secretary, and the shadowy connections that linked these three men and their conspiratorial plans would in time further aggravate the territory's turbulent political situation.[9] Jefferson's nominees for the superior court proved more predictable, but no less inclined to controversy. Lucas, a native of France who had immigrated to the United States in 1784 carrying a letter of introduction from Benjamin Franklin, quickly ascended the political ladder and won a seat in Congress representing western Pennsylvania. Albert Gallatin, Lucas's close friend and his predecessor in the House of Representatives, had recommended him for the Louisiana post. Judge Lucas ironically proved to be no friend of Upper Louisiana's French-speaking Creoles. Possessing unquestioned intellect and charm, he was also prone to passionate outbursts and disposed to carry grudges. As a condition for accepting the territorial judgeship, Lucas demanded and won a concurrent appointment as a member of Upper Louisiana's board of land commissioners.[10]

Rufus Easton, a New York lawyer who had come west to make his fortune through land speculation, was no less well connected thanks to the support of Burr, New York senator DeWitt Clinton, and Postmaster General Gideon Granger. Governor Harrison had appointed Easton to be territorial attorney general, but the American newcomer relinquished that position in order to accept his seat on the territorial superior court and to serve as St. Louis's first postmaster.[11] Easton seemed destined to occupy an influential place in Upper Louisiana's government until his outspoken criticism of the French Creoles placed him at odds with Governor Wilkinson.

The third superior court judge, Return J. Meigs, Jr., brought valuable experience to his new duties. In addition to his brief stint as commandant in the St. Charles district, he had also served as a territorial judge in the Northwest Territory and as chief justice of the Ohio Supreme Court. Unlike Lucas and Easton, however, Meigs remained only briefly in Upper Louisiana.[12]

Local leaders in St. Louis spared no effort in welcoming General Wilkinson to his new post. On his first day in the city, he dined with many of the community's leading citizens at the Auguste Chouteau residence. The general's acceptance of Chouteau's invitation to dinner before conferring with local U.S. officials miffed Maj. James Bruff, the territory's ranking military officer, who felt he had been snubbed. Wilkinson's decision to delay meeting with Bruff until the conclusion of the festivities honoring his arrival was not an inadvertent slip. Governor Harrison had cautioned the incoming governor that any appearance of taking the unpopular Bruff into his confidence would frighten some St. Louis residents out of their senses.[13]

Major Bruff's battered ego appears to have been the primary casualty of Wilkinson's otherwise highly successful entry into Upper Louisiana. The new governor's French Creole hosts delivered a laudatory address extolling his virtues as a public servant of "known principles and worth." They clearly were not bothered about the legitimacy of his republican credentials. To the contrary, they took comfort in the appointment of a high-ranking military officer to head their government, and in private conversations they found the general's views to be entirely compatible with their own. Wilkinson warmed to their lavish praises and responded with comparable rhetorical flourish by calling upon his new constituents "to expel the gall of Party spirit" and embrace "an accord in sentiment, a concert in policy, and a cheerful support of the Government."[14] For the St. Louis Creole leaders, who capped off the new administration's inauguration with a gala Fourth of July celebration featuring a dinner and grand ball, it held out every promise of being a happy marriage.

The outward gaiety of the St. Louis festivities belied the undercurrents of partisan strife already threatening to tear apart the territory's social fabric. Ensuing events soon demonstrated that the disagreements Governor Wilkinson had already encountered were too intense to be stilled by calls for cooperation and unity. The widening controversy over the validity of unconfirmed Spanish land titles lay at the heart of a conflict that pitted the mostly French claimants of extensive land holdings against a growing number of American newcomers with doubts about the legitimacy of those claims. Competition for the support of the incoming territorial officers exacerbated budding personal rivalries and widened the breach between the opposing sides. Ignoring his own advice to avoid involvement in the factional squabbles, Wilkinson joined the fray on the side of the French. By tilting in their favor, he alienated himself from several new territorial officers and many recent American settlers. In the process, he also eliminated any chance for using his good offices to resolve the problems.

The task of reconciliation would have been formidable for even the most able of politicians, but Wilkinson displayed little evidence of skill or political sagacity in his handling of Louisiana's complex problems. His seeming determination to exercise complete control over the territory, strengthened no doubt by Jefferson's occasional references to the establishment of a military government; his attempts to develop a cadre of followers personally loyal to him; his efforts to remove any officials who disagreed with him; and his predisposition to favor one faction over the other—all had the effect of intensifying the local instability.

Not surprisingly, the mining district became the scene of the territory's most heated and violent disputes over land claims. Nearly everyone there went about armed with pistols and knives, which they did not hesitate to brandish in a menacing manner at the slightest provocation.[15] The situation was ripe for conflict. Under the Spanish regime, the mines had been viewed as common property, open to exploitation by anyone who wanted to dig. That changed when Moses Austin arrived. After securing a concession from the Spanish authorities, the American entrepreneur initiated a campaign to replace the old system with the modern concept of individual freeholds and exclusive rights. Austin viewed his actions to locate his 4,250-acre concession at Mine à Breton and to prevent unauthorized persons from mining on it as a reasonable attempt to protect what the Spaniards had promised. His stance, however, flew in the face of a deeply rooted tradition in the mining community and touched off angry protests among the small claimants he sought to displace. A language barrier, which prevented the feuding parties from communicating directly, added to the misunderstanding.[16]

The battle lines were clearly drawn by the time U.S. authorities took charge of the dissension-ridden mining district in 1804. In his continuing disputes over land claims and mining rights, Austin found a willing ally in Maj. Seth Hunt, the incoming American military commandant for the Ste. Genevieve district. Hunt had received orders to remove all unauthorized settlers from the public lands.[17]

Austin was not the only American with his sights fixed on the lucrative mines. The notorious speculator John Smith T, who added to his name the letter T, for his home state Tennessee, to distinguish himself from all other John Smiths, had come to the Louisiana Territory expecting to take advantage of the unsettled situation in the mining district. He purchased numerous Spanish land patents, including one ten-thousand-arpent floating concession, which he used for claiming a one-thousand-acre tract known as New Diggings that was located on public lands only two miles from Mine à Breton. Indeed, whenever a new mine was discovered in the territory, Smith T took advantage of his floating concession to stake a claim to that particular site. Smith T's attempts to claim portions of Austin's Mine à Breton tract and his campaign to secure Austin's removal as chief justice of the Ste. Genevieve court of common pleas sparked the beginning of a bitter personal feud that further inflamed tensions in the region.[18]

The well-born and well-educated Smith T was ambitious and energetic. He also had acquired a reputation for shady land dealings and a penchant for settling his disagreements by force of arms. The slender, slightly effeminate Smith T hardly looked the part of a dreaded gunslinger, but his appearance was deceiving. He had no qualms about using weapons from his well-stocked private arsenal to intimidate anyone who threatened to get in his way.[19] Despite his notoriety, Smith T had no difficulty enlisting support for his campaign against the equally audacious Austin. Israel Dodge and his son Henry eventually joined Smith T's ranks. The ambitious Dodges were among the earliest American settlers in the Ste. Genevieve district, and Israel, who raised the American flag in Ste. Genevieve at the time of the transfer to the United States, had been appointed sheriff in that district in 1804. His son succeeded him in that post the following year.[20] William H. Ashley, whose innovations revolutionized the Rocky Mountain fur trade during the 1820s, was another of Smith T's recruits. Not long after his arrival at the mines in 1802 as a penniless young entrepreneur seeking his fortune, Ashley formed a business partnership with Smith T and Robert Browne, the territorial secretary's son. Their mercantile establishment catered to the growing mining population located beyond the immediate environs of Mine à Breton, but, like so many frontier enterprises, it eventually failed. Meanwhile the Austin–Smith T feud continued to heat up as both of the protagonists marshaled private armies of supporters.[21]

Governor Wilkinson became personally embroiled in the situation in the

Ste. Genevieve district as a result of Major Hunt's attempts to halt unauthorized mining on the public domain. Acting under orders from the secretary of war, Hunt moved to prevent persons without bona fide claims from working the mines. His actions created an understandable furor among the miners, who contended that by custom the Spanish had permitted them to dig on the king's domains. Because of the intensity of their outburst, the commandant agreed to allow them to continue mining for twenty additional days in order to give him time to secure the reinforcements necessary to enforce his directive.[22]

No doubt with Austin's encouragement, Hunt had ordered Smith T to vacate the mines he was operating at Mine à Renault, located six miles north of Mine à Breton. According to the Ste. Genevieve commandant, Smith T had made an unlawful and unauthorized settlement on the basis of a floating and probably antedated claim. Smith T, in appealing to the governor to overrule Hunt's decision, stated that he had purchased the five-hundred-acre floating claim in question from Major Hunt himself and that Hunt had tried to block his attempts to locate the claim because of the interference of Austin, who had personal designs on the land. Wilkinson proved amenable to Smith T's plea and instructed Hunt to allow Smith T to remain and not to interfere further with his mining activities. Furthermore, the governor reprimanded Hunt for speculating in Spanish land claims. Shortly thereafter, Wilkinson summarily removed Austin from the Court of Common Pleas and appointed Smith T in his place.[23]

Wilkinson justified his decision to support Smith T by noting that Smith T was a man of character and property with two brothers in the army and a brother-in-law in Congress. He obviously recognized that Smith T's connections would make him a useful ally.[24] The French inhabitants of the district, who had never liked Austin, also interceded with the governor against Hunt. In the heated exchange that ensued between Wilkinson and Hunt, the Ste. Genevieve commandant accused the governor of reneging on the principles he had initially laid down regarding the exclusion of unauthorized persons from the public lands; Wilkinson responded by denouncing Hunt for speculating in land titles, for writing insulting letters to a superior, for publicly questioning Wilkinson's appointment as governor, and for general insubordination. Charging that the young officer had been "blinded by prejudice & transported by passion," the governor removed him as commandant and ordered that he be placed under arrest and brought before a tribunal for investigation.[25]

Both men overreacted, and in attempting to resolve this touchy situation between two strong-minded individuals, Secretary of War Henry Dearborn advised Wilkinson that although Hunt's conduct had disappointed Dearborn, he was unwilling to believe that the commandant was guilty of intentional wrongdoing. Dearborn did ask for Hunt's resignation, but he instructed the governor to provide a board of inquiry if Hunt should request it.[26] Hunt, who had already announced his intention to resign his post, decided against pursuing the matter in the territory, but he later traveled to Washington in an attempt to clear his name and to warn against Wilkinson's misconduct.

While the Hunt-Wilkinson controversy still raged, Aaron Burr, the former vice-president who was by this time generally discredited, arrived in St. Louis in September 1805 for talks with Governor Wilkinson. In the absence of any authoritative record of their conversations, one can only conjecture about what was said. It does seem likely that these two old friends, who had conferred at Fort Massac in the Illinois Territory for four days the preceding June, discussed the need for cultivating persons in the Louisiana Territory who could be counted upon for support in any future undertakings they might initiate. Burr's plans for creating an empire for himself in the Old Southwest appear to have been fluid and were rumored to involve a plot for separating certain western American states and territories or alternately one for launching an invasion of Mexico from St. Louis. Wilkinson was undeniably a major participant, but observers disagreed then, as historians still do, as to whether their grand scheme represented a serious threat to create an independent western state or whether it involved nothing more than the harmless musings of another band of would-be frontier filibusters.[27]

Insofar as the local situation was concerned, the Burr-Wilkinson intrigues further complicated Louisiana's already confused political climate. Rufus Easton attributed his growing estrangement from Wilkinson to the negative response he had given to Burr's overtures. Timothy Kibby, a major in the territorial militia, and Major Bruff also claimed they had suffered from the governor's anger after turning aside Burr's inquiries.[28]

By October 1805, two clear-cut factions began to emerge within Louisiana's muddled political environment. With the governor as the catalyst, the territory divided into pro-Wilkinson and anti-Wilkinson groups. The party supporting the governor embraced not only most of the territory's French inhabitants, who greatly feared the growing American influence in the province and looked to Wilkinson for assistance, but also a select group of Americans with sizable Spanish land concessions, who believed the governor would support their confirmation, and a motley collection of Burrites and miscellaneous adventurers personally attracted by James Wilkinson. Among the well-known Louisianans who could be counted upon to support the governor's cause—but not in all cases the intrigues of his ally

Burr—were Charles Gratiot, Auguste and Pierre Chouteau, Jacques Clamorgan, John Mullanphy, Bernard Pratte, Pierre Provenchere, Joseph Browne, John Smith T, William H. Ashley, Father James Maxwell, Israel and Henry Dodge, Louis Lorimier, and James Donaldson.

The opposing group, composed almost entirely of Americans who had arrived in the territory since the United States had taken control, brought together many persons who disliked Governor Wilkinson for one reason or another. A group of young and energetic American lawyers formed an important segment of this faction. These aspiring attorneys, whom Wilkinson insisted on calling "pettifoggers," sought advancement through land speculation as well as politics and played an important role in the introduction of American law and government in Louisiana.[29] They became a powerful force in territorial politics, and because they threatened Wilkinson's position and influence, they became favorite targets for his wrath. Rufus Easton, William C. Carr, and Edward Hempstead—three of the most important early members of this group—led much of the attack against the governor. They had confined their purchases to the smaller land parcels that were certain to be confirmed. By blocking confirmation of the larger Spanish tracts, they hoped to enhance their own prospects for profits in the land business. Joining them in the anti-Wilkinson party were numerous individuals who had clashed with the governor on different occasions, including James Bruff, Seth Hunt, Moses Austin, John B. C. Lucas, and Samuel Hammond.

Louisiana's political upheaval seriously jeopardized normal governmental operations within the territory. Strained relations between the governor and the judges of the superior court delayed the opening of the territorial legislature for several months while they debated whether the governor possessed an absolute veto. On 12 October 1805, Judges John B. C. Lucas and Rufus Easton urged Wilkinson to convene the territorial legislature to deal with pressing matters of public concern, but, while always avowing his readiness to cooperate with the judges for purposes of legislation, Wilkinson continually postponed the date on which the legislature was scheduled to meet.[30]

The dispute between the governor and the territorial judges spilled over into the October term of the general court. Angered by the governor's failure to meet with them to enact legislation, the judges declined on the opening day of the general court to recognize Wilkinson's appointment of James Donaldson as public prosecutor. They rejected Donaldson on the technicality that his commission designated him as district attorney, while the current law provided for an attorney general. Following their refusal to approve Donaldson under the authority of the governor's commission, the judges asked him to serve as a court-appointed prosecuting attorney so that essential judicial business could be completed, but Donaldson, a loyal Wilkinson supporter, refused on the grounds that acceptance of the judicial appointment would represent a formal renunciation of the governor's right to designate the nominee. The court then named William C. Carr to occupy the post temporarily.[31]

Unwilling to bow to the general court's decision, Governor Wilkinson sent Donaldson back to the courtroom on the following day with a commission naming him to the post of attorney general. The justices again declined to recognize Donaldson's commission, this time on the grounds that under the act of Congress the governor possessed only power to appoint district officials, and the attorney general was not a district official. They concluded that only a new law passed by the territorial legislature could authorize Wilkinson to name an attorney general for the territory. By their narrow and admittedly questionable construction of the law, the judges hoped to force the governor to come to terms with them.[32]

Infuriated by this open challenge to his authority, Wilkinson decided to alter his plan of attack in the struggle with the judicial officers and turned his attention to the selection of the grand jury for the October term of the general court. The governor instructed Sheriff Josiah McLanahan, who summoned the members of the grand jury, to call every judge and justice of the peace in the district of St. Louis for service on the jury about to be empaneled.[33] This ensured that the grand jury would be strongly pro-Wilkinson in its composition, inasmuch as the district officers whom the governor had designated for service on the jury panel were his appointees.

The indictments subsequently returned by the grand jury revealed its partisan character. Labeling the actions of the general court indecorous and insulting, the members of the jury criticized the court for restricting the jury's power to call witnesses and for forcing them to meet in unsatisfactory quarters. They also remonstrated against the judges for having failed to recognize Donaldson's appointment as attorney general. Moreover, the grand jury indicted Judge Easton on a charge of having obtained a deed for six hundred acres of land through fraudulent practices.[34] The jurors, predominantly French and for the most part holders of substantial Spanish land claims, had taken this opportunity to even the score with Easton, whose letter to Jefferson in January 1805 had seriously hampered the efforts of their agent, Eligius Fromentin, when he had gone to Washington to present a petition on their behalf.[35]

The few American members of the grand jury issued a strongly worded minority opinion denying that the evidence presented to them justified Easton's indictment. It was, they charged, "made more to gratify personal hatred and cruel Revenge."[36] They also rejected the allegation that members of the general court had treated the jurors improperly. Instead, the four dissenting members of the jury charged that the presentment had been drawn up in secrecy at a special night session to which only part of the jurors had been summoned. They insisted that this action had violated their rights as members of the grand jury.[37]

Elaborating on those allegations, William C. Carr reported that on the night before the grand jury returned its indictments, a large number of jurors, chiefly French, had been seen at the governor's residence until late at night. Although Wilkinson later denied holding any conversations with the members of the jury, there can be little doubt that the jury's actions reflected, at least indirectly, the governor's influence. A regular jury subsequently acquitted Easton of the charges contained in the indictment, but the proceedings had damaged his reputation in national circles. Even the judicial processes had been suborned by the territory's political squabbles.[38]

Following the adjournment of the general court, the major participants in the dispute directed their attention to Washington in a search for a possible cure for the territory's political ills. Since all officials of the Louisiana Territory who had taken office on 4 July 1805 had received recess appointments, their names had to be submitted to the Senate for confirmation if they were to remain in office; both sides hoped to prevent the confirmation of members of the opposing faction. As a result of the controversy that had developed around Rufus Easton, the president decided not to reappoint him, but otherwise he made no alterations in his original choices for the top Louisiana posts.

Upon receiving word that his judgeship had been terminated, Easton went to Washington armed with letters of endorsement intended to vindicate him. While in the federal city, Easton wrote directly to Jefferson, avowing the correctness of his conduct and demanding that the president reveal the nature of the charges that had caused him not to grant a reappointment. Jefferson issued a tart reply but did agree to meet with the disgruntled official. Their conference, however, failed to change the president's mind.[39]

With Easton's removal now unalterable, local residents sought to influence the outcome of the Senate's vote to confirm Wilkinson and John B. C. Lucas. Opponents of the governor described him as power hungry, as unable to distinguish between civil and military authority, and as the principal source of the territory's political woes. By emphasizing the unfortunate consequences of the combination of civil and military powers, the anti-Wilkinson forces hoped to benefit from the strong Republican aversion to the consolidation of the two offices. The general bristled at reports of his aloof bearing, his fondness for wearing a cocked hat and sword in public, and his wife's practice of parading about town in an aristocratic carriage. He was, he assured Secretary Dearborn, "as plain as any clod hopper" in his dress and deportment, and he claimed to be accessible to all kinds of people, without exception.[40]

To counter any adverse effects of such criticism, Wilkinson's supporters launched a well-orchestrated campaign designed to demonstrate his popularity in the territory. They wrote letters and bombarded Congress with petitions bearing the signatures of local citizens who wished to express their just indignation at the "injurious and scandalous reports . . . against the governor of this territory."[41] They portrayed him as a conscientious public official who stood as a bulwark against the social chaos threatening to engulf the territory. In a somewhat less organized fashion, the pro-Wilkinson group also attempted to register their unhappiness with Lucas's rigid stance on the land claims issues and to urge the senators to reject his appointment to the board of land commissioners.

The Senate confirmed the nominations of both Wilkinson and Lucas after lengthy discussion by very narrow margins. Although neither faction had been able to secure a total victory, the decision to retain Wilkinson in office represented a triumph for the pro-Wilkinson group.[42] Meanwhile, the continued squabbling among Upper Louisiana's inhabitants and the persistent questions surrounding the alleged western enterprises of Burr and Wilkinson kept the territory and its problems in the thoughts of the president and his key advisers.

CHAPTER TEN
THE TURMOIL CONTINUES

When word of Wilkinson's confirmation as governor reached St. Louis in March 1806, his friends and supporters fired cannons and rang the church bell to announce the good news. The merrymakers capped their spontaneous celebration by building a large bonfire and, to the accompaniment of a hastily organized band, dancing and drinking toasts to the governor's health long into the night.[1] The boisterous enthusiasm of his followers failed to quell the governor's growing uneasiness about his future in the Louisiana Territory. Almost as soon as the echoes of the noisy gathering had died away, rumors predicting Wilkinson's impending removal were again being whispered in the village streets.

While pleased with Judge Easton's ouster and Wilkinson's confirmation, the governor's supporters continued to press for their most cherished objective: the confirmation of all Spanish land titles. The board of commissioners created by Congress to review land claims in the Louisiana Territory had held its first session on 1 December 1805 in St. Louis. Meeting at a time when the territory's political strife had entered one of its most vitriolic phases, the commissioners found themselves caught up in the animosities engendered by the larger struggle.[2]

Under normal circumstances the tasks confronting the board would have been formidable. Even though nearly two years had elapsed since the formal establishment of American control in Upper Louisiana, U.S. authorities had been unable to determine to their satisfaction how Spanish officials had gauged the legitimacy of land titles. Moreover, many officials in Washington had grown even more hesitant to act as the result of the widely held belief that numerous antedated and forged claims threatened to defraud the United States of large quantities of land. When combined with the turbulent conditions in the territory, the obstacles blocking a satisfactory solution to the land-claims problem seemed insurmountable.

Like most other territorial officials, the first three members of the board of commissioners, James Lowry Donaldson, Clement Biddle Penrose, and John B. C. Lucas, were political appointees. Donaldson, an Irish-born lawyer, had been active in Maryland politics; Penrose was a member of the prominent Biddle family of Philadelphia and also Governor Wilkinson's nephew; and Lucas was a former member of Congress. When the influential and strong-willed commissioners began their deliberations, they failed to reach a consensus. Penrose and Donaldson, both of whom had close ties to the governor, joined forces to rule in favor of the claimants of sizable tracts.

Lucas, a territorial judge and a caustic critic of Governor Wilkinson, took vigorous exception to the decisions rendered by the Penrose-Donaldson majority. His determined opposition to the wholesale confirmation of Spanish land titles in Missouri further estranged him from the governor and earned him the universal contempt of Louisiana's larger land claimants. The rigid and doctrinaire Lucas scorned all pleas for leniency in the land-claims cases. Several factors helped shape his unyielding stance. An unhappy encounter with Pennsylvania land jobbers had made the irascible commissioner naturally suspicious of large-scale speculators, and his reading of the evidence convinced him that in Upper Louisiana the vast majority of the biggest claims were fraudulent.[3] Lucas, who had been careful in his own land purchases, was also savvy enough to realize that his substantial confirmed holdings in the vicinity of St. Louis would appreciate in value more rapidly if fewer of the suspect titles were validated.

The extent of fraud in Spanish land claims can never be fully determined. If all land claims that had failed to fulfill every requirement of the Spanish law to the letter had been judged fraudulent, then the number of valid claims would have been small. The crux of the problem was the extent of deviation to be allowed from the provisions of Spanish law. Congress wrestled with this question long after Missouri's territorial period, and even then complete agreement proved impossible.

Under the Spanish system, officials in Upper Louisiana routinely awarded land tracts to applicants, and they generally ignored the restrictions imposed on such grants by Spanish law. Low land values and the relative ease of acquiring concessions combined to make the question of titles a rather moot point before 1803. Unconcerned with the need to establish complete titles to their land, most settlers had given little thought to the problem. Many had never bothered to seek formal title to the lands they were occupying. But that changed in the wake of the American acquisition of Louisiana and the accompanying appreciation in land prices and increases in population. These sudden changes provoked a flurry of belated activity by bona fide settlers seeking to secure completed titles, but it also led to numerous attempts to secure additional lands to which the claimants had no legitimate right. Although Lucas's stand probably embodied too narrow an interpretation, the judge did have legitimate cause for opposing the indiscriminate confirmation of titles, especially in cases involving extremely large claims.[4]

William C. Carr, territorial land agent, joined Lucas in opposing the liberal interpretation favored by Penrose and Donaldson. Charged by the secretary of the treasury with investigating cases of suspected fraud and representing the United States in questions involving public lands, Carr frequently corroborated Judge Lucas's reports.

Both Lucas and Carr expressed their disapproval of Governor Wilkinson's repeated attempts to meddle in the land-claims controversy. In an obvious effort to enhance his own popularity, Wilkinson had advised territorial residents not to sell their claims in panic after promising to use his influence to secure confirmation of their grants. Wilkinson's decision to employ Antoine Soulard as the territorial surveyor general further aggravated the situation. Soulard had served in that capacity under the last two Spanish governors and was closely linked with members of the St. Louis land junto.[5] In February 1806, Congress took steps to supplant Soulard's authority by placing the Territory of Louisiana under the U.S. surveyor general's jurisdiction. Efforts by Governors Harrison and Wilkinson to retain Soulard and his assistants in their posts failed, and Surveyor General Jared Mansfield recommended the appointment of Silas Bent as Upper Louisiana's principal deputy surveyor. Following his arrival in the territory in the fall of 1806, Bent, whose sons Charles, William, George, and Robert subsequently became renowned nineteenth-century western fur traders and merchants, reported finding numerous erasures, inaccuracies, and apparent alterations in Soulard's surveys. Even after his ouster, Soulard frequently appeared before the board of commissioners to defend his surveys and to support the confirmation of individual claims.[6]

Concerned about the governor's constant interference in the land-claims cases, Secretary Gallatin wrote to Jefferson suggesting that "General Wilkinson be advised that he has nothing to do with the land business."[7] Shortly thereafter, Gallatin again warned the president that Wilkinson should be watched closely, pointing out that he had allied himself with every major Spanish land claimant in Louisiana, including Gratiot, the Chouteaus, and Soulard.[8]

With a bitter struggle currently raging within Congress and among members of the Republican party over legislative attempts to settle the long-disputed Yazoo land claims that had resulted from the Georgia legislature's corrupt dealings in the 1790s, the president and his advisers were particularly sensitive to the potential for controversy inherent in cases of alleged land fraud. Unfavorable reports on the activities of Upper Louisiana's board of commissioners increased their apprehension. Further evidence of the board's inclination to favor wholesale confirmations came when the Penrose-Donaldson majority approved the appointments of Charles

Gratiot as clerk and Philipe Marie Leduc as translator. Both Gratiot and Leduc held numerous unconfirmed Spanish titles and were intimately associated with other major land claimants. When Attorney General John Breckinridge concurred with Carr's allegations that the extreme liberality of the commissioners' decisions had injured the interests of the American government, Secretary Gallatin urged Jefferson to remove the offending officials. The president submitted the whole matter to members of his cabinet for their consideration, and, although they unanimously agreed that the decisions handed down by the commissioners had been illegal, only Gallatin and Dearborn felt that removal would be justified. Relying upon the opinions of Madison and Breckinridge, Jefferson decided that despite the commissioners' incorrect interpretation of the land laws, their errors had not emanated from improper motives.[9]

According to the president's wishes, Secretary Gallatin prepared a set of instructions for the land commissioners, informing them of the attorney general's opinion so that they could revise their decisions to conform with his rulings. Gallatin also admonished the commissioners to adhere strictly to the letter of the law in the future and to leave to Congress any attempts to liberalize confirmation policies.[10]

The commissioners modified their positions slightly as a result of Gallatin's instructions, but relations between Lucas and the other members failed to improve. Donaldson and Penrose often met to transact official business at irregular times and places without informing either Lucas or Carr of their intentions. In response to the continued complaints of improprieties, Gallatin sent a new and more detailed set of instructions to guide the commission.[11]

Unhappy with the rigid restrictions placed upon the board's right to confirm titles, Donaldson decided to go to Washington to seek a new and more favorable law for the land claimants. After his departure from the territory sometime in the fall of 1806, the business of the board of commissioners came to a virtual standstill. Since many of the board's original decisions had still not been revised in accordance with the attorney general's ruling, Commissioner Lucas angrily denounced Donaldson for having returned pertinent original documents to their owners prior to his departure from the territory. Without this evidence, Lucas maintained that the commissioners would not be able to reconsider the cases in question. He refused, therefore, to join Penrose in submitting to the secretary of the treasury a report of the decisions handed down by the board of commissioners until all necessary changes had been made. Even though he offered to meet with the remaining commissioner to record new claims, Lucas declined to render any additional decisions in specific cases.[12]

When Penrose and Donaldson demonstrated continued reluctance to adhere strictly to instructions from Washington, the president revised his evaluation of their conduct. His disgust with the two commissioners was obvious when he wrote to Gallatin, "I have never seen such a perversion of duty as by Donaldson & Penrose."[13] Jefferson removed Donaldson from his position as recorder and named Frederick Bates of the Michigan Territory as his replacement, and Secretary Gallatin directed the commissioners to suspend any further decisions on cases until Congress had completed action on a new act it was considering for adjusting Louisiana land claims.[14]

Thus, the status of the Spanish land claims remained substantially unchanged when Wilkinson left the territory in the summer of 1806. No final decisions had been handed down by the board; numerous petitions had been circulated by opposing politicians frantically maneuvering to take advantage of the situation; tempers had flared, and the emotional fervor had grown so intense that on one occasion an enraged Rufus Easton had burst into the board's proceedings and publicly caned Donaldson in retaliation for what he believed to be the commissioner's slanderous comments.[15] In the midst of such turmoil, the prospects for a speedy resolution of the land-claims issue in Louisiana were not promising.

Although the land-claims business and the local political feuding consumed most of Wilkinson's attention during his final days in office, that had not always been the case. At the outset of his administration, the governor had devoted considerable time and energy to the military and defensive matters that Jefferson had assumed would be his principal concerns. When he first arrived in St. Louis to take up his duties, Wilkinson found 150 Sac and Fox Indians waiting to confer with him about the fate of the Sac warrior whom they had turned over to Governor Harrison the previous year. Harrison had ordered the prisoner accused in the Cuivre River murders to be confined in the guardhouse at the local garrison after promising to seek a presidential reprieve for him. Jefferson approved Harrison's request for clemency and pardoned the Indian in February, but word of the president's action had still not reached the territory three months later when the hapless warrior was shot and killed while attempting to escape. The entire affair had been badly handled, and it fell to the incoming governor to make amends with members of the victim's tribe. With great ceremony Wilkinson belatedly produced the presidential pardon, which he delivered to the dead man's relatives along with a lecture suggesting that the shooting had been the Great Spirit's way of bringing the murderer to justice for spilling the blood of his white neighbors.[16]

Wilkinson proclaimed the Sacs satisfied with his explanation, but it was probably the gifts and whiskey that momentarily persuaded them to conceal their anger over the incident. The governor did acknowledge that the visiting tribal leaders had reiterated their unhappiness with the terms of the treaty their representatives had negotiated with Governor Harrison. That experience had taught the Sacs a costly lesson: the Americans wanted one thing above all else—their lands. Already aware of the widespread disaffection caused by that agreement, federal officials hoped to divert the Indians' attention and increase their dependence on the U.S. government by opening a government-sponsored trading factory and running them into debt.[17]

Secretary Dearborn instructed Wilkinson to give immediate attention to the selection of a site for the proposed government trading post that would be convenient to Indians on both the Missouri and Mississippi rivers. After conducting an extensive search, Wilkinson initially selected a tract near Florissant belonging to a Widow James. When she had second thoughts about selling her farm, he chose an alternate location on the Missouri River four miles above the Mississippi junction at the mouth of Cold Water Creek. Wilkinson had been forced to purchase land from a private owner because, as he noted, virtually all of the land on both sides of the Missouri, extending from the Mississippi to several miles above St. Charles, had been claimed by individuals.

The site was also designated as the location for a new U.S. military installation to replace the dilapidated Spanish fort in St. Louis that currently housed the army garrison. Construction on the combined facility got underway in August, and it was ready for occupancy in the fall. Cantonment Belle Fontaine, as it was called, served the region as military headquarters for the next two decades, but the adjacent trading factory was too remote from the Indians it was intended to serve to get much use. Officials eventually closed the trading house in 1808 and transferred the goods to new factories at Fort Osage, on the Missouri River a few miles east of present-day Kansas City, and Fort Madison, on the upper Mississippi near the mouth of the Des Moines River.[18]

With Lewis and Clark on the way to the Pacific in 1805, Wilkinson was keenly aware of the president's interest in exploring the nation's new western expanses. No doubt that was on his mind when he dispatched two military expeditions from St. Louis following his arrival that summer. He sent Lt. Zebulon M. Pike and his "damned rascals" to explore the upper reaches of the Mississippi. Pike's instructions called for him to collect geographical information, to purchase sites from the Indians for potential military forts, to invite selected chiefs to visit St. Louis, and to show the American flag in the region. At the same time Wilkinson sent Pierre Chouteau and a military party under the command of Lt. George Peter on a similar mission up the Osage River to confer with Osage leaders in an effort to heal the split between the Missouri and Arkansas factions. Jefferson wanted to reunite the numerous tribe in a single location in order to make room for eastern Indians.[19]

Wilkinson looked upon these expeditions as a first step in implementing broader U.S. policy objectives for the trans-Mississippi West. One paramount American goal was the reduction of Spanish and British influence among the western tribes. Under orders from Jefferson to keep Canadian-based British traders out of the territory west of the Mississippi, the governor issued stringent new regulations governing the Indian trade in the Missouri valley. In addition to an order restricting trading licenses to American citizens, he also proposed to end the use of firearms in the Indian trade. Fierce protests from local traders, led by the Chouteaus and Manuel Lisa, persuaded him that a prohibition of firearms in the fur exchange would seriously injure St. Louis–based trading operations without depriving unfriendly tribes of weapons, so he dropped the unpopular regulation.[20]

Despite Wilkinson's efforts, British influence remained largely undiminished. Like most frontier dwellers, General Wilkinson believed that the maintenance of strong military posts in the interior was the only effective means of establishing American hegemony in the region, but the economy-minded Jefferson administration repeatedly vetoed such plans, insisting that trade was the key to control.[21] The rejection of Wilkinson's proposal for building fortifications in the upper Missouri and Mississippi watersheds came too late to cancel an expedition under the command of the governor's son, Lt. James Biddle Wilkinson, that was already on its way up the Missouri. The governor had assigned his son to escort an ailing Oto chief to his village and then establish a U.S. post at the mouth of the Platte River. A hostile Kansa Indian party prevented them from reaching their destination and forced them to return to Cantonment Belle Fontaine. It was just as well, for upon hearing of the undertaking, Secretary Dearborn immediately recalled the unauthorized mission and severely reprimanded Wilkinson for having dispatched it without prior approval. Maj. Seth Hunt's allegations that the venture was a private trading expedition outfitted by Wilkinson and his friends at government expense probably triggered Dearborn's angry rebuke. Though unproven, Hunt's charges had a ring of truth to them.[22]

Lingering hostilities between the Osages and a confederation of eastern Indians led by the Sacs and Foxes continued to be a serious problem for territorial officials. Governors Harrison and Wilkinson summoned representatives of the contesting tribes to meet in St. Louis to discuss the situation in 1805. The first delegations began arriving in September, but Wilkinson found little cause for optimism. At the same time that the Sacs sent a tribal contingent to the territorial capital to negotiate, they also dispatched a war party to renew their attack on the Osages. Wilkinson blamed the continuing Sac depredations on dissatisfaction with the 1804 treaty and the influence of British traders.[23]

Representatives from the Delawares, Miamis, Potowatomis, Kickapoos, Kaskaskias, Des Moines River Sioux, Ioways, Sacs, Foxes, and Osages heeded the government's call and gathered in St. Louis. Bowing to intense pressure from U.S. officials, the tribal representatives agreed to sign a treaty pledging an end to all hostilities, but as soon as they left town, many of them cast aside the American-dictated agreement and resumed their warfare. Both Harrison and Wilkinson remained apprehensive about the safety of their respective territories and urged the federal government to send a military force to Prairie du Chien to subdue the belligerent Indians.[24]

During the ensuing winter and spring, the Sacs continued their raids against the Osages, and when they failed to locate their Indian adversaries, they occasionally turned against isolated white settlers. Sac raiding parties killed two white hunters along the Missouri, drove off cattle and destroyed Nathan Boone's saltworks in central Missouri, and murdered another salt-maker north of St. Louis. In December 1805 Wilkinson again ordered representatives of the marauding tribe to report to St. Louis, where he delivered the strongest possible warning, stating that, unless the Sacs ceased their depredations and returned all Osage prisoners, the U.S. government would withhold all trade and supplies from the tribe. But this time the well-worn threats were to no avail, and the Indian dissatisfaction grew worse by the day.[25]

Although the president had been forced to retreat from his earlier plans for closing Upper Louisiana to white settlement altogether, he continued to press proposals for removing settlers from the territory's more sparsely inhabited regions. He instructed Governor Wilkinson to investigate the possibility of transferring the residents of the scattered settlements below Cape Girardeau to more heavily settled portions of the United States.[26] By making the existing settlements more compact, Jefferson hoped to facilitate the administration of justice, strengthen western outposts against possible attacks, and create more space for displaced eastern tribes.

Even the usually aggressive Wilkinson recognized the need for caution in initiating any such program. He recommended that relocation could best be accomplished by discouraging further settlement in the affected area and by offering inducements to those already residing there to move elsewhere. After conversations with the governor, Edward F. Bond, a resident of the Cape Girardeau district, expressed enough interest in the scheme to open discussions with settlers there and in the neighboring New Madrid district.

Bond's letters to Wilkinson and Jefferson suggested that the plan could be carried out if the price was right, but he acknowledged that some old families were much opposed to it on any terms.[27]

While continuing to advise his superiors that the objective appeared attainable, providing that the government adopted the necessary measures and that all territorial officers cooperated, Wilkinson was forced to concede that securing the assistance of other territorial officials would not be easy.[28] Moses Austin spoke for most local residents when he warned high-ranking officials that unless they abandoned their quixotic schemes for depopulating the western bank, they would have "cause to regret the moment they became possessed of Louisiana."[29] Jefferson quickly discovered what his Spanish predecessors could have told him: the footloose and fiercely independent American frontier settler could not be confined to a few well-protected enclaves.

The lack of support for consolidating white settlement forced the president to move more slowly in implementing his closely related project for making the Ozarks a dumping ground for eastern Indians. In addition to resistance from nearby white settlers, the powerful Osages, who claimed most of the region, were in no mood to tolerate additional intrusions on their lands. For the moment all such plans had to be quietly shelved.

The anti-Indian prejudice and the fear of Indian violence in the white community that helped quell Jefferson's plans for relocating eastern tribes in Louisiana also hampered the tasks of officials charged with maintaining harmonious relations between the two peoples. White violence against Indians was as serious a problem as Indian violence against whites, but in the white community the standard of justice was clearly different when Indians were involved. Samuel Hammond, Jr., unquestionably overreacted when he first shot and then stabbed to death a drunken Kickapoo warrior brandishing a tomahawk in the St. Louis streets, but Attorney General James Donaldson's attempt to prosecute him drew cries of protest from outraged local inhabitants. A hastily summoned coroner's jury quickly exonerated Hammond of all charges. Although Donaldson's actions against Hammond were undoubtedly justified, the entire affair was more a matter of politics than of a concern for Indian rights. As a staunch Wilkinson partisan, Donaldson had seen an opportunity to embarrass the accused's uncle, Col. Samuel Hammond, Sr., who recently had fallen out with the governor over Hammond's refusal to sign a petition supporting Wilkinson's confirmation as governor. The handling of the Kickapoo incident intensified the enmity between them and brought the influential Hammond, who initially had been a Wilkinson defender, to the forefront of the anti-Wilkinson ranks.[30]

Slowly and painfully, the Jefferson administration had to revise its esti-mate of the obviously deteriorating situation in the Louisiana Territory. The unrelenting political quandary made it necessary to reconsider Governor Wilkinson's role, particularly in view of reports the president had begun to receive early in 1806 suggesting the possible existence of a western conspir-acy under the leadership of Wilkinson and Aaron Burr. Keenly aware of his tenuous position and obviously disturbed by rumors predicting the immi-nence of his removal, the governor wrote to the president and to Senator Samuel Smith pleading his cause.[31]

As late as 4 May 1806, Jefferson, anxious not to alienate the general's influential friends, assured Senator Smith that no immediate change was contemplated in Wilkinson's status, but it seems obvious that the decision to remove him as governor already had been made. Only two days later, on 6 May, Secretary Dearborn ordered General Wilkinson to take command of military operations in the Territory of Orleans as a consequence of threat-ened hostilities with Spain.[32]

Worsening relations between Spain and the United States caused by a dispute over the still-unresolved Louisiana-Texas boundary provided Jeffer-son with the perfect opportunity to extricate himself from a very difficult political predicament. Under the pretext that military necessity dictated Wilkinson's departure from the territory, the president ousted him from Upper Louisiana without formally removing him as territorial governor. At least partial credit for this solution to the president's dilemma must be given to Congressman Matthew Lyon of Kentucky, who had suggested such a plan to Jefferson only a short time earlier.[33]

Although Wilkinson's departure did not necessarily mean that his tenure as governor had ended, most Louisianans interpreted it that way. Upon receiving his order to go to New Orleans, the governor protested to the secretary of war that rumors emanating from Washington had anticipated his instructions far in advance of their actual public disclosure. He clearly feared that the widely accepted view that his reassignment had been designed to get rid of him was in fact true. Although he acknowledged his orders on 16 June, Wilkinson dallied in the territory for two more months, possibly waiting to see what materialized in the rapidly developing Burr intrigue. In fairness to Wilkinson, his wife's serious illness may also have contributed to the delay.[34]

In July, Wilkinson ordered Lieutenant Pike, who had returned to St. Louis in April with maps and reports from his journey up the Mississippi, on a second and ultimately more important expedition to the west. Pike was ordered to escort some Osage captives recently released by the Pota-watomis to their villages, to assist the Kansa Indians in negotiations with the Pawnees, to make overtures to the warlike High Plains Comanches, and to explore the Arkansas and Red rivers. Wilkinson's motives in dispatching Pike on this mission continue to be debated, but it is clear that the young explorer was an innocent pawn who knew nothing of Wilkinson's intrigues with Aaron Burr. Within a year's time, Pike discovered the peak that bears his name, became lost three times while exploring and mapping in the Rockies, and fell into the hands of Spanish officials, who charged him with spying. After briefly detaining the American officer in Chihuahua, the Spaniards allowed him to return to the United States in 1807. There he found himself suspected of complicity in the Burr conspiracy, which had broken into the open during his absence.[35]

When Wilkinson finally left St. Louis on 16 August 1806, the Burrite plot was reaching a critical juncture, and the Louisiana Territory loomed large in the former vice-president's secret plans. In Wilkinson's absence, Joseph Browne, Burr's brother-in-law and the territorial secretary, became Louisiana's acting governor. Taking advantage of that situation, Burr sent his chief of staff, Col. Julien de Pestre, to St. Louis in October to recruit support for his mysterious western enterprise, but the French emigre received a cool reception. Aside from Robert Westcott (who was Browne's son-in-law), Maj. James Richardson, and Dr. Andrew Steele, Colonel de Pestre found few takers in St. Louis for the proclamations and commissions he was carrying. David Delaunay, the adjutant general of the territorial militia, Maj. Pierre Provenchere, and Col. Auguste Chouteau all rejected the overtures of Burr's agent. Chouteau went so far as to attempt to throw the commission offered him into a fire. Colonel de Pestre made a hasty retreat from St. Louis to Kentucky, but Rufus Easton, Major Bruff, and other opponents wasted little time in forwarding reports of his alleged activities to officials in Washington, D.C.[36]

The end of the year saw a marked upswing in Burrite activity in the Louisiana Territory. While his recruiters sought to attract volunteers in the vicinity of New Madrid, Burr and his party of one hundred or so men—far fewer than the twelve hundred they had counted on—reached that settlement on 1 January 1807 after descending the Ohio. They remained in New Madrid only briefly before continuing down the Mississippi. When word reached St. Louis that Burr was approaching the territory, Major Westcott and Dr. Steele set out to find him, and while en route to New Madrid, they were joined in Ste. Genevieve by John Smith T and Henry Dodge. Their party failed to link up with Burr, possibly because they had learned that a presidential proclamation had been issued on 27 November authorizing Burr's arrest. Clearly Burr's plans were unraveling. Even Wilkinson had by then turned on Burr, whom he now charged with plotting to invade Mexico.

Everywhere the reports of the alleged conspiracy generated excitement and interest. When Smith T and Dodge returned to Ste. Genevieve, they were greeted with warrants issued by territorial judge Otho Shrader charging them with treason. Dodge submitted to arrest, posted bail, and then proceeded to use his fists to settle the score with several of the grand jurors who had indicted him. Smith T characteristically drew his pistol and defied the authorities to arrest him. They chose not to, and the allegations were not pursued further.[37]

Major Westcott's arrest in St. Louis on similar charges created renewed concern in that city. A resolution drafted by a local citizens group called upon Browne as acting governor to place the territorial militia on alert as a precaution against the rumored western conspiracy. Browne's stock among the local residents was slipping rapidly in spite of his assurances that he had not received "a particle of Intelligence of any kind" suggesting a threat from treason or conspiracy. When Wilkinson concluded shortly before his departure from St. Louis that his reassignment was apt to be permanent, he had openly touted Browne as his permanent replacement. At Wilkinson's urging, Auguste Chouteau had spearheaded a campaign promoting Browne's candidacy. The anti-Wilkinson forces had countered with a proposal urging that the post be given to either Return J. Meigs, Jr., or Samuel Hammond. By February, however, Chouteau's growing doubt about Browne's intentions had caused him to sign the petition calling upon Browne to take steps to combat the threatened conspiracy. Officials in Washington had long since determined that Browne should be removed from his Louisiana post, but the rapidly unfolding developments in the conspiracy temporarily side-tracked their efforts to find a suitable successor.[38]

The president finally acted on 4 February, when he commissioned Frederick Bates to replace Browne as secretary and acting governor of Louisiana. He also named Bates to succeed James Donaldson, another former Wilkinson associate, as Louisiana's recorder of land titles and as a member of the board of land commissioners. Bates's varied experience as a territorial administrator made him a good choice for his new posts in the strife-torn territory. A Virginian by birth, Bates had gone to the frontier outpost of Detroit in 1797 as an appointee in the quartermaster's department of the U.S. army. In 1800, he went into business for himself in Detroit, but his mercantile venture collapsed after a great fire swept through that village in 1805 and destroyed virtually everything he owned. Fortunately for him, Bates had been appointed as a superior court judge for the newly created Territory of Michigan shortly before the disaster. Prior to that he had held numerous local offices, including positions as deputy postmaster, receiver of public monies, and commissioner of land titles.[39]

The selection of a replacement for Governor Wilkinson was more diffi-cult. President Jefferson, urged by some members of Congress that further delays might raise suspicions of planning to retain the general in office, named Meriwether Lewis to fill the territory's top post on 3 March 1807. Because of the intense factionalism in Louisiana, Jefferson had decided to seek Wilkinson's successor outside the territory. James Monroe had been the president's first choice, but when he declined the appointment, the co-leader of the recently completed expedition to the Pacific seemed a natural choice to administer the western territory. Jefferson also appointed Lewis's partner in discovery, William Clark, as U.S. Indian agent for all tribes in the territory except the Osages and as brigadier general of the territorial militia.[40]

Lewis and Clark were bona fide national heroes following the successful completion of their seven-thousand-mile, twenty-eight-month journey. Their accomplishments had far exceeded Jefferson's expectations. The Captains of Discovery had returned to a rousing reception in St. Louis on 23 September 1806. The celebrations had continued during their triumphal return trip to the national capital. A grateful president and other officials saluted their scientific achievements and entertained their traveling companion, the Mandan chief Shahaka. Lewis and Clark had been popular in St. Louis, and most residents of the territory hailed the decision to assign them to the vacant governmental posts. For Clark, the association with Missouri would be a long and rewarding one, but for Lewis it would be only a brief interlude that would end in tragedy.[41]

For the moment, however, the time seemed right for a new start in Upper Louisiana. The Burr controversy had moved from the territory to a Rich-mond courtroom. Wilkinson was gone, and his duplicity would soon be exposed, but the resilient soldier of fortune still had other battles to wage. In the end, he died in Mexico on one final quest, far removed from the sites of his controversies in Missouri. The task of picking up the pieces and restor-ing some semblance of order in the politically divided Louisiana Territory now awaited his highly acclaimed successors.

CHAPTER ELEVEN
TERRITORY
IN TRANSITION

G overnor Wilkinson's departure in the summer of 1806 forced his allies to take stock of their situation and reassess their political associations. The conservative Creole leaders had no desire to become embroiled in conspiratorial campaigns against the United States or any other government, so despite their attachment to the former governor, they wasted little time in distancing themselves from known Burr collaborators. Their primary political objective continued to be the confirmation of Spanish land titles, but increasingly the more influential members of the French minority realized that a perpetuation of the territory's Franco-American divisions would be suicidal for them. Consequently, the pragmatic Creoles quietly moved to strengthen their ties within the growing American community.

They overcame their aversion to American pettifoggery and formed new and mutually advantageous partnerships with several energetic young attorneys, including some who had been in the forefront of the anti-Wilkinson movement. The French land claimants counted upon their new legal advisers to guide them through the unfamiliar terrain of American law. Edward Hempstead was one of the first American lawyers to appreciate the profitability of handling land adjudication cases for the Creole leaders. A New Englander by birth, Hempstead had walked from Vincennes to St. Louis in 1804, carrying his belongings in a bundle slung over his back. Following his arrival in Upper Louisiana, he took up residence in St. Charles, where he devoted much of his time to studying French. In 1805, he moved to St. Louis and began practicing law. His courtroom oratory was so successful that other lawyers attempted to imitate his sharp, peremptory speaking style, and Hempstead emerged as a rising star in the fledgling trans-Mississippi legal community.[1]

Alexander McNair, a future governor of Missouri, was another American attorney who took up the cause of the Creole land claimants. There was no love lost between McNair, a popular militia officer, and Judge John B. C. Lucas, the outspoken foe of the wholesale confirmation of the Spanish land titles. The paths of McNair and Lucas had previously crossed in Pennsylvania, where they had been on opposite sides in a speculative land venture. Other up-and-coming Americans, including Thomas Hart Benton, William

Clark, and John Scott, joined Hempstead and McNair and initially cast their lots with Upper Louisiana's Creole leaders.[2]

The emerging connections linking prominent members of the French and American communities in business and politics carried over into the salon and the ballroom, where budding romances produced a harvest of cross-cultural marriages. Hempstead's marriage to Clarissa Dubreuil helped cement his relationship with the St. Louis Creoles. His sister Susan married Charles Gratiot's son Henry; McNair wed Antoine Reihle's daughter Marguerite; Auguste Chouteau's daughter Emilie married Capt. Thomas F. Smith of the U.S. army; and in Ste. Genevieve, the American physician Dr. Walter Fenwick wed François Vallé II's daughter Julie.[3]

The gradual merging of the two cultures did not always proceed so smoothly. The French *coutume de Paris,* for example, differed significantly from the English common law. When Henry Marie Brackenridge returned to Ste. Genevieve for a brief visit in 1811, an elderly French lady retained his services to protect her share of her late husband's estate against the claims of various creditors. Brackenridge successfully drew upon the *coutume de Paris* and its more generous provisions for women in inheritance cases to defend his client's rights. While the opposing counsel cited Blackstone, Brackenridge relied on the provisions for the *douaire* in the old French civil code to persuade the American judges to rule in favor of the widow's claims. Although Brackenridge won this case, it did not take long for the Anglo-American judicial traditions to supplant the French legal codes in Upper Louisiana, and with their passing the more liberal inheritance laws for women became another casualty of the changing times.[4]

Everywhere one looked, there was similar evidence of change. Following the territory's transfer to the United States in 1804, the leisurely pace of daily life characteristic of the Spanish period began giving way to a faster tempo of activity and an atmosphere charged with excitement and expectancy. American immigrants of all descriptions had flocked to the territory hoping to profit from the tremendous opportunities that were unfolding, but once it passed under American control, Upper Louisiana began attracting a larger number of people from the upper strata of American society. Judge Lucas reported from St. Louis in the spring of 1808 that there had been an increase in immigration the previous fall and winter, and he noted that many of the incoming families owned more property and slaves than their predecessors. The steady stream of settlers boosted the territorial population from slightly more than ten thousand in 1804 to nearly twenty thousand in 1810. Land values appreciated as speculators rushed to buy all the available Spanish grants for later resale to the swelling tide of newcomers.[5]

Land speculation was not the only profitable pursuit for the enterprising

Louisianan. The expanding population created a boom for the local businesspeople, who found the task of supplying territorial needs to be increasingly lucrative. However, as the volume of business increased, so did the number of merchants. Long-time French mercantile firms experienced stiff competition from the numerous American retailers who had recently opened for business. In contrast with their French counterparts, who sold goods from their residences, the Yankee merchandisers operated stores in which they displayed their wares for customers to examine. These new American establishments could be easily identified by the signs prominently attached to the front of their buildings, and local buyers were delighted with the larger stocks from which they could make their selections.[6] American manufactured goods from the wholesale markets of Philadelphia and Baltimore comprised a greater portion of the merchandise offered for sale than in earlier times, when local merchants had relied mostly on suppliers in New Orleans and Canada.

In the territory's larger villages, public innkeepers now looked after the needs of the strangers who were arriving daily. In Ste. Genevieve a sign identifying the Green Tree Inn immediately caught Brackenridge's eye in 1810, for as he noted, "In former times private hospitality was the only recourse of the traveler." The visiting Englishman Thomas Ashe had stayed at the Green Tree in 1806 and found the accommodations to be comfortable and the coffee as good as any he had drunk in the finest European establishments.[7]

Brackenridge reported that in St. Louis in 1810 "every house is crowded, rents are high, and it is exceedingly difficult to procure a tenement on any terms." Six or seven houses had been built there the previous year, and he predicted that twice as many would be constructed in the next. In a frontier village where individuals skilled in the construction trades were in short supply and basic building materials such as glass, nails, hinges, and locks had to be imported from eastern manufacturers, that amounted to a virtual building boom. The city already had twelve mercantile stores, two schools, one English and the other French, and a printing office where the first territorial newspaper, the *Missouri Gazette*, had been printed since 1808. The Court of Common Pleas approved a petition for the incorporation of St. Louis as a town in 1807. Its nearly fifteen hundred inhabitants were an amalgam of races, classes, and nationalities. Visitors to the town could see mothers, homemakers, and domestics, both black and white; their playful children; Indian braves and squaws from nearby tribes peddling freshly killed game; Kentucky hunters straight from the backwoods; cultivated French merchants and an occasional Creole businesswoman; illiterate boatmen; metis hunters and their Indian wives; black working people, some slave and others free; brash Yankee lawyers; aspiring American entrepreneurs; assorted mechanics and laborers; and a collection of ne'er-do-wells and idlers. All commingled in the territorial capital's crowded streets, which were still confined to the compact area along the river below the hill.[8]

Old-timers justifiably complained that the influx had brought a new lawless element to Upper Louisiana. The arrival of a contingent of foot-loose, pistol-toting banditti from the United States escalated the level of violence throughout the territory. Although these reckless newcomers constituted only a small segment of the incoming American settlers, they clearly made their presence felt. In St. Louis, Ste. Genevieve, and the other villages fighting, brawling, and killing became more commonplace. In 1807 Frederick Bates informed his brother, "At the last Court, the Jury gave a countryman the sum of 102 dols. in damages against a Bravo-Erratic, who had gouged both his Eyes out." Citizens protested the laxity of local law enforcement. Silas Bent reported from St. Louis in 1812, "Much confusion prevails—murder has been openly committed in the streets of St. Louis and the murderer goes at large. The mechanicks have paraded the streets armed with muskets and bayonets threatening to burn houses." Although violence was increasing, murders were still infrequent; Bent undoubtedly was referring to the case of a riverman killed in a brothel brawl.

Conditions were most volatile in the mining district. Visitors described it as a virtual armed camp, where the pistol, the cudgel, and the dirk were all standard equipment. In other parts of the territory's less-settled interior regions, the same wayward breed of Americans defied local officials and harassed peaceful Indians. The semisavage lifestyles and erratic ways that made these rugged pioneers excellent woodsmen did not necessarily make them model citizens.[9]

The American penchant for violence was not confined solely to raucous lower-class elements, however. Within the ranks of the territory's more genteel sort, gentlemen suddenly resorted to the dueling pistol as a means for redressing personal insults and affronts. One of the earliest of these so-called affairs of honor in Upper Louisiana occurred in 1807 when Joseph McFerron shot and killed William Ogle in Cape Girardeau following a dispute. A charge of cheating in a card game resulted in a similar encounter in 1810 on "Bloody Island," the infamous locale that came to be favored by St. Louis duelists. In that episode, Dr. Bernard Farrar and James Graham were both wounded, and Graham eventually died from his injuries. The following year, Dr. Walter Fenwick fell to a bullet fired by Thomas T. Crittenden on Moreau's Island, a short distance below Ste. Genevieve.[10]

The growing American presence was even more apparent on the territory's changing cultural landscape. Gradually St. Louis and the other

French villages began to look more like American towns. Newly constructed two-story brick and frame buildings with symmetrical windows and gable roofs, reflecting the American mode of construction, intermingled with the older French-style buildings. The trend of using brick and stone was accelerated by a growing shortage of desirable timber near the principal villages. During his stay in the late 1790s, Nicolas de Finiels had observed that the "forests are getting thinner and harder to find, especially near St. Louis." The abandoned common fields on the outskirts of the capital city illustrated another important change: the transition from the traditional French village-oriented, communal agricultural system to the more typically American individualized, market-oriented production system.[11]

American modes of fashion and dress were gaining wider acceptance, especially among the younger people. English slowly replaced French as the principal language, and members of the Creole elite made sure that their offspring became fluent in the new tongue. The territory's sole newspaper, the *Missouri Gazette*, was published in English with only an occasional notice in French. It was yet another sign of the times when Father James Maxwell and the other organizers of a new academy in the territory's oldest community, Ste. Genevieve, stipulated that English and French would be taught together and that no preference would be given in the choice of trustees, professors, teachers, or students on account of religious sentiment.[12]

Outside the territorial villages, the American newcomers were inching their way into the interior, especially along the banks of the Missouri. By 1811 there were settlements adjacent to that vital artery at Femme Osage, La Charette, Loutre Island, Cote sans Dessein, and Boonslick. With the exception of two families who had taken up residence in the shadow of Fort Osage, Boonslick was the westernmost settlement in the territory prior to the War of 1812. Daniel Boone's sons had made use of one of the salt springs at the place that now bore their name as early as 1805.[13] Three years later, Col. Benjamin Cooper and his family attempted to settle the adjacent bottomland in Howard County since known as Cooper's Bottoms, but U.S. authorities quickly ordered them to vacate the Indian country pending the completion of a formal land-cession agreement with the Osages.[14]

Cooper, who had come to St. Charles County from Madison County, Kentucky, in 1806, moved back downriver and eventually joined the Sarshall Cooper and Braxton Cooper families at Loutre Island. The 1808 Osage land cession removed a major impediment to white settlement in the Boonslick country, and in the spring of 1810 Benjamin Cooper returned to Howard County with the region's first permanent white settlers. That fall Stephen Cole, his wife, and their five children, along with his sister-in-law

Hannah Cole, a widow with nine children whose husband had been killed earlier in the year by Indians, settled across the river near present-day Boonville. The peripatetic Coles had migrated from Virginia to Kentucky and finally to the Louisiana Territory. By the time Brackenridge passed through the region the following year while on his way upriver in the company of English naturalist John Bradbury and trader Manuel Lisa, he reported that there were already seventy-five families residing at the Boonslick, including many with slaves. Since they were inhabiting a "howling wilderness" filled with danger, most of these trailblazers followed the example of the early Kentucky pioneers and constructed stations—small groups of cabins arranged to form an enclosure supplemented by a strong stockade.[15]

In other less exposed parts of the territory, there was similar evidence of growth. The incoming immigrants found the Cape Girardeau district equally appealing. When Christian Schultz visited the region in 1807, he observed that "from the goodness of the soil and the well-known industry of the Germans, of which there are considerable settlements about twenty miles back, the Cape bids fair to arrive at some consequence," and at the location where Louis Lorimier had long operated his trading establishment, the new town of Cape Girardeau was beginning to take shape.[16]

The story of frontier settlement in Missouri is a composite of the individual tales of the many people who abandoned familiar surroundings and headed for the trans-Mississippi territory. For some, the trek brought success and prosperity. Brackenridge found luxuriant fields of corn and well-dressed settlers at the remote but flourishing Boonslick settlement less than a year after its founding. Frederick Hyatt, who was twenty years old when he first moved to that settlement in 1811, fondly recalled that, with the exception of the war troubles, life there had been a time "full of fun & frolic, dancing on puncheon floors, cracking jokes . . . and scarcely any natural death." For him, the Missouri frontier afforded the opportunity for a lengthy and successful public career.[17]

For other less fortunate souls, the Missouri frontier brought tragedy and despair. The roseate conditions Brackenridge found in the Boonslick country stood in stark contrast to the utter desolation he discovered at a remote American farmstead near Little Prairie in the New Madrid district. When Brackenridge first visited the sparsely populated region below New Madrid in 1810, he met a Connecticut couple with fourteen children ranging in ages from a newborn infant to eighteen years.[18] The difficulties of providing for such a large family had caused them to move from Connecticut to Ohio and finally to the isolated tract in the Louisiana Territory. Accounts of the new American territory's abundant resources had persuaded them that it was a place that could provide them a better life. Within the short space of two months, this determined pioneer family had already cleared a small area in the woods, built a cabin of rough logs, and furnished it with a homemade table and benches. Although they had escaped the burdens of rent and taxes that went with living in more settled locations, they were already experiencing the loneliness of living in a wilderness where "bears and wolves [were] their nearest neighbors and most frequent visitors."[19] But there were greater dangers than wild animals lurking in the isolated environs they had chosen for their home.

When Brackenridge again passed by their abode on his return trip nearly two years later, the cabin seemed wasted and deserted. Little progress had been made in clearing, and the spots from which the timber had been removed were growing up in weeds. As he approached, the pioneer settler crawled from his dwelling "more dead than alive" to report that his wife and four of his children had died of the fever. Neighbors at the nearby settlement of Little Prairie had taken in three of the younger surviving children, while the oldest daughter and remaining boys stayed with him to recuperate.[20]

During his travels in the Louisiana Territory, Brackenridge also stopped at another backwoods cabin below Cape Girardeau. The members of this solitary family had been residing there since about 1795, largely shut off from the outside world. After they shared their meal of hog meat and coarse hominy with Brackenridge, the husband, a veteran of the French and Indian War, regaled him with stories of Gen. Edward Braddock's star-crossed campaign. Although he was familiar with the names of Washington and Adams, the old man claimed he never had heard of Jefferson or Madison "because they never fout." Paradoxically, a Shawnee Indian leader living in the same general region knew that Madison was president and inquired of Brackenridge about the current state of relations between England and France and the likelihood of a general war.[21]

When officials of the incoming Meriwether Lewis administration arrived in the territory in the spring of 1807, they too were concerned about the dangers of war and the concomitant threat of Indian hostilities along the exposed western frontier. A host of other problems also pressed upon them, including the needs to eliminate any lingering traces of the Burr conspiracy, to diminish the political factionalism rending the territory, and to resolve the controversy over Spanish land titles and mining concessions. Lewis originally had been disinclined to accept his appointment as territorial governor, but at the president's urging he had relented and agreed to serve. Reluctant to move to St. Louis permanently, the new governor initially hoped to administer the territory in absentia. At Lewis's request,

William Clark departed at once for St. Louis to take up his duties as U.S. Indian agent and territorial militia commander and to assist incoming territorial secretary Frederick Bates in launching the new regime. Lewis instructed Clark to monitor closely the activities of the suspected Burrites John Smith T, Henry Dodge, Robert Westcott, and Joseph Browne.[22] Overall, the tasks facing Clark and Bates were formidable.

Frederick Bates was the first to arrive on the scene. He reached the territorial capital on 1 April, confident that he would be able to eliminate the divisions that had existed during the Wilkinson administration. Joseph Browne was away from the city at Colonel Smith T's lead mines, so Bates did not formally notify the outgoing territorial secretary that he had been replaced until 7 April.[23] Browne thought himself badly treated, but the urgent demands of territorial business forced Bates to set aside personal doubts about the extent of his authority as acting governor and take charge of local administration. Insofar as frontier conditions permitted, he attempted to keep the absentee governor apprised of all major developments, but he often had to act without securing Lewis's prior approval.[24] Although minor differences did arise between the governor and the secretary during this period, it was not until after Governor Lewis arrived in the territory that relations between the two men became seriously strained.

Bates wasted no time in seeking to root out the last vestiges of Burrism in Louisiana and end the territory's deep factional divisions. Having decided that the territorial discords would not be permanently silenced until the new administration dealt effectively with the principal plotters and critics, Bates ordered the immediate dismissal from all public offices of two prime suspects—John Smith T and James Richardson. He decided against removing Henry Dodge from his position as sheriff in Ste. Genevieve after concluding that he was an innocent pawn whom Smith T had misled. Robert Westcott, another alleged conspirator, had already resigned his territorial positions.[25]

Smith T's ouster produced a momentary backlash in the Ste. Genevieve district. His colleagues on the court of common pleas threatened to halt public business by resigning en masse, but when the acting governor made it clear that he would appoint new judges to take their places, the justices angrily denounced the actions against their fellow jurist and then resumed their duties. When a few militia officers did resign to protest the cancellation of Smith T's commission as a lieutenant colonel, Bates declined to reconsider his decision. By refusing to return Smith T's archrival Moses Austin to the vacant seat on the court of common pleas, the territorial secretary wisely chose not to identify the government with any particular political faction. His neutral stance had the desired effect, and the dissension in Ste. Genevieve gradually subsided.[26]

Bates convened the territorial legislature on 27 April, and it continued to meet regularly until early summer. A second session followed in October. In contrast to the Wilkinson administration, relations between the judges and the territorial executive seem to have been amiable as they worked together in revamping the territory's confused and sometimes contradictory statutes. Territorial Judge John Coburn reported finding a hodgepodge of laws combining English, French, Spanish, and American usages. This bewildering maze of statutes proved totally inadequate for the needs of a rapidly growing territory.[27]

Seeking to bring order out of this legal chaos, the acting governor and the territorial judges enacted a substantial amount of new legislation covering such diverse subjects as divorce and alimony, insolvent debtors, mortgages, orphans, local government, and courts of justice. In their legislation, they paid particular attention to judicial proceedings and the structure of the court system. In an apparent effort to further diminish discontent in the Ste. Genevieve district, the legislature agreed to hold the superior court's May session in Ste. Genevieve each year, much to the consternation of the residents in the territorial capital, St. Louis.[28]

Of the numerous tasks he performed as acting governor, Bates encountered his greatest difficulties in handling the intricate Indian problems.[29] In accordance with Governor Lewis's wishes, he relied heavily on the advice of the territory's two Indian agents, William Clark and Pierre Chouteau. Bates welcomed Clark's arrival in St. Louis in early May 1807 and immediately turned to him for assistance. Clark began by arranging for a combined military-trading expedition to escort the Mandan chief, Shahaka, to his home on the upper Missouri. The Indian leader had accompanied Lewis and Clark on their return journey and had gone with them to Washington, but the homesick chieftain now longed to rejoin his people. Clark dispatched Ensign Nathaniel Pryor, a veteran of the Pacific expedition, and fourteen soldiers to oversee his safe return. They traveled in the company of a trading party organized by Auguste Pierre Chouteau, a recent graduate of the U.S. Military Academy at West Point. Young Chouteau had resigned from the service and returned home to assist with his family's business operations at a time when members of the St. Louis trading community were showing renewed interest in opening trade with the northern tribes. Manuel Lisa had already headed up the Missouri with that objective, and the Chouteaus did not want to risk being shut out by their competitor.[30]

The Mandan chief's return was only one of numerous problems demanding Clark's attention. A band of 120 Osages was in St. Louis when he arrived, having come to protest the U.S. government's failure to live up to its promises. After reminding Pierre Chouteau, the U.S. agent to their tribe, that they were still waiting for the delivery of a grist mill and for the opening of regular trade, the Osages let it be known that Spanish emissaries had been in their villages seeking their support.

Before the Osages had departed, a Sioux delegation arrived seeking an audience with the president. Clark declined to authorize them to travel to Washington, but he did send them back to their villages with a military escort, a supply of U.S. medals and flags, and nearly $1,500 in merchandise as tokens of the American government's support. The Sacs and Foxes were equally restless. One of their bands had murdered trader Antoine Le Page during a drunken encounter at nearby Portage des Sioux the previous winter, but tribal leaders stalled when Clark demanded that they surrender the murderers to U.S. authorities.[31]

Although the machinations of Spanish and British agents were partly to blame for the unsettled conditions, the relentless pressures of an expanding white population that threatened the land, the resources, and even the existence of the Indians lay at the heart of the problem. The Shawnee and Delawares were protesting the encroachment by whites on lands belonging to them, and the Osage chieftain White Hair was experiencing increasing difficulty in controlling rebellious younger warriors enraged by the continued intrusions on their lands.[32] The Jeffersonian calculation that the trans-Mississippi West would not be heavily populated with whites for generations to come proved to be hopelessly inaccurate—tragically so for the Indian nations, who in desperation turned to rival European powers for assistance in resisting the American assault.

Clark also directed his attention to the territorial militia, which he found in a deplorable condition. He collaborated with Secretary Bates to improve the territory's state of military readiness by revising the militia laws. In September, he reported that a complete reorganization had been effected, but even after the implementation of those changes Clark continued to worry, estimating that half of the territory's 2,433 militiamen were still unarmed and widely scattered. Should an Indian war erupt, he confided to Jefferson, "they would be in a very defenceless State." Clark's concerns were legitimate. In addition to the shortage of weapons, many of the independent backwoodsmen resented being summoned for compulsory military duty. Christian Schultz observed that many inhabitants "do not relish the idea of traveling sixty or a hundred miles, to attend to other people's quarrels; or of carrying a gun and cartouch-box the same distance for *one man to look at,* and then bring it home again."[33]

After spending two and a half months in the territory, Clark left for Kentucky to visit friends and relatives. His absence posed a problem for Bates, who again found himself forced to deal with the ongoing Indian problems. During the summer of 1807, reports of a steadily deteriorating Indian situation along the upper Mississippi intensified local anxieties. The most ominous accounts concerned alleged attempts by Tecumseh and his brother Tenskwatawa, the Shawnee Prophet, to organize a coalition of eastern tribes for an attack against the United States. Although Bates considered the local rumors exaggerated, he ordered all men in the territory to arm themselves in compliance with the new militia law.[34]

Worsening relations between the United States and Great Britain made stories of British attempts to incite the Indians against the Americans seem even more foreboding. Unconfirmed and often distorted reports of Indian hostilities circulated daily on the streets of the various territorial villages. Word of the unprovoked British assault upon the *U.S.S. Chesapeake* added to the local unease during the summer of 1807, and residents braced themselves for a British-sponsored attack in the event that the United States declared war on Great Britain.[35]

Bates continued to believe that anxious local inhabitants had exaggerated the immediate dangers, but in view of the tense international situation he took the precaution of ordering about one-third of the territorial militiamen to muster at their respective parade grounds, ready to march at a moment's notice. Although the acting governor believed that his action would alleviate his constituents' fears, the unexpected return of Ensign Pryor and the party assigned to accompany Shahaka to the Mandan villages again revived the local gloom. A band of hostile Arikara and Sioux warriors had forced them to turn back before they could deliver the Mandan chief to his destination. For the moment the unhappy Indian leader from the upper Missouri had to be satisfied with the quarters he was provided at Cantonment Belle Fontaine.[36]

The persistent threat of Indian attack was not sufficient to quell the escalating conflict over mineral rights in the Ste. Genevieve district. Disturbed by continuing reports of unauthorized diggings on public lands, Congress had acted to protect U.S. interests by excluding lead mines and saline springs from private ownership and barring the confirmation of any claims to those valuable properties. This legislation, approved on 3 March 1807, empowered the president to lease mineral lands for a term not in excess of three years under conditions he deemed appropriate.[37]

In the fall of 1807, Bates authorized several persons to operate lead mines on government-owned land for a three-year period in accordance with the new law's provisions. The leases stipulated that the U.S. was to receive one-tenth of all minerals taken from the mines. Bates predicted that the leasing policy would end speculation and also supply the American government with substantial monetary returns, but in order to ensure that the government received full value from these agreements, he suggested that it establish furnaces and a storehouse for processing its share of the lead.[38]

Even though the president approved the contracts negotiated by Bates and indicated a willingness to endorse additional leases, he recommended that they be made for as short a time as possible. Furthermore, he rejected Bates's suggestion that the U.S. erect its own furnaces and proposed instead to make the government's share payable in the future in metal rather than mineral.[39]

In practice, the new leasing system was a total failure. Holders of Spanish concessions encompassing the valuable mineral properties condemned the measure and vowed to carry on their fight against the government's denial of their claims. Unauthorized intruders who had long mined on public lands without formal permission took an equally dim view of the government's efforts to monopolize the lead lands. Individuals from both groups frequently harassed and intimidated federal leaseholders attempting to dig lead on the disputed tracts.[40] "The mine country," traveler Christian Schultz observed following his 1807 visit there, "is a very unpleasant place of residence, as the continued broils and quarrels among the workmen, as well as the proprietors, keep up a constant scene of warfare."[41] A motley assortment of speculators, gamblers, fortune hunters, and adventurers described by Henry Brackenridge as "some of the rudest and most savage of the uncivilized portion of civilized society" kept the place in a state of perpetual anarchy.[42]

From his post in St. Louis, nearly sixty miles from the mines, the acting governor had neither the time nor the means to enforce the government's leases. In the absence of additional federal assistance, Bates was powerless to check the flagrant disregard of governmental authority, and the leaseholders were left to fend for themselves. Despite the system's shortcomings, the government waited until 1829 to abandon it.[43]

As white settlers quarreled among themselves over rights to the territory's valuable real estate, the Indians inhabiting the region remained convinced that it belonged to them. The external dangers caused by a worsening international situation added another element of uncertainty to the mounting problems awaiting Governor Lewis on the eve of his much-delayed arrival in the territory.

This document was originally written in French by surveyor Antoine Soulard and dated 22 November 1813; it was translated and copied by Frederick Bates in his role as recorder of land titles. The French system of long lots is clearly shown. Courtesy Missouri State Archives.

John B. C. Lucas. Courtesy Missouri Historical Society.

Edward Hempstead. Courtesy Missouri Historical Society.

Frederick Bates. Courtesy Missouri Historical Society.

Rufus Easton. Courtesy Missouri Historical Society.

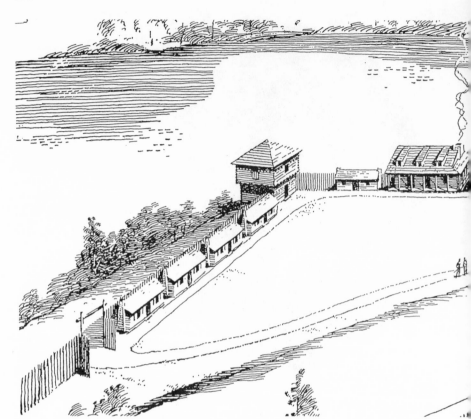

George Sibley. Permission to reproduce courtesy Lindenwood College.

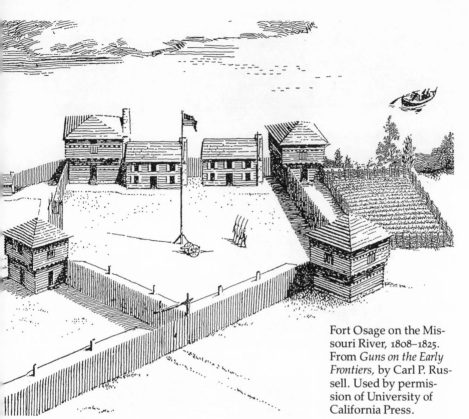

Fort Osage on the Missouri River, 1808–1825. From *Guns on the Early Frontiers*, by Carl P. Russell. Used by permission of University of California Press.

Pawhuska (White Hair), chief of the Big Osages. Portrait by C. B. J. F. de Saint-Mémin, 1806. Courtesy The New-York Historical Society.

Meriwether Lewis. Portrait by C. B. J. F. de Saint-Mémin. Courtesy Missouri Historical Society.

Manuel Lisa. Courtesy Missouri Historical Society.

William Clark. Portrait by Chester Harding. Courtesy Missouri Historical Society.

Nathan Boone. Courtesy Missouri Historical Society.

Sac and Fox Indians near St. Louis. Engraving by Karl Bodmer. Courtesy State Historical Society of Missouri.

Interior of the Nathan Boone House near Defiance. Photograph by Martha Kusiak. Courtesy Missouri Department of Natural Resources.

CHAPTER TWELVE
AN UNEASY
INTERLUDE

Although he had been appointed governor on 3 March 1807, Meriwether Lewis did not arrive in Louisiana to take charge of the government until 8 March 1808. The governor's long-awaited appearance brought welcome relief to the overloaded territorial secretary, but it also temporarily resurrected old political rivalries as the principal protagonists vied for the new executive's favor. Unlike Governor Wilkinson, however, Lewis displayed little interest in local politics, preferring instead to focus his attention on military and Indian matters. The continental pathfinder directed his gaze westward, not eastward. As Richard Dillon notes, for Meriwether Lewis the things that mattered most were "exploration, science, trade, Indians, furs." In those subjects he excelled.[1]

When he finally reached St. Louis, Governor Lewis found Upper Louisiana's Indian affairs in a state of disarray. The Sacs were on a rampage. They had murdered several Ioway and Sioux families, stolen horses and slaughtered livestock belonging to frontier settlers, and repeatedly ignored demands to deliver to U.S. authorities the culprit responsible for killing the French trader at the mouth of the Missouri. The situation with the Osages was only slightly better, as members of the Arkansas faction continued to defy the American government's efforts, in cooperation with the Chouteau brothers, to reunite the divided Indian nation under White Hair's (Pawhuska's) control. Even a few dissidents within the ranks of the normally pro-American Missouri Osages had embarked on a campaign of stealing horses, killing cattle, and harassing isolated territorial settlers. The growing disaffection of the once-dominant Osages was understandable, as they watched their territories being invaded by land-hungry white settlers and well-armed eastern tribes, notably the Cherokees. Some of the Osage renegades challenged White Hair's authority and joined with representatives of the Kansa, Republican Pawnee, and Pawnee tribes in a meeting with Spanish agents. And if all that were not enough, the governor learned that an Ioway party had murdered two traders traveling by canoe down the Missouri in the vicinity of the Grand River. Governor Lewis and General Clark, who had returned to St. Louis in June 1808 with his new bride, both blamed British and Spanish agents for inciting the Indians.[2]

Without hesitation, the governor initiated actions to force the errant tribes to come to terms with the United States. He ordered all trade with the

Osages halted and refused to issue any new licenses for trading with other tribes along the lower Missouri pending the establishment of permanent U.S. trading posts in the region. At the same time, he declared that the Osages no longer enjoyed the American government's protection and invited tribes friendly to the United States to war against them and drive them from the territory. The governor also offered a six-hundred-dollar reward for the apprehension and delivery of the Ioway murderers and sent a party of twenty-seven infantrymen to the Sac villages to force that tribe to surrender the French trader's alleged assassin. Anticipating that his superiors in the national capital might consider such measures unnecessarily harsh, Lewis wrote to Secretary of War Dearborn, suggesting that in the federal government's concern for the welfare of the Indians, it should not lose sight of the precarious position of the white settlers along the frontier.[3]

The governor predicated his policies upon the assumption that the Indians' love of merchandise and their fear of punishment afforded the most effective means for controlling them. Most local residents heartily endorsed his strong stand in handling Indian problems, but officials of the Jefferson administration remained more reserved in their assessment of the situation. While approving Lewis's general course of action, the president advised him to avoid, if at all possible, any military coercion of the Indians. Jefferson held that "commerce is the great engine by which we are to coerce them, & not war."[4]

Operating under this philosophy, federal officials hoped to regain the Indians' friendship by establishing more government trading factories that offered good merchandise at reasonable prices. Because the existing factory at Cantonment Belle Fontaine had not been readily accessible to the region's numerous tribes, the War Department decided to construct a new factory near the Osage villages, and another on the upper Mississippi at the mouth of the Des Moines River. Secretary Dearborn also instructed the troop commander at Belle Fontaine to establish military forts adjacent to each of the new trading stations, manned by enough soldiers to protect them.[5]

By late summer the necessary arrangements had been completed. When Governor Lewis and General Clark suggested that the proposed site for the factory on the Osage River was inaccessible, Secretary Dearborn agreed to shift its location to a point on the Missouri River approximately three hundred miles upstream from the Mississippi. In early August 1808, a keelboat expedition under the command of Capt. Eli Clemson set out from Cantonment Belle Fontaine carrying men and supplies for the new Missouri River installation. A short time later, Clark traveled overland with Capt. Nathan Boone's company of mounted dragoons from the St. Charles district to join Clemson's force at the Missouri River site.[6]

Clark had selected a spot on a high bluff overlooking the winding Missouri near the present town of Sibley in Jackson County. The location's unobstructed view of the surrounding countryside had been a decisive factor in its choice. When he arrived on the scene, Clark directed construction of an upright log palisade and four blockhouses, a connected two-cabin factory store with a cellar, barracks for the soldiers, and assorted other buildings. As the log structures began to take shape, Clark dispatched Captain Boone and the mixed-blood interpreter Paul Loise to the Osage towns to inform tribal members of his arrival and invite them to take up residence near the new fort. Territorial officials had decided to follow a carrot-and-stick strategy in their dealings with the out-of-favor Osages. While threatening them with war, they simultaneously used the new U.S. trading factory as an inducement to lure them back into the American fold. The Osages accepted Clark's invitation to confer at the site of the new fort, known to them as Fire Prairie.[7]

During the ensuing negotiations, the Osages agreed to a treaty in which they relinquished to the United States an immense tract of land between the Missouri and Arkansas rivers within the Louisiana Territory in return for promises of trade and protection. Clark, whom the Indians referred to as the Red Head, won them over with his assurances that the transfer of the tract to the U.S. government would make the area more secure from eastern tribes seeking to occupy it. Clark returned to St. Louis with the agreement, but the ink on the document was barely dry when an Osage delegation came to the territorial capital expressing its displeasure with the treaty's contents. They maintained that White Hair and the other signers had lacked authority to bind the tribe because they had failed to secure consent from the tribal council. Their objections irritated Clark, who insisted that he and the interpreters had carefully reviewed every provision with the Osage leaders before they signed the treaty. Lewis believed that the treaty had been accurately represented to the tribesmen, but he consented to its renegotiation to forestall future problems.[8]

Lewis personally drew up a new treaty designed to eliminate Indian objections to the previous agreement. In drafting the document, he consulted Pierre Chouteau, but he rejected the Osage agent's request for an article confirming Chouteau's Spanish title to thirty thousand arpents of land in the ceded area. When he completed the revised treaty, Lewis directed Chouteau to secure Osage approval for it. The Indian agent presented the new agreement to tribal leaders, and at his urging they accepted its provisions on 10 November 1808. In return for the title to the ceded lands, the American government agreed to establish a permanent trading factory to supply the tribe with merchandise, to erect a blacksmith shop and mill for use by the Indians, to grant annual $1,500 stipends to the tribe, and to restore the Osages to the protection of the United States.[9]

The Osage call for the inclusion of a provision in the revised treaty validating Chouteau's title to the lands they had given him in 1792 caused Clark to conclude that it was the French trader who had persuaded the Indians to reject the original agreement. George Sibley, the U.S. factor at Fort Osage, also castigated Chouteau's handling of the negotiations, but in fact, although Chouteau undoubtedly encouraged the Indians to press for the proviso concerning his lands, the Indians based their objections to the treaty on more than a concern for Chouteau's private interests. Once they understood the magnitude of the concessions they were making, it was little wonder that they registered their objections to the original treaty. At their insistence, the provision for the $1,500 annuity was inserted in the revised document, along with additional articles concerning hunting grounds, the surrender and punishment of Indian and white criminals, and the recovery of stolen property. The completion of Fort Osage in 1808 and the formal signing of the revised treaty in St. Louis on 31 August 1809 marked the official return of the Osages into the American fold, and when the test came during the critical years of the War of 1812, they continued to support the United States.[10]

As the westernmost U.S. outpost, Fort Osage was a busy place following its establishment in 1808. A segment of the Osages had settled near the new installation, and Indians from other nearby tribes came to trade, to confer with American officials, and in some instances to smoke the peace pipe. Most were friendly, but some were more menacing. The visitors ran the gamut. A lone, grief-stricken Osage man came to exchange two skins for a piece of blue cloth that he planned to use as his dying wife's burial garment. A sullen Kansa delegation, numbering nearly one thousand, demanded to transact business, but when they became insolent and threatening, Sibley simply closed up shop. River travelers, including such illustrious members of the fur trading community as Manuel Lisa, Andrew Henry, Pierre Chouteau, Pierre Menard, Ramsay Crooks, and Wilson Price Hunt, periodically anchored their boats at the fort's landing and made their way up the hill to pay their respects and pass along the latest news from St. Louis or from upriver. Mary Easton Sibley, the official hostess at Fort Osage, often favored her Indian and white guests with the tunes she played on a piano brought upriver from St. Louis.[11]

Attempts to establish a similar government factory along the Mississippi at a site fifteen miles above the mouth of the Des Moines River did not go so well. Work at Fort Madison, situated in the heart of territory long dominated by British traders, proceeded much more slowly. The Americans found Indians there generally unreceptive. Despite their desire to secure a trading factory, the Indians in that region strongly disliked having regular military forces in their midst. An unusually harsh winter further retarded progress on the fort. When spring finally arrived, Fort Madison remained uncompleted. Alarmed by increasing Indian activity in the area, the commanding officer at the post sent an expedition to St. Louis requesting assistance, but before any reinforcements could arrive, a band of Sac Indians, after pretending friendship, attempted unsuccessfully to storm the still-unfinished fortification.[12]

In St. Louis the situation seemed more ominous than ever in the spring of 1809. The urgent pleas from Fort Madison offered graphic proof of continuing Indian hostility along the Mississippi. Reports that the Shawnee Prophet was increasing his anti-American activities added to the local uncertainty, as did the unfounded rumors that the United States had already declared war on both France and Great Britain. In response to these conditions, Governor Lewis attempted to shore up territorial defenses by dispatching two volunteer companies of militia to relieve the beleaguered garrison at Fort Madison. As an added precaution he placed members of the territorial militia on alert, and on 21 April he ordered companies from the districts of Cape Girardeau, Ste. Genevieve, St. Louis, and St. Charles to rendezvous on 4 May in St. Louis and St. Charles, equipped with proper arms and good horses.[13]

Although Lewis's measures struck a generally responsive chord in the territory, his attempts to control the Indians through trade restrictions occasionally roused protests from local fur traders. They particularly objected to his temporary suspension of the issuance of licenses for trading with the Indians.[14] Profits from the fur trade had been steadily declining in the Louisiana Territory since the late eighteenth century, and St. Louis's staid, conservative merchants had lost ground to their more aggressive British counterparts. Since the collapse of Jacques Clamorgan's ill-fated Company of Explorers of the Upper Missouri, the St. Louis traders had been content with operating in the same areas year after year.

The situation remained unchanged until Lewis and Clark returned bearing reports of the rich supply of furs along the upper Missouri. This news rekindled interest in opening trade with tribes in that region. One of the first of the St. Louis traders to catch a glimpse of the rich potential of the northern and far-western trade was Manuel Lisa. Considered to be something of a maverick by the small group of St. Louis merchants who had managed to monopolize the traffic in furs for many years, Lisa joined forces with Clamorgan in an unsuccessful attempt to open trade with Santa Fe in 1806. Although that venture failed, it convinced Lisa that a trading expedition to the rich beaver areas in the Rockies would be profitable. The underfur from the luxurious beaver pelts was in great demand in Europe, where it was utilized in making fashionable felt hats.[15]

Unable to secure financial support for the undertaking in St. Louis, Lisa entered a partnership with two prominent Kaskaskia merchants, Pierre Menard and William Morrison, to sponsor the first planned American trading and trapping expedition to the upper Missouri. With many recruits from Lewis and Clark's recently returned crew, Lisa organized and directed a force of more than fifty men that headed up the Missouri in the spring of 1807. After enduring the hardships and privations of living in the wilderness for over a year, Lisa returned to St. Louis in the summer of 1808 with enough beaver skins to show a modest return on the original investment. Based upon what he had seen, Lisa reported that tremendous profits awaited those willing to take the necessary risks. In fact, many of his men had chosen to remain in the mountains for the upcoming fall hunt.[16]

Lisa's successful venture created a dilemma for his St. Louis competitors, who now realized that they either must enter the race to capture the rich trade on the upper Missouri or run the risk of losing their dominant position in the fur business. Already numerous American merchants, including John Jacob Astor, were making plans to enter the trans-Mississippi trade, and at Michilimackinac a coalition of traders had recently affiliated themselves with the powerful North West Company. Moreover, the St. Louis group, headed by the Chouteaus, faced the bleak prospect of a further reduction in the present revenues as the unwelcome competition from the two newly constructed government trading factories threatened their long-time dominance in the lower Missouri trade.

After carefully considering the various alternatives, the principal traders decided to join Lisa and his partners in the formation of the St. Louis Missouri Fur Company. With the additional capital that the new organization could provide, the founders hoped to fully exploit the rich trade in the upper Missouri valley. Under the Articles of Association and Co-Partnership drafted in St. Louis during the winter of 1808–1809, each partner agreed to go on the first expedition or provide an acceptable substitute. Some of the most prominent members of the St. Louis business community joined Lisa, Menard, and Morrison in launching the new company. They included Pierre Chouteau, Sr.; his son Auguste Pierre; Reuben Lewis, the governor's brother; William Clark; Benjamin Wilkinson, the former governor's nephew; and Andrew Henry, a Ste. Genevieve entrepreneur. The group designated Clark to act as the firm's agent in St. Louis.[17]

Even before the final Articles of Agreement had been approved, the company had signed a contract with Governor Lewis to escort Shahaka, the

Mandan chief, to his home. In return for a payment of $7,000, the company agreed to supply a force of 120 men to guarantee the Indian leader's safe return. If the trade did not go as well as the members anticipated, they still could count on the substantial government payment. As an added incentive, the governor promised not to grant any licenses for trading in the area above the Platte River until after the company's scheduled departure date, thereby assuring the Missouri Company's traders a head start. Altogether, the company dispatched approximately 350 men up the river in May and June 1809 with the knowledge that they enjoyed the governor's confidence. In point of fact, their benefactor Lewis was probably a secret partner in the venture.[18]

In view of the expedition's quasi-commercial nature, the administration took a dim view of the governor's actions, especially his decision to pay the company for its assistance. Secretary of War William Eustis, a penny-pinching bureaucrat, agreed to honor the sum stipulated in the contract, but he declined to approve an additional $500 payment authorized by Governor Lewis for purchasing gifts for the Indians. In refusing to pay the amount in question, Eustis censured Lewis for having failed to secure authorization in advance for this costly project.[19] The federal government required local officials to seek prior approval for all large expenditures so that it could closely regulate territorial expenses, and economy-minded federal officials tended to be conservative in the amounts they allowed local officers to spend. In 1809, Eustis pared the Indian agency's proposed budget after chiding Clark that his recommended expenditures for Indian affairs in the Louisiana Territory amounted to four times the sum allotted for civil administration.[20]

Both Lewis and Clark considered these latest reprimands unjustified. Lewis previously had argued that in view of their distance from the seat of government, territorial officials needed broader discretion in handling local problems. Noting that it took at least two months for him to receive a reply to his most urgent inquiries, he pointed out that unexpected situations sometimes required him to act without consulting his superiors in the executive branch.[21]

The absence of regular channels of communication in frontier communities posed a perennial problem for territorial administrators, and more than any of his predecessors Governor Lewis sought to alleviate this deficiency in Louisiana. Irregular and undependable postal service was a constant source of irritation to territorial residents and officials. Post riders, under contract, carried the mails on horseback. Working under difficult and sometimes dangerous conditions, these frontier couriers often failed to make their scheduled rounds. The territory was supposed to receive mail once a week from the East, but to the disgust of local residents, several weeks often elapsed between deliveries. Despite Governor Lewis's attempts to improve the system, postal service in the territory remained erratic.[22]

The governor also took the lead in securing a territorial newspaper. Recognizing the need for a printer who could publish Louisiana's newly enacted statutes, Lewis encouraged Joseph Charless, a hot-headed Irishman, to come to St. Louis to establish a newspaper. Thanks in part to the financial assistance provided by Lewis, the initial issue of the *Missouri Gazette*, the first newspaper published west of the Mississippi River, went on sale in St. Louis on 12 July 1808.[23]

A growing impatience among local residents with the American government's seeming inability to solve perennial frontier problems—unsettled land claims, disputed mining rights, inadequate defenses, poor postal service, and deficient transportation systems, to name a few—led to increased criticism of the existing territorial government and spawned demands for advancement to second-class territorial status. The dual attractions of greater self-government and new opportunities for local public office brought added support to the movement.

As early as February 1808, Frederick Bates referred to local desires for a second-grade territorial government, but the campaign to advance Louisiana's territorial status appears not to have begun in earnest until 1809. The editor of the *Missouri Gazette* reported in January that he intended to publish in an upcoming issue a letter he had received proposing that Louisianans apply to the general government for advancement to a second-grade territory, but he cautioned his readers to consider carefully the consequences of such a step. The editor suggested that the change would increase taxes and extend the governor's powers in the territory while lessening his responsibility to the national government. Charless's arguments provided the basis for much of the later campaign against the proposed shift.[24]

Following Charless's opening blast, the *Gazette* printed a copy of a petition to Congress seeking the change in territorial status. Basing their demands upon the 1803 Treaty of Cession and the U.S. Constitution, the petitioners claimed that Louisiana's current system of government excluded them from the full enjoyment of the rights and privileges guaranteed to all American citizens. Furthermore, the petitioners reminded Congress that the Territory of Orleans already had been granted the territorial status they now sought for Upper Louisiana.[25]

The editor's opposition to the proposed change set off a major debate in the *Gazette*'s columns over the assets and liabilities of second-class territorial status. "A Subscriber" accused Charless of resisting modification in Louisiana's government because, as territorial printer, he feared loss of executive patronage. After questioning the editor's motives, the author then enumerated the advantages that the higher grade of government would provide. Appealing to the growing demands for representative government, "A Subscriber" reasoned that local residents were best equipped to solve their own problems and that this measure would pave the way for increased self-government.[26]

Charless refused to budge from his original position, insisting that the changes would not be worth the greatly increased costs. Using arguments similar to those that had been advanced by opponents of second-class status in other territories, he contended that the increased costs of the new government would discourage immigration to the territory. Like Charless, the chief antagonists of the second-grade government continually stressed that such a change would necessitate a large increase in local taxes. Whereas the territorial legislators currently received their salaries from the federal treasury, the costs of the new legislature would have to be borne by the local taxpayers, particularly the property holders.[27]

While the debate continued to rage, copies of the petition printed in the *Gazette* had been circulated throughout the territory for signatures and were forwarded to Congress in January 1810. Since Louisiana's organic act of 1805 had not provided for automatic advancement to second-class status when the territory reached a population of five thousand adult males, congressional authorization was necessary prior to this step. However, a bill introduced in the House of Representatives on 22 January 1810 calling for the creation of a second-class government for the Territory of Louisiana failed to gain approval at that session. A shortage of time rather than any organized opposition apparently caused Congress to delay action on the measure. Despite this temporary setback, the supporters of the higher classification had resurrected the earlier debate over representative government and its merits.[28]

As had been the case since Upper Louisiana had passed under American control, land claims continued to dominate local political discussions, and the board of land commissioners remained at center stage in the ongoing controversy. Because of James Donaldson's absence, the board had discontinued all regular proceedings during the winter of 1806–1807, but following the arrival of Donaldson's replacement, Frederick Bates, in the spring of 1807, the commission resumed its deliberations.[29] In the meantime, Congress had passed new legislation liberalizing certain restrictions previously placed upon confirmation of titles. No longer did the claimant have to produce written permission for claims of less than 800 arpents if he or she could demonstrate they had occupied and cultivated the lands for not less than ten years prior to 20 December 1803. Subsequently, Congress increased the amount allowable from 800 to 2,000 arpents. In addition, it granted the board of commissioners full power to confirm titles in accordance with the laws and established usages and customs of the French and Spanish governments.[30]

Upon resuming its regular proceedings, the board made several crucial decisions. It replaced its controversial clerk, Charles Gratiot, with William Christy, and following Christy's resignation, Thomas Riddick assumed those duties. Furthermore, in order to expedite the land-claims proceedings and to accommodate claimants in remote regions, the commissioners decided to hold regular sessions in various parts of the territory for the purpose of recording claims and receiving testimony.[31] The originally scheduled hearings, however, had to be postponed to a later time, probably because of inclement weather. This gave the board an opportunity to reconsider its decision, and its members decided that only one of them need visit the outlying regions to take testimony. The commissioners designated Frederick Bates to make the trip. He went to Cape Girardeau in late May of 1808 and subsequently visited the districts of New Madrid and Arkansas.[32]

While in Arkansas, Bates encountered numerous difficulties in carrying out his assigned duties. He found the isolated and uneducated settlers in that remote district "entirely unacquainted with every kind of business, except of that of the chase" and ignorant of even the most elementary legal procedures.[33] Following Bates's return from his journey, the board initiated a serious review of the claims that had been registered during the preceding two and one-half years. The commissioners issued their first formal decisions on 8 December 1808, but the work was tedious and the progress was slow. On 1 February 1810, the commissioners reported to the secretary of the treasury that they had recorded 3,056 claims and taken testimony in 2,699 of those cases. They had issued certificates of confirmation on only 323 claims, authorized an additional 167 for survey, and rejected 139.[34]

The slow-paced decisionmaking process and the unpopular guidelines governing confirmation irritated the territory's land claimants. In January 1808 holders of unapproved land grants called upon Congress to order the confirmation of every concession issued by the Spanish government except for those that could be proved to be antedated or fraudulent. The following December, they repeated their demands and protested rules that required actual habitation and cultivation of claimed lands, that limited the maximum size of grants, and that voided all grants made after 1 October 1800.[35]

When Congress failed to respond to their demands, the land-claimant group created an ad hoc committee in St. Louis similar to the one they had used to protest Upper Louisiana's attachment to the Indiana Territory in 1804. In an effort to present the appearance of a united front, they called for the formation of a new general committee representing all districts of the territory to petition Congress for action to resolve the impasse over land claims in the Louisiana Territory.[36]

Their efforts culminated with the opening of a general convention in Ste. Genevieve in August 1809. The delegates designated Edward Hempstead, a popular St. Louis attorney specializing in land-claims cases, the notorious John Smith T from the Ste. Genevieve district, and Hugh McDermed from the St. Charles district as a committee of three to draft a memorial to Congress seeking more favorable terms for confirmation. The convention members adopted two additional resolutions: one recommending that other territorial residents join them in seeking a second-class government, and another calling for John B. C. Lucas's removal as a land commissioner.[37]

The effort to oust Lucas reflected the popular belief among claimants that the judge's rigid stance was the principal reason that their claims had not been approved. As early as 1807, Lucas reported sporadic attempts were underway to secure his removal as a commissioner, but the campaign to unseat him that materialized in mid–1809 was highly organized and well orchestrated. The *Missouri Gazette* contained a notice naming the persons in the various districts designated to receive the anti-Lucas petitions that were being circulated throughout the territory. In St. Louis a slanderous attack calling upon the people to rid themselves of this "little Robespierre" appeared on the church door for all to read.[38]

Lucas sought to counter the vitriolic attacks against him with a barrage of letters to members of the administration in Washington. He invited President Madison to institute an inquiry into his official conduct if Madison believed it was necessary. Lucas insisted that he had been attacked simply because his opinions had been less favorable to the claimants than those of the other two commissioners. He reported that he had resisted all attempts at bribery and added wryly that, had he succumbed to such offers, Madison would never have heard any complaints against him. The president must have agreed since Lucas remained on the board of land commissioners until it completed its work.[39]

Lewis chose not to involve himself in the ongoing debate. Indeed, the preoccupation with the land-claims disputes partially obscured the growing differences of opinion between Governor Lewis and Secretary Bates. Relations between the two men had been strained since shortly after the governor's arrival in the territory. They disagreed on most major policy matters, including the removal of officials, the handling of lead leases, and the issuance of trading permits, and their mutual dislike for one another kept them from reconciling their differences amicably. Lewis's habit of ignoring Bates and turning to Clark and others for advice regarding significant territorial matters especially rankled the jealous secretary, who made little effort to hide his disdain for the governor.[40]

When Bates refused to speak to Lewis at a public ball in St. Louis, a duel might have ensued had it not been for William Clark's intervention. Bates attributed many of Lewis's problems to his military habits, and he once confided to his brother that the governor had acted like "an overgrown baby."[41]

Their differences undoubtedly contributed to the governor's growing mental depression, but it was Secretary of War Eustis's decision to disallow the payment of certain expenditures authorized by Lewis that further demoralized the despondent official. Lewis left for Washington, D.C., in early September 1809, intent on clearing himself of any possible taint of improper conduct and securing approval to pay the protested bills. Tragically, the journey ended with Lewis's violent death at Grinder's Tavern on the Natchez Trace. Although the circumstances surrounding his death remain clouded, Lewis in all likelihood took his own life. Upon hearing of their friend's untimely passing, both Clark and Jefferson assumed that it had been suicide.[42]

For Lewis the governorship had become a burden, and had he lived, it is doubtful that he would have returned to St. Louis.[43] Nonetheless, in view of the paucity of means at his disposal for carrying out the government's policies, the governor had accomplished as much as could reasonably have been expected of him. To his credit, Meriwether Lewis had done much to acquaint officials in Washington with the persistent problems facing the exposed western territory, and he had laid the groundwork for Missouri's successful defense during the forthcoming War of 1812.[44] But for the moment, the threat of war with Great Britain and its Indian allies clouded the horizon, and territorial residents braced themselves for an uncertain future.

CHAPTER THIRTEEN
DEFENDING THE AMERICAN REPUBLIC'S WESTERN BORDER

The inhabitants of the Louisiana Territory kept an anxious eye on developments in the Indian country as rumors of an impending war with Great Britain fueled speculation that British agents from Canada were fomenting Indian unrest and turning the disgruntled natives against the Americans. Governor Lewis's death was an unexpected blow that added to the prevailing uncertainty. Territorial residents had appreciated his insistence on firmness in dealing with hostile Indians and his willingness to challenge the Jefferson administration's philanthropic notions. Although federal officials had not always found themselves in agreement with the governor's Indian policies, they had come to recognize the dangers confronting the occupants of the American republic's exposed western border.

For that reason, President Madison took his time in selecting someone to replace Lewis as governor. He had no shortage of applicants from which to choose. At least thirteen names were offered for the chief executive's consideration, but not all of them were willing to serve. Lewis's partner and friend, William Clark, was probably the first to be offered the post, but he turned it down, most likely because he considered himself lacking in the necessary political experience.[1] Frederick Bates, whose name was also mentioned, decided against seeking the appointment because it would have meant a pay cut for him. The combined remuneration he received from his positions as territorial secretary and recorder of land titles was greater than the governor's salary.[2] Most of the other prospective candidates were not so reticent. John B. Scott, who had served briefly as military commandant in the Cape Girardeau district, and John Coburn, a member of the territorial superior court with strong local backing, both waged vigorous but unsuccessful campaigns for the appointment.[3]

Madison ultimately gave the nod to Benjamin Howard, a popular Kentucky lawyer-politician with substantial military experience. Howard, who was serving in the U.S. House of Representatives at the time of his selection, resigned from that body in April 1810 to accept the new post. Although Howard considered his appointment as governor of the Territory of Louisiana a step forward politically, he later regretted his decision. He always preferred his native state over St. Louis as a place of residence, and when his term as governor expired, he declined reappointment to accept a commission in the regular military.[4]

Howard's brief tenure as governor came at a crucial period. During the summer of 1810, British traders had stepped up their activities among tribes east of the Mississippi; those actions, in combination with the ongoing work of the Shawnee Prophet and Tecumseh, were threatening to turn the principal tribes of the Old Northwest against the United States. Major segments of the Shawnee, Potawatomi, Winnebago, Kickapoo, and Sac nations seemed ready to defy the American authorities, and the spreading unrest brought leaders from undecided neighboring tribes scurrying to St. Louis to take the measure of the American government's intentions.[5]

The growing possibility of open conflict with the Indians forced officials in the War Department to reexamine the condition of the nation's western military fortifications. Since his arrival at Cantonment Belle Fontaine the previous June, Lt. Col. Daniel Bissell had complained that the old installation was a "mass of rotting timbers" whose location along the low-lying river bank made it both unhealthy and vulnerable to attack. The secretary of war took note of Bissell's reports and authorized the construction of a new fort on the hill overlooking the original post. Work on the structure began almost immediately, and the following summer the army garrison occupied the new Fort Belle Fontaine at its more commanding site.[6]

The president signed Howard's appointment as governor on 18 April 1810, but the new territorial chief executive did not reach St. Louis until 17 September.[7] When he did get there, he found conditions in the territorial capital tense. In July a band of renegade Potawatomis had stolen a number of horses from settlers at Loutre Island on the Missouri and then murdered four members of Stephen Cole's party when they set out to retrieve the stolen property.[8] The uneasy St. Louisans welcomed the incoming governor and feted him with a lavish public dinner and dance, but despite their gracious hospitality, the new chief executive stayed in the territory only briefly before returning to Kentucky.[9]

Although the winter months brought a seasonal respite as the warring Indians took refuge in sheltered camps to escape the inclement weather, the arrival of spring touched off a new wave of violence. Settlers east of the Mississippi bore the brunt of the revived attacks, but residents in the Louisiana Territory had cause for alarm. The Ioways and the Osages were warring over hunting grounds. In May a band of Osage warriors burst into George Sibley's bedchamber at Fort Osage in the middle of the night, dangling the head of an Ioway intruder whose body they had just hacked to pieces. The agitated braves had caught the enemy spy lurking within three hundred yards of their encampment outside the isolated fort.[10] Such disturbances were not restricted to the Indian country. During the same month a party of vagabond Indians ventured within the confines of St. Louis and set fire to a barn belonging to Pierre Chouteau.[11]

Not all Indians in the territory were hostile. Unlike their tribal kinfolk in Ohio, the Missouri Shawnee were making a concerted effort to remain on good terms with their white neighbors. The Shawnee women made baskets and moccasins and sold them to the local whites, and it was not unheard of for Indian and white inhabitants of the region to hunt together. Elizabeth Musick, who settled in Upper Louisiana in 1800, was well acquainted with members of a Shawnee band who resided peacefully along the banks of the Meramec not far from St. Louis. "The Indians were kind," Mrs. Musick recalled in later years. The situation was similar in other sections of the territory. The Hancock children in Perry County played with Indian children from nearby villages, and in the Bellevue Valley, the Russells remembered the Indians as friendly. In the Ozarks and elsewhere, the eastern Indian immigrants sometimes intermarried with whites. The eldest daughter of James Rogers, a mixed-blood Shawnee chieftain, had two white husbands at different times, and Rogers's son Lewis decided against marrying a white woman who had shown interest in him only after he found her to be slovenly and untidy. Indian men did sometimes have white wives. Timothy Flint, a Presbyterian minister and author, met a "full-blooded American . . . fair and pretty" who was the wife of a young warrior. Far more commonplace, of course, was the white trader—William Gilliss, for example—who had one or more Indian wives.[12]

Mrs. Musick's high regard for Rogers and his Shawnee associates Powder Horn and Little Captain scarcely fit the image of the bloodthirsty savage that many Indian-hating pioneers sought to attach to all redskinned peoples. Even the rabidly anti-Indian editor of the *Missouri Gazette,* Joseph Charless, must have had second thoughts when Rogers advised the newspaper's readers in 1809 that he had found a sorrel horse and would return it to anyone who could furnish proof of ownership.[13] It was little wonder that U.S. Indian agent William Clark characterized this particular band of transplanted easterners as "a peaceable and well disposed people . . . of great service to our frontier settlements."[14]

Yet in spite of the tribe's friendly demeanor, leaders from the Shawnee towns on the Meramec and on the lower Mississippi above Cape Girardeau repeatedly had to ask U.S. officials for assistance in securing their lands against unlawful white encroachment and in halting illegal liquor sales by white traders.[15] White assaults against friendly Indians were at least as serious as Indian depredations against peaceful white settlers. In April 1809, Governor Lewis ordered an end to white encroachment on Indian lands within the territory. Lewis warned that the intruders' unlawful acts would lead to disturbances and disrupt the current peace and tranquility with the friendly tribes. The governor's proclamation had little effect.[16] Two years later, Rogers and the Meramec Shawnees again appealed to their Great Father in Washington for protection from the unprovoked aggression of their white neighbors. They also asked President Madison to grant them permission to mine lead in the vicinity of their village. Noting that the buffalo and elk had disappeared from the region and that even the deer were getting scarce, the Shawnee petitioners complained that they could no longer secure enough skins to feed and clothe their families.[17]

Secretary of War Eustis responded to the Indian petitioners' appeal by authorizing them to begin digging for lead on a three-square-mile tract to be reserved for their use. He also instructed Clark to expel any white interlopers from the Indian lands according to law. It was a well-intentioned if largely futile gesture, but through it all the Missouri Shawnees resisted efforts to entice them into joining the powerful, anti-American coalition headed by their tribal brother Tecumseh.[18]

Although some Indian bands maintained an uneasy truce with their American neighbors, the danger of a bloody confrontation between the United States and the more defiant Indian nations remained. Governor Howard returned to the territory in July 1811 to inspect Missouri's northern frontier and take charge of local defensive preparations. With assistance from Clark, who was reappointed brigadier general of the territorial militia, the governor directed the organization of additional militia companies and superintended the construction of several blockhouses in remote sections of the territory. One contemporary observer described the fortifications in the vicinity of Loutre Island as "simply strong log houses, with a projecting upper story, and with loopholes for musketry."[19] Having put the territory in a state of military preparedness, Howard again departed for Kentucky in September. Two months later, Acting Governor Bates ordered the territorial militia companies to be ready to repel a possible Indian invasion. On 7 November, Gen. William H. Harrison's troops had clashed with a coalition of Indian forces at Prophetstown. The Battle of Tippecanoe was hardly the great military victory that Harrison's backers made it out to be in his successful 1840 presidential campaign, but the destruction of Prophetstown was a serious blow to the fortunes of the defiant eastern Shawnee leaders.[20]

Six weeks after the clash at Prophetstown, the already jittery residents of the Louisiana Territory experienced terror of a different sort when a series of devastating earthquakes whose effects were felt as far away as the Atlantic seaboard literally tore the region apart. The first of three major sequences of shocks began on 16 December 1811, when a "distant rumbling noise resembling carriages running over pavement" roused inhabitants throughout the territory from their sleep.[21] The settlements of Little Prairie and New Madrid were hardest hit. The terrified inhabitants of those communities fled from their rolling and jostling homes amid the sounds of the quake's thunderous roaring, falling trees, collapsing chimneys, screeching birds, and screaming people. Following the initial shocks, Little Prairie lay in ruins, and the town's entire population abandoned their settlement and headed northward, where the damage was rumored to have been less serious. When the nearly one hundred refugees from Little Prairie reached New Madrid, they found many of the people there camping in tents in open fields.[22]

A second series of tremors started on 23 January, and the final and most severe set of shocks followed on 7 February. In the center of the quake zone, buildings collapsed, great fissures appeared in the earth's surface, some land sank and other land uplifted, rivers and streams altered their courses, and entire forests came crashing down. The quakes, which were equivalent to, if not greater than, those that destroyed San Francisco a century later, rearranged parts of the midwestern landscape. Reelfoot Lake in western Tennessee serves as a contemporary reminder of their unbelievable force. At various times, the New Madrid tremors caused furniture to move, church bells to ring, and clocks to stop in such distant places as Charleston, South Carolina, Richmond and Newport, Virginia, and Washington, D.C. Likewise, the impact of immense quantities of debris crashing into the rivers created such enormous swells that rumors persisted for many years that the Mississippi and the Ohio actually ran backward during the initial series of shocks. One of the quake's more bizarre consequences was the unearthing in Kentucky of the skull of a black man who had been murdered by Thomas Jefferson's nephews.[23]

By late spring the aftershocks had gradually diminished, but in the forlorn New Madrid district only the hardiest souls remained after the former inhabitants scattered in every direction. Remarkably, the loss of life had not been great. The known casualties included a woman killed by a falling log, another who allegedly died of fright, a black man who drowned in a sinkhole, and six Indians buried by a collapsing bank. An unknown number of river travelers also perished, but the region's low population held down the death toll.[24]

The territory's other settlements fared considerably better than New Madrid and Little Prairie. In Cape Girardeau, the residents reported numerous demolished chimneys and cracked walls and a few ruined brick and stone houses. The situation was even less serious in St. Louis, where the damage was confined to split walls and toppled chimneys. Still, Frederick

Bates worried that with all of the adverse publicity about earthquakes, Indians, and epidemics, Missouri would in a few years "be nothing but a place of exile for Robbers & Outlaws."[25]

Governor Howard had been in St. Louis when the tremors struck the territory. Fearful that Harrison's bloody encounter with the Shawnee and their allies in the Indiana Territory might trigger a general Indian uprising along the frontier, he had hurried back to the territorial capital in early December to take charge. He immediately dispatched spies to watch for any unusual activity, but they were helpless to prevent isolated attacks. In February 1812, a band of Kickapoo or Potawatomi Indians, after pretending to be friendly, murdered nine members of the Neal family, who resided on the Salt River in the St. Charles district.[26] Conditions had become so serious by early 1812 that Governor Howard recommended a full-scale campaign against the "marauding savages." Both Howard and Clark followed the lead of Meriwether Lewis by consistently advocating the use of force against the hostile Indians and their British collaborators.[27]

This latest surge in Indian depredations was simply the most recent episode in the ongoing struggle that pitted whites against Indians in a contest to determine who would control the valuable lands stretching across the North American continent. There were many atrocities and brutalities on both sides, but none of the participants seemed able to find a permanent solution that did not require the other's destruction. Despite a genuine desire to save the Indians, U.S. officials always eventually acquiesced to the demands of the more powerful white settlers. Their plans for persuading the Indians to abandon their traditional ways and to adopt those of the white world were unrealistic and doomed to fail.

In fact, the American government took advantage of the growing Indian dependency on white goods and merchandise and of the concurrent loss of tribal economic self-sufficiency to deprive the Native Americans systematically of millions of acres of land. In return for the Indian land cessions, federal officials sought to compensate them with tribal annuities. But those payments further undermined Indian independence and set them on a path destined to make them virtual wards of the government. Blinded to the true causes of the Indian anger and resentment, frontier officials persisted in placing the blame for what they considered to be the Indians' savage behavior on British provocation. At the same time, the majority of their pioneer constituents could only see their Indian neighbors as barriers to progress and civility. For their part, the Indians alternated between favoring a course of violence and one of acquiescence. When they resorted to the former, the Americans responded in kind.

To help subdue the warring tribes that were threatening residents of the

Louisiana Territory in early 1812, Governor Howard authorized, on his own initiative, the formation of a company of mounted riflemen to act as rangers. These special militia groups were raised at federal expense to patrol sparsely populated frontier regions. While he was still seeking enlistments for the new unit, Howard learned from a story in the Washington, D.C., *National Intelligencer* that Congress had approved the raising of six ranger companies, one of which was designated for the Missouri Territory. He immediately altered the terms for enlistment to correspond with the new law's provisions. To speed the recruitment process, Howard did make one major modification: he called for three-month enlistments rather than the one-year terms provided for in the congressional measure. The rangers were to be paid seventy-five cents per day when on foot and one dollar per day when mounted.[28]

With Capt. Nathan Boone in command, the new ranger unit immediately advanced to the northern frontier, where it patrolled from the Salt River on the Mississippi to Loutre Creek on the Missouri. Boone, described by one of his contemporaries as "a remarkable woodsman who could climb like a bear and swim like a duck," was a popular choice for the difficult assignment. Boone's rangers and a company of regular soldiers from Fort Belle Fontaine constructed Fort Mason on the Mississippi, near present-day Hannibal, about fifteen miles above the Salt River.[29] Elsewhere in the exposed St. Charles district, the settlers erected a string of crude forts, extending from Fort Mason to Cooper's Fort at the Boonslick. The editor of the *Missouri Gazette* praised those efforts and hailed Boone's rangers to be "as fine a body of hardy woodsmen as ever took the field." Following the expiration of their original three-month hitch, the rangers returned to their homes, but many agreed to reenlist for a full year when their leader raised the congressionally authorized company in June 1812.[30]

Military recruitment was a difficult task for Louisiana's territorial officials. Lt. Col. Auguste Chouteau had been forced to convene a court-martial and fine several citizens after they failed to respond to Governor Lewis's call to arms in the spring of 1809.[31] The situation did not improve when it became common knowledge that men previously summoned to duty had not been paid for their services. The federal government's failure to compensate the troops Lewis sent to relieve Fort Madison in 1809 popularized the notion that men called into service could be certain of payment only if the governor had received advanced authorization to recruit them. The reluctance to volunteer was serious enough to compel Governor Howard to issue his personal pledge that the enlistees would be paid.[32]

The growing danger of war and the constant problems of Indian defense in the Louisiana Territory led to an intensified campaign for a second-class government. Most Louisianans believed that the new form of government would offer them a more satisfactory means for making their views known to federal officials. In their renewed efforts to build popular support for the measure, proponents of the change in status pointed out that it would give the residents a voice in making their own laws through the creation of an elected territorial house of representatives. Other desirable features they touted included the right to send a delegate to Congress and the separation of local legislative and judicial authority.[33]

The renewed impetus for a second-grade government benefited from the popular belief that the general government was badly misinformed about territorial conditions. Since the political structure for first-class territories provided no means for regular, direct communication between the local citizenry and their government in Washington, the prospect of electing a congressional delegate appealed to many territorial residents as a way to keep Congress better informed about their needs and concerns. Such a dialogue, they reasoned, would be a first step in settling perennial territorial problems caused by unconfirmed land titles, inadequate defenses, unsatisfactory mail service, and similar matters.[34]

As in the earlier attempt to secure a higher territorial classification, much of the debate focused on the issue of territorial finances. A letter from "Old Farmer" in the *Missouri Gazette* revived Joseph Charless's earlier charge that the proposed change in governments would necessitate a ruinous increase in local property taxes. Predictions that the search for additional revenue might force officials to tax uncultivated lands particularly alarmed speculators with extensive holdings. Supporters of the proposed change countered all such dire projections with complicated statistical data purporting to show that the costs of the higher stage of government would not be prohibitive. They reasoned that the expected increases in population would bring in sufficient additional revenues to offset the higher costs.[35]

But the fear of increased taxes was not the only reason opponents resisted advancement to a second-class territory. Realizing that the U.S. electoral system would likely favor the champions of the ambitious, land-hungry American newcomers at their expense, the old-guard French Creole leaders struggled, as they always had, to prevent full implementation of democratic government in their territory. They remained comfortable with the 1805 arrangements placing Upper Louisiana under the authority of a governor, a secretary, and three judges, all appointed by the president. Any change in governmental forms seemed certain to further diminish their ability to influence local decisions. For them the old way was clearly the best, but the tide of history and immigration was against them.[36]

Their efforts to postpone the change were destined to fail. The American commitment to self-government and the firmly established pattern of territorial advancement virtually assured success for those seeking to raise Louisiana to the higher classification. When Congress again considered a bill granting Louisiana a second-class government in November 1811, proponents of the measure introduced numerous petitions signed by territorial residents supporting the change. Once the bill reached the floor, members briefly debated whether to grant freehold or universal suffrage. The legislation then cleared both houses unopposed, and President Madison signed it into law on 4 June 1812, three days after he had asked Congress to declare war on Great Britain.[37]

The new territorial law also authorized a name change: the Territory of Louisiana became the Territory of Missouri. Henceforth, Missouri was to bear the name of the great river that had done so much to shape its history. All that remained was for the people of the territory and later the state to decide how to pronounce it. Was it "Missouruh" or "Missouree"?[38]

If, as Missourians generally believed, the advancement in territorial status held out the promise of improved defenses, the measure came at an opportune moment. On 18 June, Congress approved a formal declaration of war against Great Britain. When word of the decision to go to war reached the territory in early July 1812, local residents reacted to the news with mixed feelings. Because their exposed location on the frontier made them vulnerable to attack, they pondered what new dangers the conflict was apt to bring. But they also hoped that a showdown with the British and their Indian allies would eventually lead to a general pacification of the territory. Recalling the glory days of the Revolutionary War, the bombastic westerners rallied around the Stars and Stripes to the strains of a ditty sung to the tune of Yankee Doodle:

> The tocsin sounds, to arms my boys,
> Our ancient foe's for fighting,
> Tis time to quit these wordy wars,
> And treat with home made lightning.
> Saratoga to them all,
> Bunker Hill confound them,
> Soon the Canadas shall fall,
> When Freedom's Sons surround them.[39]

As residents of the Missouri borderland braced for a new outbreak of hostilities, Governor Howard inspected conditions in the exposed St. Charles district. Meanwhile, hastily convened meetings in St. Louis and St. Charles unanimously adopted resolutions supporting the war and calling upon the U.S. government to provide greater military and financial assistance.[40]

During the opening months of the war, the situation along Missouri's extended frontiers failed to improve. Reports reaching St. Louis indicated that the Winnebago, Kickapoo, Potawatomi, Shawnee, and Miami Indians had declared war on the United States during a council held at the Rock River Sac villages. Several other nearby tribes reportedly were still pondering their course of action. Within the territory a party of about seventy hostile Winnebagos, Ioways, and Otos roamed the countryside between the Boonslick settlements and Fort Osage, and more than one hundred unfriendly Sacs were camped a short distance above the Salt River.[41]

The governor dispatched Pierre Chouteau to Prairie du Chien in late July to take stock of the situation along the upper Mississippi. Chouteau returned in mid-August, warning that the British in Canada might soon launch a general offensive against the United States.[42] On the heels of this dismal news came reports that the American attempt to split the Canadian forces and isolate England's Indian supporters had collapsed with Gen. William Hull's capitulation and the seizure of the U.S. forts at Mackinac, Chicago, and Detroit. With so much bad news, the St. Louis board of trustees urged Governor Howard to send Pierre Chouteau to the Osage villages to invite that tribe to declare war on all tribes hostile to the United States. But Howard had already taken measures to secure the territory with the deployment of four militia companies. According to Colonel Bissell, the commander at Fort Belle Fontaine, the governor's skillful use of those forces had kept the Indians in awe and saved the frontier for the current season.[43]

In the fall of 1812, Missourians launched an intensive campaign to bring their plight to the attention of federal authorities. They asked Governor Howard to go to the national capital to press for greater federal participation in the western campaigns. Although Howard initially agreed, he altered his plans and remained in Kentucky. Howard, who said only that circumstances prevented him from making the trip, may have been considering returning to his native state permanently. Judge John B. C. Lucas reported from Louisville that the governor had been sizing up prospects there for a seat in the U.S. Senate. Howard did, nonetheless, write a lengthy letter to Secretary of War John Armstrong urging improvements in the Missouri Territory's defensive posture as the best way for averting another military disaster comparable to the Hull debacle.[44]

At the same time, Howard proposed a major offensive campaign against the belligerent western tribes designed to end their depredations once and for all. He argued that in the long run his plan would be less costly to the U.S. government, but the secretary of war declined to underwrite such an ambitious undertaking.[45] The national government's reluctance to move strongly against the Indians was a sore point with territorial Missourians, who considered it unrealistic to assume that an adequate defensive force could be raised locally. Benjamin Cooper and the Boonslick settlers reacted angrily when William Clark, the commander of the territorial militia, informed them following the outbreak of the war that he could not spare any men to defend their remote settlements. They rejected his suggestion that they relocate in more secure areas and defiantly vowed to stand their ground in their fortified enclaves.[46]

Although they remained willing to do their part, the backwoods pioneers believed that added federal help was essential. They particularly objected to the U.S. army's failure to maintain a large permanent contingent of regular troops in their territory. At the outset of the war, there were fewer than 250 regular soldiers stationed in all of the American posts west of the Mississippi.[47]

When Missourians went to the polls for the first time in November 1812 to elect a nonvoting delegate to Congress, all of the candidates promised to work for increased federal assistance for territorial defense. Edward Hempstead, Rufus Easton, Samuel Hammond, and Matthew Lyon declared themselves in the race, but the real contest pitted Hempstead against Easton. Hempstead enjoyed the backing of the French Creoles and the long-established Americans, and Easton drew his support principally from the territory's southern districts and the newer American arrivals. Hempstead emerged victorious, and for the moment the old elite that had long dominated territorial affairs remained in control.[48] True to his word, the new territorial delegate lobbied vigorously in Washington, D.C., for added military support in the Missouri Territory. In January, Hempstead confidently predicted that by spring his constituents would have a force adequate for defense and for chastising the Indians. His optimism seemed justified, for in mid-February he announced that Congress had agreed to authorize the raising of ten companies of rangers, including three for the Missouri Territory. But the mails were slow, and that news did not reach St. Louis for another month.[49]

In the meantime, reports of suspicious Indian activity in the vicinity of Fort Mason and predictions of a pending British-Indian attack kept territorial Missourians in a state of agitation. Public meetings were held in St. Louis to explore ways of preparing their town for the expected assault. During a preliminary gathering on 15 February, several concerned citizens approved the creation of a committee to formulate a plan of action. Two days later at a town forum, the committee presented its hastily drawn report, which called for the creation of a local committee of public safety vested with unlimited authority to adopt measures for defending the city. The participants at the second session endorsed the committee's recommendations. Among their resolutions was an unconsciously ironical proviso declaring that since they constituted a free and voluntary association for objects of mutual concern, those who failed to cooperate would be treated as enemies of the territory.[50]

Remembering, no doubt, that similar preparations had saved the city in 1780, Auguste Chouteau agreed to head the public safety committee. Its members first conferred with Frederick Bates, who in Howard's absence was again serving as acting governor. Bates informed them that he was attempting to gauge the accuracy of reports predicting the territory would soon be attacked, but he cautioned the St. Louis group against expecting any direct assistance from his office inasmuch as he had not been empowered to authorize additional expenditures for St. Louis's defense.[51] Bates's reluctance to sanction an emergency appropriation undoubtedly stemmed in part from his recollections of the difficulties Governor Lewis had encountered in seeking federal reimbursement for unauthorized expenditures.

Chouteau's committee next appealed to the St. Louis board of trustees for assistance, but they declined on the grounds that they lacked legal authority to compel citizens to erect or repair military fortifications. Having concluded that private efforts would be required to supplement their city's defenses, the committee initiated plans for digging trenches around the town's outskirts, repairing three or four of the dilapidated Spanish blockhouses, mounting the few available cannons, and surrounding the village with a palisade.[52]

For their part, the St. Louis trustees called upon the acting governor to order additional military forces to their town to ward off the impending assault. Bates declared any such action premature, but he did instruct the volunteer militia companies to muster on 20 March 1813, with the stipulation that thereafter they should be prepared to report for active duty at a moment's notice.[53]

In the midst of the adversity and uncertainly unleashed by the War of 1812, the territory needed a strong and effective leader at the helm. Had Governor Howard remained in St. Louis for longer periods of time, he might have provided that leadership, but his frequent absences from the territory contributed to an unevenness in military and administrative operations. Howard may have been a more serious offender than most of his counterparts, but absentee officials were a perennial territorial problem, aggravated by the practice of appointing outsiders to fill territorial offices. Designating the territorial secretary to serve as acting governor in the absence of the regular executive offered only a partial solution.[54]

In the Missouri Territory, Governors Lewis and Howard were the most serious offenders in that regard. Whereas Lewis's prolonged absences had been a nuisance, wartime conditions made Howard's frequent departures from the territory potentially more serious. In the midst of the mounting crisis in early 1813, Bates advised the absent governor, "We are almost in despair on account of your silence."[55] Howard's absenteeism occasioned some criticism, but his success in defending the territory with the limited resources at his disposal allowed him to retain his local popularity. Even in the darkest moments, territorial Missourians chose to ascribe their woes to the federal government's inaction rather than the governor's inattention.[56]

Governor Howard was away from the territory when word of a Potawatomi murder at nearby Portage des Sioux reached St. Louis in March 1813. The incident prompted Bates to send Indian agent Pierre Chouteau to the Osage villages to confirm the tribe's continuing support for the United States and to recruit a body of warriors to oppose the pro-British Indians reportedly massing for an attack against the trans-Mississippi region. Following his return to the territory, the governor countermanded Bates's instructions for raising Indian troops, but by the time Chouteau learned of these latest orders he had assembled a party of 260 well-armed braves at the mouth of the Osage River. Though Chouteau trusted his Osage friends, others did not share his assessment. Governor Howard considered the presence of a large, armed Indian force in the vicinity of St. Louis too great a risk to take for any help they might render, and Edward Hempstead, Missouri's territorial delegate, went so far as to warn the War Department that the "savage allies . . . might without much risque destroy those they came to protect."[57]

The decision to dismiss the Osages embarrassed Chouteau and complicated his efforts to secure Osage acquiescence to the decision to evacuate Fort Osage. Despite their disappointment, the Osages remained loyal to the United States, thanks in large part to Chouteau's exertions.[58] It would be hard to overstate the importance of that tribe's continuing support, for, as William Clark later advised Secretary of War James Monroe, "Should only the half of their force be turned against these Territories, the scattered population within it will not be adequate to their defence against such a herd of Savages."[59]

Since the outbreak of the war, federal officials had favored closing Fort Osage and removing the trading factory there to a new and less exposed location. Governor Howard and Colonel Bissell finally ordered the installation's evacuation in the spring of 1813. George Sibley, the factor at the fort, arrived in St. Louis in early June with his goods.[60] As part of a general plan to shorten the line of territorial defenses, Howard and Bissell also decided to construct a blockhouse at Portage des Sioux. Following its completion, the installation served as the principal base camp for subsequent military operations in the territory. With numerous militia companies on duty along the northern frontiers and with armed gunboats simultaneously patrolling the rivers, the momentary hysteria that had gripped the Missouri Territory began to subside.[61] In mid-March, Hempstead's letter informing his constituents of the congressional decision earlier in the year to authorize the recruitment of three new companies of rangers for the Missouri Territory further eased the tensions. In light of these favorable developments, the people of St. Louis felt secure enough to abandon their costly plans for picketing their town.[62]

The War Department also moved to improve the general conduct of its military operations by reorganizing the entire army command structure. The new system divided the United States into nine military districts. The eighth military department, which encompassed the states of Kentucky and Ohio and the territories of Indiana, Illinois, Michigan, and Missouri, was placed under the command of Gen. William H. Harrison.[63] To direct military operations in the western part of the eighth district, President Madison issued a special commission to Governor Benjamin Howard, making him a brigadier general in the U.S. army and placing him in charge of all forces in the territories of Missouri and Illinois. Madison had given Howard the option of either taking the new military position or of continuing in his current post as governor of the Missouri Territory. Having already decided not to seek reappointment as governor, Howard immediately accepted the military commission and surrendered his office as Missouri's territorial chief executive. In accordance with the president's wishes, William Clark reconsidered his earlier refusal to accept the governorship and agreed to serve as Howard's replacement.[64]

Despite these elaborate precautions, periodic outbreaks of violence served as unpleasant reminders of the continuing dangers of living in the American outback, where the constraints of civilized society were loosened and where life was often a struggle. Such was the case in August 1813 when a Sac war party attacked several men and boys sowing turnips in their fields not far from Fort Howard, a stockade fort in present-day Lincoln County. The marauding Indians escaped across the Mississippi, but General Howard subsequently organized and led a military expedition up the Mississippi and Illinois rivers to chastise the warring tribes inhabiting those regions.[65]

While Howard was pursing hostile Indians in the Illinois Territory, U.S. officials invited Sac and Fox factions more favorably disposed to the United States to vacate their villages along the Mississippi and take up winter quarters on the south bank of the Missouri in Moniteau County. In relocating these friendly Indians in the heart of the Missouri Territory, the American authorities hoped to sequester them from the influence of designing British agents and belligerent tribes. In late September, 155 canoes carrying the migrating Sacs and Foxes rendezvoused near Portage des Sioux, where their leaders conferred with Governor Clark and received supplies of beef, pork, salt, and flour. In return for Sac promises to live in peace with their old enemies the Osages, the U.S. agreed to establish a trading factory on Little Moniteau Creek under the agency of John Johnson.[66] At the same time, Governor Clark dispatched George Sibley to Arrow Rock, where he erected a similar facility to replace the one recently closed at Fort Osage. By November, Sibley announced he was ready to do business with the Osages at his new location on the Missouri.[67] Initially the transplanted Sacs settled peacefully into their new surroundings. Samuel Cole recalled that as a boy, he and young Black Hawk, the great future Sac leader, often hunted together on the Moniteau.[68]

The successful resettlement of the Sacs and Foxes on the Missouri, the reopening of the trading factories in mid-Missouri, General Howard's selection to superintend territorial defenses, and the deployment in St. Louis of the First Regiment of the U.S. infantry brought renewed hope to the war-conscious residents. Experience had taught them, however, that they could not afford to let down their guard. They kept a watchful eye on developments both nationally and locally, and their mood fluctuated according to the changing tide of combat. The welcome news of Oliver Hazard Perry's great naval victory on Lake Erie lifted their sagging spirits. His military triumph signaled that U.S. prospects seemed to be improving at last, and in a spontaneous celebration, a group of revelers set a canoe on fire and drew the blazing craft through the St. Louis streets in a torchlight procession.[69]

The upbeat mood persisted despite the announcement that the American troops at Fort Madison in Iowa had been forced to abandon their post. General Howard's return from his successful campaign in the Illinois Territory and the news that the dreaded Indian organizer Tecumseh had been killed in combat had been sufficient to blunt the impact of the report disclosing the fort's surrender. In October, General Harrison sent word that he had arranged a truce with many of the warring tribes, and by the end of 1813 there was even talk in St. Louis that the war might soon be over.[70]

The scenario was all too familiar when the temporary euphoria at year's end gave way to renewed anguish and alarm with spring's return. In contrast to the positive developments during the closing months of 1813, a series of unforeseen happenings in early 1814 again dashed the hopes of the war-weary Missourians. In January, General Howard received orders to report to General Harrison at Cincinnati.[71] The popular and successful general's removal and, more importantly, the withdrawal of a portion of the regular troops recently stationed in St. Louis again left the territory heavily dependent upon its own limited forces. Territorial residents reacted immediately to the news of the new orders. A group of disgruntled St. Louis citizens convened a town meeting on 2 February to express their displeasure with this latest turn of events and to remonstrate against the federal government's failure to provide adequately for their defense.[72]

Primary responsibility for the unpopular changes must be laid at the feet of General Harrison. It had been his idea to send General Howard to Detroit as a replacement for Gen. Lewis Cass. General Harrison had informed Secretary of War Armstrong that it was possible to dispense with Howard's services in the Missouri Territory because Governor Clark's military talents and his superb knowledge of Indians qualified him to direct operations there. He also indicated that a single ranger company in St. Louis could provide adequate local protection.[73] The secretary of war agreed to Harrison's recommendation reassigning General Howard, but he decided to consult the western commander concerning the number of rangers needed for service in Missouri.[74]

At his post in the national capital, Territorial Delegate Edward Hempstead vigorously pressed Missouri's cause with members of Congress and the executive department. Eventually the combined effect of Hempstead's relentless efforts, the strongly worded memorials from territorial residents to federal officials, Governor Clark's urgent requests for more assistance, and a letter from General Howard corroborating the validity of these various petitions persuaded the War Department to countermand its earlier order and return General Howard and his troops to St. Louis.[75]

In Howard's absence, Governor Clark had assumed responsibility for directing military operations in the western territories. Acting on his own authority, he dispatched an expedition up the Mississippi for the purpose of securing Prairie du Chien, a post located on the river about five hundred miles above St. Louis in what is today southern Wisconsin. The governor believed that an American military garrison at that site would effectively isolate the Indians on the lower Mississippi from their British allies in Canada and thereby forestall renewed Indian hostilities in the valley the following spring. Clark informed Secretary Armstrong that he had most of the necessary provisions for the undertaking on hand and that all other expenses could be paid out of the Indian fund. Armstrong privately questioned the advisability of establishing a post in the heart of enemy country, but he made no move to stop the force, which by that time had already departed from St. Louis.[76]

Governor Clark personally took charge of the expedition, which arrived at Prairie du Chien on 2 June 1814. Once the initial stages of construction at the fort had been completed, he turned the command over to Lt. Joseph Perkins and headed back downriver.[77] Soon after Clark's return to St. Louis,

General Howard, who had backed the plan for stationing a military garrison at the northern outpost, requested authorization to send reinforcements to guarantee the safety of the troops assigned there. His action came too late, however, to save the fortification, which was overrun by a combined British-Indian force on 19 July.[78]

The news closer to home was no better. Settling the Sacs along the banks of the Missouri and removing the trading factory from Fort Osage to Arrow Rock had spawned growing ill will among the Osages. When one of their war parties killed Elijah Eastwood along the Gasconade in 1814, territorial officials immediately sent Pierre Chouteau to apprehend the culprits and repair the damaged relations between the U.S. and its Osage allies.[79] Continuing Osage support seemed especially crucial after Sac renegades committed a series of murders and mutilations in several remote settlements.[80]

Pro-British Sac dissidents from the Rock River villages were the primary instigators of this latest mayhem. Following their arrival at the Sac village on the Missouri during the spring of 1814, they hoisted a British flag and demanded several bottles of whiskey as their price for taking it down. Later in the summer, the same band unsuccessfully attempted to raise the British Union Jack at an Osage village. In the wake of the renewed killing and violence, John Johnson and George Sibley closed their trading factories at Little Moniteau Creek and Arrow Rock, packed up the merchandise and equipment, and returned to the relative safety of St. Louis.[81] The settlers living on the south side of the river abandoned their homes and took refuge at Cooper's Fort, Kinkaid's Fort, or one of the other stockade forts on the north shore.[82] Unarmed slaves were especially at risk. Indians killed Joe, a black man, while he was working alone near McLain's Fort, and during a later attack at Cote sans Dessein, Barney Farmer, a young black, remembered that he and several other unarmed slaves had been left in one of the forts with the women and children. When Manuel Lisa visited the Boonslick settlements in early August 1814, he sent word that the Indians were still on a rampage, roaming about the countryside killing isolated settlers, stealing horses, and shooting cattle for food. The settlers, he reported, were barricaded in their forts.[83]

General Howard dispatched three militia companies under Col. Henry Dodge's command to Cooper's Fort in Howard County, where they joined forces with Capt. Benjamin Cooper's local militia outfit. A party of friendly Shawnee Indians, recruited by Kaskaskia merchant Pierre Menard from the Apple Creek village, accompanied the Dodge expedition as guides and scouts. The combined military units pursued the enemy Indians, who melted into the surrounding woods. Dodge's men, with assistance from their Shawnee allies, took a number of the fleeing Miamis as prisoners with the clear understanding that the captives would not be killed. The subsequent discovery of a rifle in the possession of one of the Indian prisoners that had belonged to a man murdered during a recent attack prompted the aroused Boonslick volunteers to call for the Indian's immediate execution. Emotions reached a fevered pitch when Colonel Dodge attempted to shield the Indian prisoner in accordance with the original surrender terms. The men in Capt. Sarshall Cooper's company threatened to kill all of the prisoners in retaliation, but despite a few tense moments Colonel Dodge held firm and insisted on honoring the original agreement to spare the Indians.[84]

General Howard's death in September came as an added shock to the war-weary inhabitants of the Missouri Territory. They had respected the popular general's military savvy.[85] His loss, combined with the recent military reverses, gave rise to the notion that in the absence of some dramatic move by the U.S. forces, the territory was doomed to endure a long and bloody conflict. An exasperated St. Louis merchant, Christian Wilt, called upon the Americans to rise en masse and drive the British from North America and slay every Indian from St. Louis to the Rocky Mountains.[86] Governor Clark employed less graphic language, but his message was the same as he urged the national government to render immediate additional military assistance.[87]

While Clark called for stronger action from his post in Missouri, Rufus Easton had moved to Washington to step up efforts in the capital city for added federal support. Easton, who was making a political comeback following the reverses he had suffered during the Wilkinson years, had replaced Hempstead as the territory's delegate to Congress in 1814. Like his predecessor, who had declined to seek reelection, Easton took his duties seriously, often working in close tandem with other territorial representatives.[88] With each year, it was becoming increasingly difficult to raise a fighting force locally. The repeated calls to arms had taken their toll, and the U.S. government's failure to pay many of the militiamen for services rendered in 1812 and 1813 had roused widespread resentment among the veterans of frontier fighting. In early 1815 Col. Alexander McNair traveled to the federal city to plead in person for funds to compensate the unpaid rangers and militia.[89]

The sudden announcement of the war's end caught territorial residents off guard. Word that Gen. Andrew Jackson and his Kentucky riflemen had soundly trounced a larger British force at New Orleans set off celebrations in St. Louis and the other settlements, but the subsequent disclosure of the terms of the Treaty of Ghent, signed by the American commissioners to conclude formally the War of 1812, did not occasion similar popular acclaim. Article IX of the treaty, which called for immediate cessation of hostilities against the Indians and a return of the rights and privileges to which the Indians had been entitled before the war—providing that they also refrained from any further belligerence—generated intense criticism in Missouri.[90] The idea of suspending all further military operations against the Indians ran counter to convictions held by both the military and civilian sectors of the population. Christian Wilt reiterated his earlier view that "it is the Opinion of the People here that we shall not have peace with the Indians until we drub them soundly into it."[91]

The close of the conflict left the warring Indian tribes equally angry and bewildered. They had expected their British allies to continue to fight until the Americans had been driven back to their earlier boundaries. Britain's sudden withdrawal from the contest greatly altered their situation. In their confused state, the tribes debated what course to follow. Some remained determined to push ahead with the fight against their American adversaries; others displayed uncertainty.

The reluctance of warring parties on both sides to lay down their arms added to the confusion and mutual mistrust. In mid-April, Governor Clark advised the secretary of war that Indians had killed ten men on the frontier since 20 March and that the situation showed no signs of improvement.[92] On 20 May, a party of Rock River Sacs and Foxes massacred a family of five on the Missouri near Femme Osage, and four days later militia units engaged an Indian force in the bloody Battle of the Sink Hole near the Cuivre River.[93] These continuing depredations complicated the tasks facing Governor Clark, Governor Ninian Edwards of the Illinois Territory, and Auguste Chouteau—the three commissioners appointed by President Madison to negotiate a settlement with the various Indian tribes. Chouteau had been tapped to serve with the governors after Col. Alexander McNair, who later became the state of Missouri's first governor, declined the post and recommended the venerable French Creole leader. The commissioners wasted no time in condemning the latest Indian atrocities and calling upon federal authorities to use force against the belligerent tribesmen.[94]

Meanwhile, the American negotiators dispatched thirty-seven messages to various Indian nations, summoning them to meet at Portage des Sioux in July 1815 for a general council to terminate all hostilities.[95] When the three commissioners arrived at the military headquarters in early July, between two and three thousand Indians were camped nearby. The diverse array of temporary Indian lodges and the distinctive tribal costumes created a colorful spectacle as members of the Sioux, Omaha, Ioway, Shawnee, Delaware, and other tribes gathered to confer with the U.S. authorities. Some tribes were conspicuously absent, notably the Rock River Sacs and Foxes, the Winnebagos, the Ioways, and the Kickapoos.[96]

To forestall any possible trouble from the sizable assemblage, the American commissioners had arranged to station nearby two fully manned gunboats and a force of 275 regulars under the command of Col. John Miller.[97] The formal proceedings began on 6 July with the ritualized oratory and gift exchanges that were standard for all such occasions. The U.S. government supplied the commissioners with thirty thousand dollars worth of merchandise to help grease the wheels of the diplomatic machinery.[98] Some tribes agreed to terms quickly, and others took their time in accepting the settlements offered them. The negotiations continued throughout the summer as tribal delegations came and went at Portage des Sioux. When the peace commissioners finally returned to St. Louis in October, there were still a few holdouts, but the vast majority of tribes had submitted to U.S. authority.[99]

Not everyone in the white community was pleased with the handling of the negotiations. Many Missourians continued to press for forcible coercion to chastise properly the errant tribes, and they openly complained about the government's alleged lavish spending on the Indians and the "Indian treaty-men."[100] The mounting public criticism lessened William Clark's popularity and may have contributed to his loss to Alexander McNair in the 1820 gubernatorial campaign, but for the careful observer of the events during the summer of 1815, the message was clear: the Indians' days in the Missouri Territory were numbered. Having lost their British allies, they could not resist the encroachment of the hordes of settlers already beginning to pour into the territory. "You need not be alarmed about the Indians—they will never venture upon this quarter of the world—the country is populating too rapidly to fear them," wrote land speculator Justus Post from the Missouri Territory in November 1815.[101] Post's prediction proved remarkably prescient. Although sporadic Indian outbursts would continue in the territory during the succeeding years, a steady influx of new settlers—the true frontier soldiers—accomplished what inadequate military forces had been unable to achieve. After 1815 the Indian threat steadily declined in Missouri.

The years of uncertainty, intermittent fighting, and general confusion had, nonetheless, taken their toll. Between 1804 and 1810 the territorial population had doubled, but the threat of war with Great Britain, the concomitant fear of renewed Indian raids, and the destructive and demoralizing New Madrid earthquakes combined to impede territorial development and expansion between 1810 and 1815. A few hardy souls had come to Missouri during the war years, but the constant talk of Indian attack caused others to flee the territory. Settlers in the more remote frontier areas had been forced to abandon temporarily their homesteads and withdraw to safer areas. Even seasoned pioneers like the Coles retreated from the Boonslick for a brief period in 1815. Those who remained in the exposed interior regions huddled in stockade forts, reduced to subsisting on dried meat because their hunters were afraid to venture far beyond their fortified enclosures.[102]

Local businesspeople had also experienced numerous hardships. Prices fluctuated wildly in response to wartime economic dislocations, and unstable markets both nationally and locally made it difficult to secure supplies and to conduct routine commercial transactions. The repeated demands for service in militia and ranger units and the diminution in immigration combined to exacerbate the territory's chronic labor shortages. Specie, always in short supply on the frontier, grew even scarcer during the war years. Moses Austin advised against shipping much new merchandise to the territory because it would be apt to go begging for buyers. The economic hard times, he noted in early 1813, had forced many local residents to clothe themselves in Indian-dressed buckskin instead of broadcloth.[103]

The situation was particularly hard on Austin and Missouri's other lead producers. Despite an increased demand for lead and lead shot created by the war, the Potosi entrepreneur reported in late 1812 that economic stagnation, local labor shortages, and unusually severe weather conditions had brought work at the mines to a virtual standstill.[104] In an effort to stimulate economic activity and help alleviate the chronic shortage of capital, Austin joined with Auguste Chouteau, Manuel Lisa, and other prominent members of the territorial business community in spearheading a drive to establish a local bank. They secured a charter from the legislature in 1813 for the Bank of St. Louis, but the bank's directors failed to raise enough money through stock subscriptions to allow it to begin operation during the war.[105] Meanwhile, the mining business remained depressed locally until late in 1814. The British domination of the high seas interrupted commerce and effectively blocked the only feasible way of shipping Missouri lead to the eastern seaboard for sale.[106]

The war also adversely affected Missouri's important fur trade. After an attempt to revive its lagging fortunes through a general reorganization in 1812, the Missouri Fur Company formally went out of business in 1814.[107] In addition to its complicated organization and internal disagreements, the company also had to overcome added wartime burdens that played havoc with all trading operations. Indian hostilities, scarce supplies of trade goods, difficulties in carrying on business with Canadian-based firms, unpredictable international markets disrupted by the fighting in Europe and America, and a shortage of *engagés* to assist in transporting the goods to market were among the handicaps confronting the beleaguered traffickers in fur. The war forced a general retrenchment in trading operations until, by the war's end, Missouri traders found themselves confined to regions they had occupied prior to 1804. In 1814 Charles Gratiot, a St. Louis trader and businessman, informed John Jacob Astor in New York that whereas in normal years traders in St. Louis could expect to receive as many as 1,000 packs of deerskins and assorted fine furs, only 120 deerskin packs reached the territorial capital that year.[108]

To offset losses from the shrinking fur trade, many territorial merchants turned their attention to the task of supplying the U.S. government's local needs. In addition to the normal federal expenditures for routine frontier operations, the greatly expanded military efforts opened new opportunities for the business community. Equipping the militia was an especially profitable venture. Since the law required each member of the militia to provide himself with a good musket or rifle, a knapsack and pouch, cartridges or powder horn, powder and balls, and other miscellaneous items, territorial merchants did a land-office business whenever companies formed to go out on patrol, often selling the merchandise at higher prices than usual. Capitalizing upon the wartime demand for gunpowder, William H. Ashley made use of the potassium nitrate he discovered in an Ozark cave to establish a powder factory at Mine Shibboleth. For the moment, the gunpowder business was more promising than the lead business, and between his periodic militia tours, Colonel Ashley devoted much of his attention to producing the scarce commodity.[109]

Although territorial residents chronically complained about the inadequacy of the national government's contribution to the war effort, it is clear that federal subsidies played a vital role in sustaining the local economy during these troubled years. Officials often purchased provisions for the militia and trade goods for the Indians from local firms, and the payment of the troops always stimulated business activity in the territory. When the monies were delayed, the local merchants complained bitterly.[110]

During peacetime the situation was somewhat different. Federal authorities constantly sought to minimize territorial expenses. The national government paid only the salaries of officials appointed by the president. It also paid for miscellaneous clerical and office expenses, but the combined costs of civil administration seldom exceeded ten thousand dollars a year in the Missouri Territory.[111] Congress tended to be more liberal in authorizing expenditures for adjusting land claims and, although allocations proved adequate for that purpose, they could hardly be termed excessive. Indian business and frontier defense always constituted the bulk of federal expenditures in the territory. Since the army maintained only a small complement of regular troops in Missouri, the regular military expenses remained limited. William Clark estimated that the federal government spent approximately thirty-four thousand dollars per year for all Indian expenses in the Missouri Territory.

Administration officials in Washington frequently warned territorial officers not to exceed the amounts appropriated by Congress for their expenses, and they sometimes refused to approve payment of expenditures authorized by local officials without prior clearance. Territorial residents, who always overestimated the national government's resources, undoubtedly exaggerated the paucity of federal assistance. Nevertheless, with the exception of the war years, direct federal subsidies played a proportionately lesser role in the settlement and development of Missouri than in later territories, where governmental expenditures sometimes became the mainstay of the local economy.[112]

The long-awaited upturn in economic activity closely followed the end of the war, and the year 1815 witnessed a dramatic reversal in Missouri's economic fortunes. The flow of incoming settlers, which had slowed to a trickle after 1810, suddenly became a virtual tidal wave. Rangers who had roamed through the hills of mid-Missouri in pursuit of Indians during the war came back with glowing tales of the richness of the land; many now returned to settle permanently.[113] Land prices rose so rapidly that even land speculators wished for a temporary leveling off in the boom so they could acquire additional lands and take full advantage of the situation.[114] By the end of 1815 it was clear that Missouri had turned a corner and that the territory had entered a new and final phase prior to achieving statehood.

CHAPTER FOURTEEN
A LAND
OF PROMISE

Immediately following the War of 1812, everything in the Missouri Territory seemed to be in motion as emigrants flooded into the region in unprecedented numbers. They traveled on foot, on horseback, by wagon, and sometimes part of the way by flatboat. Caravans of movers, predominantly from Kentucky, Tennessee, Virginia, and the Carolinas, regularly crossed the Mississippi seeking new homes in the territory's productive unsettled lands. To frontier preacher John Mason Peck, Kentucky and Tennessee appeared to be breaking up and moving west.[1] An observant St. Charles resident watching the newcomers passing on their way to unoccupied lands in Missouri's Boonslick and Salt River regions left this account of the colorful spectacle: "The tinkling of bells, the cloud of dust, the throngs of hogs and cattle, the white headed children, the curly headed Africans, smiling infancy, blooming virgins, athletic manhood and decrepit age, altogether form groups too interesting to be painted by the pencil of Teniers."[2]

The territorial population increased from an estimated twenty-five thousand in 1814 to more than sixty-six thousand in 1820. The newcomers were a cross section of humanity, predominantly from lowland regions in the upper South, especially the Tidewater and Piedmont areas of Virginia and the Carolinas, the Kentucky Bluegrass region, and the Nashville basin. Many were small farmers who headed west with their families anticipating that they could acquire cheaper and more productive land than was available in the older states. In the popular imagination, the Missouri Territory was a land of promise: any country with land good enough to attract so many Kentuckians had to have a great deal to offer.[3] The absence of antislavery restrictions further enhanced the region's drawing power in the Old South. The numerous plain folk flooding into Missouri in search of a better life found themselves in the diverse company of ambitious entrepreneurs, energetic professionals, reckless adventurers, and fleeing felons, all eager to profit from unfolding opportunities in the burgeoning territory.

The ranks of Missouri's newcomers included many well-educated individuals with substantial means. Thomas Hart Benton, Beverly Tucker, Justus Post, Henry Vest Bingham, and Thomas and John Hardeman were typical of this group. Benton, a rising young lawyer-politician whose budding career in Tennessee had come to an abrupt end following a bloody brawl with Andrew Jackson in a Nashville hotel, arrived in St. Louis in 1815 desiring a new start. His first acquaintance there was Charles Gratiot, who invited him to take up residence in his home. Benton's friendship with the Creole leader gave him an immediate entree into the best circles in the territorial capital and initiated his close early association with members of the St. Louis establishment.

The same year Tucker, an affluent Virginian and a graduate of the College of William and Mary, sold his interest in property he had inherited and set out for the Missouri Territory with his wife Polly, their two children, and several slaves. Tucker, who was intent on replicating a true Virginia settlement with its hierarchal social system, found the preponderance of southerners among the incoming settlers to his liking. But despite the commonality of their origins, Tucker's elitist notions were clearly at odds with the more democratic Jeffersonian vision of simple yeomen on frontier freeholds espoused by most of his rank-and-file Missouri neighbors.[4]

Not everyone entering the flourishing territory came from south of the Mason-Dixon line. The Posts were prosperous Yankee emigrants who arrived in St. Louis in 1815. Eliza Post may have had some doubts about moving to "that wilderness among the Indians," but her husband, a West Point graduate, was confident that he could make a fortune through land speculation.[5] Despite their northern backgrounds, the Posts quickly adapted to the prevailing southern ways. Post advised his brother in Vermont, who was considering a move to the Missouri Territory, "There is one thing you must reconcile your mind to when you get in this region, that is the owning of slaves." Post had already acquired five black women, and he intended to purchase two black males, whom he pledged to provide with three things: "victuals, clothes & work in abundance."[6]

Bingham first came west from his native Virginia in 1818 searching for somewhere to relocate his family. During that brief reconnaissance trip, he concluded that the Missouri Territory was the place for them, and the following year the Binghams settled in Howard County. Henry, the father of artist George Caleb Bingham, quickly won acceptance in the booming community of Franklin, where he operated a popular tavern-hotel north of the public square. He subsequently purchased a farm near Arrow Rock, began cultivating tobacco, and established a factory for processing it.[7]

Thomas Hardeman was sixty-six years old in June 1816 when he again yielded to the wilderness call and headed for the Missouri Territory. The pioneer's wanderings already had taken him from his Virginia birthplace to North Carolina and from there to Tennessee, where he and his numerous progeny had established themselves as successful planters, merchants, and politicians. Once Hardeman saw the Boonslick country, he determined to make it his new home. He immediately purchased land and set about to replicate his success as a slaveholding Tennessee planter. Various family members followed him to the booming territory. His son John, an experienced merchant with capital, opened a store in Franklin and established an experimental farm on the north bank of the Missouri River that won acclaim as a botanical showplace.[8]

The wealth of these "respectable families," while not opulent, enabled them to acquire improved properties with substantial frontier residential dwellings and tracts of cleared land. With their farms and their slaves, they were well on their way to establishing themselves in the familiar style of the small southern planter, raising grain, stock, tobacco, and hemp for export, and in the process putting down roots and creating new communities to replace those they had left.

Like the Binghams and the Hardemans, many of the postwar newcomers went directly to the territory's less populous interior sections. With the danger from serious Indian depredations rapidly subsiding, the Boonslick country was especially popular with the new emigrants. In 1816 there were fewer than a thousand persons residing on both sides of the Missouri between the mouth of the Osage and the western Indian boundary, but four years later the same region boasted a population in excess of twenty thousand, including more than three thousand Afro-American slaves. The rich loess soil, the plentiful supply of timber, the salt springs, the accessibility of the Missouri River, and the draw of the Boone family name made the Boonslick country a favorite choice among westering American settlers.[9]

In selecting a place to locate, the pioneers looked for timbered land of good quality that could be easily cleared for cultivation. They initially avoided prairie lands, which prevailing theories held to be inferior agriculturally and which they found difficult to break with their shovel plows because of its thick sod. They chose instead the sparsely forested regions situated near the edge of the prairies. This gave them the best of both worlds—there were fewer trees to remove for farming, and their livestock had ready access to the nearby prairie land for grazing. Kinship, place of origin, and religious affiliation also strongly influenced the decision on where to settle and helped foster the strong sense of community and mutual cooperation that was a part of the frontier experience. The interdependent migration of families from one region to another over a period of time was a common characteristic of settlement patterns in frontier Missouri, as it was elsewhere.[10] The Coopers, Hancocks, Berrys, Browns, Wolfscales, and Thorpes, for example, all came to the Boonslick country from Madison County, Kentucky, and Benton and the Hardemans initiated a sequential migration of kith and kin from Williamson County, Tennessee, that included a well-known dispenser of pills, Dr. John Sappington.[11]

The booming town of Franklin, situated on the north bank of the Missouri, epitomized central Missouri's rapid growth in the postwar period. In the short span of three years after its founding in 1816, the county seat of Howard County had developed into a thriving settlement boasting numerous stores, two mills, a federal land office, a post office, a court house, a two-story log jail, a printing office and newspaper, and a horse-racing track. With a population of well over one thousand, it became almost overnight one of the territory's largest towns. Across the river, Boonville had not yet begun its growth spurt, but as one 1819 traveler correctly noted, the bluff town's more advantageous location destined it one day to surpass its low-lying neighbor.[12]

Town promotion was a thriving business in central Missouri. Along the river and at choice locations in the interior, speculators and promoters laid out towns that they confidently predicted would become flourishing metropolises. Arrow Rock, Warrington, Smithton, Rocheport, Chariton, Nashville, Rectorville, Persia, and Bluffton were only some of the places that competed with Franklin and Boonville for the prestatehood emigrants. Some succeeded, while others did not, but the failed ventures did not dissuade other hopeful entrepreneurs from trying their hand at town building. Timothy Flint, who claimed he had read over one hundred town-promotion advertisements in the local press, lampooned the art and ingenuity employed by these boosters "in devising new ways of alluring purchasers, to take lots and build in the new town."[13]

The rush of immigrants to the Boonslick country prompted some prospective Missouri settlers to begin looking for alternate places to locate. Five persons from Bourbon County, Kentucky, moved on to the Salt River country north and west of St. Charles in 1817 after finding the Boonslick settlements "considerable crowded and all the desirable locations taken up."[14] By 1819 the Salt River had become the latest "pole-star of attraction," and the attendant influx led to the founding of towns at Louisiana and New London.[15]

The cultural homogeneity of the incoming immigrants facilitated the perpetuation of emerging upper-south cultural traditions in the rapidly expanding territory's newly settled sections.[16] The plainer folk lived simply and frugally, raising corn, hogs, and cattle and supplementing their diet with wild game from the surrounding woods. They had little money to spend, so they learned to make their own maple sugar and salt. Neighbors stood ready to help one another with tasks that were too much for a family to accomplish on its own. They cooperated in building cabins, smoke-houses, and barns, and when misfortune or tragedy struck, they were ready to offer assistance.[17]

A combination of hard work with cooperative effort, and occasionally a little good luck, enabled many of these pioneers to prosper on the Missouri frontier. Well-cultivated, fenced fields, thriving orchards, kitchen gardens, and sizable livestock herds were the hallmarks of successful yeomen farmers. With the profits from their labors they acquired additional land, purchased slaves, ventured into hemp and tobacco production, and entered the ranks of the local gentry. Their new-found affluence also allowed them to begin replacing their original humble log structures with larger and more elaborate brick, stone, and frame dwellings. These new structures dotting the frontier landscape provided yet another sign of the territory's rapid economic development. The Thomas Hickman brick house in Howard County, which dates from 1819, and the Nathan Boone stone residence in St. Charles County, built about 1816, are among the few extant prestatehood examples of these early vernacular structures reflecting the southern building traditions that became so commonplace in nineteenth-century Missouri.[18]

The movement of people into the Ozarks was less spectacular than the influx into the central and northeastern sections of the territory, but when geologist and ethnologist Henry Rowe Schoolcraft traveled through the region in 1818 and 1819, he found settlements extending from older, well-established communities like Potosi in the eastern mining district to scattered, newer settlement pockets along the upper White and James rivers in southwest Missouri.[19] The rugged, more heavily timbered lands south of the Missouri River generally attracted a different breed of immigrant. The Ozark hills had greater appeal for persons from the highland areas of the upper South, in contrast with other sections of the territory which lured people predominantly from lowland regions in the older states. Many of the incoming Ozark pioneers were descendants of Scotch-Irish stock lacking traditions of literacy, institutional affiliations, and social experiences in cosmopolitan societies. The uneducated hunter-trapper who engaged only minimally in subsistence agriculture and grazing was a familiar Ozark occupant.

Their lives revolved around hunting. It was the primary topic of conversation among women and men alike, for as Schoolcraft observed, "The rude pursuits and coarse enjoyment of the hunter state [is] all they know."[20] They had little contact with schools, religion, learning, or the polite arts. Most of these scattered settlers cultivated a small patch of corn but did not keep a vegetable garden. Corn and wild meats—deer and bear—were the staples of their diet. The crude single-pen log cabins, which often had only an earthen floor, usually appeared ill-kept to the outside observer. The interior walls were hung with rifles, shot pouches, dried meat, animal skins and horns, and assorted articles of greasy buckskin clothing. The hunting motif continued outside the cabin, with animal skins, hides, and carcasses hanging on poles and trees, and the ever-present packs of barking dogs.[21]

It was a lifestyle that appealed to those who valued leisure over material possessions. In choosing to settle for this more primitive existence, they managed to avoid what many of them considered to be the excessive toil of daily living. But this seemingly idyllic way of life had its share of drawbacks. One Ozark woman told Schoolcraft that she had lost four children, all before they reached the age of two. Her family frequently moved and had not lived in a cabin with a wooden floor for several years. Whatever hardships they may have faced, these independent, backwoods people were, for the most part, hospitable and willing to share their meager fare with strangers passing by their door.[22]

Not all early Ozarks settlers were crude hunter-trappers. There were cultivated Scotch-Irish inhabiting such places as the Bellevue Valley in the eastern Ozarks and literate Palatinate Germans residing in the interior. Micajah Harris and his wife Sally, for example, settled with their three children along Six-mile Creek in what is now Ripley County in 1814. They had resided at Little Prairie until the Mississippi River devoured their land during the 1811–1812 earthquakes. Their new home in the Ozarks border was located adjacent to the Natchitoches Trace, a major overland route that linked Cape Girardeau with Natchitoches, Louisiana. Like many Ozarks families, they raised livestock. During his travels, Schoolcraft observed that there was no country in the world where cattle and hogs could be raised with so little expense and trouble. The animals feasted on the prairie grasses in summer, and in the winter they retreated to the more protected river bottoms, where they ate cane and rushes. The Harrises enjoyed a modicum of prosperity. They had access to a variety of trade goods and owned a collection of refined English earthenware ceramics. Micajah served as a justice of the peace, road commissioner, and militia captain at various times prior to his death in 1821.[23]

Bands of westward-migrating Indians, vacating the more crowded eastern Ozarks, joined the pioneer hunters, farmers, and stockmen in the interior Ozarks. The emigrant tribes generally traveled in the company of itinerant white traders. Like the Harrises, these traders participated in commercial networks that reached far beyond the Ozarks. The legendary Yocums of Ozark folklore and William Gilliss, later an important Kansas City promoter, were among the early frontier entrepreneurs who ventured into southwest Missouri for the purpose of trading with the Delawares,

Shawnees, Kickapoos, Piankashaws, Peorias, Weas, and other tribes who settled in the Gasconade, Jacks Fork, and James river valleys.[24]

In the Missouri Territory's older-settled regions adjacent to the Mississippi, the steady flow of newcomers was producing equally far-reaching changes. St. Louis, the territorial capital, proudly claimed more than three thousand residents by 1818, twice the number of only three years earlier. A stroll through many of that city's more than forty retail stores revealed the increasing affluence of its residents. From the well-stocked shelves of those establishments, the shopper could choose from a wide selection of luxury items, including fancy silk shawls, parasols, elegant glass bowls, fine china cups and saucers, high-quality stationery, and such palatable delicacies as figs and raisins. The thriving frontier metropolis also contained several manufacturing concerns, a market house, a post office, a federal land office, two newspapers, two banks, a courthouse, several schools, a theater, three churches, and a museum.[25]

To accommodate the growing influx of newcomers, Auguste Chouteau and John B. C. Lucas subdivided their properties on the hill immediately west of the original village in 1816 and offered them for sale. Lots in the new addition sold well, and when Henry Bingham visited the town two years later, he remarked, "There are some good buildings on the hill which I think will soon be the hansomest part of the town."[26] Conditions were crowded, and St. Louis builders still could not keep pace with the demand created by the steady stream of newcomers. Auguste Chouteau advised his son Gabriel Sylvestre, who had been away tending a trading post upriver, that he would scarcely recognize his home town. Chouteau reported, "Cellars, haylofts, and all the small inns are full not only of people, but of merchandise," and John Mason Peck similarly noted, "Every house and room that could shelter persons was occupied."[27]

On 2 August 1817, a large crowd turned out in St. Louis to welcome the *Zebulon M. Pike*, the first steamboat to ascend the Mississippi above the Ohio. The onlookers vigorously cheered as the boat docked at the foot of Market Street, and those who could afford it paid the captain a dollar to go aboard and personally inspect this new technological marvel. In comparison with the later steamboats that regularly plied the western waters, the *Pike* was rather dinky—its low-pressure engine sometimes required assistance from the crew using poles to move it against the Mississippi's swift current—but its arrival in St. Louis on that summer day marked a momentous occasion in the history of the city and of the territory.[28]

Less than two years later, the *Independence* headed up the Missouri for Franklin to inaugurate steamboat traffic on that stream, but the river's more treacherous waters made regular service along its upper reaches impractical for another decade. By 1819, however, steamboat arrivals and departures had become commonplace on the Mississippi at St. Louis, and the splash of the churning paddlewheels increasingly replaced the songs of the boatmen straining to propel heavy boats upstream against the strong river currents. The promise of speedy and economical transportation further brightened the rapidly developing territory's future prospects.[29]

In nearby St. Charles, the changes were similar. The village once noted for its primitive appearance had taken on a new look with "a long and handsome street of spacious and neat brick houses," some of which can still be found along South Main Street.[30] Local builders made good use of bricks from the town's two kilns, and lumber floated downriver from sawmills operating on the Gasconade. Amid these signs of St. Charles's new-found affluence, agriculture was supplanting the Indian trade as the local economic mainstay.[31]

Along the Mississippi south of St. Louis, Moses Austin and Samuel Hammond established the town of Herculaneum in 1808 as a depot for lead shipments from Mine à Breton. It was five miles closer to the mines than Ste. Genevieve and also provided more convenient access to the Mississippi. John Maclot completed the territory's first shot tower there on the bluffs overlooking the river in 1809, and a decade later the village had three such manufactories.[32]

In the mining district, Mine à Breton and Potosi, situated on opposite sides of Mine Creek, formed one continuous settlement containing about eighty buildings, including several handsome dwellings, a courthouse, a post office, three stores, two distilleries, two flourmills, one sawmill, and nine lead furnaces. Potosi had been designated as the county seat of the newly formed Washington County in 1814, and the commissioners appointed by Governor Clark to procure a courthouse directed the construction of an impressive brick edifice complete with Doric columns, despite the protests of John Andrews, who had advised his fellow commissioners to "rent some old cabin to hold court" before submitting his resignation.[33]

Alexander Craighead, a Scotch-Irish immigrant from Tennessee and a business partner of Andrew Henry, laid out the town of Caledonia in the Bellevue Valley of Washington County in 1818. American settlers of Scotch-Irish descent had begun moving into the valley as early as 1798, and Craighead believed that the time had come to establish a village in the thriving and cultivated rural agricultural community, which also boasted the territory's largest Presbyterian church. Murphy's Settlement (now Farmington) had become an equally prosperous neighborhood of industrious farmers with framed houses clapboarded in the eastern style and well-cultivated fenced fields.[34]

Although Herculaneum had supplanted Ste. Genevieve as the principal river port for territorial lead shipments, Missouri's oldest settlement continued to flourish as an agricultural and commercial center. Its mercantile firms were the major suppliers for the developing interior Ozarks trade. The still-influential Vallés joined forces in 1817 with prominent Kaskaskia merchant Pierre Menard to form a company that successfully monopolized much of the Ozarks Indian trade until the last Indians left the state during the 1830s. More than the other original settlements, Ste. Genevieve retained its distinctive French character. Although many of the town's newer buildings reflected the American modes of construction, local builders also continued to erect structures in the traditional French fashion well into the nineteenth century. Ste. Genevieve also held onto its reputation as a rustic and slightly rowdy place.[35]

The town of Cape Girardeau suffered a major setback when the Board of Land Commissioners refused to confirm Louis Lorimier's original Spanish land grant in 1807. At the time of Lorimier's death in 1812, the issue remained unresolved, and with virtually all of the town's land titles in doubt, would-be settlers understandably chose to locate elsewhere. In 1815, county officials moved the county seat to the new town of Jackson, situated in fertile upland soil ten miles west of Cape Girardeau. By 1818 Jackson was a growing town of three hundred persons with sixty to seventy houses, five stores, two shoe shops, a tannery, and two schools. The next year the *Missouri Herald* became the town's first newspaper, and in 1821 the first public lands went on sale at the newly established U.S. Land Office. Further to the west along the Whitewater River, the prosperous Bollinger settlement with its sturdy stone houses, well-built barns, and fenced fields continued to mirror the German heritage of its inhabitants.[36]

The residents of New Madrid County had slowly begun to recover from the aftereffects of the disastrous 1811–1812 earthquakes. In 1815 Congress authorized the district's inhabitants to exchange their lands for alternate tracts in other portions of the territory, but despite the hubbub created by speculation in New Madrid claims, a surprising number of people chose to return to the region once the tremors subsided. Although the territory's southernmost county did not draw significant numbers of new immigrants after the quakes, its population does not appear to have declined. In the town of New Madrid, property values made a partial comeback, and residents gradually replaced the destroyed buildings. The earthquakes had taken a toll, but the area's numerous poorly drained swamplands constituted a far more serious obstacle to future economic development than the adverse publicity created by the earthquakes. Inland, a collection of traders, stockmen, and farmers had settled along the St. Francis and Black rivers at places like Greenville. John Hardeman Walker, who came to the region from Tennessee in about 1810, acquired extensive cattle herds that roamed the swamplands in present Pemiscot County, and at the time of statehood he successfully lobbied for the inclusion of the Bootheel as a part of Missouri.[37]

As more settlers moved into Missouri's interior regions, territorial officials found it necessary to create new counties for the purpose of administering the burgeoning territory. Following the territory's advancement to second-class status in 1812, Governor Howard formally described the boundaries of the five original counties—St. Charles, St. Louis, Ste. Genevieve, Cape Girardeau, and New Madrid. The next year, the new territorial legislature authorized the establishment of Washington County in response to complaints from residents in the mining district west of Ste. Genevieve about the distance separating them from the county seat.[38]

In 1815 the territorial lawmakers created sprawling Lawrence County from a portion of New Madrid County, and early the following year they approved the formation of Howard County in the Boonslick country. At the time of its creation in 1816, Howard County encompassed the entire northwest quadrant of the Missouri Territory and included land on both sides of the Missouri. The continuing influx of people coupled with the opening of public land sales in the territory prompted the legislators to approve the creation of eight new counties in December 1818: Jefferson, Wayne, Franklin, Lincoln, Madison, Montgomery, Pike, and Cooper. No additional counties were formed until Missouri's first General Assembly added ten more in November 1820.[39]

The Missouri Territory may have been a land of promise for the hordes of new white settlers pouring into the region, but it was a very different story for the various Indian peoples still residing within its borders. According to Governor William Clark's 1816 report, there were nearly 5,000 Indians living within the confines of present-day Missouri, and at least twice that number occupying adjacent regions. Those in the first category included approximately 200 Piankashaws residing about 60 miles west of the mouth of the Ohio River near the Mississippi swamps; 1,300 Shawnees inhabiting three towns near Cape Girardeau, a village 150 miles west of St. Louis on the Meramec, and two more on the St. Francis River; 840 Delawares occupying one village near Cape Girardeau, three towns on the White River, and a scattering of small camps near St. Louis; 50 Peorias living in a village on the St. Francis River about 100 miles southwest of St. Louis; 1,600 Great Osages residing on the Osage River three miles west of the recently surveyed treaty line; and an unspecified number of Ioways, Sacs, and Foxes living on the Grand River and at other undesignated locations west of the Mississippi and north of the Missouri.[40]

The constant pressures from expanding white settlement placed the tribal remnants remaining in the territory increasingly at risk. White encroachment on Indian lands in the Missouri Territory was a continuous problem for federal officials, who vainly attempted to compel unlawful white intruders to vacate Indian properties. Shortly after Governor Clark ordered white interlopers removed from certain Indian lands in late 1815, a correspondent in the *Missouri Gazette* pointed out that it had never been U.S. policy to renounce a district once acquired, no matter how wrongfully. In petitioning Congress to allow the settlers to remain, the territorial assembly proposed a plan for adjusting the tribal claims by giving the Indians vacant lands in unsettled parts of the territory. The completion in 1816 of the line marking the 1808 Osage land cession to the U.S. effectively removed that large and powerful tribe from all but the westernmost portions of present-day Missouri.[41]

The Osage removal had been intended to make space available in the Ozarks for the displaced eastern tribes. For example, under the provisions of the 1818 St. Marys, Ohio, treaty, the eastern Delawares surrendered their lands in Indiana and agreed to move west of the Mississippi. Governor Clark decided that since there was already a sizable Delaware contingent residing near the James River in southwest Missouri, that would be a good location for a Delaware reservation. The influx of Delawares, Kickapoos, and other emigrant tribes into the interior Ozarks eventually brought more than 8,000 Indians to southwestern Missouri and northern Arkansas. Since most of the retreating Indians received federal annuities as compensation for their land forfeitures, their presence attracted white traders eager to capitalize on the lucrative Indian-supply business.[42]

The westward-moving Indians found only a brief respite in the Ozarks. The resentful Osages vigorously challenged the eastern tribes' claims to the traditional Osage hunting grounds, while the advancing white settlers kept up their pressures throughout the territory. Within little more than a decade after statehood, the final contingents of Missouri's original inhabitants had left the state.

The intense competition for land that ultimately sealed the Indians' fate in Missouri steadily drove territorial real estate prices upward. Since the federal government did not begin offering public lands for sale in the territory until 1818, the contest over the confirmation of Spanish land titles continued to divide the territory. The perennial complaints against the commissioners and the national government for their failure to approve all of the Spanish claims could be heard in all parts of Missouri. New petitions demanding additional concessions circulated throughout the territory, and the columns of the territorial newspapers were filled with letters on the subject.

Confronted with these persistent outpourings of discontent, Congress labored to reach a satisfactory solution to the problem. In January 1812, the Board of Land Commissioners had issued its final report containing a resumé of its actions, including a list of every claim that had been filed with the recorder and a summary of the verdict on each claim. The board had examined over 3,000 private claims, and it had confirmed 1,342 of them. Most of the claims approved by the board were small, with only five containing more than 500 acres. In submitting the report to the secretary of the treasury, board member Clement Penrose explained that the board's task had been greatly complicated by the failure of Spanish officials to adhere to any systematic procedures in making land grants. He outlined various types of claims which the board had not been authorized to confirm, but which he believed should be granted.[43]

Congress acted speedily on the recommendations. Less than a month after the board officially communicated its decisions to the House of Representatives, the president approved a bill for the further settlement of land claims in the Missouri Territory. The act confirmed most of the classes of claims that Penrose had recommended for approval. It also empowered the recorder of land titles to review once again all private claims still not confirmed and to issue a final opinion on those. In its eagerness to settle the land-claims question fairly, Congress adopted a liberal policy of confirmation. An additional law approved by the president on 12 April 1814 confirmed most French and Spanish concessions made prior to 10 March 1804, except those judged antedated or fraudulent, but even this did not satisfy completely the Missouri claimants.[44]

As a consequence of the growing congressional liberality, many claimants greatly expanded their confirmed holdings. Auguste Chouteau's real estate increased from 9,000 acres and 7 town lots in St. Charles and St. Louis to 23,500 acres and 12 town lots as a result of the 1814 revisions. His brother Pierre's confirmed possessions went from a total of 500 acres to more than 22,700 acres. Philip Marie Leduc expanded his confirmed holdings from a single town lot in New Madrid to nearly 13,000 acres. Similar increases were experienced by other large claimants.[45]

Frederick Bates, the recorder of land titles, spent nearly four years reexamining the unsettled private claims before presenting Josiah Meigs, the commissioner of the General Land Office, with a final report on 2 February 1816. Although the recorder had approved for confirmation a great many additional Spanish titles, he had rejected a large number of others. Therefore, following the conclusion of Bates's lengthy investigation, the clamor from the remaining claimants continued largely unabated.[46]

Still confronted with a barrage of petitions and memorials demanding further action on the subject, the U.S. House of Representatives requested the secretary of the treasury to submit copies of all reports compiled by the various commissioners appointed to settle and adjust land claims in the Missouri Territory. Secretary William H. Crawford forwarded copies of all such communications to the House on 5 February 1816, but, after only briefly considering the problem, the House referred the entire matter back to Crawford with instructions for him to review all pertinent memorials and petitions and then to prepare yet another plan for the final adjustment of the Spanish claims.[47]

At the next session of Congress, the secretary reported to the House, "It is extremely improbable that injustice has been done by the rejection of claims which ought to have been confirmed."[48] Crawford noted that Congress had consistently relaxed the requirements for confirmation in the past, and therefore he believed that no further concessions were necessary. However, the secretary did suggest that one final opportunity be given claimants to file previously unrecorded claims for consideration.[49] After receiving Crawford's recommendations, the House decided against further action.

There were few truly disinterested parties when it came to land claims in the Missouri Territory. Speculation in Spanish titles was a big business that affected the vast majority of early territorial residents in one way or another. Even officials designated to adjudicate the disputed titles—John B. C. Lucas and Frederick Bates, for example—dabbled in land speculation. Beyond that, the absence of authoritative records made it virtually impossible to determine the number of bona fide claims that remained unconfirmed. Some legitimate claims may not have been approved, but even if Congress had approved every known title, many of which were clearly fraudulent, it is unlikely that the problem would have been resolved. Such an action would only have encouraged the filing of a large number of additional claims and would have brought further demands for greater leniency from Congress. Thus, when Missouri's territorial period came to a close in 1820, the Spanish land-claims controversy remained a hotly contested issue, and it would continue to stir up dissension for years. All frontier territories encountered serious problems arising from foreign land titles, but the contest in Missouri had been particularly intense.[50]

The attempt to gauge the legitimacy of the Spanish grants was only one aspect of the land-titles question in the Missouri Territory. An 1815 congressional measure further complicated matters for officials charged with disposing of the federal lands by authorizing persons owning lands that had been damaged by the New Madrid earthquakes to relocate at no charge on the same quantity of land on any of the U.S. public lands approved for sale.

The law did limit New Madrid claimants to 640 acres of new land, and it also prohibited relocation on mineral lands.[51]

Upon receiving word that this measure had been approved, speculators poured into the New Madrid area in the spring of 1815 seeking to purchase titles to damaged lands from unsuspecting residents before they learned about the new law. Even Governor Clark was tempted to take advantage of the situation; he authorized Theodore Hunt and Charles Lucas to purchase titles to damaged lands for him shortly after the new act had been adopted. Speculation in New Madrid claims became so widespread that U.S. Attorney General William Wirt finally ruled in 1820 that New Madrid claims could not be transferred from the original owner except by death, and then only to one's heirs.[52]

Although the New Madrid relief measure had been designed to alleviate suffering in the devastated area, most Missourians believed that its principal beneficiaries had been the speculators. Their attempts to claim the choicest lands in central Missouri with New Madrid certificates aroused the wrath of persons already residing in the region. The situation became especially serious when Secretary Crawford determined that the right of preemption, extended to the Missouri Territory by Congress in 1814, did not apply to Howard County because at the time it was still a part of the Indian country. Congress had attempted to deal with the rapidly escalating number of unauthorized entries on the public domains by enacting the nebulous statute extending the right of preemption to all persons residing in the Missouri Territory on 12 April 1814.[53]

With thousands of squatters, including virtually all of the settlers in the Boonslick country, waiting to claim the lands they had occupied and improved as soon as the U.S. government offered them for sale, Crawford's ruling excluding Howard County came as a serious blow. By denying residents already established in that region any priority in the purchase of land, the decision in effect opened all lands in central Missouri to claims by the holders of the New Madrid certificates. Samuel Hammond, the U.S. receiver of public monies in St. Louis, reported that as a result of the secretary's action, claims had been filed to cover the best improved farms in Howard County and the already-flourishing villages of Franklin and Boonville.[54]

Squatting on the public lands until they were opened to sale was a way of life on the American frontier, and opposition to Crawford's interpretation was immediate and intense. The territorial assembly's memorial to Congress declared that Crawford's instructions were "not only arbitrary and unauthorized by law, but most unjust, cruel and oppressive, towards a people who have fought and bled for the Soil they cultivate." The hostility became so strong in Howard County that John Mason Peck, who was preaching in the area during the height of the crisis, reported that he "could not call at a cabin without being accosted: 'Got a New Madrid claim?' 'Are you one of these land speculators stranger?' "[55]

In the face of such opposition, Secretary Crawford quickly retreated from his original ruling. He informed the commissioner of the land office on 14 December 1818 that since Congress was considering the possibility of extending the right of preemption to Howard County, all lands so claimed should not be offered for sale, thereby removing them from the potential grasp of the New Madrid claimants. On 21 January 1819, the secretary capitulated and agreed to apply the provisions of the 1814 law to Howard County. Taking no chances, Missouri's territorial delegate to Congress, John Scott, had secured the passage of a law, finally approved on 3 March 1819, which formally extended the preemption provisions of the earlier act to include Howard County specifically.[56]

As competition for available lands in the territory grew, pressure increased rapidly on the federal government to open Missouri's public lands for sale. Although in 1811 Congress had authorized the president to take such a step whenever he thought it necessary, not a single acre of Missouri's public lands had been offered for sale by 1816.[57] Several factors accounted for the administration's tardiness in approving the sale of lands in Missouri, including the intervention of the War of 1812, the unresolved Spanish land-claims issues, the difficulties in extinguishing Indian titles, the failure to complete land surveys, and the lingering reluctance by some members of the administration to encourage settlement west of the Mississippi.

Governor Clark's efforts to remove all intruders from Indian lands and President Madison's directive evicting the illegal settlers from the unsold public lands unleashed another barrage of angry protests from territorial residents. In fact, the removal edicts were unenforceable. Col. Alexander McNair flatly stated that the territorial militia would refuse to march against the intruders. The president quickly retreated from his initial order and approved a law on 25 March 1816 permitting settlers to remain on the public lands until they were offered for sale.[58]

As the land hunger pushed speculation in private holdings to new heights, the campaign to bring Missouri's public lands into the market gained momentum. Proponents of the sale of the public lands in Missouri predicted that their proposal would enrich the national treasury, end unlawful intrusions on the public domain, and increase the population to the point that the region could defend itself against any enemy.[59] The long-awaited announcement of the opening of public land sales in Missouri appeared in the *Missouri Gazette* on 5 June 1818. President James Monroe ordered the sales tō begin in St. Louis on the first Monday in August 1818 and in Howard County on the first Monday in September. In accordance with the provisions of federal land statutes, Missouri's public lands were offered for sale at public auction to the highest bidder. Federal law fixed the minimum price at two dollars per acre, and although the smallest quantity that could be purchased was 160 acres, the government granted prospective buyers liberal terms of credit.

The first sales opened on schedule in St. Louis, but they had to be postponed in Howard County because of the tardy arrival of that region's land-office officials. As soon as the sales got underway, local newspapers reported feverish bidding and high prices. In 1819, improved lands in the vicinity of St. Louis averaged between four and twelve dollars an acre. One particularly good section of land near Franklin brought over twenty-six dollars an acre. In response to prodding from Missouri's territorial delegate, John Scott, the U.S. Land Office in Jackson finally offered lands for sale in 1821. The easy credit system that permitted purchasers to obtain sizable tracts of public lands with only minimal down payments added to the speculative mania. President Monroe proposed curbing land speculation by raising the minimum price, but local residents strongly objected to any such move.[60]

While the lure of cheap lands attracted growing numbers of settlers to the territory, the scarcity of labor remained a serious local problem. During the war years the shortage had been especially acute, but even after the conflict had ended, competition for the limited labor supply remained keen. "Smart young men are the scarcest articles to be found in this place," Christian Wilt had informed his uncle in 1814. Employers complained about having to tolerate incompetent and unreliable hired hands; skilled workers were particularly difficult to find. By 1817, bricklayers, masons, and carpenters received three dollars per day for their services, while unskilled workers generally were paid at least half that amount.[61]

One important segment of the territorial population did not benefit from the high prevailing wage levels. Missouri slaves remained unpaid for their labors. Black slave emigrants accompanying their migrating southern owners added their numbers to the territory's long-established slave population. Blacks consistently made up roughly 15 percent of territorial Missouri's total population, but in some counties the proportion of blacks was considerably higher. At the time of statehood, for example, one-fourth or more of the people in Ste. Genevieve and Howard counties were of African ancestry. Missouri's slave population increased from 3,000 in 1810 to nearly 10,000 in 1820. During that same period, however, the territory's free black population declined dramatically. In 1810 there were approximately 600 free blacks among the territory's more than 20,000 inhabitants, but by 1820, even though the territorial population had jumped to 66,000, the number of free blacks had dropped to about 375. The decrease was temporary, however, and following statehood, the free black population in Missouri started to grow, as it did in most other border states.[62]

Although territorial Missouri's slave population was proportionately smaller than in slave states and territories in the deep South, the fear of slave lawlessness and insurrection caused territorial authorities to enact strict black codes regulating the activities of both slaves and free blacks. Even after the enactment of the 1804 Black Code, complaints persisted that the local laws were inadequate. An 1813 critic took the territory's first elected legislative body to task for failing to correct flaws in the territorial statutes that he alleged allowed blacks belonging to scheming masters to rob at will. In St. Louis, where blacks constituted about 20 per cent of the city's growing population, the concerns were most evident. Officials in that city adopted ordinances in 1808–1809, 1811, and 1818 designed to restrain slaves from drinking, holding public gatherings, and mixing socially with free blacks and whites, especially at night. The 1818 St. Louis statute stipulated that any slave found in public between 9:00 p.m. and daylight could be whipped or jailed. A similar ordinance enacted by the board of trustees in Franklin in 1819 established patrols and authorized them to lash Negroes at their discretion.[63]

Whippings continued to be a common form of slave punishment. The slave system invited mistreatment, but slaveowners deemed guilty of un- reasonable acts in disciplining their slaves were sometimes censured pub- licly. A report of an especially blatant case of slave abuse caused the *Missouri Gazette's* editor to query, "Is there no punishment for such crimes?"[64] Nonetheless, only in the most extreme cases, usually involving the murder of a slave, were masters held accountable for their actions, and even then the scales of justice seem to have been weighted heavily in the white owner's favor. Authorities in St. Louis did bring William Henderson to trial in 1815 after he stabbed and killed his slave Joe during an argument, but the accused successfully claimed self-defense, despite the testimony of one witness alleging that Henderson had sworn to kill the slave even if it cost him his life.[65]

Few whites condoned excessive physical abuse of slaves, but with rare exceptions, they accepted the notion of black and Indian inferiority as a matter of course. Even so, the relationships between blacks and whites in early Missouri were varied and complex. Slavery in Missouri was different from slavery in the cotton and sugar regions of the lower South. Most Missouri slaveholders owned only a small number of slaves, frequently only one or two. Unlike plantation field hands whose principal contact with whites was with an overseer, Missouri's slaves usually lived in close association with the families of their owners. They frequently worked side by side and occasionally even ate at the same table. But their close proximity with their masters was often a mixed blessing, especially when the owners were hard-driving and ambitious and demanded much from themselves and from their slaves.[66]

Some slaves fared better than others. Frederick Bates advised his mother that even without an overseer or direct daily supervision, his slaves were raising a most promising crop. Stephen Hempstead was more solicitous of his slaves' welfare than many Missouri slaveholders. His daily journal contained frequent references to his slaves and to their activities. On a spring day in 1820, his overseer and his slaves took time off to go fishing, and in 1814 Hempstead gave them a pig to roast for their New Year's festivities. Hempstead's diary entry for 2 January 1816 noted, "Moses had caught cold agoing to Belle Fontaine and frolicing all night Christmas and New Year."[67]

Even for slaves with sympathetic masters who allowed them occasional moments for merriment, life was still onerous. Forced to perform the least desirable chores without compensation for their services, Missouri's slaves found numerous ways to remonstrate against their unhappy lot. The columns of the territorial newspapers often contained notices advertising for the return of missing slaves. With slaves valued at between $300 and $500 each, the loss of a slave represented a serious financial blow to the owner. For slaves residing in counties adjacent to the Mississippi, the freedom of Illinois across the river stood as a great temptation. In 1816, John B. C. Lucas offered twenty-five dollars for the return of a bilingual slave whom he described as "artful and plausible." Lucas cautioned that the runaway probably carried a forged pass identifying him as a free Negro.[68]

Runaway slaves often bore the marks of their service. Daniel Bennet, who fled with his wife from their Franklin County master in 1820, took with him numerous scars and "a few marks of the whip on his back." Not all of the scars were physical. The frequent mentions of serious slave drinking problems and speech impediments were indicators of how the peculiar institution sometimes marked its victims psychologically. Missouri slaves especially feared threats to send them down the river to join a plantation slave gang. In 1819 Governor Clark's slave Scipio shot and killed himself because he believed he was about to be transported to New Orleans.[69]

Some slaves chose other ways to strike back against the system and their owners. Pierre Chouteau attributed the loss of his lavish St. Louis home by fire in 1805 to the action of a disgruntled slave, and in 1818 officials charged a slave named Elijah with conspiracy to poison his master's family. Similar accusations against Moses Austin's slave Lyd caused her to be sent downriver with a male slave companion. The Scypions embraced a very different strategy for securing their freedom: they took their masters to court.[70]

Owners often hired out their slaves to earn extra income. Moses Austin leased a number of slaves to work at his mines and smelter, while his archrival John Smith T kept two highly skilled blacks who manufactured flintlock rifles and pistols. Christian Wilt paid a free black man, Henry Cauld, thirty-five dollars a month to perform the hazardous and difficult job of coloring lead at his factory.[71]

Manufacturing in the Missouri Territory remained limited and small scale, with a lack of capital proving to be the greatest single deterrent to the development of local industry. Conservative monied interests generally considered commerce and real estate better investments than manufacturing. Designed only to supply the local market, most territorial factories grew up in conjunction with merchandising operations and remained small concerns.[72]

The heavy demands for building materials led to the construction of sawmills to provide lumber and brickyards to supply bricks. Since its bulkiness made furniture a costly item to import, local craftsmen began producing chairs and other pieces to satisfy territorial needs. Tinsmiths and coppersmiths sold kettles and miscellaneous utensils. Even though most places enjoyed the services of one or more blacksmiths, the vast majority of the iron that they worked came from outside the territory. The earliest successful iron smelter in Missouri was the Tong-Asherbranner works established in 1815 or 1816 on Stout's Creek in the east Arcadia Valley near present-day Ironton. This small and primitive operation, which produced bar iron and castings for several years before depressed economic conditions forced its closing, was a multicultural venture uniting French Creole capital with English and German know-how. During the summer of 1817, the *Missouri Gazette* also reported that several Washington County entrepreneurs were erecting an ironworks to take advantage of the excellent local ores.[73]

Ready-made clothing did not reach the area until the 1820s, but shortly after the United States acquired the territory, tailors and hatters offered their services to local residents. Jewelers opened shops in which they made jewelry and repaired watches and clocks, and flour millers, bakers, meat packers, soap and candle makers, tanners, brewers, and distillers also operated within the territory. In the midst of the interest in steam power generated by the *Zebulon Pike*'s arrival on western waters, Manuel Lisa in 1817 investigated the possibility of acquiring a steam engine large enough to work two pairs of millstones and three saws.[74]

At the end of 1814, lead production in the Missouri Territory emerged from the wartime doldrums following a dramatic rise in lead prices. Moses Austin heralded this upturn as the dawn of a new day for the depressed industry. He expanded his operations to meet the increased demand, but the resurgence was short-lived. The return of more normal conditions in the lead market, the collapse of the Bank of St. Louis, and the general economic decline caused by the Panic of 1819 forced Austin into bankruptcy in 1820. With his once-substantial financial empire in disarray, Austin turned his attention to the new vistas of Texas and left the task of revitalizing Missouri's lead industry to others. Meanwhile, critics of the federal government's lead policies attributed the continued low production at the mines to the unpopular leasing system.[75]

The fur trade's immediate postwar recovery was even less spectacular. Because of the tremendous amounts of capital necessary to reopen operations in the upper Missouri valley, the St. Louis merchants continued to trade primarily with the more accessible tribes along the lower Missouri. The unhappy traders placed much of the blame for the declining fur traffic on the government-operated trading posts, which they called upon Congress to eliminate. Efforts to revitalize the lagging fur business proved to be very disappointing. An ill-fated attempt by Auguste Pierre Chouteau and Jules De Mun to expand operations into the far southwest landed the two St. Louis traders in a Spanish prison for forty-eight days and cost them thirty thousand dollars in confiscated property. President Monroe's announcement of plans to erect a military post on the Yellowstone River in order to establish American control in that area temporarily rekindled interest among the St. Louis traders in 1819, but the failure of the *Western Engineer* to reach its destination doomed the project and temporarily dashed hopes for a quick return of American traders to the upper Missouri. The specially constructed steamboat, designed to resemble a large smoke-breathing dragon in the belief that it would frighten hostile Indians, made it only as far as Council Bluffs, where the river, not the Indians, did it in.[76] Despite these disappointments, it was only a matter of time until the fur trade would revive.

The continuing scarcity of capital on the Missouri frontier frequently hampered local development, and the absence of a regular financial institution within the territory complicated even routine financial transactions with eastern merchants. Hoping to remedy these difficulties, Auguste Chouteau had spearheaded a drive by St. Louis businesspeople to establish a bank within the territory in 1813.[77]

Because of wartime dislocations, the bank failed to secure enough subscriptions for its stock to enable it to begin operations immediately. Following its long-awaited opening on 13 December 1816, the Bank of St. Louis began making sizable real estate loans by issuing large amounts of its own bank notes to borrowers. In a short time the bank had overextended itself and appeared to be headed for disaster. Several of the bank's original backers, including Chouteau, had already dissociated themselves from the venture, and some of the more conservative remaining directors accused the institution's officers of mismanagement. They directed their criticism against the bank's cashier, John B. N. Smith, for his role in the issuance of unauthorized bank notes. Although the disgruntled minority succeeded in forcing Smith's removal, they failed to win support for a fundamental alteration in the bank's policies. To dramatize their disaffection with the current practices, three dissenting directors resigned.[78]

The dispute among the directors soon widened to include many of the bank's stockholders. On 11 February 1818, a group led by Joshua Pilcher, Thomas Hart Benton, and Elias Rector gathered in front of the bank and held an impromptu stockholders meeting, at which they adopted a resolution demanding the keys from bank officials. When the officers refused to surrender the key to the safe, the protesters ordered everyone out of the bank and padlocked its doors. After taking this step, the insurgents announced that the bank would not be permitted to reopen until the directors had taken steps to safeguard the interests of the stockholders. Prompt legal action by the directors secured a return of the keys and a court-enforced ban against any further interference with the bank's operations, but the institution remained closed while the feuding officials attempted to put its troubled affairs in order. The Bank of St. Louis finally reopened early in 1819, but after operating only a few months, it had to close its doors permanently in the summer. A combination of internal divisions, poor management, and overextended credit had finally forced its liquidation.[79]

Although the Bank of St. Louis's policies had been popular with land speculators and rising young entrepreneurs in need of substantial amounts of capital, many of the territory's established businessmen and small farmers had been hurt by the freewheeling issuance of paper money. Even before the Bank of St. Louis had opened, Auguste Chouteau, Manuel Lisa, and several other original backers had withdrawn their support and launched a drive to establish a second bank guided by more fiscally conservative principles. Directors of the Bank of St. Louis did everything possible to block the chartering of a rival institution, but even a series of last-minute parliamentary maneuvers by opponents in the territorial legislature failed to prevent the enactment of a measure authorizing the creation of a new bank.[80]

The Bank of Missouri actually had been operating on a limited basis since the fall of 1816, but early in 1817 it welcomed customers in the basement of

Auguste Chouteau's St. Louis mansion as a fully chartered institution. Reflecting the more conservative policies of its backers, the bank, in contrast with its local competitor, offered to redeem its notes in specie. After the U.S. government designated it as a federal depository, the bank seemed destined for success, but even this solidly based financial institution found itself in trouble when the Panic of 1819 belatedly reached Missouri. Extensive loans to its directors, in violation of the charter, compounded the bank's woes and forced its closing in 1821. The unhappy experience of Missouri's two territorial banks produced a strong public reaction against all banks that blocked the creation of another state-chartered financial institution until 1837.[81]

The full effects of the Panic of 1819 were delayed in reaching the Missouri frontier, but as the territorial period drew to a close, the postwar expansion momentarily slowed. Immigration decreased, property values plummeted, local sheriffs sold property at public auction for back taxes, businesses folded, and farmers found it difficult to sell their surplus produce. The situation was especially serious in St. Louis, where a city lot contracted at a price of $1,000 in the spring of 1820 sold for $140 one year later. But the momentary economic downturn proved to be only a pause before a new surge of emigrants rushed to take advantage of Missouri's promise following the state's admission to the Union in 1821.[82]

TO THE PUBLIC.

WHEN a man makes his appearance before the public, upon occasions of this kind, it is necessary, that his grounds should be good.— Mr. Wm. Smith, a *Merchant* of this place, and formerly of Lexington, Kentucky, (a man much larger than myself) assailed me on monday last, in the Missouri Bank, in the most villanous and infamous manner, with a large club.—Circumstances prevented me from calling on Mr. S. until to day; when he, in the MOST COWARDLY AND DASTARDLY manner, refused to give any satisfaction, for the outrage committed on my person and reputation.

I therefore pronounce the aforesaid *William Smith*, to be a most infamous SCOUNDREL, RASCAL, & COWARD, and notify the world accordingly.

W. THARP.

St. Louis, (Saturday) Sep'r. 27th 1817.

This dispute between William Tharp, a laborer, and William Smith, a merchant, ended with Tharp shooting and killing Smith on a St. Louis street. Courtesy Missouri State Archives.

The *Zebulon Pike* became in 1817 the first steamboat to travel up the Mississippi to St. Louis. This modern rendering of the event by Norbury Wayman is used by permission of the artist.

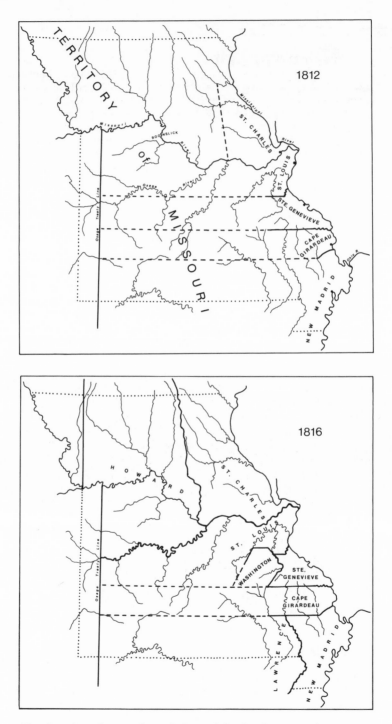

The changing of county boundaries and the development of new counties between 1812 and 1821 are shown in this sequence of four maps.

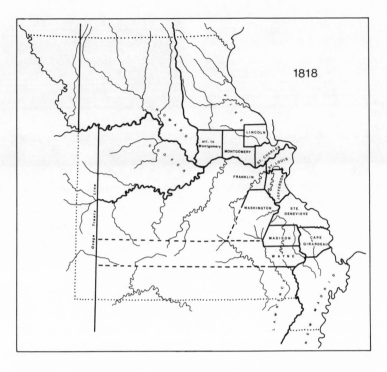

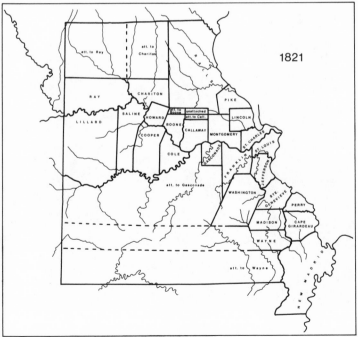

Marguerite Reihle McNair. Courtesy State Historical Society of Missouri.

Governor Alexander McNair. Courtesy Missouri Historical Society.

The Old Academy in Ste. Genevieve. Photograph by Theodore LaVack for the Historic American Buildings Survey, Washington, D.C.

Mine à Breton, as sketched in 1826 by Charles Alexander LeSueur. Moses Austin's impressive home, Durham Hall, is at right. Courtesy State Historical Society of Missouri.

McKendree Chapel, Cape Girardeau County. Photograph by Gerald Massie. Courtesy State Historical Society of Missouri.

50 DOLLARS REWAD.

Ranaway from the subscriber, on the 28th of March last past, a negro man named

S.A.M.

Five feet seven inches high, about 24 years of age, good features, stoop shoulders, very long fingers, large feet; his skin about his wrists, ears, arms, and legs very scaly and rough ; has an intelligent countenance, is artful and plausible; he had on when he went away a big blanket capo without a cap, a pair of deerskin overalls, a flannel shirt and an old fur hat; he pronounces English well and speaks some French, it is probable that he will procure himself a forged passport as a free negro ; he is the same fellow who about two years ago roamed for some months in the settlements of Turkey-hill and Rich-lands. The above reward will be paid on the delivery of the said negro to the subscriber at St. Louis, or on the delivery of said negro in any jail in the Missouri or Illinois territory, so soon as the subscriber will take possession of the same.

JOHN B. C. LUCAS.

St. Louis, Mri. Ter.

April 1st, 1815.

Missouri slaves sometimes crossed the Mississippi to Illinois seeking freedom. From *The Underground Rail Road*, by William Still (1871). Courtesy State Historical Society of Missouri.

100 DOLLARS REWARD.

Ranaway from Mr. O'Fallen's mill near, the Missouri, last July, a negro man named JUBAR,

about twenty four years of age, five feet nine or ten inches high, strongly formed, when walking throws out his knees more than men usually do; he has a scar in one of his eye brows, and when confused he flutters a little in talking : he was in and about this town a few weeks ago and had in his possession at that time a new shot gun. Whoever will take up the said runaway negro and secure him in the jail of this county, shall receive the above reward.

Wm. CLARK.

March 29, 1816.

These two notices from the *Missouri Gazette* offered a reward for the return of slaves to prominent owners. Courtesy State Historical Society of Missouri.

Mother Philippine Duchesne. Courtesy Missouri Historical Society.

Thomas Hart Benton. Portrait by Matthew Harris Jouett. Courtesy The Cleveland Museum of Art, Gift of Mrs. Otto Miller, 41.597.

Bethel Baptist Church, Cape Girardeau County. Courtesy State Historical Society of Missouri.

These two watercolors by Anna Maria von Phul, who arrived in St. Louis in 1818, are titled *Scene Near St. Louis, 1818* and *Creole Cart and Driver.* Courtesy Missouri Historical Society.

CHAPTER FIFTEEN
BEYOND
THE SABBATH

T he varied textures of life in the Missouri Territory made it a land of stark contrasts. Urbane French Creoles and cultivated Americans coexisted with eye-gouging ruffians and untutored woodsmen during the years of swift and uncontrolled expansion that preceded statehood. Within that setting, dedicated women and men labored to sustain civility, cultural refinement, and traditional values against the forces of violence and cultural regression. When Harvard-educated Timothy Flint came to the Missouri Territory in 1816 under the aegis of the Missionary Society of Connecticut, he reported that it was a common proverb that persons who cross the Mississippi "travel beyond the Sabbath." At the same time, however, the Presbyterian parson hastened to take exception with fellow New Englander Timothy Dwight's observation that Missouri was becoming "a grand reservoir for the scum of the Atlantic states."[1]

Flint described typical backwoods people as amiable and virtuous, but the transplanted easterner found plenty to criticize in the rawboned frontier environment, where whiskey flowed freely and roughnecks resorted to fist fights at the drop of a hat.[2] The editor of the *Missouri Gazette* complained in 1815 about the vagabonds who roamed the St. Louis streets after decent folks were in bed, and four years later Graf von Phul advised his sister, "We have scarcely any news here but such as you would rather dispense with hearing—of fighting in the streets, shooting at one another, handbills &c."[3]

The problem was most prevalent in the river towns along the waterfront, where idle boatmen and assorted hangers-on often whiled away their time drinking, gambling, pitching quoits, shooting at targets, and engaging in generally rowdy behavior. Mike Fink, the legendary riverman, and his sidekick Bill Carpenter were familiar faces along the St. Louis riverfront. The hard-drinking duo, both of whom were renowned marksmen, frequently demonstrated their prowess with a Kentucky rifle by shooting a tin cup off one another's head or off the head of their frequent companion Pittsburg Blue, a woman who shared their fondness for the bottle. Their high jinks ended tragically during the 1823 Ashley expedition when Fink killed Carpenter with a shot in the head and then fell victim himself to a bullet fired during a dispute with another crewman.[4]

Swearing and profane language were commonplace. During an 1819 trip to the Boonslick region, Englishman Henry Bousfield observed, "Here are some of the most outrageous swearers I ever heard, our host a Kentuckyan is very guilty of this bad practice, he allows he swears, but says he never curses." Even John Scott, the well-educated and popular Ste. Genevieve lawyer and territorial delegate in Congress, allegedly was unable to deliver a speech without uttering profanities.[5] But bad as he believed these other vices were, Timothy Flint considered dueling the most barbarous frontier custom. Flint observed that during the brief time he had been in the territory, the practice had already claimed the lives of two acquaintances. Territorial lawmakers attempted to curb the local excesses by imposing fines on individuals found guilty of gambling, dueling, and failing to keep the sabbath.[6]

Although the Missouri frontier had its share of lawlessness and vice, the territory never verged on the brink of savagery. Its well-established upper class continued to enjoy the comforts of polite society, and the vast majority of territorial residents remained hardworking, law-abiding citizens. Nonetheless, the booming region's unsavory reputation in the East made it a popular field for mission work. Before the War of 1812, the Baptists and Methodists actively recruited new members in the Missouri Territory. Both groups initially bypassed the traditional Roman Catholic village strongholds and concentrated their proselytizing activities among the scattered American elements in outlying areas.

The Baptists, who did not require their ministers to have a formal education, often "raised up" preachers from within a local church. Some individual Baptist congregations attempted to monitor their lay preachers. For example, when a Brother Smith believed he had been called by God in 1807, the leaders of his local church agreed to grant him "liberty to exercise either in preaching or exhorting in the bounds of the Church, but not out of the said bounds without a member with him." Since they normally had to support themselves by working during the week, usually as farmers or hunters, the part-time preachers frequently joined the tide of American immigrants moving westward. Even before the Louisiana Purchase, Thomas Musick, who had been preaching since he was seventeen, traveled to Upper Louisiana from his native North Carolina. Following his arrival in the vicinity of St. Louis during the Spanish regime's waning days, Musick quietly assembled Baptist families for social meetings and preaching. Like most other Baptist ministers, he received no salary and had to rely on gifts from the folk to whom he ministered.[7]

The earliest Baptist church formed in Missouri was the Tawapitty Baptist Church, established in the Cape Girardeau district in 1805. The following year, David Green organized the Bethel Baptist Church near Jackson, and in 1812 the congregation erected the first Protestant meetinghouse west of the Mississippi, a hewed-log structure measuring thirty by twenty-four feet. The Boonslick country was another center of Baptist activity. David McLain, the proprietor of McLain's Fort, was an early preacher in that region whom Samuel Cole remembered as a mighty good man with "acceptable" preaching skills.[8]

Women were especially active in the crusade to tame the wilderness and bring religion to the frontier. Sarah Murphy, wife of a Baptist minister and sister of noted Missouri political figure David Barton, taught one of the first Sunday school classes in the territory at the Murphy Settlement beginning around 1807. She came to the territory after a conversion at the feet of the militant evangelicals in the Virginia mountains, and she remained active in the Missouri Baptist movement. In 1814 the Widow Murphy arbitrated a religious dispute on the Current River in modern Shannon County. She typified the Anti-Mission Baptists (also called Primitive or Hard Shell Baptists), who formed an important cultural core among the highly individualistic, open-range hill people in the southern Missouri Ozarks. When Thomas Musick established the Fee Fee Baptist Church in St. Louis County, his initial congregation consisted of five females, and the early rolls of frontier churches frequently included a disproportionate number of women members. Women also played a principal role in creating church-based charitable organizations and mite societies.[9]

Although individual Baptist congregations were independent, as their numbers increased they frequently formed voluntary associations. Six Baptist churches in the vicinity of Jackson formed the Bethel Association in 1816. Similarly, Baptist congregations in the St. Louis area established the Missouri Association in 1817, and the following year the churches in the Boonslick region organized the Mount Pleasant Association. In 1817 the Baptist Triennial Missionary Convention dispatched John Mason Peck and James E. Welch to carry forward the church's work in the Missouri Territory. Both of these well-educated clergymen assumed important leadership roles in early Missouri Baptist affairs. Peck, who became one of the most active of the frontier evangelists, also gained recognition for his literary and historical works. Welch, a popular Baptist preacher, founded the First Baptist Church of St. Louis in 1818. The arrival of the missionaries from the East provoked a backlash among some local churchpeople, though. Peck's condescending attitude toward the unschooled local preachers fed the development of an anti-missionary faction within the Baptist church.[10]

The Methodists also entered Missouri at an early date. John Clark, whose switch in religious affiliation from Methodist to Baptist has enabled both groups to claim him, had preached in Upper Louisiana prior to American acquisition. Shortly after Louisiana's transfer to the United States, the

Western Conference of the Methodist Church sent Joseph Oglesby west to assess the need for preachers in the trans-Mississippi territory. On the basis of his findings, conference officials appointed John Travis in 1806 to form a Missouri circuit extending from present-day Pike County in the north to Pemiscot County in the south. After his first year's work in Missouri, Travis reported a membership of 100. By 1810, the Methodist Church had established five circuits with 528 members.[11]

Unlike the self-supporting Baptist ministers, who typically lived in the communities they served, early Methodist preachers were itinerants paid by church conferences in more settled areas to preach full-time on the frontier. The church assigned each of these pioneer evangelists to work in a specific area. Known as circuit riders, they traveled from settlement to settlement preaching and ministering to the people in the region they had been designated to serve. Once the circuit had been completed, the minister returned to his original point of departure and began the journey again. Between visits from the circuit rider, local Methodists often met to worship and to study.

Circuits were long and difficult—one Missouri circuit encompassed an area one hundred miles in length and two hundred miles in width. Frequently the roads linking the isolated settlements on the circuit disappeared into the wilderness. Along with the hardships of frontier travel, circuit riders also endured personal privation. Their low pay barely provided enough for minimal personal necessities. Even though settlers frequently welcomed them into their homes for the night, the itinerant preachers sometimes failed to find accommodations and had to sleep on bare ground in the open. Because they had no regular meeting places, the circuit riders preached wherever they could—outdoors, in barns, in taverns, and in courthouses. Drunks and troublemakers sometimes attempted to disrupt the meetings, as did rowdies employing a crude form of humor. Many circuit riders lacked formal education. Some young recruits gained their training by riding with experienced ministers who tutored them in basic church teachings and preaching techniques. These "brush college graduates," as they styled themselves, then received circuits of their own to cover. Through this system, the Methodists attempted to reach Missouri's widely scattered settlements.[12]

William McKendree, an early American Methodist bishop, Jesse Walker, a frequent circuit rider and later the founder of St. Louis's first Methodist body, and John Scripps, an active organizer of churches in the Boonslick country and an outspoken critic of slavery, were among Missouri's leading Methodist pioneers. The first Methodist church building in Missouri was constructed in the Bellevue Valley about 1814. That structure has long since disappeared, but the chinked-log Old McKendree Chapel, built in 1819 near Jackson at an oak grove long used for camp meetings, remains today as a remarkable survival of frontier Missouri's early religious life. The one-room, hewed-log structure, with its shingle roof and its good plank floors—Missouri's oldest surviving Protestant church building—served as the location for the 1819 meeting of the Missouri Conference of the Methodist Church, the first such session held west of the Mississippi.[13]

Since church buildings were a rarity on the early frontier, itinerant ministers representing various denominations frequently conducted camp meetings. John Clark organized one of the earliest of these gatherings in the Missouri Territory at the Coldwater Creek area north of St. Louis sometime around 1805. People traveled for miles to attend these frontier revivals, bringing provisions for camping out since they normally lasted for several days. After the crowds had assembled, the soul savers exhorted their listeners to repent or risk spending eternity in a bottomless pit of fire. Those who accepted the invitation gathered at the mourners' bench as the noisy and often confused proceedings reached a frenzied climax during which repentant sinners sometimes shrieked, shouted, barked, wept, shook, and jerked.[14]

Frontier evangelists debated the religious benefits of such emotional outbursts, but the camp meeting became an important frontier social institution that gave isolated settlers an opportunity to escape the loneliness and boredom of their daily existence. It allowed women, men, and children, white and black, to visit widely scattered neighbors and to make new acquaintances. People came to camp meetings for disparate reasons, including some of a worldly nature: women came to socialize and gossip, children came to engage in play, men came to enjoy robust fellowship and perhaps to gamble and drink, single people came to court members of the opposite sex, politicians came to electioneer, merchants came to sell their wares, and criminals came to fleece unsuspecting victims. Whatever their virtues and faults, these religious gatherings offered a valuable social outlet for frontier inhabitants.[15]

Aside from a momentary aberration in early 1812 when backsliding Christians flocked to religious services in the areas most affected by the earthquakes, overall church membership declined in the Missouri Territory during the tumultuous years between 1810 and 1815.[16] The diminution of Indian hostilities and the resumption of immigration into the territory at war's end enabled Baptists and Methodists to recoup temporary membership losses and after 1815 to register substantial gains. Eastern churches rushed to send missionaries to augment local endeavors to organize churches and win the souls of frontier men and women. These clerical imports came prepared to engage in evangelical activities and to combat the immorality and irreligion they assumed to be rampant on the American frontier.

The Presbyterians were among the first Protestants to join the Methodists and Baptists in Missouri. The Philadelphia Bible and Missionary Society sent Samuel J. Mills and Daniel Smith to the West in 1814. The two Presbyterian ministers drew large crowds for their sermons in St. Louis, and before leaving the territory, they helped generate local support for the establishment of a society to distribute Bibles. Following their departure, Stephen Hempstead, whose son Edward already had made a name for himself as an influential local attorney and politician, actively worked to secure a permanent Presbyterian minister for the Missouri Territory.[17]

Hempstead's appeals to church leaders in his native Connecticut produced results the following year when the Connecticut Missionary Society dispatched Salmon Giddings and Timothy Flint to the territory. Shortly after his arrival in 1816, Giddings visited the Scotch-Irish settlement in the Bellevue Valley, where he helped organize Missouri's first Presbyterian church, the Concord Church. Subsequently the energetic Giddings helped establish other Presbyterian congregations at Bonhomme (1816), St. Louis (1817), Richwoods Settlement (1818), Buffalo (1818), St. Charles (1818), and Franklin(1821). The group he organized in St. Louis in 1817 was that city's first Protestant congregation. That same year, church leaders also created the Presbytery of Missouri. Emphasizing the need for an educated clergy, Presbyterianism appealed most to the territory's better-educated inhabitants.[18]

So did the Episcopal Church, which clung to its Virginia–Upper South traditions when it entered Missouri near the end of the territorial period. In October 1819, John Ward conducted the first Episcopal service west of the Mississippi in St. Louis. The following month, Ward, with the aid of such prominent charter members as Alexander McNair, Thomas Hart Benton, and William Clark, helped organize Christ Church in St. Louis.[19]

The Cumberland Presbyterians, a group that separated from traditional Presbyterians following a disagreement over the church's stringent educational requirements for the clergy, conducted several meetings in St. Louis in 1817. Salmon Giddings, hardly an unbiased observer, attended some of those services and afterward proclaimed the preacher from the rival Presbyterian sect to have the manner of a "hollering Methodist." Missouri's earliest full-fledged Cumberland Presbyterian church was established in Pike County in 1820. The Disciples of Christ, commonly referred to as the Christian Church, was another denomination born on the western frontier that arrived in Missouri prior to statehood. Tennessean Thomas McBride was one of the earliest Christian Church preachers in the territory. The

Disciples organized their first Missouri congregation in 1817 in Howard County, where the group had a strong following.[20]

After Upper Louisiana's transfer to the United States in 1804, the Roman Catholic Church declined steadily in Missouri. With the end of governmental support for the church, each congregation had to assume responsibility for maintaining local operations. Most Missouri parishes suddenly found themselves without the services of a regular priest as Catholic clergymen left the territory in order to retain their stipends from the Spanish crown. Amos Stoddard went so far as to propose that the priests at Ste. Genevieve, St. Louis, and St. Charles should be put on the U.S. payroll and given a salary of three hundred dollars per year in order to keep them from leaving. When American officials said no, only Father James Maxwell elected to remain at his post. The English-speaking Ste. Genevieve cleric fared well under the new regime. Along with his priestly duties, Father Maxwell acquired substantial landholdings and later was elected the first president of the territorial Legislative Council.[21]

As late as 1818, only the churches at Florissant and Ste. Genevieve had regular clergymen. Father Henry Pratte, the pastor in Ste. Genevieve at the time, was the first native-born Missourian to become a priest. Other Missouri parishes had to depend upon the visiting priests who occasionally came to administer the sacraments. The prolonged period of neglect had a disastrous effect upon the church. Bishop Benoit Joseph Flaget of Kentucky found evidence of indifference and apathy among Missouri Catholics when he first visited the territory in 1814. Other priests who came to the area conveyed an equally dismal account of the general state of the Catholic Church in Missouri.[22]

Bishop William Louis DuBourg's arrival in the territory in 1818 revitalized the moribund local parishes. DuBourg, who had been consecrated bishop of Louisiana and the Floridas in 1815, had decided to establish his residence temporarily in St. Louis because of the opposition in New Orleans to his appointment as bishop. Despite the discouraging reports he had heard concerning the situation in Missouri, the new bishop received an enthusiastic welcome in Ste. Genevieve and St. Louis. Bishop DuBourg, whom Ann Lucas Hunt described as a person of "very great sense, learning, and eloquence," immediately launched an energetic drive to revive the church and to establish an educational program.[23] In addition to the town's French Creoles, DuBourg's St. Louis flock also included a growing number of Irish parishioners, including well-to-do businessmen Jeremiah Connor, Thomas Brady, Thomas Maguire, and John Mullanphy. In October 1819, several members of the local Irish community established an Irish Society, which soon raised the issue of language for the Sunday sermons. The French,

Irish, and a few Anglo-Americans had joined, however, in a subscription drive to help finance a new church building to replace the decaying 1776 log chapel that DuBourg described as a "poor stable." Although a shortage of funds prevented the completion of its interior, St. Louis's new cathedral, constructed on the corner of Market and Second streets, opened for services on Christmas Day 1819.[24]

To assist him in the work of the church, Bishop DuBourg had recruited a number of talented young European clerics, including Fathers Felix de Andreis and Joseph Rosati. With their assistance, members of the parish of St. Marys of the Barrens, located in Perry County south of Ste. Genevieve, in 1818 established a seminary of the Congregation of the Priests of the Mission of St. Vincent de Paul to train badly needed priests. Bishop DuBourg actively promoted Catholic educational institutions throughout his diocese. With the bishop's support, Father Francis Niel opened the St. Louis Academy, a Latin school for boys, in 1818. The next year, DuBourg approved the transformation of the academy into the College of St. Louis. Moreover, at DuBourg's invitation the Order of the Sacred Heart sent five of its members to establish a school for girls in the Missouri Territory. With Mother Philippine Duchesne in charge, the nuns arrived in St. Louis in August 1818. From there the sisters traveled to St. Charles, where they opened a school for girls, but it failed to attract many students. Handicapped by a scarcity of funds, the nuns lived and worked in the most primitive frontier conditions during their first winter in St. Charles. In letters written to relatives and friends in France, Mother Duchesne wrote, "We have had the privilege of doing without bread and water . . . . The Missouri is almost frozen over, and it is so cold that the water freezes beside the fire, as does the laundered linen hung there to dry." In 1819 they moved their school to Florissant, where they also opened a novitiate.[25]

Clerics and missionaries of all denominations agreed about the enormity of the challenges that faced them in the Missouri Territory, but the competition for converts sometimes caused the rival sects to take aim at one another rather than at the irreligion and immorality they were seeking to combat. New Englander Salmon Giddings objected to attempts by sectarian rivals to label a proposed Bible Society a "Yankee trick . . . designed by Presbyterians to unite church and state," and he later alleged that while preaching at a camp meeting in Bellevue, Methodist Bishop McKendree "did little else in his sermons than scold or whip the Presbyterians and Presbyterian missionaries."[26] In the Catholic stronghold of St. Louis, Graf von Phul reported that there was considerable anti-Catholic prejudice among the newcomers. Von Phul, who was not a Catholic, sought to diminish those sentiments by advising a fellow Protestant that the sermons of the local

Catholic priests "breathe only the most evangelical spirit."[27] In a few instances, the cooperative frontier spirit enabled members of competing denominations to rise above their differences and join to achieve a common goal. At Bellevue, the Baptists and the Presbyterians collaborated in the formation of a county auxiliary of the American Sunday School Union, and in St. Louis the Episcopalians supported Presbyterian efforts to construct a meetinghouse with the understanding that both groups would be able to use the building.[28]

The overall impact of religious and missionary activity in the Missouri Territory is difficult to assess: although they were not always consistent, the frontier churches and pastors exercised considerable powers of moral suasion over their flocks and provided an important stabilizing influence in the territory. Individual congregations frequently called delinquent members to account for offenses ranging from drunkenness, gambling, and profane swearing to espousing erroneous doctrine. Some church members accepted the admonitions of their fellow believers, while others paid them little heed. The church's influence in spiritual matters generally did not extend to the political and economic domain. It was one thing for frontier preachers to condemn the sins of the flesh, but it was quite another matter for them to venture into what their parishioners deemed to be the political arena.[29]

For many members of the clergy, the slavery question posed a particularly thorny problem. Some of Missouri's fastest-growing churches, including the Baptists, Methodists, and Presbyterians, originally opposed slavery in principle, but gradually members of those denominations in slaveholding areas modified their stance in order to win more white converts. Clerics, especially those with southern backgrounds, defended the peculiar institution and admonished their black hearers to accept their lot as slaves and serve their masters. Their insistence, however, that God would hold slaveowners accountable for the spiritual and material welfare of their human charges helped ameliorate slave conditions and rein in at least some excesses of abusive slaveholders. Most denominations accepted blacks as members, with Catholics, Presbyterians, Baptists, and Methodists leading the way. The Bethel Baptist Church in Cape Girardeau County, for example, baptized blacks as early as 1806, and twelve years later when the slavery question became a major issue in Missouri, the congregation created a separate seating section for its black members. Timothy Flint noted that a black man was examined and accepted when the Presbyterians conducted what was in all likelihood the first Protestant communion service in St. Louis. Blacks, of course, had long participated in the sacraments of the Catholic Church.[30]

John Mason Peck was especially active in working with blacks in St. Charles and St. Louis. He conducted special Sunday evening services for them, and they attended his Sunday schools. Over the protests of many, Peck was a proponent of black education and opened the doors of his regular school to black children. But even this popular preacher had to be careful not to exceed the proper limits in his pulpit. When the debate over slavery threatened Missouri's bid to become a state, Peck vigorously denied that he had spoken out on the controversial subject in his sermons: "Whatever my private sentiments on the subject of slavery itself or the policy or expediency of its limitation, I have too much regard for the cause of religion, the interests of the country, and my own public and private character, to preach on slavery or any other subject of party politics."[31] Methodist John Scripps adopted a different course and spoke out strongly against the retention of slavery in Missouri before departing for Illinois.[32]

Peck's attempts to provide schools for blacks was part of a larger concern among religious leaders for education. Since the concept of public, tax-supported education had not yet won general acceptance, the churches performed vital educational functions. Catholic priests and nuns and Protestant ministers were key providers of educational opportunities in territorial Missouri.

Some members of the Protestant clergy matched Bishop DuBourg's sponsorship of educational activity. Protestant Sunday schools offered instruction in reading and writing along with traditional Bible stories. Many ministers, most of whom were superior to the lay teachers in the territory, organized schools. Salmon Giddings, Timothy Flint, John Peck, James Welch, and Jesse Walker all ventured into the educational field. In 1819 the governing body of the Presbyterian Church in Missouri issued a list of recommended books for use in schools, including the Bible, *Webster's Spelling Book*, *Murray's English Reader*, and *Christian Orato*.[33]

Educational levels in the territory varied widely. Missouri boasted many highly educated and well-informed citizens, but it contained larger numbers of semiliterate and illiterate individuals too busy with the daily tasks of frontier living to be concerned that their children were growing up in ignorance. Salmon Giddings observed, "Not more than one-third of the inhabitants of the territory can read. Such people take but little pains to educate their children. When I converse with them on the subject, they say I cannot read & they can do as well as I have done without learning."[34] Henry Schoolcraft discovered that indifference to education was commonplace in the Ozarks. In one instance a family in Lawrence County had received a legal summons, but since none of the household members could read, they had simply ignored it. In another case a backwoods traveler shrugged off his complete ignorance of the hotly contested statehood issue by observing that he had "never troubled his head" about such matters.[35]

For most territorial residents, education was a private matter. Except for the tacit agreement that some provision should be made for educating indigent children, Missourians expected parents to assume full financial responsibility for the instruction of their offspring. Children of well-to-do, prominent families enjoyed substantially greater educational opportunities than those of the average frontier family. A greater variety of educational experiences could be found in the larger territorial communities than in outlying settlements. As one would-be schoolmaster lamented, the mode of dispersed settlement in the territorial hinterland "is very prejudicial to civilization—it makes it extremely difficult to have schools."[36]

Private schools in the larger towns offered formal instruction in subjects ranging from languages, geography, and higher mathematics to music, drawing, dancing, and fencing. St. Louis had the largest number of these educational establishments with the greatest variety of offerings, but prior to statehood most settlements had at least some type of school promising instruction in the basics. Some competent, well-qualified teachers provided their pupils with a sound educational program, while others left much to be desired even by nineteenth-century standards. Stiff competition for the limited number of local scholars able to afford the tuition produced a rapid turnover among these fledgling schools. Teachers had to supplement their income. Frederich Schewe, a German schoolmaster in St. Louis, sold candles on the side. Because of the schools' uneven quality and the uncertainty of their duration, some wealthy residents continued to send their children to schools outside the territory.[37]

Proposals seeking public support for the maintenance of schools failed to make much headway during the territorial period. Shortly after the Louisiana Territory came under American control, the special convention convened in St. Louis to protest the framework of government being suggested for Upper Louisiana called upon the U.S. government to provide funds to support a French and English school in each county. The petitioners also requested the establishment of a seminary that could offer instruction in French, English, the dead languages, mathematics, mechanics, natural and moral philosophy, and the principles of the U.S. Constitution. Congress ignored their appeal, but local community leaders occasionally attempted to broaden educational opportunities by establishing academies. Ste. Genevieve was the first Missouri settlement to undertake the creation of an academy, which proposed to offer instruction in English and French, along with such other languages and sciences as the funds would permit. A subscription drive in 1807 netted pledges of nearly three thousand dollars.

The academy's influential backers elected Father James Maxwell to chair the board of trustees.[38]

In 1808 the territorial legislature granted the academy a charter, but that was the extent of its assistance to the struggling educational enterprise. The subscribers planned to educate indigent and Indian children at no charge. The academy's articles of incorporation prohibited religious discrimination in instruction and in the selection of professors. Attempts to secure a federal land grand to help finance the academy failed. Although the trustees built a large stone building to house the academy, a shortage of funds prevented it from becoming the type of institution that its founders had envisioned and forced its untimely closing. The territorial legislature also incorporated academies for Potosi, Jackson, St. Charles, and Franklin, but the story of those institutions differed little from the unhappy experience of the Ste. Genevieve Academy.[39]

Attempts were also made to provide educational facilities for women. In the vicinity of St. Louis, several girls' schools offered instruction in traditional academic subjects and the domestic arts, with an emphasis on the latter. Outside the territorial capital, the educational opportunities for young women were more limited. The trustees of the Ste. Genevieve Academy had promised to admit females whenever funds were available, but the needed monies never materialized. The expense of maintaining separate schools discouraged the creation of women's schools in most places, but there were coeducational schools at Potosi, Jackson, and Franklin before the close of the territorial period.[40]

Since the only prerequisites for creating a school were a teacher, a room, and some students, the quality of territorial educational institutions varied greatly. Standards were generally low, although in announcing the opening of the St. Louis Academy, the founders did stipulate that "none will be received before he can read at least tolerably well."[41] Most schools could not afford to be so discriminating. The advertisements that regularly appeared in the *Missouri Gazette* promised innovative techniques to make learning easier. Not inclined to understate their own abilities, most schoolmasters claimed European training and proclaimed themselves competent to offer instruction in many widely divergent fields. Although Timothy Flint could hardly qualify as an unbiased observer since he had attempted to open a school himself, his caustic commentary on frontier schools contains a good deal of truth:

I have been amused in reading puffing advertisements in the newspapers. A little subscription school, in which half the pupils are abecedarians, is a college. One is a Lancastrian school, or a school of "instruction mutuelle." There is the Pestalozzi establishment, with its appropriate emblazoning. There is the agricultural school, the missionary school, the grammar box, the new way to make a wit of a dunce in six lessons, and all the mechanical ways of inoculating children with learning that they may not endure the pain of getting it the old and natural way.[42]

Despite the inadequacies and shortcomings of territorial Missouri's educational system, it probably compared favorably with those in other early nineteenth-century frontier areas.

Schools did not have a monopoly on cultural and intellectual activities in the territory. A small group of St. Louis residents organized an amateur thespian society in 1814, and the following year they presented their first performance in a former blacksmith shop, which they had converted into a theater. They continued to offer amateur productions for the entertainment of local audiences throughout the territorial period, and in 1818 a company of professional actors began performing. In addition to the theatrical productions, territorial residents could attend public debates, lectures, concerts, acrobatic performances, and patriotic celebrations. Typical of such occasions was the commemoration of American independence celebrated in St. Louis in 1819. At 3:00 p.m. on 5 July, a large crowd turned out to enjoy the festivities, which featured a full-length portrait of General Washington, along with a living eagle that periodically spread its wings to their full six-foot extent. The venerable Auguste Chouteau presided over a "sumptious dinner" followed by numerous toasts to patriotic events and personalities and a rousing rendition of "Yankee Doodle."[43]

Even though St. Louis's first commercial museum did not open until after the territorial period, William Clark often permitted visitors to view his extensive private collection. As one would expect, Clark's exhibits included many of the Indian relics that he had accumulated, along with a collection of unusual animal skins and such miscellaneous oddities as a stuffed pelican and elephant tusks.[44]

Reading matter was not totally lacking on the Missouri frontier. After its establishment in 1808, the *Missouri Gazette* provided its subscribers with tidbits of local news, letters from readers commenting on local political issues, reports on the latest Indian activities, lengthy national and international items reprinted verbatim from eastern periodicals, and a variety of feature articles on such topics as "Are the Planets Inhabited or Not?" Near the end of the territorial period, the rapidly growing population spawned the establishment of a second newspaper in St. Louis, along with similar publications in Jackson and Franklin.

At least some territorial Missourians continued to have access to a wide selection of books. Many St. Louis establishments offered books for sale to their customers, but Christian Wilt's lament that he had a fifty-year supply of *Love's Labours Lost* suggests that books were not fast movers. A few Missourians maintained substantial personal libraries that they allowed private borrowers to use. Bishop DuBourg opened his library of eight thousand volumes to students at the College of St. Louis. Attempts to establish a public library in St. Louis failed before statehood, but a Franklin group did organize a semiprivate library in 1819. Joseph Charless invited readers to come to the *Gazette* office, and in 1818 a "Reading Room & Punch House" opened nearby. While some Missourians undoubtedly availed themselves of these opportunities, reading was a luxury for which most residents had neither the time nor the inclination. Aside from a select group of well-educated citizens, few persons had any book other than the Bible, and many could not even afford it.[45]

Missouri's literary and artistic output was equally sparse. Henry Marie Brackenridge, who had been educated in Ste. Genevieve and had spent several years in the territory, probably ranks as early Missouri's leading literary figure. Timothy Flint, Henry Rowe Schoolcraft, John Bradbury, John Mason Peck, and Christian Schultz also published accounts of their travels in the Missouri Territory. Pierre François Regnier, a minor poet who lived in St. Louis and Ste. Genevieve between 1802 and 1821, wrote several poems in French.[46] Anna Maria von Phul was a local folk artist who came to St. Louis with her older brother Henry in 1818. Although she did not consider herself a serious painter, her sketches and watercolor drawings provide an extraordinary glimpse of people and places in early St. Louis. A few individuals collected European artwork. Bishop DuBourg's collection was one of the larger ones, but with the exception of a French painting of the martyrdom of St. Bartholomew, Graf von Phul adjudged them rather ordinary. He did admire a painting of St. Peter belonging to Auguste Chouteau.[47]

To label territorial Missouri as a cultural wasteland would be erroneous, but cultural and intellectual pursuits remained the special province of a small segment of the territorial population.[48] The world of poetry and drama would have been alien to most Missouri pioneer farmers, who toiled to clear their lands and raise their crops. These frontier people preferred to leave such heady matters to the territory's social and cultural elite. In the tradition of the eighteenth century, they also deferred to their so-called betters in political matters, but in the days prior to statehood, change was in the air. Ordinary people were beginning to claim their political prerogatives in the name of democracy.

CHAPTER SIXTEEN
MISSOURI
COMES OF AGE

The arrival of so many new settlers presaged the beginning of an era in Missouri politics that manifested the rising tide of political democracy sweeping across nineteenth-century America. Advocates of the new democratic order in the Missouri Territory initially found themselves matched against well-entrenched factions whose dominance was rooted in a political culture that blended eighteenth-century American republicanism with the vestiges of French and Spanish elitism and hierarchical authority. During the early years of American incumbency, the tempo of political change was slow, but as Missouri approached statehood, the popular forces gradually gained the ascendancy.

Missouri's second-stage territorial government, which took effect in 1812, was patterned after the general form established in the Northwest Ordinance of 1787. Local citizens gained the right to elect members of the territorial House of Representatives. Representation in that body was apportioned according to population, with one representative allotted for each five hundred inhabitants. The U.S. president appointed the nine members of the Legislative Council from a list of eighteen names selected by members of the lower house of the territorial assembly. The president also continued to name the governor and three justices of the superior court, but territorial voters—adult white males—were empowered to elect a nonvoting delegate to Congress.[1]

The advancement to second-class territorial status marked an important step in Missouri's political evolution. Politics had traditionally been the province of a small group of influential citizens. The introduction of the electoral process generated considerable popular interest and forced the local politicos to pitch their campaigns in the direction of ordinary voters. In the 1812 elections, candidates representing the long-dominant business and commercial leaders and large Spanish land claimants triumphed in the contests for delegate to Congress and for seats in the territorial legislature. Although the old-line leaders could claim victory, there were also signs that change was in the air.

Edward Hempstead, who was elected territorial delegate, had to turn aside charges that "fifteen or twenty great folks in St. Louis wanted to dictate and govern the territory."[2] Hempstead's opponents especially took aim at his close association with influential members of the small but politically powerful French-speaking community. He successfully deflected those allegations, but the fact remained that not a single French Creole was elected to the lower house of the territorial assembly. It was a sobering message. Even so, within the confines of St. Louis, the French elements remained dominant, and they retained friends in high places. Hempstead was their ally, and so was William Clark, whom President James Madison had just appointed to replace Benjamin Howard as Missouri's territorial governor.[3]

The Creoles could still muster some American support, but more and more of the territorial newcomers shared Frederick Bates's anti-French bias. The territorial secretary, who was serving as acting governor until Clark arrived, had confided to his brother Richard that "the very name of *liberty* deranges their [the Creoles'] intellects, and it appears absolutely impossible for them to form accurate conceptions of the rights which Justice creates on the one hand, and the obligations which it imposes on the other."[4] Under the circumstances, it was little wonder that the French inhabitants and their American supporters took strong exception to a ruling by Bates in 1812 that Missouri's new organic act had vacated all territorial offices held under gubernatorial appointment. In effect, the acting governor claimed authority to select his own slate of local territorial officials.

Two prominent incumbents, Louis Labeaume and Silas Bent, openly challenged Bates's interpretation of the statute, and several other St. Louis County officials joined them in refusing to surrender their positions. The local judicial system seemed poised on the verge of bedlam as rival sets of justices competed. Finally the territorial superior court intervened and declared the original officeholders entitled to continue in their posts. That ruling resolved the immediate legal problem, but it failed to reassure the early settlers, who saw their power and influence waning.[5]

When Auguste Chouteau subsequently resigned his seat on the St. Louis Court of Common Pleas in order to accept a presidential appointment to the territorial Legislative Council, Judge Bent urged him to reconsider. The American jurist warned his friend and colleague, "Your loss will be severely felt by the French people, for I am convinced that those Americans who declare the most inveterate hatred to the French and manifest a disposition to govern . . . will likely be appointed to office."[6] Chouteau decided, however, that he could accomplish more good for the French cause as a member of the Legislative Council.

Sectional jealousies further complicated territorial politics. Residents of the southern counties resented the preponderant influence exercised by the politically dominant clique of influential St. Louis leaders—both French and American. When the newly elected territorial House of Representatives met to select its list of nominees for the upper legislative chamber, the anti–St. Louis sentiment was apparent. Representatives from the southernmost counties—Ste. Genevieve, Cape Girardeau, and New Madrid— united to oppose resolutions favored by the St. Louis and St. Charles delegations calling for the apportionment of representation in the upper house according to population and for congressional authorization to choose Legislative Council members in a popular election. The delegates from the lower districts feared that the proposed measures would perpetuate St. Louis's domination of territorial affairs. After extended debate, the assembly endorsed a resolution recommending that the president give each of the four largest counties equal representation. In filling the posts on the nine-member council, President Madison complied with their wishes and appointed two persons each from St. Louis, St. Charles, Ste. Genevieve, and Cape Girardeau counties and the remaining one from New Madrid County. In this instance, the representatives from the southern counties had not allowed democratic impulses to get in the way of protecting their particular interests. The concerns about representation stemmed, at least in part, from a realization that local officeholders would have a greater voice in shaping territorial laws and policies under the new governmental framework.[7]

Shortly after the president announced his appointments to the Legislative Council, Governor William Clark convened both houses of the General Assembly in St. Louis. Clark cautioned the new and mostly inexperienced lawmakers against initiating unnecessary reforms and urged them to make modifications in the territorial code only where experience had shown material defects in the existing statutes.[8] The governor's admonition notwithstanding, rapidly changing local conditions necessitated frequent alterations in Missouri's territorial statutes. As in other frontier territories, the subject of local government and its organization commanded a disproportionate share of the legislature's time.[9]

The shift to representative government was not always smooth. Critics openly lambasted territorial legislators for wasting time and failing to address urgent local needs.[10] Edward Bates advised his brother Frederick, who was then in Washington, D.C., on business, that the legislature had been busily engaged in altering previous legislation but, he noted, "they create very little, and in fact their character for prudence and wisdom is not at all advanced in my estimation."[11]

When it appeared that persons circulating counterfeit banknotes in the territory would escape punishment because the Missouri statute governing that crime had been improperly drawn, a group of self-styled regulators in St. Louis County took it upon themselves to see that justice was done. The situation quickly threatened to get out of hand as the self-appointed vigilantes broadened the scope of their activities and began interrogating culprits suspected of gambling, hog stealing, and arson, even though those subjects were covered in the territorial statutes. Responsible citizens rallied to rein in the extralegal actions, but not before much of the blame for the episode had been laid at the legislature's doorstep.[12]

The territory's inadequate road system was a constant source of irritation to residents, who had to make their way along poorly marked traces connecting the scattered frontier settlements. The problem increased as more settlers moved away from the rivers and into Missouri's interior. In its legislation on the subject, the territorial assembly assigned county author- ities the primary responsibility for establishing and maintaining public roads. To help minimize the costs, the legislature authorized local officials to require able-bodied males between sixteen and forty-five to devote a spec- ified number of days each year to road construction and upkeep. The system's critics contended that it placed a hardship upon the poorer resi- dents, who could not afford the fines levied for failing to render the required service, but many settlers made the best of it and turned the compulsory work parties into quasi-social gatherings commonly known as road bees.[13]

The territorial assembly claimed an equally limited role for itself in other areas. It placed the burden for managing poor relief on county authorities, and it left to local groups the responsibility for creating schools. Aside from chartering several academies, all of which failed for want of sufficient financial support, and creating a board of trustees to oversee schools in St. Louis, the territorial legislature adopted a hands-off policy regarding public education.[14]

Governmental operations in the Missouri Territory remained modest in conformity with the Jeffersonian precepts of frugal and limited govern- ment. Those policies were well suited to a developing territory with limited financial resources. The popular aversion to higher taxes made territorial lawmakers wary of providing a broader range of governmental services. While most taxpayers favored better roads and schools, few wanted to bear the added costs necessary to provide them. Even with the General Assem- bly's conservative fiscal policies, the change in territorial status necessitated greater governmental expenditures. Salaries for public officials accounted for most of the increase, and local critics frequently complained about the amounts allocated for compensation. A legislative decision to pay territorial circuit judges $1,200 a year evoked especially strong criticism.[15]

Rising governmental costs forced the territorial legislature to search for new sources of income. Initially, the territory had no general property tax, only a series of special property taxes. In 1814, for the first time, the legislature added uncultivated lands in amounts up to eight hundred arpents to the list of taxable property in Missouri. The following year, the General Assembly completely revised the territorial revenue system and imposed a tax on all land in the territory, including lands claimed under preemption rights. Fines and fees, license charges on certain occupations and activities, a poll tax levied on able-bodied single men with limited property, and taxes on slaves, pleasure carriages, houses, and similar improvements constituted additional sources of territorial income.[16]

The so-called bachelor tax applied to all unmarried white males between the ages of twenty-one and fifty. Men far outnumbered women in early Missouri, and the legislators apparently enacted this legislation in the belief that it would encourage marriage, the family, and social stability and also would ensure that the footloose single male populace would contribute its share to the general welfare. Legislation such as this was not uncommon in frontier areas. The Spaniards had sometimes refused to grant land in Upper Louisiana to single men, and in a few instances they even warned incoming males that they would have to marry within two years or leave. The General Assembly repealed the bachelor tax in 1822, but the stigma against bachelors did not disappear so quickly. Despite the complaints from the legislature's critics against this tax and others, the overall tax burden in the territory remained light.[17]

The growing public debate over territorial issues further intensified local political factionalism. Joseph Charless, the *Missouri Gazette*'s combative editor, launched an assault against a St. Louis–based junto of lawyers, land claimants, judges, and military officers. The targets of Charless's journalistic jibes countered by establishing a rival St. Louis newspaper, the *Western Journal*, as a forum for their viewpoints.[18] The territory's overwhelming Republican majority and the diminished level of national party activity during the so-called Era of Good Feelings mitigated against the formation of nationally based political parties within the territory. In their absence, local issues and personal rivalries shaped the increasingly angry political squabbles between special-interest groups battling to direct the territory's destinies and enrich personal fortunes.

Political partisans routinely resorted to name calling and slander in discrediting opponents, and political disagreements often degenerated into bitter personal feuds. Charless, a principal combatant in the territory's political strife, lamented the personal animosity that converted "peaceful actors in an election into so many furious gladiators." Why, Charless asked, should a political rival be a personal enemy? The outspoken Irishman spoke from personal experience. During the course of his journalistic career he endured threats to burn his newspaper office, a fight with rival editor Isaac Henry, and a shot fired at him while he was working his garden.[19]

The St. Louis junto, which stood in the center of the territorial political battleground, drew most of its support from the coterie of French families who had long dominated affairs in that town. This tightly knit network of Creole families with their extensive fur trade and commercial enterprises and their numerous unconfirmed Spanish titles formed the junto's nucleus. Through the effective use of their wealth and influence, they had won the allegiance of some powerful American allies, including Governor Clark, Edward Hempstead, John Scott, and Thomas Hart Benton.

The junto's opposition came primarily from a rival group of land speculators who objected to the confirmation of the large unapproved Spanish grants. Composed principally of Americans who entered the territory after 1804, the faction's most vocal members included Charless, Rufus Easton, William Russell, John B. C. Lucas, his son Charles, and David Barton.

These opposing groups of influential businessmen and property holders continued to be the principal combatants in the political arena. Despite their bitter disagreements over the issue of private land claims, the rival groups had much in common. Both opposed the U.S. government's policy of reserving lead mines and saline lands for itself. Since the lead-leasing system had never operated satisfactorily, Missourians universally supported its abandonment in favor of the sale of the mineral and saline lands to private interests. Similarly, the junto and the anti-junto both called for the abolition of the government-operated Indian-trading factory system. Missouri traders blamed the unpopular government factories for contributing to the St. Louis–based fur trade's precipitous decline. Members of both factions also called for increased federal support for transportation and public schools.

When Edward Hempstead declined in 1814 to seek reelection as delegate to Congress, the territorial voters chose Rufus Easton to take his place. Easton's election came as a blow to the St. Louis junto, and its members took immediate steps to see that the new incumbent would be turned out of office at the next election. In an effort to neutralize Easton's strength in the southern counties and defuse the anti-St. Louis bias of voters outside the territorial capital, the junto selected Ste. Genevieve attorney John Scott as its candidate. Eight months before the 1816 election, junto supporters had already taken to the hustings in support of Scott. In their efforts to rally popular support behind their candidate, they directed their appeal to the widening territorial political constituency. Scott issued a circular letter in March 1816 in which he promised to work for the sale of government lead and saline lands, the abolition of the U.S. factory system, Missouri's speedy admission to statehood, the prompt sale of public lands in smaller quantities and at reduced prices, the establishment of new schools and roads, and a halt in the practice of forcibly removing squatters from the public domain.[20]

Junto members portrayed Easton as a do-nothing incumbent who had accomplished little for his constituents. They particularly criticized Easton's record on land claims, suggesting that he consistently opposed the legitimate interests of the Spanish land claimants. They also accused him of delaying the opening of public land sales in the territory to allow him time to sell his extensive private landholdings at inflated prices.[21]

The opposition frantically scrambled to refute the junto's unfavorable picture of Easton's record by crediting the first-term delegate with an impressive list of legislative accomplishments, including increased military protection, a new law preventing the removal of settlers from the public lands, relief for the sufferers of the New Madrid earthquake, Missouri's advancement to third-class territorial status, and a law confirming additional private land claims. At the same time that they accused the junto of misrepresentation and slander, Easton's adherents portrayed Scott as a profane gambler aligned with a faction of lawyers, colonels, and majors in St. Louis bent on dominating the territory and fleecing the public of its money, goods, and offices.[22]

Following the hotly contested 1816 election, Governor Clark, whose preference for Scott was well known, declared the Ste. Genevieve attorney the winner by a margin of fifteen votes. However, in certifying Scott's election, the governor had accepted a set of contested returns from Cote sans Dessein in St. Charles County, delivered to St. Louis by the victorious candidate himself, before they had been certified by the local election judges. The *Missouri Gazette*, which had endorsed Easton, printed a barrage of protests against the governor's actions.[23]

Easton went to Washington seeking to reverse the governor's decision, armed with a lengthy report detailing various irregularities and inaccuracies in the returns submitted by Clark. After reviewing his charges, the Committee on Elections in the U.S. House of Representatives recommended that Easton be seated by the House in Scott's place.[24] The committee's report triggered a lengthy debate, with some members attempting to sidestep the issue by arguing that the election of territorial delegates did not come under the House's jurisdiction since they were merely agents afforded the courtesy of sitting and speaking in the lower chamber.[25]

Although a majority of the House members rejected that interpretation, they did vote to recommit the report to the Committee on Elections for reconsideration. On 10 January 1817, the committee requested that it be relieved of further deliberation in the matter since it could not accurately determine the validity of the disputed returns in the Missouri election. After rejecting the committee's original recommendation that Easton be certified to sit as the delegate from Missouri, the House voted to declare the seat vacant and to order a new election on the grounds that the original election had been illegally conducted.[26]

While members of the U.S. Congress debated what to do about the contested Missouri election, members of the territorial assembly were embroiled in a bitter fight over the campaign to charter a second bank in the territory. As previously noted, the Bank of St. Louis's freewheeling and highly speculative approach had caused many of its more fiscally conservative original backers to withdraw their support and seek permission to create a rival financial institution guided by policies more to their liking.

Supporters of the Bank of St. Louis vigorously lobbied against the creation of a second local bank, but their efforts failed, and the territorial legislators voted to grant the Bank of Missouri a charter. William Neely, the president of the Legislative Council and an opponent of the new bank, refused to sign the bill and resigned his post in protest of the legislative action. The new bank's opponents frantically maneuvered to keep the legislation from reaching the governor's desk for a signature, but refusing to be denied their victory, the bill's supporters snatched it from the feuding officers of the upper chamber and delivered it to Governor Clark, who promptly signed it into law. Clark's detractors protested the unorthodox manner in which the bill had been handled, but the measure stood. While the efforts to win the charter succeeded, both banks soon failed, brought down by poor management and the aftereffects of the Panic of 1819.[27]

When word reached the territory in mid-summer 1817 that Congress had voided the previous year's election for territorial delegate, Governor Clark issued a call for a special election on the first Monday in August. Upon hearing the news, William Russell, a former soldier and land speculator now turned farmer, advised Easton that he was ready to spend time and money to keep Scott, Hempstead, and Benton out and to secure the election of either Easton, Frederick Bates, or Barton.[28] Following a careful evaluation of the situation, both the junto and the anti-junto groups decided to stick with the candidates they had supported in the original race. Both sides resorted to their well-worn arguments during the brief but intense campaign, and even before all of the votes had been tallied the results were being called into question.

The *Missouri Gazette* proclaimed it a "MILITARY ELECTION!!!" "On Monday last," the editor wrote, "an election for delegate to congress took place in the several districts of this territory. In this town, the election was conducted in the most violent, turbulent and savage manner." Charless listed a vast array of irregularities, including voter intimidation, military interference, buying votes with liquor, and excessive gubernatorial partisanship in the contest.[29]

Charless's tirade mirrored his frustration with Scott's easy victory over Easton in the rematch, but the evidence does indicate that conditions in St. Louis on election day had been far from ideal. According to the *Gazette's* account, a militia recruiting party paraded through the streets carrying signs supporting Scott. Although a military court of inquiry exonerated the militiamen of official misconduct, their actions obviously had increased local tensions. Tempers were at or near the boiling point as the voters assembled to cast their ballots. Capt. John O'Fallon, Governor Clark's nephew, engaged Easton supporter Dr. Robert Simpson in a shouting and shoving match at the polling place on election day, and several days later the officer pummeled Simpson during a heated exchange in the streets.[30]

Another election-day altercation had more tragic consequences. When Charles Lucas challenged Thomas Hart Benton to prove that he had paid his taxes before he voted, the hypersensitive Benton disdainfully referred to young Lucas as a "puppy." Lucas demanded the satisfaction due one gentleman from another for such an indignity, and Benton accepted. Once the necessary arrangements had been made, the two men met on the infamous Bloody Island in the Mississippi. Even though Benton seriously wounded Lucas during their first encounter, he insisted on a second meeting, and in that meeting he killed Lucas. The prominent young politician's death intensified the personal animosities and widened the already deep divisions in the political arena.[31]

The very next day, St. Louisans witnessed a second shooting, also due to personal animosities and political differences. In this instance, William Tharp, a laborer, shot and killed merchant William Smith on a St. Louis street corner following a confrontation. Smith had struck Tharp with a cane a few days earlier in the Bank of Missouri, but he had declined Tharp's demands that he be given satisfaction. Tharp responded by posting handbills declaring Smith to be "a most infamous SCOUNDREL, RASCAL, & COWARD," thereby precipitating the encounter that resulted in Smith's death. Tharp was indicted for murder, but a local jury subsequently acquitted him. Lucas and Smith were not the only prominent St. Louisans to be struck down in their prime during that summer. Two days prior to the first Benton-Lucas duel, Edward Hempstead had died from injuries sustained in a fall from his horse.[32]

Despite the turmoil surrounding the 1817 special election, Scott took his seat in Congress, and with his victory the St. Louis junto reclaimed its dominant position in the local political arena. As territorial delegate, Scott vigorously labored in support of the agenda he had outlined in his 1816 circular letter. Although he failed to secure congressional approval for most of those programs, he remained popular among his constituents, who continued him in office as Missouri's representative in the U.S. House until 1827.[33]

Governor Clark's open identification with the St. Louis clique made him a favorite target for the barbs of the anti-junto faction. They viewed his undisguised support for Scott as prima facie evidence of improper executive interference in the political processes. Rightly or wrongly, Clark's loyalty to long-time friends and members of the territorial establishment, coupled with his belief that their continuing support was in the national interest, guided his political choices. Ultimately his close association with individuals representing the old order in a rapidly changing territory turned out to be a serious liability. Clark's political instincts may have been flawed, but his considerable talents as an Indian diplomat, territorial administrator, and military commander, his conscientious devotion to official duties, and his consistent commitment to the welfare of the territory and its inhabitants earned him the distinction of being Missouri's best territorial governor.[34]

With new American farmers arriving daily, the changes in Missouri's cultural landscape and its political outlook became increasingly apparent. Missouri's new agrarian majority, which was concentrated in the territorial hinterland, increasingly embraced the emerging democratic impulses of nineteenth-century America. Proponents of this new order were less concerned with choosing judicious leaders than with choosing leaders who would faithfully represent their values and interests.[35] For those accustomed to the old ways, the new ones were sometimes difficult to fathom. John Heath, a resident of Boonslick, was indignant when President Madison bypassed his nomination for the territorial Legislative Council and appointed instead Benjamin Cooper, "a very ignorant old man, in his dotage," who could neither read nor write.[36] Cooper, the pioneer of settlement in central Missouri and apostle of the new order, was hardly the dolt Heath painted him to be, but he was a far cry from the sort of leader who once would have been called upon to take up the challenges of governance.[37] So was the rough-and-tumble Samuel Cole, scion of another early mid-Missouri pioneer family and member of the General Assembly, who physically prevented Governor McNair from breaking up a fist fight between two members of the legislature shortly after statehood.[38]

The final days of the territorial period represented the end of one era and the beginning of another. The old guard managed to hold its own against the popular new forces until statehood, but the field was not uncontested. When the territorial legislature appointed William Clark, Thomas Hart Benton, Auguste Chouteau, Alexander McNair, Jean P. Cabanné, and William C. Carr to serve as trustees for the St. Louis schools in 1817, they had to defend themselves against charges that a free people should have the right to elect such a board.[39] Some Missouri politicians—Alexander McNair, for instance—correctly read the signs, disengaged themselves from the old politics, and embraced the new democratic order.

The swelling population that helped transform Missouri politically also accelerated the drive for statehood. In 1816 Congress had advanced Missouri to the third and highest territorial grade and authorized its voters to elect members of the Legislative Council. On that happy occasion, Rufus Easton, the territorial delegate at the time, advised his constituents, "It is now admitted with few exceptions that our settlements ought to be fostered to the extent of such district of territory as will form us into a State; and I rejoice that the period is not far distant, when we will form a free and independent State government."[40]

Despite the building statehood fever, Easton's optimistic predictions proved a bit premature. Private petitions calling for statehood began circulating during the fall of 1817, and in November 1818 the territorial assembly drafted a memorial to Congress praying for Missouri's admission to the Union. Not inclined to understate their case, the Missouri legislators claimed a population of nearly one hundred thousand souls when in fact it was only approaching sixty-five thousand, but that was still more than enough for statehood. On 18 December, Speaker of the House Henry Clay laid their petition before the U.S. House of Representatives. After the bill was assigned to a select committee, Missouri's territorial delegate, John Scott, pressed for action. On 13 February 1819, the committee reported out a statehood bill, but during the ensuing debate in the House, Missouri's drive for statehood suddenly came untracked. New York congressman James Tallmadge succeeded in attaching an amendment to the Missouri bill restricting the further introduction of slaves and providing that all slaves born in Missouri after the territory became a state should be freed at age twenty-five. The Senate refused to accept Tallmadge's restrictions, and Congress remained deadlocked on the issue when the session ended.[41]

The congressional attempts to restrict slavery as a condition for admission to statehood aroused a storm of protests in the Missouri Territory as its people—slaves and free blacks excepted—rallied around the cause of statehood without restriction. In newspaper editorials, letters to the editor, grand jury presentments, and public meetings, the antirestrictionists indignantly condemned the congressional interference. Some even went so far as to proclaim it a plot by easterners to halt the westward flow of settlement.[42] The Mount Pleasant Baptist Association in Howard County, while expressing regret over the existence of slavery, declared it an issue belonging solely to the states and beyond congressional purview. In fact, it seems clear that the great majority of white Missourians in 1819 favored the perpetuation of slavery. The few brave souls who dared to raise their voices in dissent invited the wrath of their neighbors. In one such case, Humphrey Smith of Franklin was forced to flee the territory to avoid prosecution for inciting slaves to rebellion. The devout Methodist leader had questioned publicly how a church member could be a slaveowner.[43] In St. Louis, Thomas Hart Benton, the editor of the *St. Louis Enquirer,* took pains to reassure his readers following reports of a 5 June meeting at the home of Elisha Patterson in the St. Ferdinand township of St. Louis County. Patterson and his friends had adopted a resolution supporting the Tallmadge amendment and labeling the slave system a great evil, but Benton editorialized that no bona fide St. Louis citizens supported the congressional right to restrict slavery. According to him, all such talk came from newcomers not yet qualified to vote.[44] Nobody thought to poll Missouri's black residents on the subject.

The Missouri statehood controversy became a national issue as the debate over the Missouri question raged throughout the country. Jonathan Roberts, a member of the U.S. House of Representatives from Pennsylvania, advised his friend in St. Louis, John B. C. Lucas, that the "Missouri question . . . runs far wider than Missouri."[45] Slavery's defenders viewed Senator Rufus King's lengthy 26–27 February speech supporting Tallmadge's proposal as the debut of constitutional antislavery. Sentiment favoring the restriction of slavery had been steadily building in the more populous northern states, but with the number of slave and free states equally divided at eleven apiece, the outnumbered southerners were unwilling to consider breaking the balance in the Senate. Some members of Congress openly questioned whether this difficult issue could be resolved, but under Henry Clay's skillful guidance the feuding combatants eventually struck a compromise. They agreed to maintain the equality between free and slave states by admitting Missouri as a slave state without restriction and Maine, which also had applied for admission to the Union, as a free state. In addition, Clay's Missouri Compromise included a provision forever banning slavery from all remaining portions of the Louisiana Purchase above 36°30′ north latitude, the westward extension of Missouri's southern boundary. The measure's final approval cleared the way for Missouri's admission to the Union, but the bitter dispute over slavery portended a troubled future for the American republic. Former president Thomas Jefferson, who had favored restriction in 1784 but now opposed it, declared from his home at Monticello that the Missouri crisis, "like a firebell in the night, awakened and filled me with terror."[46]

President James Monroe signed the Missouri Enabling Act on 6 March 1820, and when the news reached Missouri a little over two weeks later, it touched off spontaneous public celebrations throughout the territory. The Enabling Act defined the boundaries for the proposed new state and authorized the people of Missouri to elect a convention to draft a state constitution. The elections to choose delegates to the constitutional convention were held during the first week in May and were open to all free, white males who had reached the age of twenty-one and had resided in the Missouri Territory for three months prior to the voting day. The forty-one delegates were apportioned among the territory's fifteen counties.[47]

When a few citizens in the territory had the temerity to question if Missouri should consider limiting the further introduction of slavery, the proslavery majority raised a hue and cry against the menace of restrictionism. The most outspoken statement in support of restriction came from a meeting in Herculaneum attended by the well-known antislavery crusader Benjamin Lundy. Lundy, who resided only briefly in Missouri, chaired a committee that drafted an address to the voters of Jefferson County branding black servitude as a "dangerous system of cruelty and injustice." It questioned the assumption that the state would benefit economically from slavery and advised the voters that the upcoming election might be their only opportunity to "oppose the horrible system with effect."[48]

The fears about restrictionism in Missouri were greatly overblown. The issue was raised in only five of the territory's fifteen counties, and no restrictionists were elected. The few bona fide candidates who supported some future limitation made it clear that they had no intention of interfering with those slaves already in the territory. John B. C. Lucas, who ran as a restrictionist candidate in St. Louis County, was himself a slaveholder. For him and most others supporting eventual restriction, the issue was economic, not moral. He touted the advantages of free labor over slave labor in promoting the new state's long-term economic development. Lucas, like all other restrictionist candidates, was trounced in the election, but he did garner the support of members of two small abolitionist Baptist congregations near St. Louis.[49]

Joseph Charless unsuccessfully tried to refocus the political debate by insisting that the two crucial issues in the contests for the constitutional convention were whether voting should be restricted to freeholders, as some reportedly favored, and whether elections should be conducted viva voce or by ballot.[50] The preoccupation with the slavery question resulting from the bitter battle in Congress seems to have preempted any attempts to make the election a referendum on broadening participation in the political process. The conservative, commercially oriented territorial leaders successfully seized upon the antislavery fears and positioned themselves as the champions of the antirestrictionist majority. For the moment, statehood and the future of slavery in Missouri were the paramount issues, and a majority of the voters played it safe by selecting well-known, proslavery property holders to represent them in the constitutional convention, which convened on 13 June in St. Louis's Mansion House Hotel.[51]

The forty-one delegates could be loosely divided into three factions— liberal, conservative, and moderate. The fourteen members who could be classified as liberals favored frequent elections, no property qualifications for voting, and popular election of judges, sheriffs, and coroners. They were more democratically inclined than the conservative majority and worked unsuccessfully, under the leadership of Joseph McFerron of Cape Girardeau County, to limit executive power in favor of greater popular control. The sixteen-member conservative bloc, which represented the St. Louis junto and was known in the convention as "the caucus," managed to curtail most of the liberal measures. The smaller moderate group mediated between the opposing factions.[52]

David Barton, a St. Louis lawyer and junto member, presided over the convention and saw to it that lawyers who shared his conservative views gained seats on key drafting committees. According to historian Floyd Shoemaker, Barton, Edward Bates, John Cook, John Rice Jones, Jonathan Findlay, Duff Green, and John Scott were the principal architects of the final document, which was completed in only five weeks. Since the convention members decided against submitting their handiwork to the voters for ratification, they forwarded the new constitution directly to Congress for its inspection.[53]

Missouri's 1820 Constitution was essentially a conservative document. It did provide for universal manhood suffrage, and it allowed the legislature to override a governor's veto with an absolute majority of each house after it considered the executive's objections. But over strenuous objections from the liberals, the constitution provided for a strong, independent judiciary, with state judges appointed by the governor for life. It set the minimum salary for the governor and judges at two thousand dollars a year and included a stipulation that those amounts could not be reduced during an official's term of office. Since many persons considered the minimum salaries outrageously high, that provision aroused considerable public comment.[54]

The framers took great pains to protect slavery. They prohibited the legislature from authorizing emancipation without the owner's consent and from restricting the importation of new slaves into the state. They went so far as to include a constitutional provision mandating the General Assembly to enact legislation to prevent free blacks and mulattos from entering the state. With the exception of questions relating to slavery, the architects of the constitution imposed few limitations on the General Assembly's legislative authority. Even constitutional amendments did not have to be ratified by the people. They could be proposed by a two-thirds majority of both houses and ratified by the same margin during the first session of the succeeding legislature. As previously noted, the framers chose not to submit the completed document to the people for approval.[55]

The conservative factions had carried the day in the convention, but the issues raised by the liberals during the deliberations loomed large when the voters went to the polls in August to select a governor, lieutenant governor, representative to the U.S. Congress, and members of the General Assembly. In the gubernatorial contest, Alexander McNair, who had parted company with his former allies in the little junto and voted with the liberal faction in the convention, announced his candidacy. William Clark also declared his intent to seek the governorship with the junto's backing. McNair openly criticized the new constitution's undemocratic features and campaigned throughout the state in an effort to win the rural support. His opponents accused the well-liked militia leader of using his "greatest exertions in the tippling shops." By making the unpopular salary-guarantee clause a major issue in his campaign, McNair became one of the few candidates in the annals of American politics who tried to convince voters that, if elected, he would be overpaid.[56]

Clark, whose wife, Julia, had died in Virginia in June, was out of the state during the campaign. Not attuned to the changing territorial political climate, he referred anyone with questions about his suitability for the office to the old inhabitants and early settlers, with whom he had long been on friendly terms. His close identification with that group and the unpopularity of his Indian policies sealed his fate with the growing number of voters outside St. Louis. When the returns were in, McNair had swamped his opponent, 6,576 to 2,656.[57]

Many of the constitutional convention delegates who had been associated with the caucus also were defeated, as the fully enfranchised adult white males of Missouri made their presence felt in a dramatic way once the statehood and slavery issues had been resolved. In the lieutenant governor's race, William H. Ashley, a prominent businessman and popular militia leader, defeated Nathaniel Cook, a southeast Missouri politician and constitutional convention member with strong ties to the junto. Of the junto's statewide candidates, only John Scott managed to survive as he retained the right to represent Missouri in the U.S. House of Representatives. In the face of these unexpected results, junto members reordered their ranks in order to ensure victory in the upcoming contest in the

General Assembly to select U.S. senators. The caucus managed to hold off the popular onslaught and secure the election of David Barton and Thomas Hart Benton. Shortly after statehood, Benton would break ranks with the junto and proclaim himself a champion of the common people in opposition to his Whiggish senatorial colleague, David Barton.

But a final obstacle remained to be overcome before statehood could become a reality for Missourians. When the state's new constitution was placed before Congress in November 1820, opponents of Missouri's admission as a slave state challenged the constitutional provision requiring the General Assembly to enact legislation to keep free blacks and mulattos from moving into the state. Claiming that this stipulation violated the rights of free blacks who were recognized as citizens by some northern states, they sought to delay Missouri's entry.

Missourians protested that many states had similar provisions in their constitutions, and Henry Clay, who had been influential in drafting the first Missouri Compromise, moved to piece together a face-saving formula that would remove this final obstacle. Under the terms of that second compromise, Congress authorized President James Monroe to approve Missouri's admission upon receipt of assurance from the state's General Assembly that it would never construe the offending clause as sanctioning the passage of any law abridging the privileges and immunities of U.S. citizens. The Missouri legislators hastily complied and adopted the required statement with tongue in cheek. Once that gesture had been completed, President Monroe made it official on 10 August 1821 and proclaimed Missouri the twenty-fourth state in the Union amid sighs of relief and shouts of jubilation. With the completion of that final territorial rite of passage, the one-time wilderness outpost had come of age.[58]

EPILOGUE
THE LEGACY OF COLONIAL AND TERRITORIAL MISSOURI

A t first glance, today's Missouri has little resemblance to the sparsely populated, premodern frontier territory that became a state in 1821. Despite the dramatic transformation Missouri has undergone since joining the Union, many of its distinguishing characteristics were already discernible in the years preceding statehood. For centuries Indian peoples, and then rival European powers, had competed to control the vital region situated at the confluence of North America's great central river system in the continental heartland. Most of these diverse groups left remnants to mark their presence, and by the time Missouri came under the aegis of the American republic in 1803, it could lay claim to a rich cultural heritage containing Indian, French, Spanish, African, Anglo-American, and other scattered strains.

The Louisiana Purchase signaled the beginning of a new era for Missouri's ancient inhabitants, who unexpectedly found themselves caught up in Thomas Jefferson's designs for expanding "Freedom's Empire" into the vast trans-Mississippi domains. The creative mixing of diverse peoples in Missouri's frontier environment produced folkways that extolled cooperation, democratic values, and material success. But not all early Missourians were equal partners in the emerging order. The Indians were systematically pushed beyond the territory's western border, and the vast majority of prestatehood blacks were enslaved and treated as chattel.

Missouri's location at the North American crossroads also gave it a unique niche in the broader scheme of national immigration patterns. The migrants from the Old South, who began coming to Missouri during the waning days of the Spanish era and continued flocking to the state well into the mid-nineteenth century, represented the northernmost extension of southern culture in the United States. This substantial southern influx reinforced the territory's slave base, established its future as a border state, and ultimately gave Missouri a cast different from other midwestern states.

Missouri's fertile soil and its economic opportunities likewise drew substantial German and Irish elements, placing the state at the southern periphery of midwestern German and Northern European settlement. The great surge in German and Irish immigration occurred after statehood, but a vanguard of both groups reached Missouri well in advance of 1821. So did the early Scotch-Irish pioneers who entered the Ozarks. They brought southern Appalachian hill culture to its westernmost limits in the United States and added yet another dimension to Missouri's multifaceted image.[1]

Missouri and its people occasionally found themselves at center stage in national and international developments. When the subject of slavery stirred up increased contention among Americans nationally, Missouri became a focal point in the early controversies surrounding the troubling issue. Missouri's application for statehood in 1818 precipitated a major crisis over slavery extension, which, in the words of Jefferson, sounded an alarm "like a firebell in the night." Jefferson's fears proved well founded as the debate over slavery persisted both within Missouri and beyond its borders. By the eve of the Civil War, a clash over slavery and the Union between Missouri's long-dominant southern elements and its growing Germanic and Yankee populace brought devastation and made Missouri the mirror image of a divided nation.

As the gateway to the West, Missouri played an equally vital role in the settlement and development of the western half of the North American continent. Not only did it serve as the point of departure for vast numbers of westering Americans, but it also became a depot and warehouse for much of that region's produce. The annals of the West are filled with the names of early Missouri men and women who symbolize the pioneering spirit. Etienne de Bourgmont, Auguste and Pierre Chouteau, their mother Marie Thérèse Bourgeois Chouteau, Manuel Lisa, Daniel and Rebecca Boone, Moses Austin, Mike Fink, Meriwether Lewis, William Clark, and William H. Ashley are only a few of the celebrated figures of western lore with significant links to prestatehood Missouri.

It is little wonder that confusion still exists concerning Missouri's proper identity. Many northerners consider Missourians to be unreconstructed rebels, while southerners are apt to classify the Show-Me state's inhabitants as Yankees. Easterners think of Kansas City as a cowtown on the western prairies, but westerners associate the state with the eastern establishment. Not clearly situated in any of the four national geographic sections, and yet a part of all, Missouri and its people personify American pluralism.

Even at this late date, tangible reminders of Missouri's colonial and territorial era continue to surround modern Missourians. Although the Indians departed long ago, their presence remains permanently enshrined in the state's name and in the names of many other Missouri places—Kansas City, Moniteau County, and the Osage River, to cite only a few. The Indian heritage also persists in the blood of numerous present-day residents. According to the 1980 U.S. Census, nearly 250,000 Missourians claim some Indian ancestry. Not surprisingly, these modern descendants of the Osage,

Shawnee, Delaware, Cherokee, and Kickapoo people are heavily concentrated in the Ozarks region, which their ancestors once called home.[2]

Colonial Missouri's French legacy lives on in places like Ste. Genevieve and Old Mines. Ste. Genevieve, Missouri's oldest permanent settlement, is a national treasure. Its restored French-colonial structures, many built before 1821, and its warm and engaging residents recreate the ambience of Missouri's earliest days. In the rugged terrain of the nearby mining district in the vicinity of Old Mines, a handful of dedicated people continue to speak the Old French of their eighteenth-century forebears.

The Creole buildings have long since disappeared in St. Louis, but the distinctive street patterns based on the outlines of common fields and irregularly shaped land grants, the French place names, and the coterie of descendants of the river town's founding families remain as reminders of the beginnings of Missouri's largest city. So does the majestic, modern Gateway Arch, situated on the bank of the Mississippi at the spot where Pierre de Laclède and Auguste Chouteau constructed the city's original structures. In nearby St. Charles County, Nathan Boone's restored dwelling bears witness to the Anglo-American pioneers who flooded into Missouri in the late eighteenth and early nineteenth centuries. Across the state near Kansas City, the reconstructed Fort Osage, standing on the bluff overlooking the state's other great river, calls to mind the days when the wilderness region was primarily the haunt of Indians and their trading partners.

The southern traditions of many of Missouri's frontier settlers live on in the Democratic politics and vernacular architecture of central Missouri's river counties, still commonly referred to as Little Dixie. The state's capital city appropriately bears the name of Thomas Jefferson, the founding father whose vision of America's future extended to the new world beyond the Mississippi.[3] To the south, in the scenic Ozark landscape, vestiges of the hill culture that took root in Missouri's earliest days persist in out-of-the-way places, where a few still cling to the old ways. Elsewhere in the Ozarks, the legends of lost silver mines and the lore of the Yocum family, used now to lure tourists and their dollars into the region, perpetuate familiar Ozark tales dating from the pioneer era.[4]

Missouri's colonial and territorial legacy is also manifested in less obvious ways. The cooperative spirit of helping one's neighbors, a commonplace on the early Missouri frontier, still persists in many parts of the state, but especially in its small towns and rural areas. The roots of Missouri's traditional fiscal conservatism, low-tax mentality, and cautionary approach to resolving its problems likewise predate statehood. But the most enduring legacy of Missouri's earliest days is its racially and culturally diverse population. Then as now, Missouri's people are its greatest resource.

Missourians share a rich heritage. The state's amalgam of peoples, cultures, and traditions, its strategic geographic location in the American heartland, its involvement with major national and international historical developments, and its economic, political, and social diversity make its story a vital chapter in U.S. history. Missouri emerged from its wilderness origins to become, in the words of historian Lawrence Christensen, "the most American of states . . . a microcosm of the nation."[5]

NOTES

ABBREVIATIONS

Bates Papers: The Life and Papers of Frederick Bates, edited by Thomas M. Marshall. 2 vols. St. Louis: Missouri Historical Society, 1926.

BLC: Before Lewis and Clark: Documents Illustrating the History of Missouri, 1785–1804, edited by Abraham P. Nasatir. 2 vols. St. Louis: St. Louis Historical Documents Foundation, 1952.

BMHS: Bulletin of the Missouri Historical Society.

Draper MSS: Draper Manuscripts, State Historical Society of Wisconsin, Madison.

MHR: Missouri Historical Review.

MVHR: Mississippi Valley Historical Review.

SMV: Spain in the Mississippi Valley, 1765–1794, edited by Lawrence Kinnaird. 3 vols. Annual Report of the American Historical Association for the Year 1945. Washington, D.C.: Government Printing Office, 1946.

SRM: The Spanish Regime in Missouri, edited by Louis Houck. 2 vols. Chicago: R. R. Donnelley, 1909.

Territorial Papers: The Territorial Papers of the United States, edited by Clarence E. Carter. Vol. 13, *Louisiana-Missouri, 1803–1806* (1948); vol. 14, *Louisiana-Missouri, 1806–1814* (1949); vol. 15, *Louisiana-Missouri, 1815–1821* (1954). Washington, D.C.: U.S. Government Printing Office.

PREFACE

1. "The Discovery of Americans," 443.
2. See William E. Foley, "Antebellum Missouri in Historical Perspective."

CHAPTER 1. EXPLORING THE WILDERNESS

1. See Virgil J. Vogel, "The Origin and Meaning of 'Missouri,'" and Donald M. Lance, "The Origin and Pronunciation of 'Missouri.'"
2. Charles E. Burgess, "The DeSoto Myth in Missouri."
3. For an overview of Spanish colonization in North America, see John Francis Bannon, *The Spanish Borderlands Frontier, 1513–1821*, and Charles Gibson, *Spain in America*.
4. W. J. Eccles, *France in America*, 14–15, 19–24.
5. Eccles, *The Canadian Frontier, 1534–1760*, 104–5.
6. Ibid., 106.
7. Ibid.
8. Marquette's career is covered in Joseph P. Donnelly, *Jacques Marquette, S.J., 1637–1675*, and John Francis Bannon, "Jacques Marquette, 1637–1675." For Jolliet's life, see Jean Delanglez, *Life and Voyages of Louis Jolliet (1645–1700)*. Documents pertaining to Marquette, Jolliet, and the preparations for their expedition can be found in Reuben Gold Thwaites, ed., *The Jesuit Relations and Allied Documents*, 58:95, 59:88–91.
9. Thwaites, ed., *Jesuit Relations*, 59:91, 107, 109–25.
10. Ibid., 139–41. The mysterious bluff painting first mentioned by Marquette and later known as the Piasa Bird was located on the Mississippi's east bank near present-day Alton, Illinois. For details, see Wayne C. Temple, "The Piasa Bird: Fact or Fiction."
11. An excellent summary of early efforts to chart the Missouri's course is W. Raymond Wood, "Mapping the Missouri River Through the Great Plains, 1673–1895," 30–34.
12. Thwaites, ed., *Jesuit Relations*, 59:159–61.
13. Donnelly, *Marquette*, 230–32; Delanglez, *Jolliet*, 135ff.; and Eccles, *Canadian Frontier*, 107.
14. Donnelly, *Marquette*, 236, 249–52, and 259–60.
15. Eccles, *Canadian Frontier*, 109; *France in America*, 86–89.
16. Peter H. Wood, "La Salle: Discovery of a Lost Explorer," 310.
17. Ibid., 294–323. Wood suggests that inaccurate maps and poor geographic knowledge were major causes for La Salle's final fiasco in the Texas wilderness.
18. Eccles, "The Fur Trade and Eighteenth-Century Imperialism," 342–45.
19. Ibid.
20. James Axtel, *The Invasion Within: The Contest of Cultures in Colonial North America*, 43, 72–90.

21. Ibid.; Gabriel Marest to Father Germon, 9 November 1712, in Thwaites, ed., *Jesuit Relations*, 66:219.

22. A brief study of Father Marest can be found in John Francis Bannon, "Black Robe Frontiersman: Gabriel Marest, S.J." For the story of the River Des Peres settlement, see Mary Borgia Palm, *Jesuit Missions in the Illinois Country, 1673–1763*, 36–41; Temple, *Indian Villages of the Illinois Country*, 34–35; Gilbert J. Garraghan, "First Settlement on the Site of St. Louis"; Roger W. Taylor, *Watershed–1: Swamp Hawk*; and Thwaites, ed., *Jesuit Relations*, 65:69.

23. Father Gabriel Marest to Father Germon, 9 November 1712, in Thwaites, ed., *Jesuit Relations*, 66:231.

24. Palm, *Jesuit Missions*, 36–41; Taylor, *Watershed–1*, 31–32.

25. Palm, *Jesuit Missions*, 40–41; Norman W. Caldwell, "Charles Juchereau de Saint-Denis: A French Pioneer in the Mississippi Valley."

26. Report of Father Jacques Gravier, 14 February 1694, in Thwaites, ed., *Jesuit Relations*, 64:171; Gilbert Din and Abraham P. Nasatir, *The Imperial Osages: Spanish-Indian Diplomacy in the Mississippi Valley*, 29–30; *BLC*, 1:16–17; and Willard H. Rollings, "Prairie Hegemony: An Ethnohistorical Study of the Osage from Early Times to 1840" (Ph.D. diss., Texas Tech University, 1983), 189.

27. Frank Norall, *Bourgmont: Explorer of the Missouri, 1698–1725*, 4–13. This carefully researched new study stands as the definitive work on Bourgmont and his activities.

28. An excellent account of the Missouri Indians is Robert T. Bray, "The Missouri Indian Tribe in Archaeology and History." A brief summary of Missouri life and culture is also found in Carl H. Chapman and Eleanor F. Chapman, *Indians and Archaeology of Missouri*, 99–106.

29. Norall, *Bourgmont*, 15–24. See also Marcel Giraud, "Étienne Veniard De Bourgmont's 'Exact Description of Louisiana,' " and Robert T. Bray, "Bourgmond's Fort d'Orleans and the Missouri Indians."

30. Norall, *Bourgmont*, 24–28. Guillaume Delisle used Bourgmont's data to draw the first accurate map of the lower Missouri. Complete translations of both the "Exact Description" and the "Route to Ascend the Missouri" can be found in ibid., 99–123.

31. Ibid., 28–30, 168n; Commission of Bourgmont as Captain of Infantry in Company of Indies, 26 July 1720, photostatic copy in Sieur de Bourgmont Papers, Missouri Historical Society.

32. The most thorough and complete historical assessment of the Osages is Rollings, "Prairie Hegemony." A good brief summary can be found in Chapman and Chapman, *Indians and Archaeology of Missouri*, 106–17. Din and Nasatir's *Imperial Osages* provides a comprehensive account of Spanish-Osage diplomacy.

33. Rollings, "Prairie Hegemony," 39, 177–79.

34. Ibid., 174–76.

35. Ibid., 31–35.

36. Ibid., 57, 181; Chapman and Chapman, *Indians and Archaeology of Missouri*, 110–14.

37. Rollings, "Prairie Hegemony," 47–51, 83–87, 109–12. When Dutisné visited the Osage village in 1719, he observed that the chief's powers were "not very absolute." See Mildred Mott Wedel, "Claude-Charles Dutisné: A Review of His 1719 Journeys," part 1, p. 15.

38. Rollings, "Prairie Hegemony," 10–16.

39. Ibid., 105–7, 202–3, 220–21.

40. Eccles, *Canadian Frontier*, 136, 142, and *France in America*, 158–61; Giraud, *A History of Louisiana, Vol. I: The Reign of Louis XIV, 1698–1715*, 249–50.

41. Eccles, *France in America*, 161–63; Giraud, *History of Louisiana*, 1:250–55; and Natalia M. Belting, *Kaskaskia Under the French Regime*, 16.

42. Wedel, "Claude-Charles Dutisné," part 1, pp. 7–9; John E. Rothensteiner, "Earliest History of Mine La Motte," 199–202.

43. Rothensteiner, "Earliest History of Mine La Motte."

44. Ibid.; Crozat as quoted in Marc de Villiers du Terrage, *The Last Years of French Louisiana*, edited by Carl A. Brasseaux and Glenn R. Conrad, translated by Hosea Phillips, 15.

45. Eccles, *France in America*, 163–64.

CHAPTER 2. MISSOURI'S FRENCH FOUNDATIONS

1. Marc de Villiers du Terrage, *The Last Years of French Louisiana*, 15; Natalia M. Belting, *Kaskaskia Under the French Regime*, 16; and Glenn R. Conrad, "The French Administrative Controversy Over the Illinois Country" (unpublished paper), 4–5.

2. Villiers du Terrage, *Last Years of French Louisiana*, 15–16; Conrad, "French Administrative Controversy," 4–5.

3. Villiers du Terrage, *Last Years of French Louisiana*, 15–16; Belting, *Kaskaskia Under the French Regime*, 16–19; W. J. Eccles, *France in America*, 164–66; and Anna Price, "The Three Lives of Fort de Chartres: French Outpost on the Mississippi."

4. John E. Rothensteiner, "Earliest History of Mine La Motte," 203–8.

5. Ibid., 209–10; Carl Ekberg, "Antoine Valentin de Gruy: Early Missouri Explorer," 137, and *Colonial Ste. Genevieve: An Adventure on the Mississippi Frontier*, 145–46; Ekberg et al., *A Cultural, Geographical and Historical Study of the Pine Ford Lake Project Area, Washington, Jefferson, Franklin, and St. Francois Counties, Missouri*, 10–15.

6. "Memoir of sieur de Guis [*sic*] Concerning Lead Mines in the Illinois Country," 1743, in Ekberg, "Antoine de Gruy," 147–48.

7. Report of Des Ursins, 10 July 1719, in Rothensteiner, "Mine La Motte," 206.

8. Ibid. Apparently following Henry Rowe Schoolcraft's account, Louis Houck stated that Renault brought five hundred slaves with him. Existing records indicate that this number is much too large. The 1726 French census credited Renault with owning twenty slaves. See Ekberg, *Colonial Ste. Genevieve*, 199–200; and "Memoir de sieur de Guis," in Ekberg, "Antoine de Gruy," 146–47.

9. De Gruy reported that more than 2,200 of the 60- to 80-pound lead bars were produced at Mine La Motte in both 1741 and 1742. He also stated that frequent Sioux and Fox Indian assaults had caused Renault to abandon his mines at the Mineral Fork. See "Memoir de sieur de Guis," in Ekberg, "Antoine de Gruy," 146, 148; and Ekberg, *Colonial Ste. Genevieve*, 146–47.

10. Mildred Mott Wedel, "Claude-Charles Dutisné: A Review of His 1719 Journeys," part 1, pp. 11–12.

11. Ibid., 12–17, and part 2, 147–48; Claude-Charles Dutisné to Bienville, 22 November 1719, in Henri Folmer, "French Expansion Toward New Mexico in the Eighteenth Century" (M.A. thesis, University of Denver, 1939), 70–77; and Tanis Chapman Thorne, "People of the River: Mixed-Blood Families on the Lower Missouri" (Ph.D. diss., UCLA, 1987), 138–39.

12. Wedel, "Claude-Charles Dutisné," part 2, 152.

13. Ibid., 156–63.

14. Alfred Barnaby Thomas, *After Coronado: Spanish Exploration Northeast of New Mexico, 1696–1727*, 36–39; Folmer, "French Expansion Toward New Mexico," 92, 124.

15. Bienville to the Council of Regency, 25 April 1722, in Folmer, "French Expansion Toward New Mexico," 124.

16. Robert T. Bray, "Bourgmond's Fort d'Orleans and the Missouri Indians," 14.

17. Instructions to Bourgmont, 17 January 1722, in Folmer, "French Expansion Toward New Mexico," 127–28; Frank Norall, *Bourgmont: Explorer of the Missouri, 1698–1725*, 29–37.

18. Bray, "Bourgmond's Fort d'Orleans," 15; Gilbert J. Garraghan, "Fort Orleans of the Missoury," 376; and Norall, *Bourgmont*, 39–42.

19. Bray, "Bourgmond's Fort d'Orleans," 18–19; Bourgmont to Commissaries of the Colony, 11 January 1724, in Folmer, "French Expansion Toward New Mexico," 150. The best guess is that Fort Orleans was located about two-and-a-half miles south-southeast of the present town of Wakenda, but the exact location has never been verified. Changes in the course of the river and major levee work in the 1930s make it unlikely that any of the original traces can be found at this late date. Norall, *Bourgmont*, 47.

20. Bray, "Bourgmond's Fort d'Orleans," 19–22; Folmer, "French Expansion Toward New Mexico," 158.

21. Journal of De Bourgmond's Voyage to the Padoucas, 1724, in Folmer, "French Expansion Toward New Mexico," 158–85.

22. See Norall, *Bourgmont*, 81–88, and Richard N. Ellis and Charlie R. Steen, eds., "An Indian Delegation in France."

23. Ibid.

24. Bray, "Bourgmond's Fort d'Orleans," 24.

25. Bray, "The Missouri Indian Tribe in Archaeology and History," 219.

26. Clarence W. Alvord, *The Illinois Country, 1673–1818*, 167.

27. Folmer, "French Expansion Toward New Mexico," 226ff.; Noel M. Loomis and Abraham P. Nasatir, *Pedro Vial and the Road to Santa Fe*, 52–57.

28. BLC, 34–40; Gilbert J. Din and Abraham P. Nasatir, *The Imperial Osages: Spanish-Indian Diplomacy in the Mississippi Valley*, 45–49; and Charles E. Hoffhaus, *Chez Les Canses: Three*

Centuries at Kawsmouth, 53–85. According to Hoffhaus, Fort Cavagnal was located just north of present-day Fort Leavenworth, Kansas.

29. David Denman, "History of 'La Saline': Salt Manufacturing Site, 1675–1825," 307–15; Rothensteiner, "Earliest History of Mine La Motte," 202; and Sale of La Saline, 16 and 30 November and 14 December 1766, St. Louis Archives, Missouri Historical Society, St. Louis. A member of La Salle's ill-fated expedition reported visiting the Saline in August 1687. See Henry Reed Stiles, ed., *Joutel's Journal of La Salle's Last Voyage, 1684–1687,* 186.

30. Ekberg's award-winning account of colonial Ste. Genevieve provides an authentic portrait of life in Missouri's earliest permanent settlement. For a thorough review of the evidence concerning the date of its founding, see Ekberg, *Colonial Ste. Genevieve,* 12–25.

31. Ibid., 26–29, 35, 41–42, 44.

32. E. Wilson Lyon, *Louisiana in French Diplomacy: 1759–1804,* 13–44; William R. Shepherd, "The Cession of Louisiana to Spain"; Arthur S. Aiton, "The Diplomacy of the Louisiana Cession"; Allan Christelow, "Proposals for a French Company for Spanish Louisiana, 1763–1764"; Arthur Whitaker, "The Retrocession of Louisiana in Spanish Policy"; and John Preston Moore, *Revolt in Louisiana: The Spanish Occupation, 1766–1770,* 33–36. Although there was little fighting in the Illinois Country during the French and Indian War, French inhabitants from the region did participate in the eastern campaigns. Jean Gabriel Cerré, for example, was present at the 1755 rout of British general Edward Braddock's forces in southwestern Pennsylvania. See Ekberg and Foley, eds., *An Account of Upper Louisiana by Nicolas de Finiels,* note 103.

33. John Francis McDermott, "The Exclusive Trade Privileges of Maxent, Laclède and Company." James Neal Primm's *Lion of the Valley: St. Louis, Missouri* is an excellent history of the city.

34. McDermott, "Myths and Realities Concerning the Founding of St. Louis," in his *The French in the Mississippi Valley,* 8–15. Although it was written long after the actual event, Auguste Chouteau's "Narrative of the Settlement of St. Louis" is the primary source for details concerning the city's founding. That document, hereafter citied as "Chouteau's Narrative," is located in the St. Louis Mercantile Library's Archives. An exact translation can be found in McDermott, *The Early Histories of St. Louis,* 47–49. Laclède's relationship with the Chouteau family is spelled out in Foley, "The Laclède-Chouteau Puzzle: John Francis McDermott Supplies Some Missing Pieces." The most comprehensive treatment of Auguste Chouteau's career is Foley and C. David Rice, *The First Chouteaus: River Barons of Early St. Louis.*

35. "Chouteau's Narrative."

36. Ibid.

37. Alvord, *The Illinois Country,* 262.

38. "Chouteau's Narrative"; Thorne, "People of the River," 73–74. Laclède occupied the original trading headquarters until 1768, when he leased it to Spanish officials for use as the Government House. In 1789 Auguste Chouteau purchased the structure, and after a major renovation and enlargement it was converted into the city's most elegant residence. For the complete story of the historic structure see Foley and Rice, "'Touch Not a Stone': An 1841 Appeal to Save the Historic Chouteau Mansion."

39. "Chouteau's Narrative."

40. Aubry to the Minister, 12 March 1766, in Clarence W. Alvord and Clarence E. Carter, *The New Regime, 1765–1767,* 185; Capt. Thomas Stirling to Gen. Thomas Gage, 15 December 1765, in ibid., 125–26; and Journal of Capt. Harry Gordon, August 1766, in ibid., 300.

41. Frederic L. Billon, *Annals of St. Louis in Its Early Days under the French and Spanish Dominations, 1764–1804,* 27–29.

42. Ekberg, *Colonial Ste. Genevieve,* 336–38.

43. BLC, 60–63; Billon, *Annals of St. Louis,* 50–51.

CHAPTER 3. CREATING A SPANISH BARRIER

1. John Preston Moore, *Revolt in Louisiana: The Spanish Occupation, 1766–1770,* 18–20, 37–38, 42–44.

2. Ibid., 2–11, 60–70.

3. Secret Instructions of Antonio de Ulloa to Francisco Ríu, 7 January 1767, in SRM, 1:20–28; *Estado* given by Loyola, 16 January 1767, in Moore, *Revolt in Louisiana,* 76; and Gilbert C. Din and Abraham P. Nasatir, *The Imperial Osages,* 59.

4. Carl J. Ekberg, *Colonial Ste. Genevieve,* 54, 338, 342.

5. Secret Instructions of Ulloa to Ríu, 7 January 1767, in SRM, 1:20–28.

6. Minutes of Council of War in St. Louis, 2 October 1767, in ibid., 1:29–31.

7. Din and Nasatir, *Imperial Osages*, 61.

8. Frederic L. Billon, *Annals of St. Louis in Its Early Days*, 54–57; George Morgan to Baynton and Wharton, 11 December 1767, in Clarence W. Alvord and Clarence E. Carter, *Trade and Politics, 1767–1769*, 135–36; Thomas Gage to Gen. Frederick Haldimand, 26 April 1768, in ibid., 272–73; and Ulloa to Marquis de Grimaldi, 4 August 1768, in *SRM*, 1:32–34.

9. Ríu's Trade Regulations [June 1768], in *SRM*, 1:35–36; St. Louis Merchants to Ríu, 15 January 1769, in ibid., 1:37–38; St. Ange's Report on Ríu's Conduct, 2 March 1769, in ibid., 1:39; Ulloa to Grimaldi, 4 August 1768, in ibid., 1:33–34; and Din and Nasatir, *Imperial Osages*, 62–63, 66.

10. Moore, *Revolt in Louisiana*, 103–7, 111–23, 143–64; Pedro Piernas to Alejandro O'Reilly, 31 October 1769, in *SRM*, 66–69; Transfer of Fort Don Carlos to Piernas, 10 March 1769, in ibid., 1:49–52; and Din and Nasatir, *Imperial Osages*, 67–68.

11. Moore, *Revolt in Louisiana*, 185–210.

12. Oath of Allegiance to Spain, 19 November 1769, in *Louisiana Historical Quarterly* 4 (April 1921): 205–6; Ekberg, *Colonial Ste. Genevieve*, 339.

13. Piernas to O'Reilly, 31 October 1769, in *SRM*, 1:66–75.

14. Ibid., 70–72.

15. Ibid., 72–75.

16. Fernando de Leyba to Bernardo de Gálvez, 16 November 1778, in *SMV*, 1:312–13.

17. John Francis McDermott, "Paincourt and Poverty."

18. Father Bernard to Bernardo de Gálvez, 30 June 1777, Archivo General de Indias, Papeles Procedentes de Cuba, Legajo 190. Photostatic copy in John Francis McDermott Collection, Lovejoy Library, Southern Illinois University-Edwardsville; Pedro Piernas to Alejandro O'Reilly, 31 October 1769, in *SRM*, 1:73.

19. In the Kaskaskia Records, François Vallé signed his name with a mark, and only after he came to Ste. Genevieve did he begin using a signature. Carl Ekberg has concluded that Madame Vallé in all likelihood taught him to sign his last name. A short summary of Laclède's activities can be found in John Francis McDermott, "Myths and Realities Concerning the Founding of St. Louis," 8–15. Sale of house and lot by Joseph Lefebvre to François Eloy, 27 June 1766, and sale of house and lot by Julien Le Roy to Joseph Lefebvre, 1767, both in St. Louis Archives, Missouri Historical Society, St. Louis.

20. St. Ange to O'Reilly, 23 November 1769, as quoted in Din and Nasatir, *Imperial Osages*, 69; Ordinance of Francisco Cruzat, 25 February 1781, in *SRM*, 1:242–43.

21. O'Reilly's instructions to Lieutenant Governor of Upper Louisiana, 17 February 1770, in *SRM*, 1:76–83.

22. Ekberg, *Colonial Ste. Genevieve*, 348–57.

23. William Cronon and Richard White, "Indians in the Land," 23–24.

24. Piernas to O'Reilly, 31 October 1769, in *SRM*, 1:73–74; Inventory of Indian presents, 27 November 1787, in ibid., 268–69; Report of Various Tribes Receiving Presents in St. Louis, 2 May 1769, in ibid., 1:44–45.

25. Instructions to Francisco Ríu, 1767, in ibid., 1:14; Nasatir, "The Anglo-Spanish Frontier on the Upper Mississippi, 1786–1796," 158–59; Willard H. Rollings, "Prairie Hegemony: An Ethnohistorical Study of the Osage from Early Times to 1840" (Ph.D. diss., Texas Tech University, 1983), 124–25; and O'Reilly's Proclamation Regarding Indian Slavery, 6 December 1769, in *SMV*, 1:125–26.

26. Din and Nasatir, *Imperial Osages*, 58–59; McDermott, "The Myth of the 'Imbecile Governor': Captain Fernando de Leyba and the Defense of St. Louis in 1780," 354–55; and Jean Baptiste Martigny to [Gálvez], 30 October 1779, as quoted in *BLC*, 1:71.

27. Nasatir, *Borderlands in Retreat*, 15–16, 25; Thomas Gage to Lord Shelburne, 24 April 1768, in Carter and Alvord, *Trade and Politics*, 267; and letter in *Quebec Gazette*, 18 August 1768, quoted in Harold A. Innis, *The Fur Trade in Canada*, 172–73.

28. Piernas to Unzaga, 30 July 1772, in *SMV*, 1:206–7; Din and Nasatir, *Imperial Osages*, 81–82.

29. Din and Nasatir, *Imperial Osages*, 73–84.

30. Nasatir, "Ducharme's Invasion of Missouri: An Incident in the Anglo-Spanish Rivalry for the Indian Trade of Missouri," part 1, 3–14.

31. Ibid.

32. Ekberg, *Colonial Ste. Genevieve*, 88–89; Cruzat to Unzaga, 10 December 1775, AGI, PPC, Leg. 2385, photostatic copy in McDermott Collection.

33. Bernardo de Gálvez to José de Gálvez, 27 January 1778, in *SRM*, 1:152–53; Francisco Cruzat to Bernardo de Gálvez, 8 December 1777, in ibid., 1:153–54; Bernardo de Gálvez to José de

Gálvez, 9 June 1778, in ibid., 1:154–55; and Decree of Bernardo de Gálvez, 19 February 1778, in ibid., 1:155–57.

34. Din, "Protecting the 'Barrera': Spain's Defenses in Louisiana, 1763–1779," 201–11; Leyba to Clark, 8 July 1778, in Kinnaird, ed., "The Clark-Leyba Papers," 94.

35. Leyba to Gálvez, 16 November 1778, and Leyba to Gálvez, 18 October 1779, in Kinnaird, ed., "The Clark-Leyba Papers," 102, 111–12; Chouteau's receipts dated 19 November 1778, Clark Family Papers, Missouri Historical Society.

36. Ekberg, *Colonial Ste. Genevieve*, 59; Joseph P. Donnelly, *Pierre Gibault, Missionary, 1737–1802*, 63–85.

37. Leyba to Gálvez, 16 November 1778, in McDermott, "Myth of Leyba," 331–33; Gálvez to Leyba, 13 January 1779, in *SMV*, 1:230.

38. Leyba to Gálvez, 21 July 1778, in *SMV*, 1:298–99.

39. Charles Gratiot to John Kay, 26 April 1779, Charles Gratiot Papers, Missouri Historical Society; Leyba to Gálvez, 11 July, 21 July, and 25 July 1778, in *SMV*, 1:296–97, 298, 300; Leyba to Gálvez, 13 July and 28 October 1779, in ibid., 346–47, 361; and J. B. Martigny to Gálvez, 30 October 1779, in *BLC*, 1:71.

40. Din, "Protecting the Barrera," 209–11; Nasatir, *Borderlands in Retreat*, 26–27; Patrick Sinclair to Capt. Diedrick Brehm, 1780, in Reuben Gold Thwaites, ed., "Papers from Canadian Archives," in *Collections of the State Historical Society of Wisconsin* 11 (1888): 144; and Sinclair to Haldimand, 29 May 1780, in ibid., 151–52.

41. John Montgomery to George Rogers Clark, 18 February 1780, Clark Family Papers; Leyba to Gálvez, 13 July 1779, in *SMV*, 1:348; and St. Louis Militia Roster, 9 November 1779, in McDermott, "Myth of Leyba," 373–80.

42. "Documents Relating to the Attack Upon St. Louis in 1780," 44–46; Leyba to Gálvez, 8 June 1780, in Nasatir, "St. Louis During the British Attack of 1780," 1:243–51.

43. Leyba to Gálvez, 8 June 1780, in Nasatir, "St. Louis During the British Attack of 1780," 243–51.

44. Ibid.; Testimony of Jean Baptiste Rivière *dit* Baccane in Theodore Hunt, Testimony before the Recorder of Land Titles, 1825, in Missouri State Archives, Jefferson City (hereafter cited as Hunt's Minutes), book 2, 56.

45. Leyba to Gálvez, 8 June 1780, in Nasatir, "St. Louis During the British Attack of 1780," 243–51; Martin Navarro to José de Gálvez, 18 August 1780, in *SRM*, 1:167–69.

46. Leyba to Gálvez, 8 June 1780, in Nasatir, "St. Louis During the British Attack of 1780," 243–51.

47. "Virtutis, Veritatisque Amicus" to Bernardo de Gálvez, 12 June and 23 June 1780, and the People of Illinois to Gálvez, 1780, both in McDermott, "Myth of Leyba," 363–72.

48. "Virtutis, Veritatisque Amicus" to Gálvez, 23 June 1780, in ibid., 366–67.

49. Din and Nasatir, *Imperial Osages*, 128; Inhabitants of St. Louis to Cartabona, 2 July 1780, in Nasatir, "St. Louis During the British Attack of 1780," 254–57.

50. Nasatir, "The Anglo-Spanish Frontier in the Illinois Country during the American Revolution, 1779–1783," 325–28.

51. Gálvez to Cartabona and Gálvez to Cruzat, 25 July 1780, in *SRM*, 1:171–74; Navarro to Cruzat, 15 February 1781, in ibid., 1:197–206; and Leyba to Gálvez, 11 July 1778, in ibid., 1:161.

52. Inhabitants of St. Louis to Cruzat, September 1780, in Nasatir, "St. Louis During the British Attack of 1780," 258–59; Cruzat to Gálvez, 2 December and 19 December 1780, in *SRM*, 1:175–77; and Pierre Chouteau to James Wilkinson, 12 April 1806, Pierre Chouteau Letterbook, Missouri Historical Society.

53. Cruzat to Gálvez, 18 December 1780, in *SMV*, 1:408–9.

54. Kinnaird, "The Spanish Expedition Against Fort St. Joseph in 1781: A New Interpretation."

55. Esteban Miró to Gálvez, 5 June 1782, and Testimony of Madame Cruzat, 30 May 1782, in *SRM*, 1:211–34.

56. William E. Foley and C. David Rice, *The First Chouteaus: River Barons of Early St. Louis*, 37–40.

CHAPTER 4. YOU CANNOT LOCK UP AN OPEN FIELD

1. Gilbert Din, "The Immigration Policy of Governor Esteban Miró in Spanish Louisiana," 161; Arthur P. Whitaker, *The Spanish-American Frontier, 1783–1795*, 7–9, 68–77.

2. Din, "Immigration Policy of Miró," 155–64; Lawrence Kinnaird, "American Penetration into Spanish Louisiana," 1:214–17.

3. Din, "Immigration Policy of Miró," 155–64; Kinnaird, "American Penetration into Spanish Louisiana," 1:214–17; Esteban Miró to Peter Paulus, 7 March 1789, in ibid., 1:233–34; and Whitaker, *Spanish-American Frontier*, 102–6.

4. The two best biographies of Wilkinson are Thomas Robson Hay and M. R. Werner, *The Admirable Trumpeter: A Biography of General James Wilkinson*, and James Ripley Jacobs, *Tarnished Warrior: Major-General James Wilkinson*.

5. Whitaker, *Spanish-American Frontier*, 98; Din, "Immigration Policy of Miró," 164–66; and William R. Shepherd, "Wilkinson and the Beginnings of the Spanish Conspiracy," 494–99.

6. Din, "Immigration Policy of Miró," 164–68.

7. Ibid., 167–68; Whitaker, *Spanish-American Frontier*, 98–101; and Decision of Council of State, 20 November 1788, and Wilkinson's Second Memorial, 17 September 1789, in William R. Shepherd, ed., "Papers Bearing on James Wilkinson's Relations with Spain, 1787–1789," 749–50, 751–52.

8. Max Savelle, *George Morgan: Colony Builder*, 18–75, 203–4; Din, "Immigration Policy of Miró," 169.

9. Savelle, *George Morgan*, 205.

10. Ibid., 205–8; Thomas Jefferson to George Washington, 2 April 1791, in Andrew A. Lipscomb, ed., *The Writings of Thomas Jefferson*, 7:161.

11. Savelle, *George Morgan*, 206–11; Morgan to Miró, 14 April 1789; John Dodge, Peter Light, David Rankin, et al. to Turnbull and Company, 14 April 1789; Morgan to Gardoqui, 20 August 1789; Morgan's General Directions for New Madrid, 6 April 1789; and Pérez to Miró, 27 March 1789; all in *SRM*, 1:279, 279–83, 286–99, 302–6, and 310–12. Testimony of Robert McCoy, in Hunt's Minutes, book 2, 154–55, Missouri State Archives, Jefferson City.

12. Savelle, *George Morgan*, 211–14; John Dodge, Peter Light, David Rankin, et al. to Turnbull and Co., 14 April 1789; Morgan to Gardoqui, 20 August 1789; and Morgan's General Directions for New Madrid, 6 April 1789; all in *SRM*, 1:279–83, 292–95, 302–6.

13. Morgan's General Directions for New Madrid, 6 April 1789, in *SRM*, 1:303.

14. Ibid., 1:305.

15. Morgan to Gardoqui, 20 August 1789, and John Dodge, Peter Light, David Rankin, et al. to Turnbull and Co., 14 April 1789; both in ibid., 1:295, 282.

16. Esteban Miró to Antonio Valdes, 20 May 1789; Morgan to Gardoqui, 20 August 1789; and Miró to Morgan, 29 May and 26 June 1789; all in ibid., 276–78, 297–99, 308.

17. Morgan to Gardoqui, 20 August 1789, in ibid., 290–99; Savelle, *George Morgan*, 224–27.

18. "Statement of Inhabitants who have come from the American side to settle in the District of Illinois" between 1 December 1787 and 31 December 1789, in *SMV*, 2:290.

19. Din, "Immigration Policy of Miró," 171–74.

20. Carl Ekberg, *Colonial Ste. Genevieve*, 95.

21. Miró to Francisco Cruzat, 15 May 1787, in *SMV*, 2:201.

22. Henri Peyroux de la Coudrenière to Miró, 12 March 1788, in ibid., 2:247; Ekberg, *Colonial Ste. Genevieve*, 95–96; and Din and Nasatir, *The Imperial Osages*, 184–85, 187.

23. Grant Foreman, ed., "Notes of Auguste Chouteau on Indian Boundaries of Various Indian Nations," in Missouri Historical Society's *Glimpses of the Past* (October-December 1940), 126.

24. Shawnees to the President of the United States, 29 March 1811, Letters Received by the Secretary of War Relating to Indian Affairs, 1800–1816, M271, National Archives; Capt. Alexander McKee to Sir William Johnson, 2 June 1784, in Thwaites, ed., "The British Regime in Wisconsin, 1760–1800," *Collections of the State Historical Society of Wisconsin* 18 (1908): 435; and Cruzat to Miró, 19 March 1782, in *SRM*, 1:209–10.

25. Nicolas de Finiels affirmed Lorimier's mixed-blood status in his "Notice sur la Louisiane Supérieure." See Carl J. Ekberg and William E. Foley, eds., *An Account of Upper Louisiana by Nicolas de Finiels*, 35. Nasatir, *Spanish War Vessels on the Mississippi, 1792–1796*, 71–72; "Louis Lorimier," in *Dictionary of American Biography*, 11:413; *Wisconsin Historical Collections*, 18:435n; George Sharp and Thomas Sheperd to Hugh Heward, 4 May 1787, in Houck, *A History of Missouri*, 2:172–73; and Testimony of François Duchoquet in Hunt's Minutes, book 2, 134–35. Meriwether Lewis commented on Lorimier's long queue of hair after visiting him while en route to St. Louis in 1803. See Lewis's journal entry for 23 November 1803 in Gary E. Moulton,

ed., *The Journals of the Lewis & Clark Expedition,* 2:107–8. One Shawnee who migrated to Missouri was Methoataske, the mother of Tecumseh and Tenskwatawa (the Prophet). Only one of her children, her second daughter, accompanied her across the Mississippi. That daughter, Tecumseh's older sister, later married François Maisonville, a French Creole from New Madrid, and the couple had a large family. See R. David Edmunds, *Tecumseh and the Quest for Indian Leadership,* 22, and Lynn Morrow, "New Madrid and Its Hinterland, 1783–1826," 242.

26. Morgan to Gardoqui, 20 August 1789, and Trudeau to Louis Lorimier, 8 August 1792 and 1 May 1793, all in *SRM,* 1:292, 2:47, 50–51; and Trudeau to Carondelet, 28 September 1793, in *BLC,* 1:203.

27. Trudeau to Carondelet, 8 June 1794; Trudeau to Gayoso, 20 December 1797, both in *BLC,* 1:232–33, 2:529.

28. Carondelet to Marquis de Branceforte, 7 June 1796, in ibid., 2:440.

29. Carondelet to Count de Aranada [1793], in *SRM,* 2:12–13.

30. Din, "Spain's Immigration Policy in Louisiana and the American Penetration, 1792–1803," 255–57; Nasatir, *Spanish War Vessels,* 9–12, 20–21.

31. Din, "Spain's Immigration Policy," 257–58; Ekberg, *Colonial Ste. Genevieve,* 461–62.

32. Ekberg, *Colonial Ste. Genevieve,* 445–50. Ekberg's account details the fascinating story of the royalist emigre's frontier experiences in colonial Missouri. Austin recorded Madame de Luzières' comments in the journal he kept during his reconnaissance trip to Louisiana in 1796–1797. See George P. Garrison, ed., "A Memorandum of Moses Austin's Journey, 1796–1797," 541. See also Testimony of Charles Dehault Delassus in Hunt's Minutes, book 2, 179.

33. Nasatir, *Spanish War Vessels,* 29–32.

34. Ibid., 177n; "Miró's Appointment of Foucher as Commandant at New Madrid," 28 July 1789, in *SRM,* 1:309.

35. Carondelet to Trudeau, 22 December 1792, in *SMV,* 3:107–8; and Nasatir, *Spanish War Vessels,* 62–64.

36. Fernando de la Concha to Trudeau, 7 October 1792; Diary of Pedro Vial from Santa Fe to St. Louis, 21 May to 3 October 1792; and Pedro Vial from St. Louis to Santa Fe, 14 June to 16 November 1793; all in Noel M. Loomis and Nasatir, *Pedro Vial and the Road to Santa Fe,* 369–407.

37. Carondelet to Las Casas, 31 May 1794, in *SRM,* 2:100–101; F. R. Hall, "Genêt's Western Intrigue, 1793–1794"; and E. Wilson Lyon, *Louisiana in French Diplomacy, 1759–1804,* 69–75, 101–9.

38. Nasatir, *Spanish War Vessels,* 76–88; François Vallé to Louis Lorimier, 18 March 1793, and Louis Lorimier's Journal, 1793–1795, both in *SRM,* 2:49, 59–99; and Ekberg, *Colonial Ste. Genevieve,* 72–74.

39. Trudeau to Carondelet, 8 June 1794, in *BLC,* 1:231.

40. Carondelet to Las Casas, 31 May 1794, in *SRM,* 1:100–101; Din and Nasatir, *Imperial Osages,* 221–24.

41. Trudeau to Carondelet, 25 July 1792, in *BLC,* 1:156–57.

42. Carondelet to Trudeau, 22 December 1792, and Trudeau to Carondelet, 10 April 1793; both in *SMV,* 3:107, 148.

43. Trudeau to Carondelet, 2 March 1793 and 28 September 1793, in *BLC,* 1:167–68, 197–203; Proclamation of Zenon Trudeau, 23 June 1793, typescript copy in Ste. Genevieve Papers, Missouri Historical Society.

44. Din and Nasatir, *Imperial Osages,* 252–54; Contract between Chouteau and Carondelet, 18 May 1794, in *SRM,* 2:106–10.

45. Din and Nasatir, *Imperial Osages,* 255–75; Carl H. Chapman, "The Indomitable Osages in Spanish Illinois (Upper Louisiana), 1763–1804," 300–308.

46. Willard H. Rollings, "Prairie Hegemony: An Ethnohistorical Study of the Osages from Early Times to 1840" (Ph.D. diss., Texas Tech University, 1983), 138–44; Trudeau to Carondelet, 15 January 1798, in *BLC,* 2:538. For a full account of the Chouteaus' trading activities, see William E. Foley and C. David Rice, *The First Chouteaus: River Barons of Early St. Louis.*

47. Nasatir, *Borderlands in Retreat,* 58.

48. Trudeau to Carondelet, 20 October 1792, in *BLC,* 1:160–61.

49. Trudeau to Carondelet, 31 May 1794, in ibid., 1:229–30.

50. Carondelet's Instructions to Trudeau, 28 March 1792, and Regulations for the Illinois Trade, 15 October 1793, both in ibid., 1:151–53, 186–94.

51. Distribution of Missouri Trading Posts, 1–3 May 1794, and Trudeau to Carondelet, 18 April 1795, both in ibid., 1:209–11, 320–21.

52. Nasatir, "The Formation of the Missouri Company"; Carondelet to Trudeau, 27 May 1794, Articles of Incorporation of the Missouri Company, May 1794, and Trudeau to Carondelet, 31 May 1794, in *BLC*, 1:212, 217–28, 228–29.

53. Nasatir, "Jacques Clamorgan, Colonial Promoter of the Northern Border of New Spain"; Report of Jacques Clamorgan, 8 July 1795, and Trudeau to Gayoso, 20 December 1797, both in *BLC*, 1:335–37, 2:525. Little is known about Clamorgan's background. He was probably of mixed Welsh, Portuguese, and French blood, with perhaps a trace of Afro-American ancestry. See Lawrence Christensen, "Cyprian Clamorgan, The Colored Aristocracy of St. Louis," 5.

54. Report of Jacques Clamorgan, 8 July 1795, and Trudeau to Carondelet, 15 July 1795, both in *BLC*, 1:335–40, 341–43; Nasatir, *Borderlands in Retreat*, 78–79; and Nasatir, "Jacques d'Eglise."

55. James Mackay to Clamorgan, 24–27 October 1795, in *BLC*, 1:351–54; Nasatir, *Borderlands in Retreat*, 78.

56. Trudeau to Carondelet, 26 May 1797, and Trudeau to Gayoso, 20 December 1797 and 15 January 1798, all in *BLC*, 2:519–20, 525–29, 539–42; Nasatir, *Borderlands in Retreat*, 79–80; two articles by Nasatir, "James Mackay" and "John T. Evans"; and Gwyn A. Williams, *Madoc: The Making of a Myth*.

57. W. Raymond Wood, "The John Evans 1796–97 Map of the Missouri River"; James P. Ronda, "Dreams and Discoveries: Exploring the American West, 1760–1815," 151–52.

58. Minutes of Council of State, 27 May 1796, and Agreement between Andrew Todd and Clamorgan, Loisel and Company, 26 October 1796, in *BLC*, 2:435–36, 464–69.

59. Nasatir, "Jacques Clamorgan," 111–12; Account of Daniel Clark, Jr., with Auguste Chouteau relative to affairs of Clamorgan, Loisel and Company, 27 July 1798–1 December 1800, in Chouteau Collections, Missouri Historical Society.

60. Nasatir, *Spanish War Vessels*, 291n.

61. Ernest R. Liljegren, "Jacobinism in Spanish Louisiana, 1792–1797"; Trudeau to Carondelet, 2 October 1793, in *BLC*, 1:204; Gayoso's Diary, 6 October 1795–8 December 1795, and Gayoso's Report, 1795, both in Nasatir, *Spanish War Vessels*, 291–314, 331–41.

62. Nasatir, *Spanish War Vessels*, 119–31; Whitaker, *Spanish-American Frontier*, 117, 190–97.

63. Whitaker, *Spanish-American Frontier*, 197–209.

64. Nasatir, *Spanish War Vessels*, 130–31.

65. Ibid., 307n; Nasatir, *Borderlands in Retreat*, 61; George W. Kyte, "A Spy on the Western Waters: The Military Intelligence Mission of General Collot in 1796"; and Georges-Victor Collot, *A Journey in North America*, 2:1–6.

66. Jack D. L. Holmes, ed., *Documentos Inéditos Para La Historia de la Luisiana*, 361–63. A manuscript copy of Finiels' "Notice sur la Louisiane Supérieure" can be found in the John Francis McDermott Papers, Lovejoy Library, Southern Illinois University-Edwardsville. Carl J. Ekberg has prepared an English translation, which is contained in Carl J. Ekberg and William E. Foley, eds., *An Account of Upper Louisiana by Nicolas de Finiels*. Also consult W. Raymond Wood, "Nicholas de Finiels: Mapping the Mississippi and Missouri Rivers, 1797–1798."

67. Carondelet to Carlos Howard, 26 November 1795 [1796], in *SRM*, 2:123–32.

68. Nasatir, *Spanish War Vessels*, 137–40.

69. Kinnaird, "American Penetration of Louisiana," 221–22.

70. Jo Tice Bloom, "Daniel Boone: Trailblazer to a Nation," 36–38; Lyman Draper's 1851 interview with Nathan Boone, in Draper MSS, 6S, 214–17, 221–23.

71. Garrison, "Memorandum of Moses Austin's Journey," 539. A good brief account of Austin's Missouri years is David B. Gracy II, "Moses Austin and the Development of the Missouri Lead Industry."

72. Din, "Spain's Immigration Policy," 271; Trudeau to Gayoso, 15 January and 6 May 1798, and James Mackay to Gayoso, 28 November 1798, all in *BLC*, 2:543, 559, 587–88.

73. Victor Collot to Talleyrand, 6 November 1801, in ibid., 2:670.

74. Amos Stoddard, *Sketches, Historical and Descriptive of Louisiana*, 225.

75. Arthur P. Whitaker, *The Mississippi Question, 1795–1803*, 176–77. Godoy as quoted in ibid., 180.

76. Ibid., 176–86.

77. Ibid., and Lyon, *Louisiana in French Diplomacy*, 101–9.

78. Summary of Distribution of Trade Licenses by Delassus, 1799–1804, in *BLC*, 2:590–93.

CHAPTER 5. VILLAGES AND FARMSTEADS

1. The brother of the St. Louis commandant, St. Ange, was, for example, married to the daughter of an Indian woman. On this subject see Tanis Chapman Thorne, "People of the River: Mixed-Blood Families on the Lower Missouri" (Ph.D. diss., UCLA, 1987).

2. Henry Marie Brackenridge, *Views of Louisiana*, 119; Carl J. Ekberg and William E. Foley, eds., *An Account of Upper Louisiana by Nicolas de Finiels*, 62. Records in the St. Louis Archives at the Missouri Historical Society show that the typical town lot was one-fourth of a city block and measured 120 feet by 150 feet.

3. There are a number of excellent works on Mississippi valley French architecture and material culture. The pioneering studies in the field were done by Charles Peterson. See his *Colonial St. Louis: Building a Creole Capital;* "Early Ste. Genevieve and Its Architecture"; and "The Houses of French St. Louis." Also useful is Charles Van Ravenswaay, "The Creole Arts and Crafts of Upper Louisiana." Two recent studies of great value are Susan Green, "The Material Culture of a Pre-enclosure Village in Upper Louisiana: Open Fields, Houses, and Cabinetry in Colonial Ste. Genevieve, 1750–1804" (M.A. thesis, University of Missouri–Columbia, 1983), and Melburn D. Thurman, *Building a House in 18th-Century Ste. Genevieve.*

4. Peterson, "Houses of French St. Louis," 19–21; Thurman, *Building a House in 18th-Century Ste. Genevieve.*

5. Green, "Material Culture of a Pre-Enclosure Village," 42–50, 75–78.

6. Ibid., 67–90; Foley and C. David Rice, " 'Touch Not a Stone': An 1841 Appeal to Save the Historic Chouteau Mansion," 14–19.

7. Miscellaneous ordinances published by Francisco Cruzat, 1780–1787, in *SRM*, 1:240–52; Ordinance for Draining Streets, 1 May 1778, Manuscript of Miscellaneous Reports for St. Louis, 1770–1780, St. Louis History Collection, Missouri Historical Society; and Ekberg and Foley, *Account of Upper Louisiana*, 62.

8. Ekberg and Foley, *Account of Upper Louisiana*, 64–65.

9. Baron de Carondelet to Count of Aranda, 1793, in *SRM*, 2:12–13.

10. On dog-trot construction, see Terry G. Jordan and Matti Kaups, "Folk Architecture in Cultural and Ecological Context."

11. Walter A. Schroeder's intensive analysis of settlement patterns in the Ste. Genevieve District, undertaken as a part of the University of Missouri's Ste. Genevieve project, offers the most comprehensive study of settlement patterns in the pre-American period. His findings point to the variety of settlement forms in colonial Missouri. See his "Settlement of the Historic Ste. Genevieve District 1790–1819," unpublished paper, University of Missouri–Columbia, 1985.

12. Ekberg and Foley, *Account of Upper Louisiana*, 109.

13. Fernando de Leyba apologized to his superiors in New Orleans for sending his proposals for fortifying St. Louis written in French: "There is not at this post anyone who can write Spanish even moderately well, unless it be a soldier, of whose services I have not availed myself because of the many errors which he makes." Leyba to Bernardo de Galvez, 16 November 1778, in *SMV*, 1:310–12. See also Walter B. Douglas, "The Spanish Domination of Upper Louisiana," 90. An interesting attempt to assess the impact of the city planning ordinances of the Laws of the Indies on St. Louis can be found in Dora P. Crouch, Daniel J. Garr, and Axel I. Mundingo, *Spanish City Planning in North America*, 116–55.

14. Ekberg, *Colonial Ste. Genevieve*, 450.

15. Ekberg and Foley, *Account of Upper Louisiana*, 119.

16. George P. Garrison, ed., "Memorandum of Moses Austin's Journey," 535.

17. Amos Stoddard to Mrs. Samuel Benham, 16 June 1804, Stoddard Papers, Missouri Historical Society.

18. Ekberg and Foley, *Account of Upper Louisiana*, 120.

19. James Neal Primm, *Lion of the Valley: St. Louis, Missouri*, 65–67.

20. Ibid.; Ekberg and Foley, *Account of Upper Louisiana*, 55–56.

21. Primm, *Lion of the Valley,* 66; Ekberg and Foley, *Account of Upper Louisiana*, 70.

22. Primm, *Lion of the Valley,* 66; Ekberg and Foley, *Account of Upper Louisiana*, 70–71.

23. Primm, *Lion of the Valley,* 67; James Mackay to Manuel Gayoso de Lemos, 28 November 1798, in *BLC*, 2:588; Houck, *History of Missouri*, 2:72; Nasatir, "James Mackay," 200–207; Stoddard, *Sketches*, 221; and John Bradbury, *Travels in the Interior of America*, 5:41.

24. Ben L. Emmons, "The Founding of St. Charles and Blanchette Its Founder"; Ekberg and Foley, *Account of Upper Louisiana*, 74.

25. An excellent article by Daniel H. Usner, Jr., "The Frontier Exchange Economy of the

Lower Mississippi Valley in the Eighteenth Century," offers insights into the importance of small-scale trading operations in Louisiana.

26. *A Journey in North America*, 1:277.

27. Ekberg and Foley, *Account of Upper Louisiana*, 74–77.

28. Houck, *History of Missouri*, 2:88–90; Lewis C. Beck, *A Gazetteer of the States of Illinois and Missouri*, 310; and Ekberg and Foley, *Account of Upper Louisiana*, 76–77.

29. Houck, *History of Missouri*, 2:91–92.

30. *American State Papers, Public Lands*, 2:396; Interview with Nathan Boone by Lyman C. Draper, Draper MSS, 6S, 213–15, 221–26.

31. Jo Tice Bloom, "Daniel Boone: Trailblazer to a Nation," 36–38; Ekberg and Foley, *Account of Upper Louisiana*, 76–77.

32. Ekberg, *Colonial Ste. Genevieve*, 416–30; Testimony of Julien Labrière in Hunt's Minutes, book 2, 225.

33. Ekberg, *Colonial Ste. Genevieve*, 436–40.

34. Brackenridge, *Views of Louisiana*, 126.

35. Ekberg and Foley, *Account of Upper Louisiana*, 47–50, 119; Spanish Census for 1800 in *SRM*, 2:414.

36. Spanish Census for 1800 in *SRM*, 2:414.

37. Ekberg, *Colonial Ste. Genevieve*, 433–35, 444–54; Ekberg and Foley, *Account of Upper Louisiana*, 45–47.

38. Ekberg and Foley, *Account of Upper Louisiana*, 44–45; Schroeder, "Settlement of the Historical Ste. Genevieve District."

39. Schroeder, "Settlement of the Historical Ste. Genevieve District."

40. Moses Austin to Judather Kendall and Elias Bates, December 1797, in Eugene C. Barker, ed., *The Austin Papers*, 38–39; testimony of Elias Bates, Pierre Boyer, and John Stewart, all in Hunt's Minutes, book 2, 64–65, 87–88, 199; and David B. Gracy II, *Moses Austin: His Life*, 59–66.

41. According to an account by Austin's son Stephen F. Austin, "The first family who settled permanently at 'Mine a Breton' and in what is now called Washington County, in the State of Missouri, was that of Elias Bates, a nephew of my father, who moved there from Ste. Genevieve in the fall of 1799" (quoted by George P. Garrison in the Introduction to his "A Memorandum of Moses Austin's Journey," 519). See also testimony of Elias Bates, Pierre Boyer, and John Stewart in Hunt's Minutes, book 2, 64–65, 87–88, 199; Gracy, *Moses Austin*, 71–73, 91, 111–13; Carl Ekberg et al., *A Cultural, Geographical and Historical Study of the Pine Ford Lake Project Area*, 34; and Brackenridge, *Recollections*, 212.

42. Russel L. Gerlach, *Settlement Patterns in Missouri*, 13; Robert Flanders, "Caledonia: An Ozarks Village, History, Geography, Architecture."

43. Houck, *History of Missouri*, 1:375.

44. Schroeder, "Settlement of the Historic Ste. Genevieve District."

45. Ibid.

46. Floyd Shoemaker, "Cape Girardeau, Most American of Missouri's Original Five Counties"; Houck, *History of Missouri*, 2:167–92.

47. Ibid.; Ekberg and Foley, *Account of Upper Louisiana*, 36–37.

48. Peter Anthony Laforge to Charles Dehault Delassus, 31 December 1796, in Frederic Billon, *Annals of St. Louis in Its Early Days*, 264–65. Although 1783 is traditionally cited as the date when the Le Sieur brothers established their trading post at L'Anse à la Graisse, Robert McCay testified that while he was en route to New Orleans from Post Vincennes in December 1786, there was no living person at the place where New Madrid now stands, but when he passed by that location on his return in the spring of 1787, Joseph Le Sieur was in residence there, trading with the Indians. See testimony of Robert McCay in Hunt's Minutes, book 2, 154–55.

49. Laforge to Delassus, 31 December 1796, in Billon, *Annals of St. Louis in Its Early Days*, 267–71.

50. Charles Dehault Delassus to Capt. Amos Stoddard, 30 March 1804, in Billon, *Annals of St. Louis in Its Early Days*, 373–74; and Ekberg, *Colonial Ste. Genevieve*, 122–23. Officials generally discouraged the execution of Indian criminals in order to avoid the unsettling effects and attempts at retaliation.

51. La Forge to Delassus, 31 December 1796, in Billon, *Annals of St. Louis in Its Early Days*, 271.

52. According to Robert McCay, Little Prairie was settled by François Le Sieur in 1794 or 1795. See Testimony of Robert McCay in Hunt's Minutes, book 2, 154–55.

53. Ekberg and Foley, *Account of Upper Louisiana*, 53–54.

54. Ibid., 31–32.

55. Ibid., 30–31.

56. Leyba to Bernardo de Gálvez, 11 July 1778, in *SRM*, 1:161.

57. See Leland D. Baldwin, *The Keelboat Age on Western Waters*.

58. Brackenridge, *Views of Louisiana*, 127–28.

59. Amos Stoddard, *Sketches, Historical and Descriptive of Louisiana*, 228–30; Israel Dodge to Charles Dehault Delassus, 5 December 1800, and letter from Delassus de Luzières, 8 December 1800, in *American State Papers, Public Lands*, 8:49; Ekberg and Foley, *Account of Upper Louisiana*, 77; John Ashton, "History of Shorthorns in Missouri Prior to the Civil War," 33–34; and Ashton, "A History of Hogs and Pork Production in Missouri," 27–28. As early as 1739, French inhabitants of the Illinois Country attempted to drive cattle from Fort de Chartres in southern Illinois to Fort St. Francois on the Arkansas River. See Margaret Kimball Brown, "Allons, Cowboys!"

60. Ibid.; John G. Clark, *New Orleans, 1718–1812: An Economic History*, 211–12. Though the shipments from Spanish Illinois were increasing, Clark points out that they did not begin to satisfy the needs of New Orleans.

61. Stoddard, *Sketches*, 297–98. Most of the furs were shipped through Canada; only about $80,000 worth of furs reached New Orleans each year. See Clark, *New Orleans*, 212.

62. Ekberg, *Colonial Ste. Genevieve*, 154–58.

63. Gracy, *Moses Austin*, 81–85; Ekberg, *Colonial Ste. Genevieve*, 153–54; James Gardner, "The Business Career of Moses Austin in Missouri, 1798–1821," 237–38; Clark, *New Orleans*, 212; and Moses Austin, "Report on Lead Mines in Upper Louisiana," in *American State Papers, Public Lands*, 1:191.

64. Houck, *History of Missouri*, 2:255–56; Clark, *New Orleans*, 211; Michael J. O'Brien et al., *Grassland, Forest, and Historical Settlement: An Analysis of Dynamics in Northeast Missouri*, 91–92; and Ekberg and Foley, *Account of Upper Louisiana*, 44–45, 78.

65. The Chouteaus epitomized Upper Louisiana's frontier mercantile capitalists. See Foley and Rice, *The First Chouteaus*.

66. Stoddard, *Sketches*, 230, 282; Ekberg and Foley, *Account of Upper Louisiana*, 121. For the characteristics of the frontier exchange economy, see Usner, "Frontier Exchange Economy."

67. Brackenridge, *View of Louisiana*, 138–39; Ekberg and Foley, *Account of Upper Louisiana*, 125.

68. Ekberg and Foley, *Account of Upper Louisiana*, 125.

69. Ibid., 50–51, 68–69, 125. An excellent study of Upper Louisiana's legal and judicial systems is Morris S. Arnold, *Unequal Laws Unto a Savage Race: European Legal Traditions in Arkansas, 1686–1836*.

70. Amos Stoddard to Henry Dearborn, 10 January 1804, in *American State Papers, Public Lands*, 1:177.

71. Ibid.; Albert Gallatin to Thomas Jefferson, 5 January 1807, Jefferson Papers. The Spanish authorities rewarded Austin and Dodge for their special contributions to the region's development. Austin helped revolutionize the lead mining activities, and Dodge was credited with having erected several mills, distilleries, and breweries in the Spanish territory.

CHAPTER 6. GALLERIES, GUMBO, AND "LA GUIGNOLÉE"

1. Carl J. Ekberg and William E. Foley, eds., *An Account of Upper Louisiana by Nicolas de Finiels*, 50, 67, 118, 120; Henry Marie Brackenridge, *Views of Louisiana*, 135, 137; and Belting, *Kaskaskia Under the French*, 68–69.

2. In St. Louis the Guignolée custom died out in the nineteenth century, but it still lingers in Ste. Genevieve, Old Mines, and Prairie du Rocher in Illinois. The King's Night Ball does survive in St. Louis as the Veiled Prophet Ball. See Rosemary Hyde Thomas, "La Guillonnée: A French Holiday Custom in the Mississippi Valley."

3. Ekberg and Foley, *Account of Upper Louisiana*, 114.

4. Ekberg, *Colonial Ste. Genevieve*, 382–94. Ekberg's account carefully documents Father Hilaire's curious activities. Father Bernard to unidentified person, 30 June 1777, AGI, PPC, Leg. 190, photostatic copy in John Francis McDermott Collection, Lovejoy Library, Southern Illinois University-Edwardsville. Cruzat's presence in the crowded sanctuary quarters was made less of a problem by the lieutenant governor's infrequent attendance at mass. See also John E. Rothensteiner, *History of the Archdiocese of St. Louis*, 1:103, 115, 125–26, 131, 141.

5. Manuel Pérez to Esteban Miró, 10 September 1770, in *SMV*, 2:378; Ekberg, *Colonial Ste. Genevieve*, 407–13. When thirteen families from Ste. Genevieve and New Bourbon petitioned

for a land concession at St. Michel, there were hints that they were dissatisfied with Father Maxwell's performance. See unpublished paper by Walter Schroeder, "Settlement of the Historic Ste. Genevieve District, 1790–1819."

6. Inhabitants of Ste. Genevieve to Pedro Piernas, 6 June 1774; Piernas to Luis de Unzaga, 16 November 1774; and Unzaga to Piernas, 20 February 1775; all in *SRM*, 1:121–25.

7. Brackenridge, *Views of Louisiana*, 135; Houck, *A History of Missouri*, 3:201–4.

8. Leyba to Gálvez, 16 November 1778, in *SMV*, 1:353.

9. *Views of Louisiana*, 135.

10. Ekberg and Foley, *Account of Upper Louisiana*, 67–68, 115, 118–20; Foley and C. David Rice, "Touch Not a Stone," 15–19. In his overview of small communities, Darrett Rutman points out that in those places stratification sharpened with growth and diversification ("Assessing the Little Communities of Early America," 174).

11. Ekberg and Foley, *Account of Upper Louisiana*, 118; Susan Boyle, "Opportunities and Inequality: Wealth Distribution in Early Ste. Genevieve" (unpublished paper).

12. Banishment of Amable Litourneau, 15–24 August 1770, and Banishment of Jeanot, 17 September 1770, in Manuscript of Miscellaneous Reports for St. Louis, 1770–1780, St. Louis History Collection, Missouri Historical Society; and Leyba to Gálvez, 9 December 1778, in *SMV*, 1:316.

13. Ekberg, *Colonial Ste. Genevieve*, 56.

14. Leyba to Gálvez, 11 July 1778, 6 August 1778, and 13 July 1779; all in *SMV*, 1:295–96, 302, 349. Piernas was listed as retired when he attended a council of war in St. Louis on 9 July 1782; see Minutes of Council of War, in ibid., 2:42. Miscellaneous ordinances published by Francisco Cruzat, 1780–1787, in *SRM*, 1:240–52.

15. Tanis Chapman Thorne, "People of the River: Mixed-Blood Families on the Lower Missouri" (Ph.D. diss., UCLA, 1987), 70–80.

16. Susan Boyle, "Did She Generally Decide? Women in Ste. Genevieve, 1750–1805," 778–79; Ekberg, *Colonial Ste. Genevieve*, 191, 246.

17. Thorne, "People of the River," 94–95.

18. Ekberg and Foley, *Account of Upper Louisiana*, 116–17.

19. Brackenridge, *Recollections of Persons and Places in the West*, 18; Natalia M. Belting, *Kaskaskia Under the French*, 46–47; and Charles Delassus to Carondelet, 6 March 1797, quoted in Ekberg, *Colonial Ste. Genevieve*, 305. A superb kitchen history of Missouri featuring a collection of recipes contributed by some of Missouri's finest cooks, including a section entitled "Setting the Table, French Colonial Style," is Jean Rissover, editor and illustrator, *Missouri History on the Table: 250 Years of Good Cooking and Good Eating*.

20. Auguste Chouteau to Carondelet, 8 December 1796, and Chouteau to William Grant, 8 May 1797, both in Chouteau Collections; Zenon Trudeau to Manuel Gayoso de Lemos, 15 January 1798, and Trudeau to Carondelet, 2 October 1793, both in *BLC*, 2:538, 1:204–5; and Belting, *Kaskaskia Under the French*, 47.

21. Boyle, "Did She Generally Decide?," 783–84; Belting, *Kaskaskia Under the French*, 47.

22. Ekberg and Foley, *Account of Upper Louisiana*, 112; Brackenridge, *Views of Louisiana*, 137; and Belting, *Kaskaskia Under the French*, 48.

23. Ekberg and Foley, *Account of Upper Louisiana*, 112–13; Brackenridge, *Views of Louisiana*, 137; and Belting, *Kaskaskia Under the French*, 48, and 51.

24. Ekberg and Foley, *Account of Upper Louisiana*, 117.

25. Ibid., 131–32; Brackenridge, *Views of Louisiana*, 111; Ekberg, *Colonial Ste. Genevieve*, 204; and Perrin du Lac as quoted in ibid., 267. Ekberg's chapter "Life, Death, and Doctoring" in ibid., 240–68, is especially good on this subject.

26. Boyle, "Did She Generally Decide?," 785; Brackenridge, *Views of Louisiana*, 135.

27. Katherine T. Corbett, "Veuve Chouteau: A 250th Anniversary"; Vaughan Baker, Amos Simpson, and Mathé Allain, "Le Mari est Seigneur: Marital Laws Governing Women in French Louisiana," 14.

28. Boyle, "Did She Generally Decide?," 779–89; Baker, Simpson, and Allain, "Le Mari est Seigneur," 7–17; and Ekberg, *Colonial Ste. Genevieve*, 226–27.

29. Baker, Simpson, and Allain, "Le Mari est Seigneur," 8. The cases of Pelagie Carpentier Vallé and Marie Thérèse Bourgeois Chouteau afford prime examples of the problems encountered by women in intolerable marital situations. See Ekberg, *Colonial Ste. Genevieve*, 192–95; Foley, "The Laclede-Chouteau Puzzle: John Francis McDermott Supplies Some Missing Pieces," 18–25.

30. Ernest R. Liljegren, "Frontier Education in Spanish Illinois."

31. Ibid.; Ekberg, *Colonial Ste. Genevieve*, 276–83.

32. Regulations for New Madrid, 6 April 1789, in *SRM*, 1:304.

33. Houck, *History of Missouri*, 2:275–76.

34. Auguste Chouteau to Pierre Louis Panet, 10 May 1800, Chouteau Collections. For the complete story of young Chouteau's unhappy experience in Canada, see Foley and Rice, *The First Chouteaus*, 186–87.

35. Ekberg, *Colonial Ste. Genevieve*, 283.

36. See McDermott's *Private Libraries in Creole St. Louis* and "Culture and the Missouri Frontier."

37. Ekberg and Foley, *Account of Upper Louisiana*, 112. A marvelous collection of early Missouri French folktales carefully passed from generation to generation by French-speaking residents of Old Mines can be found in Rosemary Hyde Thomas, *It's Good to Tell You: French Folk Tales from Missouri*. For the river songs, consult Marius Barbeau, "Voyageur Songs of the Missouri."

38. Census of Spanish Illinois, 1772, in *SRM*, 1:53–54.

39. Census of Spanish Illinois, 1800, in ibid., 2:414.

40. Bernardo de Gálvez to José de Gálvez, 27 January 1778; Francisco Cruzat to Bernardo de Gálvez, 23 November 1777; and Spanish Court to Bernardo de Gálvez, 8 April 1778; all in *SRM*, 1:158–60.

41. Ekberg, *Colonial Ste. Genevieve*, 204–11.

42. Ibid.; Stephen Webre, "The Problem of Indian Slavery in Spanish Louisiana, 1769–1803," 121–22; and Hans W. Baade, "The Law of Slavery in Spanish Louisiana, 1769–1803." A 1792 report to the Spanish Council of the Indies on slavery argued persuasively that slaves received milder treatment in Spanish colonies than in the American possessions of France, England, or the Netherlands. See Baade, "The Law of Slavery," 51–53, 60.

43. Manuel Pérez to Miró, 16 February 1792, as quoted in Din and Nasatir, *Imperial Osages*, 221.

44. Ekberg, *Colonial Ste. Genevieve*, 204.

45. Ibid., 203.

46. La Frenure to Lefebre and Labauxiere, 6 August 1766, St. Louis Archives, Missouri Historical Society.

47. *Recollections*, 20.

48. Cruzat to Vallé, 11 November 1776, as quoted in Ekberg, *Colonial Ste. Genevieve*, 220.

49. Tacoua's compelling story is told in ibid., 238–39, 372–73.

50. Ordinance regarding Slavery, 12 August 1781, in *SRM*, 1:244.

51. Ordinance regarding Slavery, 15 August 1781, in ibid., 1:245.

52. Ekberg and Foley, *Account of Upper Louisiana*, 109.

53. Census of Spanish Illinois, 1800, in *SRM*, 2:414.

54. Frederic Billon's Memoranda of Emancipation of Slaves from 1767 to 1804, copied from original documents in Billon Papers, Missouri Historical Society; Louis Villars to Piernas, 2 June 1770, and Emancipation Order of Piernas, 3 June 1770, in Billon, *Annals of St. Louis in Its Early Days Under the French and Spanish Dominations*, 102; Carondelet to Thomas Portell, 5 September 1792, New Madrid Archives, Missouri Historical Society; and Ekberg, *Colonial Ste. Genevieve*, 232–33.

55. Ekberg, in *Colonial Ste. Genevieve*, 226–32, gives several examples of these exteneded black-white relationships in Ste. Genevieve, including those of Charles Vallé, Jean-François La-Buche, and Antoine Janis. In St. Louis, trader Jacques Clamorgan openly lived with several black women who bore him a number of children.

56. One of the few specific references to the activities of free blacks in colonial Missouri can be found in Ekberg and Foley, *Account of Upper Louisiana*, 108–9. Finiels, who was not particularly complimentary in his portrayal of black slaves, stated that the free blacks were generally "more active and vigorous" than whites.

57. Inventory of property of Jeanette, a free black woman, 22 October 1773; Marriage contract of Jeanette and Valentin, 22 October 1773; Manuel Pérez acting on petition of Jeanette, free negress, widow of Valentin, free negro, 10 May 1790; and Will of Juaneta Forchet, 2 January 1803; all in St. Louis Archives. The author gratefully acknowledges the assistance of Mary Seematter at the Missouri Historical Society for calling Jeanette Forchet to his attention and for providing the necessary documentation.

58. O'Reilly's Proclamation, 6 December 1769, and Luis de Unzaga to Piernas, 1770, both in *SMV*, 1:125–26, 190. The most comprehensive account of Indian slavery during the Spanish

regime is Webre, "The Problem of Indian Slavery in Spanish Louisiana." A useful overview of Indian slavery in Missouri is Russell M. Magnaghi, "The Role of Indian Slavery in Colonial St. Louis."

59. Vallé's Report of Indian Slaves at Ste. Genevieve, 28 May 1770, and Piernas's Report of Indian Slaves at St. Louis, 12 July 1770, both in *SMV*, 1:168–70, 170–72.

60. Webre, "Indian Slavery in Spanish Louisiana," 123–26.

61. Cruzat's Announcement regarding Indian Slaves, 23 June 1787, in *SRM*, 1:249–50. The case that provoked Miró to order the republication of O'Reilly's 1769 ordinance in St. Louis involved the death of Madame Marie Thérèse Chouteau's slave Baptiste. Documents pertaining to that case can be found in Billon, *Annals of St. Louis in Its Early Days*, 233–42.

62. Foley, "Slave Freedom Suits Before Dred Scott: The Case of Marie Jean Scypion's Descendants."

63. Thorne, "People of the River," 154–55.

64. Ibid., 85–86; Gary E. Moulton, ed., *The Journals of the Lewis and Clark Expedition*, 2:107–8.

65. Regarding Lisa and Mitain (the prototype of Claybasket in James Michener's *Centennial*), consult Richard E. Oglesby, *Manuel Lisa and the Opening of the Missouri Fur Trade*, 153, 162–63, 175, 178n; and Thorne, "People of the River," 155.

66. Quoted in David B. Gracy II, *Moses Austin: His Life*, 114–15.

67. *Recollections*, 26.

68. Auguste A. Chouteau to Auguste Chouteau, 26 November 1802, Chouteau Collections.

69. Ekberg, *Colonial Ste. Genevieve*, 112; Thorne, "People of the River," 77–78.

70. Ekberg and Foley, *Account of Upper Louisiana*, 35–36; Amos Stoddard, *Sketches, Historical and Descriptive of Louisiana*, 215.

71. Manuel Gayoso de Lemos to Shawnee Indians, 17 May 1799, Ste. Genevieve Archives; Ekberg and Foley, *Account of Upper Louisiana*, 36; and Ekberg, *Colonial Ste. Genevieve*, 100.

72. Perrin du Lac, as quoted in Ekberg, *Colonial Ste. Genevieve*, 112; Petition of Inhabitants of New Bourbon, 19 August 1801, Ste. Genevieve Archives.

73. Ekberg and Foley, *Account of Upper Louisiana*, 112, 118; Thorne, "People of the River," 94. Young Auguste Chouteau's request that his father, Auguste Sr., send him his bow and arrows along with his deer antlers and his Indian moccasins decorated with porcupine quills showed the strong influence of Indian culture in his native village. Auguste A. Chouteau to Auguste Chouteau, 26 November 1802, Chouteau Collections. The elder Chouteau's handsome European-style buckskin coat with quillwork decorations in Indian designs is in the Missouri Historical Society Museum Collections. One of François Vallé II's daughters sent Governor Carondelet's daughter a sample of Indian handiwork in 1794. See Ekberg, *Colonial Ste. Genevieve*, 116.

CHAPTER 7. WE ARE ALL NOW AMERICANS

1. Marshall Smelser, *The Democratic Republic, 1801–1815*, 86–89; Dumas Malone, *Jefferson the President: The First Term*, 249–50; and Lyon, *Louisiana in French Diplomacy, 1759–1804*, 147–64.

2. Malone, *Jefferson the President: The First Term*, 251, 255.

3. For the reaction in Ste. Genevieve, see Carl Ekberg, *Colonial Ste. Genevieve*, 83. Pierre Clément Laussat to Pierre Chouteau, 30 April and 24 August 1803, Delassus Collection, Missouri Historical Society. In addition, Pierre Louis Panet's 18 May 1804 letter to Auguste Chouteau (Chouteau Collection, Missouri Historical Society) suggested that the Chouteaus had expected to benefit greatly from the restoration of French control.

4. Moses Austin to James Richardson, 2 August 1803, Louisiana Purchase Papers, Missouri Historical Society.

5. Lyon, *Louisiana in French Diplomacy*, 101–26, 192–99; Smelser, *Democratic Republic*, 89.

6. Lyon, *Louisiana in French Diplomacy*, 167–88; Smelser, *Democratic Republic*, 90–91; and Malone, *Jefferson the President: The First Term*, 260–61, 264–66.

7. Malone, *Jefferson the President: The First Term*, 269–70; Smelser, *Democratic Republic*, 90–91.

8. Lyon, *Louisiana in French Diplomacy*, 191–217.

9. Ibid., 217–28.

10. Rufus King as quoted in Malone, *Jefferson the President: The First Term*, 297. For reaction to the Louisiana Purchase, see ibid., 296–97, and Jerry W. Knudson, "Newspaper Reaction to the Louisiana Purchase: 'This New, Immense, Unbounded World.' "

11. Amendment to the Constitution, 1803, Thomas Jefferson Papers, Library of Congress, Washington, D.C.

12. Ibid.

13. Ibid.

14. For a comprehensive treatment of Jeffersonian Indian policy, see Bernard W. Sheehan, *Seeds of Extinction: Jeffersonian Philanthropy and the American Indian.*

15. Jefferson to John Breckinridge, 12 August 1803, Jefferson Papers.

16. Albert Gallatin to Jefferson, 9 July 1803, Robert Smith to Jefferson, 9 July 1803, and Breckinridge to Jefferson, 10 September 1803, all in Jefferson Papers; Raymond D. Walters, *Albert Gallatin: Jeffersonian Financier and Diplomat*, 178–79; and Rufus King to Christopher Gore, 6 September 1803, in Charles R. King, ed., *The Life and Correspondence of Rufus King*, 4:302.

17. Jefferson to John Dickinson, 9 August 1803, Jefferson Papers; Everett S. Brown, *The Constitutional History of the Louisiana Purchase, 1803–1812*, 25–29; and *Annals of Congress*, 8 Cong., 1 sess., 12 (17 October 1803).

18. Treaty of Cession, in *American State Papers, Foreign Relations*, 2:507.

19. *Annals*, 8 Cong., 1 sess., 44–45, 49–52 (3 November 1803), 432–34 (25 October 1803).

20. Smelser, *Democratic Republic*, 100.

21. Joseph T. Hatfield, *William Claiborne: Jeffersonian Centurion in the American Southwest*, 102–7.

22. Lyon, *Louisiana in French Diplomacy*, 231–50.

23. Wilfrid Hibbert, "Major Amos Stoddard: First Governor of Upper Louisiana and Hero of Fort Meigs."

24. William Henry Harrison to Carlos Dehault Delassus, 2 August 1803, Delassus Collection, Missouri Historical Society. Auguste Chouteau confirmed this date in his testimony before Theodore Hunt in 1825 (Hunt's Minutes, Missouri State Archives).

25. Robert Flanders, "Caledonia: Ozark Legacy of the High Scotch-Irish," 37–38; David B. Gracy, *Moses Austin: His Life*, 93–94.

26. Delassus to Stoddard, 30 March 1804, and Stoddard to Delassus, 3 April 1804, in Billon, *Annals of St. Louis in Its Early Days*, 376–79; Ekberg, *Colonial Ste. Genevieve*, 84.

27. William C. Carr to John Breckinridge, 7 July 1804, in *Territorial Papers*, 13:30–31; Stoddard, *Sketches*, 311.

28. Delassus to Stoddard, 24 February 1804, Stoddard to Claiborne and Wilkinson, 10 March 1804, and Pierre Clément de Laussat to Stoddard, 12 January 1804, all in Stoddard Papers.

29. Order of Troops of St. Louis, 8 March 1804, Delassus Collection; Stoddard to Claiborne and Wilkinson, 26 March 1804, Stoddard Papers.

30. Juan Lavallee to Marquis de Casa Calvo and Don Juan Manuel de Salcedo, 29 March 1804, in *SRM*, 2:331.

31. Henry Dearborn to Stoddard, 7 November 1803, and Stoddard to Louisianans, 10 March 1804, both in Stoddard Papers; Dearborn to Daniel Bissell, 7 November 1803, in *Territorial Papers*, 13:9–10.

32. Stoddard to Phoebe Reade Benham, 16 June 1804, Stoddard Papers.

33. Jefferson's Message to Congress, 18 January 1803, and Jefferson's Instructions to Lewis, 20 June 1803, both in Donald Jackson, ed., *Letters of the Lewis and Clark Expedition with Related Documents, 1783–1854*, 1:10–13, 61–66; Foley, "The Lewis and Clark Expedition's Silent Partners: The Chouteau Brothers of St. Louis," 132–35.

34. Donald Jackson, *Thomas Jefferson and the Stony Mountains: Exploring the West from Monticello*, 42–43, 74–78, 117–21.

35. William Clark to William Croghan, 2 May 1804, Clark Papers, Missouri Historical Society; Foley, "Lewis and Clark Expedition's Silent Partners," 133–35; James P. Ronda, *Lewis and Clark Among the Indians*, 10–12; and Donald Chaput, "The Early Missouri Graduates of West Point: Officers or Merchants?"

36. Meriwether Lewis to Clark, 18 February 1804, and Clark to Croghan, 21 May 1804, both in Clark Papers; Foley and Rice, *The First Chouteaus*, 90–91. The full story of the Osage delegation can be found in two articles by Foley and Rice: "Pierre Chouteau, Entrepreneur as Indian Agent," 368–71, and "Visiting the President: An Exercise in Jeffersonian Indian Diplomacy."

37. Gary E. Moulton, ed., *The Journals of the Lewis and Clark Expedition*, 2:227–38.

38. Ibid., 240–44.

39. Claiborne and Wilkinson to Stoddard, 16 January 1804, Stoddard Papers.

40. Dearborn to Stoddard, 16 May 1804, in *Territorial Papers*, 13:23.

41. Delassus to Stoddard, 6 March 1804, in Billon, *Annals of St. Louis in its Early Days*, 365–71; Stoddard to Claiborne and Wilkinson, 26 March 1804, Claiborne to Stoddard, 26 June 1804, and Stoddard to Claiborne, 19 May 1804, all in Stoddard Papers.

42. Foley, "Slave Freedom Suits Before Dred Scott," 7–8; Claiborne to Stoddard, 26 June 1804, Stoddard Papers.

43. Lemont K. Richardson, "Private Land Claims in Missouri," part 1, 135–37.

44. Ibid.; Russel Gerlach, "Spanish Land Grants in Missouri," 10–11.

45. Stoddard to Dearborn, 10 January 1804, in *American State Papers, Public Lands*, 1:177.

46. Ibid. For Stoddard's subsequent view, see his *Sketches*, 255–58.

47. Stoddard to Inhabitants of Upper Louisiana, 10 March 1804, Stoddard Papers.

48. Stoddard, *Sketches*, 253.

49. Stoddard to Claiborne, 26 March 1804, Stoddard Papers; William Cronon and Richard White, "Indians in the Land," 23–24.

50. Stoddard to Claiborne, 19 May 1804, Stoddard Papers; Stoddard's Proclamation Against Muskoe or Creek Indians, 30 April 1804, copy in Ste. Genevieve Archives.

51. Stoddard to Dearborn, 3 June 1804, Stoddard Papers.

52. James Bruff to Wilkinson, 29 September 1804, Warren Cottle to James Bruff, 9 September 1804, and Mackey Wherry to Stoddard, 12 September 1804, all in *Territorial Papers*, 13:56–63.

53. Ibid.; Representative Inhabitants of New Madrid to Bruff, 19 September 1804, in ibid., 61–62.

54. Stoddard to an unidentified person, 3 June 1804, Stoddard Papers; Bruff to Wilkinson, 29 September 1804, in *Territorial Papers*, 13:59.

CHAPTER 8. THE BEGINNINGS OF REPUBLICAN GOVERNMENT

1. Thomas Jefferson to John Breckinridge, 24 November 1803, Breckinridge to Jefferson, 26 November 1803, both in Jefferson Papers.

2. A Bill Erecting Louisiana into Two Territories and providing for the temporary Government thereof, 30 December 1803, Records of the U.S. Senate, National Archives.

3. The *Annals* provide only limited information on the debate. A much more comprehensive account of the proceedings in the Senate is contained in Everett S. Brown, ed., *William Plumer's Memorandum of Proceedings in the United States Senate, 1803–1807*, 133–41. See also Jefferson to DeWitt Clinton, 2 December 1803, Jefferson Papers.

4. Brown, ed., *Plumer's Memorandum*, 139–41.

5. Ibid.

6. Amos Stoddard to Henry Dearborn, 10 January 1804, in *American State Papers, Public Lands*, 1:177; *Annals*, 8 Cong., 1 sess., 1128 (9 March 1804).

7. *Annals*, 8 Cong., 1 sess., 1186–87 (14 March 1804).

8. Although the District of Louisiana officially encompassed the territory today constituting the states of Missouri, Arkansas, Iowa, Nebraska, Kansas, North Dakota, South Dakota, Oklahoma, and parts of Minnesota, Montana, Wyoming, and Colorado, for all practical purposes governmental authority in the district was confined to limited areas along the Mississippi River in Missouri and Arkansas. See Isidor Loeb, "The Beginnings of Missouri Legislation," 57.

9. *2 U.S. Statutes at Large* (1850), 287–89.

10. Proceedings of a meeting of the inhabitants of St. Louis, 2 April 1804, in *Territorial Papers*, 13:35–37.

11. Proceedings of a meeting of the inhabitants of St. Louis, 15 April 1804, in ibid., 37.

12. Albert Gallatin to Jefferson, 20 August 1804, Jefferson Papers.

13. Thomas W. Waters to Jefferson, 23 August 1804, Jefferson Papers; Stoddard, *Sketches*, 253.

14. Committee of Inhabitants of St. Louis to citizens of Upper Louisiana, 28 July 1804, and Resolutions of a Committee of Ste. Genevieve and New Bourbon, 2 September 1804, in *Territorial Papers*, 13:33–35, 41–43.

15. John C. Miller, *The Wolf by the Ears: Thomas Jefferson and Slavery*, 142–45, 234.

16. William C. Carr to John Breckinridge, 7 July 1804, in ibid., 29–30; J. Rankin, translator, to Amos Stoddard, Translation of Petition of St. Louis Committee, 4 August 1804, and Stoddard to Auguste Chouteau, president of St. Louis Committee, 6 August 1804, Chouteau Collections.

17. Resolutions of a Committee of Ste. Genevieve and New Bourbon, 2 September 1804, in *Territorial Papers*, 13:41–43.

18. David B. Gracy II, *Moses Austin: His Life*, 91; Rufus Easton to Jefferson, 17 January 1805, Jefferson Papers.

19. Minutes of a meeting at St. Louis, 14 September 1804, in *Territorial Papers*, 13:43–46.

20. Ibid.

21. Michael Amoureaux to Albert Gallatin, 2 November 1804, and Anonymous paper

concerning the attitude of French inhabitants of Louisiana, 4 November 1804, in ibid., 64–67, 68–71.

22. Anonymous paper concerning the attitude of French inhabitants of Louisiana, 4 November 1804, in ibid., 68–71; Representation and Petition of the Representatives Elected by the Freemen of the Territory of Louisiana, Washington City, 1805, printed copy of original in the State Historical Society of Missouri.

23. Ibid.

24. *American State Papers, Miscellaneous,* 1:404–5.

25. Amos Stoddard to William Henry Harrison, 3 June 1804, Stoddard Papers; Harrison to Jefferson, 24 June 1804, and Jefferson to Harrison, 14 July 1804, Jefferson Papers.

26. James Madison to Harrison, 14 June 1804, in Logan Esarey, ed., *Governor's Messages and Letters: Messages and Letters of William Henry Harrison,* 1:96; Department of War to Harrison, 21 June 1804, as cited in Annie H. Able, "The History of Events Resulting in Indian Consolidation West of the Mississippi," 251.

27. Jefferson to Col. Richard Kennon as quoted in Stella M. Drumm, "Samuel Hammond," 410; Gallatin to Jefferson, 11 May 1804, Jefferson Papers.

28. Dearborn to Col. Samuel Hammond, Col. R. J. Meigs, Jr., Col. Richard Kennon, and Maj. Seth Hunt, 17 September and 2 November 1804, in *Territorial Papers,* 13:46–47, 54–55. Dearborn did not mention a commission for commandant of the District of New Madrid. However, according to Louis Houck, Pierre Antoine LaForge acted as commandant of New Madrid. LaForge was the only commandant who was not an army officer. See Houck, *History of Missouri,* 2:382.

29. Loeb, "The Beginnings of Missouri Legislation," 59–60.

30. Eugene M. Violette, "The Black Code in Missouri."

31. Proclamation by Governor Harrison, 1 October 1804, in *Territorial Papers,* 13:51–52; Loeb, "The Beginnings of Missouri Legislation," 65.

32. Proclamation of Governor Harrison, 1 October 1804, in *Territorial Papers,* 13:51–52; Commissions issued by Governor Harrison, 1 October 1804, Governors Papers, Missouri Historical Society.

33. Freeman Cleaves, *Old Tippecanoe,* 43.

34. Diary of Don Carlos Delassus on the Evacuation of Upper Louisiana, entry dated 17 November 1804, Delassus Collection, Missouri Historical Society.

35. Cleaves, *Old Tippecanoe,* 43; Anonymous letter, 4 November 1804, in *Territorial Papers,* 13:70.

36. For accounts of these negotiations, see William T. Hagan, "The Sauk and Fox Treaty of 1804"; Donald Jackson, *Thomas Jefferson and the Stony Mountains: Exploring the West from Monticello,* 203–22.

37. *American State Papers, Indian Affairs,* 1:693–94.

38. Ibid.; Harrison to Auguste Chouteau, 4 January 1806, Lucas Collection, Missouri Historical Society; Hagan, "The Sauk and Fox Treaty," 1–7; and Jackson, *Jefferson and the Stony Mountains,* 208–17.

39. Hagan, "The Sauk and Fox Treaty"; Jackson, *Jefferson and the Stony Mountains,* 208–17; James Bruff to James Wilkinson, 5 November 1804, in *Territorial Papers,* 13:77; and Dearborn to Jefferson, 8 January 1805, in Esarey, ed., *Messages and Letters of Harrison,* 115–16.

40. *Annals,* 8 Cong., 2 sess., 13 (8 November 1804); Moses Austin, "Report on Land Mines in Upper Louisiana," in *American State Papers, Public Lands,* 1:191; and Simeon Baldwin to David Daggett, 19 November 1804, in Simeon E. Baldwin, *Life and Letters of Simeon Baldwin,* 342.

41. Eligius Fromentin to Auguste Chouteau, 12 January 1805, Chouteau Collections; Harrison to Chouteau, 21 December 1804, in Esarey, ed., *Messages and Letters of Harrison,* 113–14.

42. Harrison indicated that the inhabitants were especially disturbed by the remarks made in Congress by Matthew Lyon. Harrison to Jefferson, 6 November 1804, Jefferson Papers; Harrison to Auguste Chouteau, 21 December 1804, in Esarey, ed., *Messages and Letters of Harrison,* 113–14.

43. Eligius Fromentin to Auguste Chouteau, 12 January and 14 February 1805, Chouteau Collections; Rufus Easton to Jefferson, 17 January 1805, Jefferson Papers.

44. Harrison to Chouteau, 19 March 1805, in Esarey, ed., *Messages and Letters of Harrison,* 116–17.

45. For an example of the reasons for this concern about the readiness of the French Creoles for republican government, see Jefferson to John Breckinridge, 22 November 1803, in Breckinridge Family Papers, Library of Congress. 2 *U.S. Statutes at Large* (1850), 331–32.

46. *2 U.S. Statutes at Large* (1850), 324–29.

CHAPTER 9. PETTIFOGGERS, RENEGADOES, AND IMPATIENT NATIVES

1. James A. Wilkinson to Henry Dearborn, 27 June, 27 July, and 8 September 1805, in *Territorial Papers*, 13:144–45, 164–65, 204–5.

2. William E. Foley and C. David Rice, *The First Chouteaus*, 116.

3. Wilkinson to Dearborn, 27 July 1805, in *Territorial Papers*, 13:164–65.

4. Wilkinson to James Madison, 28 July 1805, in ibid., 173.

5. James Jackson to Thomas Jefferson, 9 January 1803, and Joseph Anderson to Jefferson, 10 January 1803, Letters of Application and Recommendation during the Administration of Thomas Jefferson, 1801–1809, National Archives; Clarence E. Carter, "The Burr-Wilkinson Intrigue in St. Louis," 448.

6. Jefferson to Joseph Anderson, 28 December 1805, Jefferson Papers.

7. Carter, "Burr-Wilkinson Intrigue," 448; Donald Jackson, *Jefferson and the Stony Mountains*, 244, 257.

8. John B. C. Lucas to Albert Gallatin, 12 November 1805, in *Territorial Papers*, 13:269. Amos Stoddard had also found it costly to live in St. Louis. Stoddard to Phoebe Reade Benham, 16 June 1804, Stoddard Papers.

9. Gideon Granger to Rufus Easton, 16 March 1805, Rufus Easton Papers, Missouri Historical Society.

10. Hugh C. Cleland, "John B. C. Lucas, Physiocrat on the Frontier," part 3, 163.

11. DeWitt Clinton to Easton, 1 September 1803, Aaron Burr to Abraham R. Ellery, 11 March 1804, and Gideon Granger to Easton, 7 July 1804, Easton Papers.

12. William T. Utter, "Return Jonathan Meigs," in Dumas Malone, ed., *Dictionary of American Biography*, 12:509–10.

13. Wilkinson to Dearborn, 31 December 1805, and William Henry Harrison to Wilkinson, 7 June 1805, in *Territorial Papers*, 13:370, 134.

14. Citizens of St. Louis to Wilkinson, 3 July 1805, and Wilkinson to Citizens of St. Louis, 3 July 1805, in ibid., 149–51.

15. Christian Schultz, *Travels on an Inland Voyage*, 2:53.

16. Carl Ekberg et al., *A Cultural, Geographical and Historical Study of the Pine Ford Lake Project Area, Washington, Jefferson, Franklin, and St. Francois Counties, Missouri*, 34; *American State Papers, Public Lands*, 2:554; and David Gracy II, *Moses Austin*, 77–83.

17. Proclamation by Commandant of Ste. Genevieve District, 24 March 1805, and Wilkinson to Madison, 21 September 1805, in *Territorial Papers*, 13:110, 219–20; Gracy, *Moses Austin*, 99–103.

18. Moses Austin to Wilkinson, 22 July 1805, and Notice to Public [1805], in Eugene C. Barker, ed., *The Austin Papers*, 1:97–98, 123; John Smith T to Wilkinson, 8 July 1805, in *Territorial Papers*, 13:210–11; Smith T to Frederick Bates, 29 December 1807, and Bates to Secretary of Treasury, 12 June 1814, in *Bates Papers*, 1:251–52, 2:276–77.

19. Henry Marie Brackenridge, *Recollections of Persons and Places in the West*, 218; Gracy, *Moses Austin*, 100–101. John Darby reported that Smith T, who was a Princeton graduate, killed fifteen men, mostly in duels, but a sympathetic recent account contends that the reports of Smith T's killings in duels have been grossly exaggerated. According to Valle Higginbothan, only two known deaths can be definitely attributed to Smith T. See John F. Darby, *Personal Recollections of Many Prominent People Whom I Have Known*, 85–89, and Valle Higginbothan, *John Smith T: Missouri Pioneer*. A copy of the latter, which was privately printed, is in the State Historical Society of Missouri Library.

20. *Bates Papers*, 1:116n; Louis Houck, *A History of Missouri*, 2:364. The Dodges were in many ways kindred spirits with Smith T. Israel Dodge and his brother John had been considered troublemakers in American Illinois prior to their move to Ste. Genevieve in the 1780s.

21. Richard M. Clokey, *William H. Ashley: Enterprise and Politics in the Trans-Mississippi West*, 12–22.

22. William C. Carr to Gallatin, 14 November 1805, in *Territorial Papers*, 13:274.

23. Seth Hunt to Wilkinson, 30 June 1805, Smith T to Wilkinson, 8 July 1805, and Wilkinson to Hunt, July 1805, all in ibid., 208, 210–12, 212–13; Gracy, *Moses Austin*, 104–6.

24. Wilkinson to Dearborn, 21 September 1805, in *Territorial Papers*, 13:222.

25. Hunt to Wilkinson, 5 September 1805, Wilkinson to Dearborn, 8 September 1805, and Wilkinson's remarks on Hunt's letter, 4 December 1805, all in ibid., 222–25, 204–7, 313.

26. Dearborn to Wilkinson, 16 October 1805, in ibid., 241.

27. For a lengthy discussion of relations between these two men at this time, consult Carter,

"The Burr-Wilkinson Intrigue." Carter's version of the St. Louis meeting agrees substantially with the shorter account presented by Thomas P. Abernethy in *The Burr Conspiracy,* 31–32. Abernethy argues that until after Burr's departure from St. Louis, they had cooperated closely, with Burr devoting his attention to the domestic situation while Wilkinson concentrated on the Mexican venture.

28. Easton to Granger, 17 February and 18 June 1807, Easton Papers.

29. William Francis English, *The Pioneer Lawyer and Jurist in Missouri,* 21.

30. Carr to Breckinridge, 13 November 1805, in *Territorial Papers,* 13:270–71; Lucas and Easton to Wilkinson, 12 October 1805, Lucas Collection, Missouri Historical Society; Wilkinson to Lucas and Easton, 12 October 1805, Wilkinson to Lucas and Easton, 28 October 1805, and Wilkinson to Lucas and Easton, 2 November 1805, photostatic copies in James Wilkinson Papers, Missouri Historical Society. The legislature did not finally convene until the spring of 1806, when Wilkinson and Judges Lucas and Meigs enacted a series of laws encompassing such varied topics as the appointment of an attorney general, the sale of liquor to Indians, marriages, prisons, public roads and highways, the regulation of ferries, the prevention of stallions from running at large, and the regulation of taverns.

31. Opinion of the territorial court re the commission of a district attorney, 29 October 1805, and Donaldson to Wilkinson, 29 October 1805, in *Territorial Papers,* 13:256–59.

32. Opinion of the territorial court re the commission of an attorney general, 30 October 1805, in ibid., 260.

33. Deposition of Richard Caulk, 4 November 1805, Lucas Collection, and Deposition of Edward Hempstead, 11 November 1805, photostatic copy in Hempstead Papers, both in Missouri Historical Society.

34. Presentment of the Grand Jury of the Territory, October term, 1805, in *Territorial Papers,* 13:248–51.

35. Carr to Breckenridge, 24 December 1805, in ibid., 320–23.

36. Protest of a Minority of the Grand Jury, October term, 1805, Easton Papers.

37. Ibid.

38. Carr to Breckinridge, 13 November 1805, and Wilkinson to Dearborn, 17 December 1805, in *Territorial Papers,* 13:272, 307.

39. Samuel Hammond to Abraham Baldwin, 30 December 1805, and Hammond to John Archer, 30 December 1805, Easton Papers; Carr to Breckinridge, 30 December 1805, in *Territorial Papers,* 13:359–60; Easton to Jefferson, 21 February 1806, and Jefferson to Easton, 22 February 1806, Jefferson Papers. Jefferson's decision to remove Easton must have been reinforced by a letter he received from William Keteltas, a Wilkinson backer from New York, that was highly unfavorable to Easton. Keteltas to Jefferson, 19 January 1806, Jefferson Papers.

40. Lucas to Madison, 12 November 1805, photostatic copy in Lucas Collection; Lucas to Gallatin, 12 November and 19 November 1805, Carr to Breckinridge, 13 November 1805, and Wilkinson to Dearborn, 31 December 1805, in *Territorial Papers,* 13:269–70, 286–89, 270–73, 369–70.

41. Memorial to the President by Citizens of the Territory, 27 December 1805; Memorial to the President by Citizens of Ste. Genevieve, 28 December 1805; Memorial to the President by Citizens of St. Ferdinand, 28 December 1805; Memorial to the President by Citizens of St. Charles, 30 December 1805; John Bledsoe to Breckinridge, 30 December 1805; and Auguste Chouteau and others to the President, 6 January 1806; all in ibid., 329–45, 345–49, 349–51, 360–64, 364–65, 385–86. Josiah McClanahan to Samuel Smith, 13 January 1806, photostatic copy in Wilkinson Papers.

42. Lucas to unidentified person, 24 March 1806, Lucas Collection; *Plumer's Memorandum,* 392–93.

CHAPTER 10. THE TURMOIL CONTINUES

1. Louis Lorimier to Col. John B. Scott, 25 March 1806, Louisiana Territory Papers, Missouri Historical Society; Clarence E. Carter, "The Burr-Wilkinson Intrigue in St. Louis," 457.

2. Minute Books of the Board of Land Commissioners, Missouri State Archives, Jefferson City.

3. Hugh C. Cleland, "John B. C. Lucas, Physiocrat on the Frontier," 92–100.

4. Silas Bent to Jared Mansfield, 5 October and 13 October 1806, in *Territorial Papers,* 14:13–14; Amos Stoddard, *Sketches, Historical and Descriptive of Upper Louisiana,* 255–57.

5. Carr to Breckinridge, 24 December 1805, in *Territorial Papers,* 13:323–24; Lucas to Gallatin, 29 January 1806, Albert Gallatin Papers, New York Historical Society; Notification by Governor

Wilkinson, 18 September 1805, in *Territorial Papers*, 13:255–56; and Moses Austin to [Albert Gallatin?], n.d., in Eugene C. Barker, ed., *The Austin Papers*, 1:115–18.

6. William H. Harrison to Jared Mansfield, 19 April 1806, Mansfield to Gallatin, 14 June 1806, and Antoine Soulard to Board of Land Commissioners, 24 July 1806, in *Territorial Papers*, 13:492, 519, 534–35; Silas Bent to Mansfield, 5 October 1806, and Soulard to Board of Land Commissioners, 5 November 1806, in *Territorial Papers*, 14:13–14, 29–33; and Lemont K. Richardson, "Private Land Claims in Missouri," 143–44.

7. Gallatin to Jefferson, received 6 January 1806, Jefferson Papers.

8. Gallatin to Jefferson, 12 February 1806, Jefferson Papers.

9. Lucas to Gallatin, 29 January 1806, Gallatin Papers; Gallatin to Jefferson, 15 March 1806, Jefferson to Cabinet, 16 March 1806, Dearborn to Jefferson, 16 March 1806, Breckinridge to Jefferson, 22 March 1806, and Jefferson to Gallatin, 22 March 1806, Jefferson Papers.

10. Gallatin to the Land Commissioners, 26 March 1806, in *Territorial Papers*, 13:462–63.

11. Lucas to Gallatin, 5 August 1806, in ibid., 559–67; Carr to Gallatin, 1 September 1806, in ibid., 14:6–7; and Gallatin to Land Commissioners, 8 September 1806, in *American State Papers, Public Lands*, 3:356–57.

12. Lucas to Gallatin, 4 November 1806, and Lucas to Clement Penrose, 25 November 1806, in *Territorial Papers*, 14:27–29, 40–41.

13. Jefferson to Gallatin, 4 January 1807, Jefferson Papers.

14. Gallatin to Lucas and Penrose, 13 February 1807, in *Territorial Papers*, 14:97–98.

15. The first certificates of confirmation were not issued until 8 December 1808. See Eugene Morrow Violette, "Spanish Land Claims in Missouri"; Carr to Moses Austin, 12 August 1806, in Barker, ed., *Austin Papers*, 1:113–14.

16. Wilkinson to Dearborn, 27 July 1805, in *Territorial Papers*, 13:165.

17. Jefferson to Harrison, 27 February 1803, Jefferson Papers.

18. Dearborn to Wilkinson, 19 April 1805, Wilkinson to Dearborn, 27 July and 30 December 1805, in *Territorial Papers*, 13:116–17, 167–68, 358. The complete story of Fort Belle Fontaine's construction is told in Kate L. Gregg, "Building the First American Fort West of the Mississippi," and an account of the trading factory there can be found in Russell M. Magnaghi, "The Belle Fontaine Indian Factory, 1805–1808."

19. Wilkinson to Pike, 30 July 1805, and Wilkinson to Pierre Chouteau, 30 July 1805, in *Territorial Papers*, 13:184–85; Jackson, *Jefferson and the Stony Mountains*, 246–47; and Foley and Rice, *First Chouteaus*, 117–18. In a letter to Daniel Bissell, Pike informed him, "They are a Damn'd set of Rascals yet in the woods they are staunch fellows and very proper for such expeditions as I am engaged in" (Bissell Papers, Mercantile Library, St. Louis).

20. Wilkinson to Jefferson, 6 November 1805, Jefferson Papers; Wilkinson to Madison, 20 July and 24 August 1805, Wilkinson to Dearborn, 8 September 1805, Merchants of St. Louis to Wilkinson, 24 August 1805, and Proclamation by Governor Wilkinson, 26 August 1805, in *Territorial Papers*, 13:173–74, 190–91, 196–200, 202–3, 203.

21. Wilkinson to Madison, 28 July 1805, Wilkinson to Dearborn, 10 August 1805, Dearborn to Wilkinson, 16 October and 2 November 1805, in *Territorial Papers*, 13:173–74, 182–83, 239, 251–52; Paul Francis Prucha, *The Sword of the Republic: The United States Army on the Frontier, 1783–1846*, 75–76.

22. Wilkinson to Dearborn, 8 October and 10 December 1805, and Dearborn to Wilkinson, 21 November 1805, in *Territorial Papers*, 13:236, 297–98, 290.

23. Wilkinson to Dearborn, 10 August 1805, 22 September 1805, and 8 October 1805, in ibid., 183, 229–30, 234.

24. Wilkinson to Dearborn, 22 October 1805, Wilkinson and Harrison to Dearborn, 19 October 1805, and Treaty Between Tribes of Indians Called the Delawares, Miamis, et al., 18 October 1805, all in ibid., 243–44, 245, 245–47.

25. Wilkinson to Dearborn, 10 December 1805, and Wilkinson to Chiefs of the Sauk Nation, 10 December 1805, in ibid., 298–99, 300–302.

26. Wilkinson to Madison, 24 August 1805, in ibid., 189–90; Edward F. Bond to Jefferson, 17 October 1806, Jefferson Papers.

27. Edward F. Bond to Wilkinson, 2 August 1805, and Wilkinson to Madison, 24 August 1805, in *Territorial Papers*, 13:175–78, 189–90; Wilkinson to Jefferson, 6 November and 23 December 1805, Jefferson Papers.

28. Wilkinson to Madison, 26 November 1805, photostatic copy in Wilkinson Papers.

29. Austin to Gallatin, [August 1806?], in Barker, ed., *Austin Papers*, 1:122.

30. Samuel Hammond to Jefferson, 28 May 1806; Deposition of Samuel Soloman, 27 May 1806; Findings of Coroners Jury, 23 May 1806; Hammond to Wilkinson, 1 June 1806; Wilkinson to Hammond, 8 June 1806; and James L. Donaldson to Dr. William Steward, 5 July 1806; all in *Territorial Papers*, 13:514–18, 537–39. Deposition of John Alexander Michau, 26 May 1806, Lucas Collection. Territorial Supreme Court Minute Book, entries for 27 May, 4 June, and 6 June 1806, Missouri Historical Society.

31. Wilkinson to Jefferson, 29 March 1806, and Wilkinson to Samuel Smith, 29 March 1806, Jefferson Papers.

32. Jefferson to Samuel Smith, 4 May 1806, and Dearborn to Wilkinson, 6 May 1806, Jefferson Papers.

33. Matthew Lyon to Jefferson, 22 April 1806, Jefferson Papers.

34. Lucas to Col. Thomas Baird, 7 September 1806, Lucas Papers; Wilkinson to Dearborn, 17 June 1806, and Wilkinson to Samuel Smith, 17 June 1806, Jefferson Papers; *Bates Papers*, 1:26; Joseph Browne to Madison, 26 August 1806, in *Territorial Papers*, 14:3–5; and Jackson, *Jefferson and the Stony Mountains*, 254–55.

35. Jackson, *Jefferson and the Stony Mountains*, 250–54. See also Donald Jackson, ed., *The Journals of Zebulon Montgomery Pike*.

36. Carter, "Burr-Wilkinson Intrigue," 458–59.

37. Ibid., 460–61; *Bates Papers*, 116n.

38. Carter, "Burr-Wilkinson Intrigue," 461; Gallatin to Jefferson, 25 October 1806, Jefferson Papers; John B. C. Lucas to Henry Dearborn, 9 February 1807, Resolution of Citizens of Louisiana, 13 February 1807, Joseph Browne to Citizens of Louisiana, 15 February 1807, in *Territorial Papers*, 14:96–97, 99, 100; Auguste Chouteau to Jefferson, 15 July 1806, Letters of Application and Recommendation during the Administration of Thomas Jefferson, National Archives; Petitions by the People of Louisiana to the President, 4 July 1806, and Memorial to the President by Citizens of the Territory, [1806], in *Territorial Papers*, 13:550–55, 468–86; and Dumas Malone, *Jefferson the President: The Second Term, 1805–1809*, 244.

39. Commission of Frederick Bates as Secretary, 4 February 1807, in *Territorial Papers*, 14:117–18; Commission of Frederick Bates as Recorder of Land Titles, 4 February 1807, in *Bates Papers*, 1:91. For a brief account of Bates's activities in the Michigan Territory, consult ibid., 3–18.

40. Matthew Lyon to Jefferson, 22 February 1807, Jefferson Papers; Commission of Meriwether Lewis as Governor, 3 March 1807, in *Territorial Papers*, 14:107; and Carter, "Burr-Wilkinson Intrigue," 461.

41. Jackson, *Jefferson and the Stony Mountains*, 268–69.

CHAPTER 11. TERRITORY IN TRANSITION

1. John F. Darby, *Personal Recollections of Many Prominent People Whom I Have Known*, 19.

2. James Neal Primm, *Lion of the Valley*, 85; Carl J. Ekberg, *Colonial Ste. Genevieve*, 468; Ronald L. F. Davis, "Community and Conflict in Pioneer Saint Louis, Missouri," 343; and Kenneth W. Keller, "Alexander McNair and John B. C. Lucas: The Background of Early Missouri Politics."

3. Primm, *Lion of the Valley*, 85; Ekberg, *Colonial Ste. Genevieve*, 263; and William E. Foley and C. David Rice, *The First Chouteaus*, 188.

4. Brackenridge, *Recollections of Persons and Places in the West*, 206.

5. 1810 Census Figures for the Territory of Louisiana, in *Territorial Papers*, 14:431. Excluding the Arkansas settlements, the territory's population was 19,783, according to the 1810 census. John B. C. Lucas to James Mountain, 3 March 1808, Lucas Collection, Missouri Historical Society.

6. Brackenridge, *Views of Louisiana*, 120.

7. Brackenridge, *Recollections*, 200; Thomas Ashe, *Travels in America*, 288–89.

8. Brackenridge, *Views of Louisiana*, 123–24; Washington Irving, *Astoria*, rpt. in Herbert L. Kleinfield, ed., *The Complete Works of Washington Irving*, 93. Lt. Col. Daniel Bissell advised Secretary of War Eustis in 1809 that "Mechanics cannot be got, Builders, Undertakers &c are not known in the Country." He also pointed out that bricks and other building materials would be equally hard to obtain locally. Bissell to Eustis, 17 August 1809, photostatic copy in Daniel Bissell Papers, Missouri Historical Society.

9. Ashe, *Travels in America*, 290–91; Primm, *Lion of the Valley*, 87–88, 109; Ekberg, *Colonial Ste. Genevieve*, 373–75; Joseph Browne to James Madison, 26 August 1806, in *Territorial Papers*, 14:4; Frederick Bates to Frederick Woodson, 1 May 1807, and Frederick Bates to Richard Bates, 31 May 1807, in *Bates Papers*, 1:110–14, 136–37; and Silas Bent to John B. C. Lucas, 26 December 1812, Lucas Collection, Missouri Historical Society.

10. Houck, *History of Missouri*, 3:75–77.

11. Susan Green, "The Material Culture of a Pre-Enclosure Village in Upper Louisiana" (M.A. thesis, University of Missouri–Columbia, 1983), 91; Osmund Overby, "House and Home in the New Village of Ste. Genevieve" (paper presented at Ste. Genevieve Seminar, Ste. Genevieve, Mo., 3 November 1985); Brackenridge, *Views of Louisiana*, 120, 122; Brackenridge, *Recollections*, 199; Irving, *Astoria*, 93; Ekberg and Foley, *Account of Upper Louisiana*, 124; and Christian Schultz, *Travels on an Inland Voyage*, 2:39–40.

12. François Vallé sent his first son to New York to learn English, and Auguste Chouteau sent his eldest boy to Canada with instructions that he be enrolled in English classes and his second son to a Catholic college in Bardstown, Kentucky. Sons of the Vallé, Chouteau, and Gratiot families also enrolled in the U.S. Military Academy at West Point. Proposal for the Establishment of an Academy, 29 July 1807, in *Territorial Papers*, 14:177–81.

13. Brackenridge, *Journal of a Voyage Up the River Missouri*, 33–34; John Bradbury, *Travels in the Interior of America, in the Years 1809, 1810, and 1811*, 188; Walter Schroeder, "Spread of Settlement in Howard County, Missouri, 1810–1859," 8; and Lyman Draper's 1851 interview with Nathan Boone, in Draper MSS, 6S, 244–46. Apparently on the basis of Draper's material, 1806 is traditionally cited as the year that Nathan and Daniel Morgan Boone initiated their saltmaking activity in the Boonslick country, but they were already at work there in 1805. In December 1805, Governor Wilkinson advised Secretary Dearborn, "I am info[rmed] the salt works of a son of old Dan'l Boone, about one hundred fifty miles up the Missouri have been broken up." See Wilkinson to Dearborn, 10 December 1805, in *Territorial Papers*, 14:298.

14. Cooper family history in Draper MSS, 23S, 126.

15. Ibid., 126–27; testimony of Samuel Cole, Draper MSS, 23S, 65–92; and Brackenridge, *Journal*, 34. On the arrangements in the earliest Kentucky settlements, see Lewis C. Gray, *History of Agriculture in the Southern U.S. to 1860*, 2:866.

16. Schultz, *Travels on an Inland Voyage*, 79.

17. Brackenridge, *Journal*, 33–34; Bradbury, *Travels*, 188; and testimony of Judge Frederick Hyatt in Draper MSS, 22S, 141–42, 148.

18. Brackenridge, *Journal*, 33–34; Bradbury, *Travels*, 188; and Brackenridge, *Recollections*, 192–93.

19. Brackenridge, *Recollections*, 193–94.

20. Ibid., 240–41.

21. Ibid., 195–96, 198.

22. Meriwether Lewis to William Clark, 13 March 1807, Clark Papers, Missouri Historical Society.

23. Frederick Bates to Meriwether Lewis, 5 and 7 April 1807, and Bates to Joseph Browne, 7 April 1807, in *Bates Papers*, 1:98–100, 100–102, 102.

24. Frederick Bates to Richard Bates, 31 May 1807, and Frederick Bates to Lewis, 16 January 1808, in ibid., 136–37, 265.

25. Bates to Lewis, 15 May 1807, and Bates to John Smith T, 1 May 1807, in ibid., 1:115–16, 109–10; Bates to Thomas Jefferson, 6 May 1807, Thomas Jefferson Papers, Library of Congress.

26. Bates to William Hull, 17 June 1807, in *Bates Papers*, 1:144–45; John G. Westover, "The Evolution of the Missouri Militia, 1804–1819" (Ph.D. diss., University of Missouri, 1948), 34.

27. "A Journal of the Proceedings of the Legislature of the Territory of Louisiana," 3 [11] June 1806 to 9 October 1811, St. Louis Mercantile Library; Bates to Augustus B. Woodward, 18 January 1807, in *Bates Papers*, 1:147; and John Coburn to James Madison, 15 August 1807, as quoted in English, *Pioneer Lawyer and Jurist in Missouri*, 56.

28. *The Laws of the Territory of Louisiana*.

29. Bates to Lewis, 28 April 1807, in *Bates Papers*, 1:103–7.

30. Clark to Dearborn, 18 May 1807, in *Territorial Papers*, 14:122–25. For the full story of the attempts to return the Mandan chief, see Foley and Rice, "The Return of the Mandan Chief."

31. Clark to Henry Dearborn, 18 May and 1 June 1807, in *Territorial Papers*, 14:122–25, 126.

32. Louis Lorimier to Joseph Browne, 19 February 1807, and Lewis to Dearborn, 1 July 1808, in *Territorial Papers*, 14:112, 196–97.

33. Clark to Dearborn, 18 May, 1 June, and 12 September 1807, in *Territorial Papers*, 14:125, 126, 146; Clark to Jefferson, 20 September 1807, Jefferson Papers; and Schultz, *Travels in America*, 2:88.

34. Bates to Col. Thomas Hunt, 22 July 1807, Bates to Clark, 25 July 1807, and Bates to Dearborn, 2 August 1807, in *Bates Papers*, 1:163, 168, 169.

35. Bates to James Madison, 8 August 1807, in *Territorial Papers*, 14:140; Bates to William H. Harrison, 16 September 1807, in *Bates Papers*, 1:191.

36. Bates to Clark, 15 September 1807, and Bates to Augustus Woodward, 20 October 1807, in *Bates Papers*, 1:188–89, 220; Foley and Rice, "Return of the Mandan Chief," 6–8.

37. Act Re Claims to Land in the Territories of Orleans and Louisiana, 3 March 1807, in *Territorial Papers*, 14:102–6.

38. Lead Mining Contracts, October 1807, and Bates to Albert Gallatin, 6 October 1807, in *Bates Papers*, 1:211–15, 216–18.

39. Gallatin to Bates, 13 November 1807, in *Territorial Papers*, 14:152.

40. William Mathers to Bates, 29 January and 17 February 1808, and Seth Hunt to Bates, 18 February 1808, in *Bates Papers*, 1:270–72, 293–94, 295–96.

41. *Travels on an Inland Voyage*, 2:53.

42. *Recollections*, 213.

43. For a more detailed account of the operation of the lead-leasing system in Missouri, see Donald J. Abramoske, "The Federal Lead Leasing System in Missouri."

CHAPTER 12. AN UNEASY INTERLUDE

1. Bates to Robert Dickson, 8 March 1808, Bates to Timothy Kibby, 22 March 1808, Bates to Richard Bates, 24 March 1807, Moses Austin to Bates, 27 [March] 1808, in *Bates Papers*, 1:308, 314, 315, 318–19; Dillon, *Meriwether Lewis*, 300.

2. Lewis to Dearborn, 1 July 1808, and James McFarland to Lewis, 11 December 1808, in *Territorial Papers*, 14:196–203, 266–68; Foley, "Different Notions of Justice."

3. Lewis to Dearborn, 1 July 1808, in ibid., 196–202; Foley, "Different Notions of Justice."

4. Lewis to Dearborn, 20 August 1808, in ibid., 214; Jefferson to Lewis, 21 August 1808, Jefferson Papers. For evidence of Lewis's local support, see the letter from "A Bye Stander" in *Missouri Gazette*, 17 August 1808.

5. Dearborn to Thomas Hunt, 17 May 1808, in *Territorial Papers*, 14:184.

6. Clark to Dearborn, 25 June 1808, 18 August 1808, and 23 September 1808, and Lewis to Dearborn, 1 July 1808, in ibid., 14:194, 208–210, 224–28, 196. For the story of Fort Osage, see Kate L. Gregg, "The History of Fort Osage."

7. Clark to Dearborn, 23 September 1808, in *Territorial Papers*, 14:224–25.

8. Ibid.; *American State Papers, Indian Affairs*, 2:763–67; and Kate L. Gregg, ed., *Westward with Dragoons: The Journal of William Clark on His Expedition to Establish Fort Osage, August 25 to September 22, 1808*, 41.

9. Ibid.

10. Ibid.; Charles T. Jones, Jr., *George Champlin Sibley: The Prairie Puritan, 1782–1863*, 52–54. For a more detailed treatment of Osage-U.S. relations, see Willard Rollings, "Prairie Hegemony: An Ethnohistorical Study of the Osage from Early Times to 1840" (Ph.D. diss., Texas Tech University, 1983), 399–409.

11. The story of Fort Osage and the activities there can be found in Gregg, "The History of Fort Osage."

12. See Donald Jackson, "Old Fort Madison, 1808–1813."

13. Clark to William Eustis, 29 April 1809, in *Territorial Papers*, 14:264–66; *Missouri Gazette*, 12 and 26 April 1809.

14. Lewis to Dearborn, 1 July 1808, in *Territorial Papers*, 14:198–99; Bates to Eustis, 2–8 September 1809, in *Bates Papers*, 2:87–88.

15. Richard E. Oglesby, *Manuel Lisa and the Opening of the Missouri Fur Trade*, 35–39.

16. Ibid., 39–64.

17. For a full discussion of the Missouri Fur Company and its founding, see ibid., 65–75. Missouri Fur Company Articles of Agreement, 24 February 1809, copy in Chouteau Collections.

18. Ibid.

19. Eustis to Lewis, 15 July 1809, in Donald Jackson, ed., *Letters of the Lewis and Clark Expedition*, 456–57.

20. Eustis to Clark, 7 August 1809, in *Territorial Papers*, 14:289–90.

21. Lewis to Dearborn, 20 August 1808, in *Territorial Papers*, 14:212.

22. *Missouri Gazette*, 10 August 1808, 4 January and 13 September 1809, and 1 March 1810; Gideon Granger to Lewis, 29 March 1809, in *Territorial Papers*, 14:256–57.

23. Lewis to Clark, 29 May 1808, Clark Papers. For a complete account of the establishment and the early years of the *Missouri Gazette*, see William Lyon, *The Pioneer Editor in Missouri, 1808–1860*.

24. Bates to James Abbott, 23 February 1808, in *Bates Papers*, 1:301; *Missouri Gazette*, 25 January and 3 February 1809; Petition to Congress by the Inhabitants of Louisiana, referred to Congress 6 January 1810, in *Territorial Papers*, 14:357–62.

25. *Missouri Gazette*, 3 February 1809.

26. Ibid.

27. Ibid., 1 March 1809.

28. Petition to Congress by Inhabitants of Louisiana referred to Congress 6 January 1810, and A Bill for the Government of Louisiana Territory, 22 January 1810, in *Territorial Papers*, 14:357–62, 362–64.

29. William C. Carr to Charles Carr, 28 May 1807, and Bates to Gallatin, 30 May 1807, in *Bates Papers*, 1:126–28, 134–35.

30. 2 *U.S. Statutes at Large* (1850), 441.

31. Bates to Gallatin, 14 July 1807, in *Bates Papers*, 1:158–61.

32. John B. C. Lucas to Gallatin, 23 April 1808, and Bates to Gallatin, 5 June 1808, in *Territorial Papers*, 14:183, 190.

33. Bates to Gallatin, 22 July 1808, in *Bates Papers*, 2:8.

34. Report of the Board of Land Commissioners, 1 February 1810, in *Territorial Papers*, 14:366.

35. Petitions to Congress, 2 January and 18 December 1808, in ibid., 163, 246.

36. *Missouri Gazette*, 21 June 1809.

37. Ibid., 12 October 1809; Representation to Congress by a Committee of Inhabitants of Louisiana, 10 October 1809, in *Territorial Papers*, 14:323–27.

38. John B. C. Lucas to Charles Lucas, 12 November 1807, Lucas Collection; *Missouri Gazette*, 26 October 1809; Notice re John B. C. Lucas, 1809, in *Territorial Papers*, 14:335–36.

39. Lucas to Gallatin, 19 October 1809, and Lucas to Eustis, December 1809, in *Territorial Papers*, 14:334–35, 353–55; Lucas to Madison, 22 March 1810, James Madison Papers, Library of Congress.

40. Frederick Bates to Richard Bates, 15 April, 14 July, and 9 November 1809, and Frederick Bates to Eustis, 28 September 1809, in *Bates Papers*, 2:64, 68–69, 108–9, 86–87. Richard Dillon suggests that Bates was jealous of Lewis because Jefferson had selected Lewis to be his secretary rather than Bates (*Meriwether Lewis*, 297).

41. Frederick Bates to Richard Bates, 14 July and 9 November 1809, in *Bates Papers*, 2:69, 109–10.

42. Lewis to Eustis, 18 August 1809, in *Territorial Papers*, 14:291–92. Although Richard Dillon disputes the suicide claim in *Meriwether Lewis*, there is much evidence to the contrary. An excellent discussion of that evidence can be found in Donald Jackson's *Letters of Lewis and Clark*, 574–75n. Also see Dawson A. Phelps, "The Tragic Death of Meriwether Lewis," and Howard I. Kushner, "The Suicide of Meriwether Lewis: A Psychoanalytic Inquiry."

43. William C. Carr, an attorney whom Lewis had assigned to take charge of his business affairs in St. Louis, did not believe that the governor intended to return to the territory. Carr to Charles Carr, 25 August 1809, William C. Carr Papers, Missouri Historical Society.

44. For an assessment of Lewis and his contributions, see Dillon, *Meriwether Lewis*.

CHAPTER 13. DEFENDING THE WESTERN BORDER

1. The territory was popular with office seekers. The files of Letters of Application and Recommendation located in the National Archives contain numerous letters from individuals requesting an assignment in the Louisiana-Missouri Territory. Also see *Territorial Papers*, 14:365–66n, and Wilson P. Hunt to Frederick Bates, 8 March 1810, in *Bates Papers*, 2:129.

2. Frederick Bates to Richard Bates, 9 November 1809, in *Bates Papers*, 2:108–12.

3. John B. Scott should not be confused with the better-known John Scott, also from Virginia, who later became Missouri's territorial delegate to Congress. The files of the Letters of Application and Recommendation during the Administration of James Madison contain twenty-two letters supporting Coburn's appointment.

4. In endorsing Howard's candidacy for the post, Virginia congressman John W. Eppes strongly emphasized the applicant's military qualifications. Eppes to Madison, 8 February 1810, in *Territorial Papers*, 14:374. See also "Benjamin Howard," in *Biographical Directory of the American Congress, 1774–1927*, 1118. On Howard's regrets, see Sarah [von Phul] to Henry von Phul, 11 March [1813], Von Phul Family Papers, Missouri Historical Society.

5. William Clark to William Eustis, 20 July 1810, photostatic copy in Clark Papers, Missouri Historical Society; Clark to Eustis, 12 September and 28 September 1810, in *Territorial Papers*,

14:412–16; Pierre Chouteau to Eustis, 19 July 1810, Pierre Chouteau Letterbook, Missouri Historical Society.

6. Daniel Bissell to Eustis, 16 June and 17 August 1809 and 28 June 1811, and unsigned letter to Bissell, 18 April 1810, all photostatic copies in Daniel Bissell Papers, Missouri Historical Society.

7. Commission of Benjamin Howard as Governor, 18 April 1810, in *Territorial Papers*, 14:403–4; *Missouri Gazette*, 20 September 1810.

8. William Clark to Eustis, 12 September 1810, in *Territorial Papers*, 14:413; testimony of Samuel Cole in Draper MSS; Louis Houck, *A History of Missouri*, 3:98–101.

9. *Missouri Gazette*, 27 September 1810.

10. Kate L. Gregg, "The War of 1812 on the Missouri Frontier," part 1, 7.

11. *Missouri Gazette*, 30 May 1811.

12. Testimony of Elizabeth Musick, Draper MSS, 22S, 168–70; Lynn Morrow, "Trader William Gilliss and Delaware Migration in Southern Missouri," 151. Gilliss is a prime example of the Ozark trader with several Indian wives and numerous mixed-blood offspring. In addition to Morrow's article, see also Emory Melton, *Delaware Town and the Swan Trading Post, 1822–1831*, and Timothy Flint, *Recollections of the Last Ten Years in the Valley of the Mississippi*, 96, 109. Flint also mentioned that a French Creole woman who had once been the belle of Portage des Sioux was now married to a Potawatomi.

13. Testimony of Elizabeth Musick, Draper MSS, 22S, 168–70; *Missouri Gazette*, 14 June 1809.

14. Clark to Madison, 10 April 1810, in *Territorial Papers*, 14:445–46.

15. Ibid.

16. Proclamation of Governor Lewis, 16 April 1809, in *Missouri Gazette*, 12 April 1809.

17. Shawnees to President of the U.S., 29 March 1811, Letters Received by Secretary of War Relating to Indian Affairs, 1800–1816, M271, National Archives. The difficulties the Missouri Shawnees faced in sustaining their families were not unique. When John Bradbury traveled down the Mississippi in 1811, Indians along the banks were attempting to supplement their livelihoods by selling freshly killed venison and turkeys to the river travelers. See Bradbury, *Travels in the Interior of America, in the Years 1809, 1810, and 1811*, 195–97. Several years earlier, John Watson had reported that while he was en route down the Mississippi, three Delaware Indian girls came on board his boat at New Madrid with the object of bartering "their persons for biscuits, whiskey &c" ("John Watson's Diary of his Journey to New Orleans, 1804–1805," as quoted in John F. McDermott, "Travelers on the Western Waters," 278.

18. Eustis to Clark, 31 May 1811, Letters Sent by Secretary of War re Indian Affairs, M–15, National Archives; Gustavus Ste. Gem to Lyman Draper, 4 January 1855, Draper MSS, 5YY, 71.

19. Eustis to Madison, 31 January 1811, in *Territorial Papers*, 14:436; List of Civil and Militia Appointments in the Territory of Louisiana, 1 October 1810–30 September 1811, gives dates of Howard's arrivals and departures, in *Bates Papers*, 2:191, 194; and Gregg, "War of 1812," 10. The description of the blockhouses is found in Edwin James, *Account of an Expedition from Pittsburgh to the Rocky Mountains performed in the Years 1819, 1820 . . . Under the Command of Maj. S. H. Long* (London, 1823), rpt. in Reuben Gold Thwaites, ed., *Early Western Travels*, 14:134.

20. *Missouri Gazette*, 23 November 1811; R. David Edmunds, *Tecumseh and the Quest for Indian Leadership*, 159–60. Tecumseh was away from Prophetstown at the time of the battle and first learned about it while visiting the Shawnee villages near Cape Girardeau.

21. *Missouri Gazette*, 21 December 1811. A comprehensive account covering all aspects of the New Madrid tremors is James Penick, Jr., *The New Madrid Earthquakes of 1811–1812*.

22. Penick, *New Madrid Earthquakes*, 34–35, 40–41.

23. Ibid., 1–9, 57–104; Boynton Merrill, Jr., *Jefferson's Nephews: A Frontier Tragedy*, 266–67.

24. Penick, *New Madrid Earthquakes*, 1–7, 92–98, 37, 111–13.

25. *Missouri Gazette*, 21 and 28 December 1811 and 8 and 29 February 1812; Frederick Bates to William C. Carr, 31 July 1812, in *Bates Papers*, 2:232.

26. Clark to Eustis, 13 February 1812, Howard to Daniel Bissell, 13 February 1812, and Howard to Eustis, 19 March 1812, in *Territorial Papers*, 14:518–20, 522, 531.

27. Howard to Eustis, 13 January 1812, Clark to Eustis, 13 February 1812, and Howard to Eustis, 19 March 1812, in *Territorial Papers*, 14:505, 518–20, 531–34.

28. Howard to Eustis, 19 March 1812, in *Territorial Papers*, 14:531; Eustis to Howard, 28 March 1812, Letters Sent by Secretary of War, Indian Affairs, M–15.

29. Interview with Nathan Boone and testimony of Judge Frederick Hyatt, both in Draper MSS, 6S, 254–55, and 22S, 145.

30. Ibid.; Eustis to Howard, 28 March 1812, Letters Sent by Secretary of War, Indian Affairs,

M–15; *Missouri Gazette*, 21 March 1812; and Howard to Eustis, 14 June 1812, in *Territorial Papers*, 14:564.

31. *Missouri Gazette*, 19 October 1809.

32. Howard to Eustis, 14 June 1812, and Eustis to Lewis, 15 July 1809, in *Territorial Papers*, 14:566, 285.

33. *Missouri Gazette*, 8 August and 16 November 1811.

34. Ibid., 8 August, 3 October, 9 and 16 November 1811; Petition to Congress by the Inhabitants of Louisiana, 9 September 1811, in *Territorial Papers*, 14:471–79.

35. *Missouri Gazette*, 9 and 23 November 1811.

36. James F. Hull to William Clark, 28 November 1811, Clark Family Papers, Missouri Historical Society; Petition to Congress by Inhabitants of St. Louis, 9 November 1811, in *Territorial Papers*, 14:486–87; and Charles Gratiot to John Jacob Astor, 13 May 1813, Charles Gratiot Letterbook, Missouri Historical Society.

37. *Annals of Congress*, 12 Cong., 1 sess., 356–58 (19 November 1811); 398–401 (3 December 1811); 577 (18 December 1811); and 584–85 (27 December 1811). Representative John Rhea's speech to the House on 3 December summarized the prevailing view that the inhabitants of Louisiana were entitled to the same consideration that had been routinely given to other territories.

38. For discussions of that perennial controversy, consult Allen Walker Read, "Pronunciation of the Word 'Missouri' "; Howard Wight Marshall, "How to Say 'Missouri' "; and Donald M. Lance, "The Origin and Pronunciation of 'Missouri.' "

39. *Missouri Gazette*, 11 July and 8 August 1812.

40. Ibid., 18 July and 29 August 1811; Gregg, "War of 1812," part 1, 16.

41. Declaration of Mellessello, 3 July 1812, in *Territorial Papers*, 14:578–80; *Missouri Gazette*, 25 July 1812; and Gregg, "War of 1812," part 1, 17.

42. Pierre Chouteau to Eustis, 26 July 1812, Pierre Chouteau Letterbook; *Missouri Gazette*, 29 August 1812.

43. Howard to Eustis, 20 September 1812, in *Territorial Papers*, 14:593–94; Gregg, "War of 1812," part 1, 19; and Bissell to Col. Jacob Kinsbury, 19 September 1812, photostatic copy in Bissell Papers, Missouri Historical Society.

44. *Missouri Gazette*, 28 November 1812; Howard to Secretary of War John Armstrong, 10 January 1813, in *Territorial Papers*, 14:614–22; and John B. C. Lucas to Charles Lucas, 29 December 1812, Lucas Collection, Missouri Historical Society.

45. Howard to Armstrong, 10 January 1813, and Armstrong to Howard, 11 February 1813, in *Territorial Papers*, 14:614–22, 631.

46. Testimony of Col. Benjamin Cooper, Draper MSS, 22S, 235–36.

47. Joseph Charless to James Monroe, 7 February 1813, in *Territorial Papers*, 14:630–31. Within the Missouri Territory there were 63 regular soldiers at Fort Osage and 134 at Fort Belle Fontaine. There were another 44 at Fort Madison in present-day Iowa. See Gregg, "War of 1812," part 1, 16.

48. *Missouri Gazette*, 17 and 24 October 1812; *Supplement to the Missouri Gazette*, 24 October 1812; James Neal Primm, *Lion of the Valley: St. Louis, Missouri*, 105; and Edward Hempstead to David Barton, 10 September 1812, Hempstead Papers, Missouri Historical Society.

49. Extract of a letter dated 13 February 1813 from Edward Hempstead in *Missouri Gazette*, 20 March 1813. As Missouri's first territorial delegate, Hempstead compiled an impressive record during his only term as a nonvoting member of Congress. In addition to his successful efforts to improve territorial defensive measures, he also helped secure congressional approval for a more liberal land-confirmation policy that included an agreement to approve some grants issued by Spanish authorities after 1800. See Nancy Jo Tice, "The Territorial Delegate, 1794–1820" (Ph.D. diss., University of Wisconsin, 1967), 213–15.

50. *Missouri Gazette*, 20 February 1813.

51. Ibid.

52. Ibid.; Christian Wilt to Joseph Hertzog, 20 February 1812 [1813], Christian Wilt Letterbook, Missouri Historical Society.

53. *Missouri Gazette*, 27 February and 6 March 1813.

54. Although Howard had been commissioned governor on 18 April 1810, he did not reach St. Louis until 17 September 1810, according to the *Missouri Gazette*. He left the territory on 16 November 1810 and did not return again until 3 July 1811. According to a log kept by Frederick Bates, Howard left the territory again on 19 September 1811, and he returned on 2 December 1811. Howard again left for his native state in late November or early December 1812.

He was back in St. Louis on 31 March 1813. For a discussion of the reasons for absenteeism among territorial officials, see Earl S. Pomeroy, *The Territories and the United States, 1861–1890: Studies in Colonial Administration*, 9.

55. Bates to Howard, 27 February 1813, in *Territorial Papers*, 14:637.

56. *Missouri Gazette*, 19 March 1814; Lt. John Campbell to [?], 3 April 1812, as quoted in Gregg, "War of 1812," part 1, 13; and *Missouri Gazette*, 28 November and 12 December 1812.

57. Bates to Howard, 27 February 1813, Pierre Chouteau to Armstrong, 5 March and 20 May 1813, Howard to Pierre Chouteau, April 1813, and Hempstead to Armstrong, 14 June 1813, all in *Territorial Papers*, 14:638, 639–40, 671–73, 674, 676.

58. William E. Foley and C. David Rice, *The First Chouteaus: River Barons of Early St. Louis*, 148–51.

59. Clark to Monroe, November 1814, James Monroe Papers, Library of Congress.

60. Fort Osage Officers to Secretary of War, 16 July 1812, Daniel Bissell to Secretary of War, 30 March and 12 April 1813, Howard to Pierre Chouteau, 6 April 1813, and Howard to Armstrong, 20 June 1813, all in *Territorial Papers*, 14:587–90, 646–47, 662–63, 675, 680–81; Daniel Bissell to Secretary of War, December 1812, photostatic copy, Daniel Bissell Papers, Missouri Historical Society; and Gregg, "War of 1812," part 2, 191–92.

61. Clark to Armstrong, 24 February 1813, Bissell to Armstrong, 30 March and 12 April 1813, in *Territorial Papers*, 14:632–33, 646–47, 662–63; Gregg, "War of 1812," part 2, 190–91.

62. *Missouri Gazette*, 20 March 1813; Marietta Jennings, *A Pioneer Merchant of St. Louis, 1810–1820: The Business Career of Christian Wilt*, 149.

63. *American State Papers, Military Affairs*, 1:387.

64. Armstrong to Howard, 10 April 1813, Howard to James Monroe, 30 March 1813, and Monroe to Howard, 3 April 1813, in *Territorial Papers*, 14:656–57, 645–46, 655.

65. *Missouri Gazette*, 7 August 1813, and Clark to Armstrong, 12 September 1813, in ibid., 14:697–98.

66. Clark to Armstrong, 12 September 1813, in ibid., 14:687–98; *Missouri Gazette*, 18 September and 2 October 1813; and Gregg, "War of 1812," part 2, 198–99.

67. Gregg, "War of 1812," part 2, 199–200.

68. Testimony of Samuel Cole, Draper MSS, 23S, 91.

69. Christian Wilt to Andrew Wilt, 2 October 1813, Christian Wilt Letterbook; *Missouri Gazette*, 27 November 1813; and John B. C. Lucas to Mr. Leacock, 3 December 1813, memorandum of a letter, Lucas Collection.

70. Gregg, "War of 1812," part 2, 202.

71. Armstrong to Howard, 31 December 1813, in *Territorial Papers*, 14:724.

72. *Missouri Gazette*, 12 February 1814.

73. Harrison to Armstrong, 21 December 1813, in Logan Esarey, ed., *Messages and Letters of William Henry Harrison*, 2:610–11.

74. Armstrong to Harrison, 29 December 1813, in ibid., 2:614.

75. Hempstead to Armstrong, 22 March 1814, Clark to Armstrong, 28 March 1814, and Howard to Armstrong, 22 March 1814, in *Territorial Papers*, 14:744, 746–47, 737n; and Tice, "Territorial Delegate," 213, 257.

76. Clark to Armstrong, 6 January, 2 February, and 28 March 1814, and endorsement by Armstrong of Clark's letter to him dated 4 May 1814, in *Territorial Papers*, 14:727–28, 738–40, 746–47, 763.

77. Clark to Armstrong, 5 June 1814, in ibid., 768–69.

78. Howard to Armstrong, 20 June 1814, and Report of Joseph Perkins to Howard, August 1814, in ibid., 772, 784–86.

79. Clark to Sibley, 17 March 1814, Sibley Papers, Missouri Historical Society; *Missouri Gazette*, 28 May 1814.

80. *Missouri Gazette*, 7 and 14 May 1814. The deaths of Johnathan Tood and Thomas Smith at Boonslick were particularly gruesome. The Indians decapitated and dismembered the bodies and hung the parts on trees.

81. Ibid., 14 May and 25 June 1814.

82. Testimony of Samuel Cole and testimony of Judge Frederick Hyatt in Draper MSS, 23S, 85–86, and 22S, 118–26.

83. *Missouri Gazette*, 13 August 1814; testimony of Judge Hyatt and Barney Farmer in Draper MSS, 22S.

84. Gregg, "War of 1812," part 3, 336; testimony of Judge Frederick Hyatt and Gustavus Ste.

Gem to Lyman Draper, 4 January 1855, in Draper MSS, 22S, 125–26, 5YY, 71; *Missouri Gazette,* 20 August 1814; and Floyd C. Shoemaker, *Missouri and Missourians: Land of Contrasts and People of Achievements,* 1:303.

85. Clark to Armstrong, 18 September 1814, in *Territorial Papers,* 14:787–88; Christian Wilt to Andrew Wilt, 24 September 1814, Christian Wilt Letterbook; and *Missouri Gazette,* 24 September 1814.

86. Christian Wilt to Joseph Hertzog, 6 August 1814, Christian Wilt Letterbook.

87. Clark to Monroe, November 1814, James Monroe Papers, Library of Congress.

88. *Missouri Gazette,* 7 December 1814; Rufus Easton to Charles Lucas, 24 December 1814, Rufus Easton Papers, Missouri Historical Society. Like his predecessor Edward Hempstead, Easton worked hard in behalf of his constituents' interests and pressed for a variety of measures—most of them unsuccessfully. Overall, his achievements in office were modest in contrast with his predecessor's record. See Tice, "Territorial Delegate," 216–20, 245.

89. John P. Gates to William Clark, 5 March 1814, Clark Papers; Gregg, "War of 1812," part 3, 342.

90. *Missouri Gazette,* 18 February 1815; James Monroe to Indian Commissioners, 11 March 1815, in *Territorial Papers,* 15:14–15.

91. Col. William Russell to James Monroe, 12 March 1815, in *Territorial Papers,* 15–16; Christian Wilt to Joseph Hertzog, 13 March 1815, Christian Wilt Letterbook.

92. Clark to Monroe, 17 April 1815, in *Territorial Papers,* 15:25–26.

93. *Missouri Gazette,* 27 May 1815; William Russell to Monroe, 29 May 1815, in *Territorial Papers,* 15:57–58; and testimony of Judge Frederick Hyatt and testimony of Samuel Cole, Draper MSS, 22S, 118–26, and 23S, 92.

94. James Monroe to Indian Commissioners, 11 March 1815, in *Territorial Papers,* 15:14–15; Monroe to William Clark, 11 March 1815, Clark Family Papers; Foley and Rice, *First Chouteaus,* 153; and Commissioners Clark, Edwards, and Chouteau to Monroe, 22 May 1815, in *American State Papers, Indian Affairs,* 2:7.

95. Report on Activities as Peace Commissioners to Mississippi Indians, 18 October 1815, in *American State Papers, Indian Affairs,* 2:9–11.

96. Ibid.; *Missouri Gazette,* 8 July 1815.

97. Robert L. Fisher, "The Treaties of Portage des Sioux," 499–501.

98. Ibid., 499–503.

99. Foley and Rice, *First Chouteaus,* 155–57.

100. Daniel Bissell to Maj. General Andrew Jackson, 2 July 1815, photostatic copy in Daniel Bissell Papers, Missouri Historical Society; Christian Wilt to Joseph Hertzog, 13 March 1815, Christian Wilt Letterbook; and letter signed "Justice" in *Missouri Gazette,* 12 April 1817.

101. Justus Post to John Post, 26 November 1815, Justus Post Letters, Missouri Historical Society.

102. Testimony of Samuel Cole and testimony of Barney Farmer, Draper MSS, 23S, 65–92, and 22S, 219–23. Farmer was a young black slave left at Tibeau's Fort at Cote sans Dessein when it was attacked during the war.

103. Moses Austin to James Bryan, 4 January 1813, in Eugene C. Barker, ed., *The Austin Papers,* 2:222–23. Christian Wilt also reported a similar dearth of business at the same time (Christian Wilt to Joseph Hertzog, 6 February 1813, Christian Wilt Letterbook). Also see Jennings, *Pioneer Merchant,* 101.

104. Austin to Bryan, 19 October and 4 December 1812, in Barker, ed., *Austin Papers,* 2:218, 220.

105. Timothy Hubbard and Lewis E. Davids, *Banking in Mid-America: A History of Missouri's Banks,* 15–20.

106. David B. Gracy II, "Moses Austin and the Development of the Missouri Lead Industry," 47–48.

107. Richard E. Oglesby, *Manuel Lisa and the Opening of the Missouri Fur Trade,* 126–49.

108. Charles Gratiot to John Jacob Astor, 29 May 1814, Gratiot Letterbook, Missouri Historical Society; Jennings, *Pioneer Merchant,* 201.

109. Halvor Gordon Melom, "The Economic Development of St. Louis, 1803–1846" (Ph.D. diss., University of Missouri, 1947), 29; Jennings, *Pioneer Merchant,* 148, 151, 158–59, 161; and Richard M. Clokey, *William H. Ashley,* 29–32.

110. Christian Wilt to Thomas Hill, 7 January 1815, and Wilt to Joseph Hertzog, 20 March 1815, Christian Wilt Letterbook; Jennings, *Pioneer Merchant,* 151, 158–61.

111. This estimate is based upon an examination of the Auditor's Reports, 1804–1820, in the National Archives.

112. For examples of the reliance on federal subsidies in later territories, see Howard R. Lamar's landmark study, *Dakota Territory 1861–1889: A Study of Frontier Politics,* and Lewis L. Gould's *Wyoming: A Political History, 1868–1896.*

113. Justus Post to John Post, 10 December 1815, Justus Post Letters.

114. Justus Post to John Post, 26 November 1815, Justus Post Letters.

CHAPTER 14. A LAND OF PROMISE

1. Peck, *Forty Years of Pioneer Life,* 146.

2. *Missouri Gazette,* 9 June 1819.

3. For population figures, see Chelidonia Ronnebaum, "Population and Settlement in Missouri, 1804–1820" (M.A. thesis, University of Missouri, 1936). Justus Post wrote to his brother John from St. Louis in 1815, "This circumstance I suppose is sufficient to convince the people of Kentucky to leave the country so long celebrated for its excellence to inhabit the borders of Missouri" (9 November 1815, Justus Post Letters).

4. The stories of Benton and Tucker and the circumstances surrounding their moves to the Missouri Territory can be found in William Nesbit Chambers, *Old Bullion Benton: Senator from the New West,* and Robert J. Brugger, *Beverly Tucker: Heart Over Head in the Old South.*

5. Eliza Post Memorandum Book No. 1, Missouri Historical Society.

6. Justus Post to John Post, 7 October 1817, Justus Post Letters. A summary of Post's activities can be found in William E. Foley, "Justus Post: Portrait of a Frontier Land Speculator."

7. Marie George Windell, ed., "The Road West in 1818, the Diary of Henry Vest Bingham," part 1, 22, 30–32.

8. For an account of the Hardemans and their move to Missouri, see Nicholas Perkins Hardeman, *Wilderness Calling: The Hardeman Family in the American Westward Movement, 1750–1900,* 71–94.

9. Ronnebaum, "Population and Settlement in Missouri," 96; Walter Schroeder, "Spread of Settlement in Howard County, Missouri, 1810–1859," 1–3, 8–9.

10. An excellent analysis of factors influencing frontier settlement patterns can be found in Michael O'Brien et al., *Grassland, Forest, and Historical Settlement: An Analysis of Dynamics in Northeast Missouri.* See also Lewis C. Gray, *History of Agriculture in the Southern U.S. to 1860,* 2:866, and John Mack Faragher, *Sugar Creek: Life on the Illinois Prairie,* 62–66. Englishman Henry Bousfield visited the Boonslick in 1819 and commented at length on the American preference for timbered land over the fertile prairies. See Bousfield's journal of a trip through Missouri in 1819, typescript in Journals and Diaries Collection, Missouri Historical Society.

11. W. F. Johnson, *History of Cooper County, Missouri,* 65; Hardeman, *Wilderness Calling,* 77.

12. Jonas Viles, "Old Franklin: A Frontier Town of the Twenties"; Stuart F. Voss, "Town Growth in Central Missouri, 1815–1880: An Urban Chaparral," part 1, 76–80; Edwin James, *Account of an Expedition . . . Under the Command of Major S. H. Long,* rpt. in Reuben Gold Thwaites, ed., *Early Western Travels,* 14:150.

13. Voss, "Town Growth in Central Missouri," part 1, 64–80; James, *Account of an Expedition,* 146; Houck, *History of Missouri,* 3:184; and Flint, *Recollections of the Last Ten Years in the Valley of the Mississippi,* 136–37.

14. O'Brien, *Grassland, Forest, and Historical Settlement,* 92–94.

15. Ibid.; Flint, *Recollections,* 148.

16. For a brief introduction to the region's southern cultural backgrounds, see Howard Wight Marshall, *Folk Architecture in Little Dixie: A Regional Culture in Missouri,* 3–5.

17. Testimony of Elizabeth Musick, Draper MSS, 22S, 172. For comparable examples of the importance of families cooperating in communities on the American frontier, see Faragher, *Sugar Creek,* especially 130–42, and John Hebron Moore, *The Emergence of the Cotton Kingdom in the Old Southwest: Mississippi, 1770–1860,* 143.

18. James M. Denny, "Early Southern Domestic Architecture in Missouri, 1810–1840: The 'Georgianization' of the Trans-Mississippi West."

19. Schoolcraft, *Journal of a Tour into the Interior of Missouri and Arkansaw . . . in the Year 1818 and 1819.*

20. Ibid., 32.

21. Ibid., 30, 40, 49–50.

22. Ibid., 39, 49–50. The counterpart of the primitive Ozarks hunter-trapper was present in

other nineteenth-century southern territories and states. See Moore, *The Emergence of the Cotton Kingdom in the Old Southwest*, 155.

23. The recent studies of Lynn Morrow and Robert Flanders provide the most sophisticated analysis of early Ozark settlement. See Lynn Morrow, "The Yocum Silver Dollar: Image, Realities to Traditions," 160; Robert Flanders, "Caledonia, Ozarks Legacy of the High Scotch-Irish," 35–39; James Price, "The Widow Harris Cabin Site: A Place in the Ozarks"; and Carl O. Sauer, *The Geography of the Ozark Highland of Missouri*, 121.

24. Morrow, "Trader William Gilliss and Delaware Migration in Southern Missouri," 148–49; Price, "The Widow Harris Cabin Site," 6–8. Henry Rowe Schoolcraft mentioned the Yocums in *Scenes and Adventures in the Semi-Alpine Region of the Ozark Mountains of Missouri and Arkansas*, 122.

25. Schoolcraft, *A View of the Lead Mines of Missouri*, 241; Primm, *Lion of the Valley*, 107–8.

26. *Missouri Gazette*, 18 May 1816; Windell, ed., "Diary of Henry Vest Bingham," 183.

27. August Chouteau to "Cerre" Chouteau, 8 January 1818, Chouteau Collections; Peck, *Forty Years of Pioneer Life*, 84.

28. *Missouri Gazette*, 2 August 1817; Glen Holt, "The Heritage of Transportation," 48.

29. *Franklin Missouri Intelligencer*, 28 May 1819; *Missouri Gazette*, 19 May 1819.

30. Flint, *Recollections*, 153.

31. James, *Account of an Expedition*, 126–27.

32. Floyd Shoemaker, "Herculaneum Shot Tower," 215; David B. Gracy II, "Moses Austin and the Development of the Missouri Lead Industry," 124–26; and James, *Account of an Expedition*, 104.

33. Schoolcraft, *View of the Lead Mines*, 48; John Andrews to Samuel Perry, 25 February 1814, Washington County Papers, Missouri Historical Society; and Gracy, *Moses Austin*, 151–53.

34. Flanders, "Caledonia," 31–40; Schoolcraft, *Journal*, 90; Salmon Giddings to Connecticut Missionary Society, 6 July 1816, photostatic copy, and letter from Rev. David Terry to Editor, 29 June 1819, in *Boston Recorder*, 7 August 1819, photostatic copy, both in Church Papers–Presbyterian, Missouri Historical Society.

35. Morrow, "The Yocum Silver Dollar," 161, 163–64; Pierre Menard to Maj. Richard Graham, 13 June 1820, Richard Graham Papers, Missouri Historical Society; and Osmund Overby, "House and Home in the New Village of Ste. Genevieve" (paper presented at Ste. Genevieve Seminar, October 1985). The Rozier house, built in 1844, is an example of the persistence of the Creole tradition in Ste. Genevieve. On Ste. Genevieve's persistent image as a rough-and-tumble place, see William Russell to John B. C. Lucas, 8 March 1820, Lucas Collection.

36. Shoemaker, "Cape Girardeau, Most American of Missouri's Original Counties," 57–58; Flint, *Recollections*, 168, 172.

37. Leon P. Ogilvie, "Governmental Efforts at Reclamation in the Southeast Missouri Lowlands," 151–55; Morrow, "New Madrid and Its Hinterland, 1783–1826," 246–50; and Shoemaker, *Missouri and Missourians: Land of Contrast and People of Achievements*, 1:177.

38. Proclamation by Governor Howard, 1 October 1812, in *Territorial Papers*, 14:599–601; Shoemaker, *Missouri and Missourians*, 1:217–19.

39. Shoemaker, *Missouri and Missourians*, 1:219–28. Wayne County (1818) was created from Missouri's original Lawrence County (1815), and the remaining portions of Lawrence County were made a part of the Arkansas Territory. The ten new counties added in 1820 were Boone, Chariton, Cole, Lillard, Perry, Ralls, Ray, Callaway, Gasconade, and Saline.

40. William Clark, Report of the Names and probable number of the Tribes of Indians in the Missouri Territory . . . , 4 November 1816, in Letters Received by the Secretary of War Relative to Indian Affairs, 1800–1816, M-271, National Archives. Clark's report also included figures for other tribes falling within the jurisdiction of the Missouri Territory but residing outside Missouri's present boundaries. For example, according to Clark's reports, there were 2,600 Great Osages and 1,800 Little Osages on the Verdigris and Neosho Rivers in present-day Oklahoma, and 1,500 Kansa Indians on the Kansas River. His grand total for all Indians in the Missouri Territory and east of the mountains was 73,750.

41. *Missouri Gazette*, 10 February 1816; Resolutions of the Territorial Assembly, referred 24 January 1817, in *Territorial Papers*, 15:234–36.

42. Morrow, "The Yocum Silver Dollar," 161–65.

43. Lemont K. Richardson, "Private Land Claims in Missouri," part 2, 285–86; *American State Papers, Public Lands*, 2:388–603; and Clement Penrose to Albert Gallatin, 24 March 1812, in *American State Papers, Public Lands*, 378.

44. 2 *U.S. Statutes at Large* (1850), 748–52, and 3 *U.S. Statutes at Large* (1850), 121–23.

45. Richardson, "Private Land Claims in Missouri," part 3, 393–94.

46. *American State Papers, Public Lands*, 3:274–330.

47. William H. Crawford to Speaker of the House Henry Clay, 5 February 1818, in ibid., 274, and Annals of Congress, 15 Cong., 1 sess., 1744 (16 April 1818).

48. William H. Crawford to Speaker of the House Henry Clay, 7 December 1818, in *American State Papers, Public Lands*, 3:348.

49. Ibid.

50. On the persistence of land-claims problems, see Nancy Jo Tice, "The Territorial Delegate, 1784–1820" (Ph.D. diss., University of Wisconsin, 1967), 259. A discussion of the land-claims problem in the Territory of Orleans, which was quite similar to that in the Missouri Territory, can be found in Harry L. Coles, Jr., "Applicability of the Public Land System in Louisiana."

51. 3 *U.S. Statutes at Large* (1850), 211–12.

52. Agreement between William Clark, Theodore Hunt, and Charles Lucas, 18 June 1815, and William Clark to Charles Lucas, 10 October 1815, Lucas Collection, Missouri Historical Society; William Wirt to William H. Crawford, 11 May 1820, in *American State Papers, Public Lands*, 3:437.

53. William H. Crawford to Josiah Meigs, 27 November 1818, in *Territorial Papers*, 15:433–64; *Franklin Missouri Intelligencer*, 30 April 1819.

54. Samuel Hammond to Josiah Meigs, 27 December 1818, in *Territorial Papers*, 15:486–87; Schroeder, "Spread of Settlement in Howard County, Missouri," 10–15.

55. *Missouri Gazette*, 1 January 1819; *St. Louis Enquirer*, 6 January 1819; William Clark to Thomas A. Smith, 20 January 1819, Thomas A. Smith Collection, State Historical Society of Missouri; Memorial to Congress by the Territorial Assembly, referred 22 January 1819, in *Territorial Papers*, 15:503; and Peck, *Forty Years of Pioneer Life*, 147.

56. William H. Crawford to Josiah Meigs, 14 December 1818 and 21 January 1819, in *Territorial Papers*, 15:473, 499–500; 3 *U.S. Statutes at Large* (1850), 517.

57. 2 *U.S. Statutes at Large* (1850), 605.

58. Proclamation of Governor William Clark, 4 December 1815, in *Territorial Papers*, 15:191–92; Proclamation of President James Madison, 12 December 1815, in *Missouri Gazette*, 27 January 1816; Moses Austin to James Bryan, 22 January 1816, in Eugene C. Barker, ed., *The Austin Papers*, 2:254; Resolutions of the Territorial Assembly, 22 January 1816, and Alexander McNair to Josiah Meigs, 27 January 1816, in *Territorial Papers*, 15:105–9, 112; and 3 *U.S. Statutes at Large* (1850), 260–61.

59. Alexander McNair to Josiah Meigs, 16 June 1817, in *Territorial Papers*, 15:283.

60. Thomas A. Smith to Josiah Meigs, 30 July 1818; Letterbook No. 7, Thomas A. Smith Collection; *Missouri Gazette*, 28 August and 6 November 1818, 9 June 1819; *St. Louis Enquirer*, 31 March 1819; Flint, *Recollections*, 198; and Memorial from Citizens of Howard County in *Missouri Gazette*, 20 February 1820.

61. Christian Wilt to Joseph Hertzog, Christian Wilt Letterbook, 19 March 1814; Halvor Gordon Melom, "The Economic Development of St. Louis, 1803–1846" (Ph.D. diss., University of Missouri, 1947), 204.

62. Harrison A. Trexler, *Slavery in Missouri: 1804–1865*, 9–10; Arvarh E. Strickland, "Aspects of Slavery in Missouri, 1821," 509–11. Lawrence O. Christensen points out that even though Missouri had outlawed free blacks from entering the state as early as 1821, many of them continued to come to St. Louis from outside the state. See his "Cyprion Clamorgan, The Colored Aristocracy of St. Louis," 4.

63. Maximilian Reichard, "Black and White on the Urban Frontier: The St. Louis Community in Transition, 1800–1830," 5–7; *Missouri Gazette*, 4 December 1813; and *Franklin Missouri Intelligencer*, 17 December 1819.

64. *Missouri Gazette*, 13 November 1813.

65. Lloyd A. Hunter, "Slavery in St. Louis, 1804–1860," 248.

66. Strickland, "Aspects of Slavery in Missouri," 509–17.

67. Hunter, "Slavery in St. Louis," 240–41, 251; Frederick Bates to Caroline M. Bates, 19 July 1812, in *Bates Papers*, 2:228.

68. Frederick Bates to John Michie, 22 August 1810, in *Bates Papers*, 2:154; Notes in the Lucas Collection, 1816, and Lucas to Joseph Pratt, 13 May 1816, Lucas Collection.

69. Strickland, "Aspects of Slavery in Missouri," 525–26; *Missouri Gazette*, 21 April 1819; and Joseph Charless to John B. C. Lucas, 18 April 1819, Lucas Collection.

70. Pierre Chouteau to Henry Dearborn, 11 March 1806, Pierre Chouteau Letterbook;

Missouri Gazette, 4 September 1818; Gracy, *Moses Austin,* 136; and Foley, "Slave Freedom Suits Before Dred Scott: The Case of Marie Jean Scypion's Descendants."

71. Strickland, "Aspects of Slavery in Missouri," 520–22; Marietta Jennings, *A Pioneer Merchant of St. Louis: The Business Career of Christian Wilt,* 57, 115–16.

72. Melom, "Economic Development of St. Louis," 345–47.

73. Arthur B. Cozzens, "The Iron Industry of Missouri," 520–21; Keefe and Morrow, eds., *A Connecticut Yankee in the Frontier Ozarks: The Writings of Theodore Pease Russell,* 277n; and *Missouri Gazette,* 9 August 1817.

74. Primm, *Lion of the Valley,* 112; *Missouri Gazette,* 9 August 1817.

75. David B. Gracy II, "Moses Austin and the Development of the Missouri Lead Industry," 48; James A. Gardner, "The Business Career of Moses Austin in Missouri, 1718–1821," 241–47.

76. Glen E. Holt, "St. Louis's Transition Decade, 1819–1830," 369–70; Paul C. Phillips, *The Fur Trade,* 2:507–9; *Missouri Gazette,* 13 September 1817. For a description of the *Western Engineer,* see *Franklin Missouri Intelligencer,* 25 June 1819.

77. Timothy E. Hubbard and Lewis E. Davids, *Banking in Mid-America: A History of Missouri's Banks,* 14–15; Original Act to Incorporate the Stockholders of the Bank of St. Louis, 21 August 1813, reprinted in ibid., 192.

78. Chambers, *Old Bullion Benton,* 78.

79. Ibid., 79.

80. Hubbard and Davids, *Banking in Mid-America,* 20–21.

81. Ibid., 29–39.

82. Dorothy P. Dorsey, "The Panic of 1819 in Missouri," 79–83; Holt, "St. Louis's Transition Decade," 367–71.

CHAPTER 15. BEYOND THE SABBATH

1. Timothy Flint, *Recollections of the Last Ten Years,* 128–30. Dwight was president of Yale University.

2. Ibid., 129.

3. *Missouri Gazette,* 6 May 1815; Graf von Puhl to Anna Maria von Puhl, 9 August [1819], Von Phul Family Papers, Missouri Historical Society. An excellent description of pioneer conditions in Missouri can be found in Frances Lea McCurdy's *Stump, Bar, and Pulpit: Speechmaking on the Missouri Frontier,* 3–23.

4. "St. Louis and Its Men Fifty Years Ago," 1819–1822, Reminiscence by James Haley White, St. Louis History Papers, Missouri Historical Society; Testimony of Stephen Hempstead in Draper MSS, 22S, 177–78. For a full discussion of the incident on the Ashley expedition, see Hiram Martin Chittenden, *The American Fur Trade of the Far West,* 2:698–703.

5. McCurdy, *Stump, Bar, and Pulpit,* 10.

6. Flint, *Recollections,* 130–31; "Act for Preventing Vice and Immorality," published in *Missouri Gazette,* 19 February 1814.

7. Typescript of record of Bethel Baptist Church prepared by Thomas Bull, church writing clerk, entry for 12 September 1807, in Church Papers–Baptist, Missouri Historical Society; testimony of Elizabeth Musick, Draper MSS, 22S, 173–75.

8. E. W. Stephens, "History of Missouri Baptist General Association," 76–77; testimony of Samuel Cole, Draper MSS, 23S, 89; and typescript of record of Bethel Baptist Church, entries for 19 July 1806 and 12 September 1812.

9. Louis Houck, *History of Missouri,* 1:375, 3:1223; testimony of Elizabeth Musick, Draper MSS, 22S, 173–75; Salmon Giddings to Connecticut Missionary Society, 23 July 1818, photostatic copy in Church Papers–Presbyterian, Missouri Historical Society; and Lynn Morrow to William E. Foley, 22 August 1988, letter in author's possession.

10. Lucy Simmons, "The Rise and Growth of Protestant Bodies in the Missouri Territory," 296–99; Morrow to Foley, 22 August 1988. These plain folks in the southern Missouri Ozarks are Missouri's example of the group Bertram Wyatt-Brown described in "The Antimission Movement in the Jacksonian South: A Study in Regional Folk Culture."

11. Lawrence E. Murphy, "Beginning of Methodism in Missouri, 1798–1824," 371; Simmons, "Rise and Growth of Protestant Bodies," 299; Joab Spencer, "John Clark, Pioneer Preacher and Founder of Methodism in Missouri," 174–76; John Mason Peck, *Father Clark or the Pioneer Preacher,* 228–33; and Alberta H. Klemp, "Early Methodism in the New Madrid Circuit," 23–27.

12. Frank C. Tucker, *The Methodist Church in Missouri, 1789–1939,* 14–16, 41; Murphy, "Beginnings of Methodism," 376–78, 392.

13. James M. Denny, "McKendree Chapel," National Register of Historic Places Inventory—Nomination Form, Missouri Department of Natural Resources, 1984.

14. Spencer, "John Clark," 175; Marie G. Windell, "The Camp Meeting in Missouri," 256–60.

15. Charles A. Johnson, *The Frontier Camp Meeting*, 214–15.

16. James Penick, Jr., *The New Madrid Earthquakes of 1811–1812*, 117–19.

17. DeWitt Ellenwood, Jr., "Protestantism Enters St. Louis: The Presbyterians," 253–56; Stephen Hempstead to Rev. William Channing, 27 June 1815, Hempstead Letterbook, Missouri Historical Society. Also see Joseph H. Hall, *Presbyterian Conflict and Resolution on the Missouri Frontier*.

18. Ellinwood, "Prostestantism Enters St. Louis," 257–64; Flint, *Recollections*, 306n; and Salmon Giddings to Connecticut Missionary Society, 28 November 1818, published in *Boston Recorder*, 16 January 1819, photostatic copy in Church Papers–Presbyterian, Missouri Historical Society. The Buffalo settlement at which Giddings helped found a congregation was on the Mississippi north of St. Louis.

19. Charles F. Rehkopf, "The Beginnings of the Episcopal Church in Missouri, 1819–1844," 266–67.

20. Floyd Shoemaker, *Missouri and Missourians*, 1:527, 529–30; Salmon Giddings to Connecticut Missionary Society, 26 May 1817, photostatic copy in Church Papers–Presbyterian, Missouri Historical Society.

21. R. L. Kirkpatrick, "Professional, Religious, and Social Aspects of St. Louis Life, 1804–1816," 376–78; Amos Stoddard to Henry Dearborn, 3 June 1804, Letters Received by the Secretary of War, 1800–1816, National Archives.

22. John E. Rothensteiner, "The Missouri Priest," 564; William Barnaby Faherty, S.J., "The Personality and Influence of Louis William DuBourg: Bishop of 'Louisiana and the Floridas' (1776–1833)," 47–48.

23. Faherty, "Personality and Influence of Bishop DuBourg," 46–49; Rothensteiner, *History of the Archdiocese of St. Louis*, 1:271; and Ann Lucas Hunt to John B. C. Lucas, 28 January 1818, Lucas Collection. The most comprehensive treatment of Bishop DuBourg is Annabelle M. Melville, *Louis William DuBourg*.

24. Melville, *Louis William DuBourg*.

25. Faherty, "Personality and Influence of Bishop DuBourg," 49–51; Primm, *Lion of the Valley*, 97; Melville, *DuBourg*, 2:540; Faherty, "St. Louis College: First Community School," 122–26; Stafford Poole, "The Founding of Missouri's First College: Saint Marys of the Barrens 1815–1818," 1–22; and Mother Philippine Duchesne to Mother Thérèse Mailucheau, December 1818, as cited in Louise Callan, *Philippine Duchesne, Frontier Missionary of the Sacred Heart, 1769–1852*, 284. Callan's book provides a detailed account of Mother Duchesne and her work in frontier Missouri. The Roman Catholic Church formally proclaimed Mother Duchesne a saint in 1988.

26. Leslie Gamblin Hill, "A Moral Crusade: The Influence of Protestantism on Frontier Society in Missouri," 16–34; Salmon Giddings to Connecticut Missionary Society, 20 April 1816 and 23 July 1818, photostatic copies in Church Papers–Presbyterian, Missouri Historical Society.

27. Graf von Phul to John Breckinridge, 31 December 1818, Von Phul Family Papers.

28. Typescript of Diary of John Hutchings, in Church Papers–Baptist, and Salmon Giddings to Connecticut Missionary Society, 14 January 1819, photostatic copy in Church Papers–Presbyterian, both in Missouri Historical Society.

29. Leslie Gamblin Hill, "A Moral Crusade: The Influence of Protestantism on Frontier Society in Missouri," 16–34; McCurdy, *Stump, Bar, and Pulpit*, 156, 164–65. As an example, between 1806 and 1816 the Bethel Baptist Church disciplined members for the following offenses: drunkenness, gambling, profane swearing, holding erroneous doctrines and trying to lead others into the same errors, joining a Masonic Lodge, and joining a Methodist Society. They did, however, agree to permit one of their members to wear gold earrings "for the benefit of her eyes." See typescript in Church Papers–Baptist, Missouri Historical Society.

30. McCurdy, *Stump, Bar, and Pulpit*, 165–67; Strickland, "Aspects of Slavery in Missouri, 1821," 522–23; and Hugh Wamble, "Negroes and Missouri Protestant Churches," 325, 329. A brief but instructive discussion of evangelical Protestantism and the slavery issue can be found in John Hebron Moore, *The Emergence of the Cotton Kingdom in the Old Southwest: Mississippi, 1770–1860*, 85–86. In her recent work, Mechal Sobel notes that the Awakening in eighteenth-century Virginia was a mixed black-white phenomenon. According to her, "Whites who had lifetimes of intimate association with blacks did not regard it as strange that this new religious experience was a shared one. Blacks were singing and shouting and 'having a Christ' right

along with whites. In fact, from the outset, it was recognized that their emotional response and spiritual sensitivity helped whites to 'come through.'" See Sobel, *The World They Made Together: Black and White Values in Eighteenth-Century Virginia,* 189.

31. Strickland, "Aspects of Slavery in Missouri," 523; John Mason Peck, as quoted in Houck, *History of Missouri,* 3:249. Missouri did not enact formal legislation making it illegal to teach black persons to read and write until 1847. See Lorenzo J. Greene, Gary R. Kremer, and Anthony F. Holland, *Missouri's Black Heritage,* 48–49.

32. Murphy, "Beginnings of Missouri Methodism," 392.

33. Records of the Missouri Presbytery, 1817–1831, Volume 1, entry for 23 September 1819, State Historical Society of Missouri. Typescript in Church Papers–Presbyterian, Missouri Historical Society.

34. Salmon Giddings to Connecticut Missionary Society, 6 July 1816, photostatic copy in Church Papers–Presbyterian, Missouri Historical Society.

35. Henry Rowe Schoolcraft, *Journal of a Tour into the Interior of Missouri in the Year 1818 and 1819,* 32, 68.

36. Salmon Giddings to Connecticut Missionary Society, 6 July 1816, photostatic copy in Church Papers–Presbyterian, Missouri Historical Society.

37. On schools in territorial Missouri, consult Margaret McMillan and Monia C. Morris, "Educational Opportunities in Early Missouri," and John F. McDermott, "Private Schools in St. Louis, 1809–1821."

38. *Representation and Petition of the Representatives Elected by the Freemen of the Territory of Louisiana* (Washington, D.C., 1805), 23, State Historical Society of Missouri; Hugh Graham, "Ste. Genevieve Academy: Missouri's First Secondary School," 67–79; and Ste. Genevieve Academy, Louisiana Territory Papers, Missouri Historical Society.

39. Ibid.; McMillan and Morris, "Educational Opportunities in Early Missouri," 493–94.

40. See McDermott, "Private Schools in St. Louis," and McMillan and Morris, "Educational Opportunities in Early Missouri."

41. *Missouri Gazette,* 23 October 1818.

42. Flint, *Recollections,* 135–36.

43. Frederic Billon, *Annals of St. Louis in the Territorial Days from 1804 to 1821,* 73–78; Ann Hunt Lucas to John B. C. Lucas, 4 January 1818, Lucas Collection; and *Missouri Gazette,* 14 July 1819.

44. McDermott, "Museums in Early St. Louis," 129–32.

45. Primm, *Lion of the Valley,* 91–92; McCurdy, *Stump, Bar, and Pulpit,* 13–14; and McDermott, "Culture and the Missouri Frontier," 359. Two additional useful sources on the reading habits of early Missourians are McDermott, *Private Libraries in Creole St. Louis,* and Harold Dugger, "Reading Interest and the Book Trade in Frontier Missouri" (Ph.D. diss., University of Missouri, 1951).

46. Alexander De Menil, *The Literature of the Louisiana Territory;* DeMenil, "A Century of Missouri Literature," 74–125; and Charles Guenther, "An Early St. Louis Poet: Pierre François Regnier," 59–80.

47. Von Phul's sketches are in the Missouri Historical Society collections. Graf von Phul to Anna Maria von Phul, 15 March and 19 July 1819, Von Phul Family Papers.

48. See two articles by McDermott, "Culture and the Missouri Frontier" and "The Confines of a Wilderness."

CHAPTER 16. MISSOURI COMES OF AGE

1. See William E. Foley, "The American Territorial System: Missouri's Experience," 420–21.

2. "One of the Majority," in *Missouri Gazette Supplement,* 24 October 1812.

3. Ronald L. F. Davis, "Community and Conflict in Pioneer Saint Louis, Missouri."

4. Frederick Bates to Richard Bates, 17 December 1807, in *Bates Papers,* 1:241–43. Bates persisted in his views. When the Marquis de Lafayette came to Missouri in 1825, Bates, who was then governor of the state, refused to lend his support to the festivities honoring the celebrated hero of two continents and openly announced that he had no interest in meeting the visiting Frenchman.

5. Statement signed by Louis Labeaume and Silas Bent, 12 December 1812, and Silas Bent to John B. C. Lucas, 26 December 1812, in Lucas Collection; Christian Wilt to Joseph Hertzog, 29 December 1812, Christian Wilt Letterbook; and *Missouri Gazette,* 19 March and 9 April 1814.

6. Silas Bent to Auguste Chouteau, 21 February 1813, Chouteau Collections; *Missouri Gazette,* 13 March 1813.

7. *Missouri Gazette,* 26 December 1812.

8. Ibid., 31 July 1813.

9. Clarence W. Alvord, *The Illinois Country,* 432. The legislature was especially caught up in organizing and revamping the local courts. For a more complete account of the changing judicial system in territorial Missouri, see William Francis English, *The Pioneer Lawyer and Jurist in Missouri,* 46–64.

10. See letter signed "Seven-Eighths of the People" in *Missouri Gazette,* 4 December 1813, and those signed "Aldiberata Foscofornia" in ibid., 13 May, 29 July, and 21 October 1815.

11. Edward Bates to Frederick Bates, 18 December 1815, in *Bates Papers,* 2:296.

12. *Missouri Gazette,* 27 January, 17 and 24 February, 6 and 13 July 1816; Halvor Gordon Melom, "The Economic Development of St. Louis, 1803–1846" (Ph.D. diss., University of Missouri, 1947), 185–86.

13. Governor Clark's Address to Missouri General Assembly in *Missouri Gazette,* 11 December 1813; An Act Concerning Public Roads and Highways, approved 18 January 1814, in ibid., 19 and 26 March 1814; Letter of Minos Ironsides in ibid., 17 June 1815; and Resolution of Territorial Assembly seeking establishment of a public road, 15 January 1815, in *Territorial Papers,* 15:38–39.

14. Act for the Relief of the Poor, in *Missouri Gazette,* 18 February 1815; Margaret McMillan and Monia Morris, "Educational Opportunities in Early Missouri," 498; Richard C. Wade, *The Urban Frontier,* 247–48; and William F. Knox, "The Constitutional and Legal Basis of Public Education in Missouri" (Ed.D. diss., University of Missouri, 1938), 106–7. Knox notes that the territorial legislature made no clear distinction between public and private schools.

15. Paul Nagel argues persuasively that throughout their history, Missourians have consistently adopted a cautious Jeffersonian approach that extols the virtues of simple rural life, limited government, and fiscal conservatism. See his *Missouri: A Bicentennial History.* Members of the Missouri territorial assembly received three dollars per day for every day they attended actual legislative sessions, plus three dollars for every thirty miles traveled to and from the seat of government by the most usual road. In its appropriation for 1813 and 1814, the General Assembly set aside $5,000 to reimburse its officers and members and $528.87 to cover miscellaneous expenses. *Missouri Gazette,* 19 March 1814, 13 May, 24 June, 8 July, 5 August, 9 September, and 14 October 1815.

16. Frederick C. Hicks, "Territorial Revenue System of Missouri."

17. Roy D. Blunt and David D. March, *Missouri: Images from the Past,* document 5.

18. *Missouri Gazette,* 21 January 1815. St. Louis's second newspaper, the *Western Journal,* became the *Western Emigrant* and eventually the *St. Louis Enquirer.* Thomas Hart Benton edited the *Enquirer* between 1818 and 1820.

19. *Missouri Gazette,* 21 December 1816.

20. William Russell to Charles Lucas, 13 December 1815, Lucas Collection; Circular Letter of John Scott, *Missouri Gazette,* 29 March 1816.

21. *Missouri Gazette,* 27 July 1816.

22. Ibid., 27 July and 3 August 1816; Political Broadside, 26 July 1816, Lucas Collection.

23. Election returns certified by Governor Clark, 19 September 1816, in *Territorial Papers,* 15:195; *Missouri Gazette,* 21 and 28 September and 5 and 12 October 1816.

24. *Report of the Committee on Elections on the Memorial of Rufus Easton, contesting the election and returns of John Scott, the Delegate from the Territory of Missouri.* The State Historical Society of Missouri has a copy of the report.

25. *Annals of Congress,* 14 Cong., 2 sess., 414–15 (3 January 1817) and 415–19 (4 January 1817).

26. Ibid., 418–19 (4 January 1817) and 472–73 (13 January 1817); *Report of the Committee on Elections, to which was recommitted their Report of the 31st ult. on the Petition of Rufus Easton, contesting the election of John Scott,* 10 January 1817. The State Historical Society of Missouri has a copy of the report.

27. *Missouri Gazette,* 15 February 1817; Timothy Hubbard and Lewis E. Davids, *Banking in Mid-America: A History of Missouri Banks,* 20–21.

28. William Russell to Charles Lucas, 22 February 1817, Lucas Collection; Russell to Rufus Easton, [1817], Rufus Easton Papers.

29. *Missouri Gazette,* 9 August 1817.

30. John O'Fallon to Dennis Fitzhugh, 11 August 1817, Clark Papers.

31. John B. C. Lucas, Charles's embittered father, spent the remainder of his life seeking to brand Benton as a murderer. For a detailed account of the Benton-Lucas duel and its consequences, see William N. Chambers, "Pistols and Politics: Incidents in the Career of

Thomas H. Benton, 1816–1818," and Chambers, *Old Bullion Benton: Senator from the New West,* 72–76.

32. *U.S. v. William Tharp,* case file, Missouri State Archives; *Missouri Gazette,* 4 October 1817, 11 September 1818; Trial Notes on testimony in case of William Tharp, October 1817, Lucas Collection; and Chambers, *Old Bullion Benton,* 69, 72.

33. On Scott's record as territorial delegate, see Nancy Jo Tice, "The Territorial Delegate, 1794–1820" (Ph.D. diss., University of Wisconsin, 1967), 220–21, 230–31, 245.

34. The best assessment of territorial Missouri's changing political climate and William Clark's role can be found in Jerome O. Steffen, "William Clark: A New Perspective on Missouri Territorial Politics, 1813–1820," and in the same author's *William Clark: Jeffersonian Man on the Frontier.*

35. Steffen, "William Clark," 175–76.

36. John Heath to James Madison, 1 May 1816, in *Territorial Papers,* 15:133–34.

37. In his interview with Lyman Draper, Cooper recalled that after Clark had declined to provide the Boonslick Settlement with protection during the War of 1812, he had "everafter felt unfriendly to Governor Clark" (testimony of Benjamin Cooper, Draper MSS, 22S, 235–36).

38. Testimony of Stephen Hempstead, Draper MSS, 22S, 190–91.

39. Steffen, "William Clark," 187–88.

40. Circular Letter of Rufus Easton, 27 April 1816, Lucas Collection.

41. On the Missouri statehood crisis, see David March, "The Admission of Missouri"; Floyd C. Shoemaker, *Missouri's Struggle for Statehood, 1804–1821;* and Glover Moore, *The Missouri Controversy, 1819–1821.* The Memorial of Citizens of Missouri Territory, 1817, and the Memorial and Resolutions of the Legislature of the Missouri Territory can both be found in Shoemaker, *Missouri's Struggle for Statehood,* 521–28.

42. March, "The Admission of Missouri," 431–35. Beverly Tucker collaborated with Edward Bates to produce a series of articles challenging congressional restriction on constitutional grounds that were published in the *Missouri Gazette* and the *St. Louis Enquirer* between April and mid-June under the pseudonym "Hampden." For an example of allegations of an eastern plot to retard emigration, see "A Citizen of Missouri" in *Missouri Gazette,* 28 April 1819.

43. *Franklin Missouri Intelligence,* 24 September and 1 October 1819; Arvarh E. Strickland, "Aspects of Slavery in Missouri, 1821," 517.

44. *St. Louis Enquirer,* 9 June 1819; Benjamin Merkel, *The Antislavery Controversy in Missouri, 1819–1865,* 3.

45. Jonathan Roberts to John B. C. Lucas, 27 February 1820, Lucas Collection.

46. Robert McColley, *Slavery and Jeffersonian Virginia,* 171–74; William M. Wiecek, *The Sources of Antislavery Constitutionalism in America, 1760–1848,* 106–25; and Thomas Jefferson to John Holmes, 22 April 1820, in *Thomas Jefferson: Writings,* 1434.

47. Shoemaker, *Missouri's Struggle for Statehood,* 66–68.

48. Merkel, *Antislavery Controversy in Missouri,* 5.

49. *Missouri Gazette,* 5 April 1820.

50. Ibid.

51. Shoemaker, *Missouri's Struggle for Statehood,* 135–65; Rudolph Eugene Forderhase, "Jacksonianism in Missouri from Predilection to Party, 1820–1836" (Ph.D. diss., University of Missouri-Columbia, 1968), 7.

52. Forderhase, "Jacksonianism in Missouri," 17–18.

53. Shoemaker, *Missouri and Missourians: Land of Contrasts and People of Achievements,* 1:183; Steffen, "William Clark," 191–92.

54. Ibid.; Perry McCandless, *A History of Missouri, Volume II: 1820 to 1860,* 9–11.

55. McCandless, *History of Missouri,* 11–12.

56. Shoemaker, *Missouri's Struggle for Statehood,* 264; Steffen, "William Clark," 192–93.

57. Steffen, "William Clark," 193–97.

58. Shoemaker, *Missouri's Struggle for Statehood,* 290–320; Missouri's Solemn Public Act, 26 June 1821, reprinted in ibid., 360–62.

EPILOGUE

1. Russel L. Gerlach, *Settlement Patterns in Missouri,* 41–42.

2. Ibid., 7–8.

3. See Paul Nagel's fine interpretative study, *Missouri: A Bicentennial History,* for a lively discussion of the state's Jeffersonian predisposition, which he describes as "a quiet, unpreten-

tious viewpoint, marked by a determination to cherish the old and consider skeptically the new."

4. See Lynn Morrow and Dan Saults, "The Yocum Silver Dollar: Sorting Out the Strands of an Ozarks Frontier Legend," 8–15.

5. Lawrence O. Christensen, "Missouri: The Heart of the Nation," 86.

WORKS CITED

For a list of abbreviations used in this section, see the beginning of the Notes section.

BOOKS

Abernethy, Thomas P. *The Burr Conspiracy.* New York: Oxford University Press, 1954.

Alvord, Clarence W. *The Illinois Country, 1673–1818.* Springfield: Illinois Centennial Commission, 1920.

Alvord, Clarence W., and Clarence E. Carter, eds. *The New Regime, 1765–1767.* Vol. 11, Collections of the Illinois State Historical Library. Springfield: Illinois State Historical Library, 1916.

———. *Trade and Politics, 1767–1769.* Vol. 16, Collections of the Illinois State Historical Library. Springfield: Illinois State Historical Library, 1921.

Arnold, Morris S. *Unequal Laws Unto a Savage Race: European Legal Traditions in Arkansas, 1686–1836.* Fayetteville: University of Arkansas Press, 1985.

Axtel, James. *The Invasion Within: The Contest of Cultures in Colonial North America.* New York: Oxford University Press, 1985.

Baldwin, Leland D. *The Keelboat Age on Western Waters.* Pittsburgh: University of Pittsburgh Press, 1941.

Baldwin, Simeon E. *Life and Letters of Simeon Baldwin.* New Haven: Tuttle Morehouse & Taylor Co., 1919.

Bannon, John Francis. *The Spanish Borderlands Frontier, 1513–1821.* New York: Holt, Rinehart, and Winston, 1970.

Barker, Eugene C., ed. *The Austin Papers.* 2 vols. Annual Report of the American Historical Association for the Year 1919. Washington, D.C.: Government Printing Office, 1924.

Beck, Lewis C. *A Gazetteer of the States of Illinois and Missouri.* Albany, N.Y.: C. R. and G. Webster, 1823.

Belting, Natalia M. *Kaskaskia Under the French Regime.* Urbana: University of Illinois Press, 1948.

Billon, Frederic L. *Annals of St. Louis in Its Early Days Under the French and Spanish Dominations, 1764–1804.* St. Louis, 1886.

———. *Annals of St. Louis in the Territorial Days from 1804 to 1821.* St. Louis, 1888.

Blunt, Roy D., and David D. March. *Missouri: Images from the Past.* Jefferson City: Office of the Secretary of State of Missouri, 1988.

Brackenridge, Henry Marie. *Journal of a Voyage up the River Missouri.* Baltimore: Coale & Maxwell, Pomeroy & Toy, 1815.

———. *Recollections of Persons and Places in the West.* Philadelphia: J. Kay, Jr., and Brother, 1834.

———. *Views of Louisiana, Together with a Journal of a Voyage up the Missouri River in 1811.* Pittsburgh: Cramer, Spear, and Eichbaum, 1814.

Bradbury, John. *Travels in the Interior of America, in the Years 1809, 1810, and 1811.* Liverpool: Smith and Galway, 1817.

Brown, Everett S. *The Constitutional History of the Louisiana Purchase, 1803–1812.* Vol. 10 of University of California Publications in History. Berkeley: University of California Press, 1920.

———, ed. *William Plumer's Memorandum of Proceedings in the United States Senate, 1803–1807.* New York: Macmillan, 1923.

Brugger, Robert J. *Beverly Tucker: Heart Over Head in the Old South.* Baltimore: Johns Hopkins University Press, 1978.

Callan, Louise. *Philippine Duchesne, Frontier Missionary of the Scared Heart, 1769–1852.* Westminster, Md.: Newman Press, 1957.

Chambers, William N. *Old Bullion Benton: Senator from the New West.* Boston: Little, Brown, 1956.

Chapman, Carl H., and Eleanor F. Chapman. *Indians and Archaeology of Missouri.* Rev. ed. Columbia: University of Missouri Press, 1983.

Chittenden, Hiram M. *The American Fur Trade of the Far West.* 3 vols. New York: F. P. Harper, 1902.

Clark, John G. *New Orleans, 1718–1812: An Economic History*. Baton Rouge: Louisiana State University Press, 1970.

Cleaves, Freeman. *Old Tippecanoe*. New York: Charles Scribner's Sons, 1939.

Clokey, Richard M. *William H. Ashley: Enterprise and Politics in the Trans-Mississippi West*. Norman: University of Oklahoma Press, 1980.

Collot, Georges-Victor. *A Journey in North America*. 2 vols. Paris: Arthur Bertrand, 1826.

Crouch, Dora P., Daniel J. Garr, and Axel I. Mundingo. *Spanish City Planning in North America*. Cambridge: MIT Press, 1982.

Darby, John F. *Personal Recollections of Many Prominent People Whom I Have Known*. St. Louis: G. I. Jones & Co., 1880.

Delanglez, Jean. *Life and Voyages of Louis Jolliet (1645–1700)*. Chicago: Institute of Jesuit History, 1948.

DeMenil, Alexander. *The Literature of the Louisiana Territory*. St. Louis: St. Louis News Co., 1904.

Dillon, Richard. *Meriwether Lewis*. New York: Coward-McCann, 1965.

Din, Gilbert C., and Abraham P. Nasatir. *The Imperial Osages: Spanish-Indian Diplomacy in the Mississippi Valley*. Norman: University of Oklahoma Press, 1983.

Donnelly, Joseph P. *Jacques Marquette, S.J., 1637–1675*. Chicago: Loyola University Press, 1968.

———. *Pierre Gibault, Missionary, 1737–1802*. Chicago: Loyola University Press, 1971.

Eccles, W. J. *The Canadian Frontier, 1534–1760*. New York: Holt, Rinehart and Winston, 1969.

———. *France in America*. New York: Harper and Row, 1972.

Edmunds, R. David. *Tecumseh and the Quest for Indian Leadership*. Boston: Little, Brown, 1984.

Ekberg, Carl J. *Colonial Ste. Genevieve: An Adventure on the Mississippi Frontier*. Gerald, Mo.: Patrice Press, 1985.

Ekberg, Carl J., and William E. Foley, eds. *An Account of Upper Louisiana by Nicolas de Finiels*. Columbia: University of Missouri Press, 1989.

Ekberg, Carl J., et al. *A Cultural, Geographical and Historical Study of the Pine Ford Lake Project Area, Washington, Jefferson, Franklin, and St. Francois Counties, Missouri*. Normal, Ill.: Illinois State University, 1981.

English, William Francis. *The Pioneer Lawyer and Jurist in Missouri*. Columbia: University of Missouri Press, 1947.

Esarey, Logan, ed. *Messages and Letters of William Henry Harrison*. 2 vols. Indianapolis: Indiana History Commission, 1922.

Faragher, John Mack. *Sugar Creek: Life on the Illinois Prairie*. New Haven: Yale University Press, 1986.

Flint, Timothy. *Recollections of the Last Ten Years in the Valley of the Mississippi*. Boston, 1826. Rpt., edited by George R. Brooks. Carbondale: Southern Illinois University Press, 1968.

Foley, William E., and C. David Rice. *The First Chouteaus: River Barons of Early St. Louis*. Urbana: University of Illinois Press, 1983.

Gerlach, Russel L. *Settlement Patterns in Missouri*. Columbia: University of Missouri Press, 1986.

Gibson, Charles. *Spain in America*. New York: Harper and Row, 1966.

Giraud, Marcel. *A History of Louisiana, Volume I: The Reign of Louis XIV, 1698–1715*. Translated by Joseph Lambert. Baton Rouge: Louisiana State University Press, 1974.

Gould, Lewis L. *Wyoming: A Political History, 1868–1896*. New Haven: Yale University Press, 1968.

Gracy, David B., II. *Moses Austin: His Life*. San Antonio: Trinity University Press, 1987.

Gray, Lewis C. *History of Agriculture in the Southern U.S. to 1860*. 2 vols. Washington, D.C.: Carnegie Institution of Washington, 1933.

Greene, Lorenzo J., Gary Kremer, and Anthony F. Holland. *Missouri's Black Heritage*. St. Louis: Forum Press, 1980.

Gregg, Kate L., ed. *Westward with Dragoons: The Journal of William Clark on His Expedition to Establish Fort Osage, August 25 to September 22, 1808*. Fulton, Mo.: Ovid Bell Press, 1937.

Haas, Edward F., and Robert R. Macdonald, eds. *Louisiana's Legal Heritage*. Pensacola, Fla.: Perdido Bay Press for the Louisiana State Museum, 1983.

Hafen, Leroy. *The Mountain Men and the Fur Trade of the Far West*. 10 vols. Glendale, Calif.: Arthur H. Clark, 1964–1972.

Hall, Joseph H. *Presbyterian Conflict and Resolution on the Missouri Frontier*. Lewiston, N.Y.: Edward Mellen Press, 1987.

Hammond, George P., ed. *New Spain and the Anglo-American West.* 2 vols. Lancaster, Pa.: Lancaster Press, 1932.

Hardeman, Nicholas Perkins. *Wilderness Calling: The Hardeman Family in the American Westward Movement, 1750–1900.* Knoxville: University of Tennessee Press, 1977.

Hatfield, Joseph T. *William Claiborne: Jeffersonian Centurion in the American Southwest.* Lafayette: University of Southwestern Louisiana Press, 1976.

Hay, Thomas Robson, and M. R. Werner. *The Admirable Trumpeter: A Biography of General James Wilkinson.* Garden City, N.Y.: Doubleday, Doran & Company, 1941.

Higginbothan, Valle. *John Smith T: Missouri Pioneer.* N.p.: privately published, 1968. Copy in State Historical Society of Missouri Library.

Hoffhaus, Charles E. *Chez Les Canses: Three Centuries at Kawsmouth.* Kansas City, Mo.: Lowell Press, 1984.

Holmes, Jack D. L., ed. *Documentos Inéditos para la Historia de la Luisiana, 1792–1810.* Madrid: J. Porrúa Turanzas, 1963.

Houck, Louis. *History of Missouri.* 3 vols. Chicago: R. R. Donnelley, 1908.

———, ed. *The Spanish Regime in Missouri.* 2 vols. Chicago: R. R. Donnelley, 1909.

Hubbard, Timothy, and Lewis E. Davids. *Banking in Mid-America: A History of Missouri's Banks.* Washington, D.C.: Public Affairs Press, 1969.

Innis, Harold A. *The Fur Trade in Canada.* Rev. ed. New Haven: Yale University Press, 1962.

Irving, Washington. *Astoria.* Rpt. in *The Complete Works of Washington Irving,* edited by Herbert L. Kleinfield. Boston: Twayne, 1976.

Jackson, Donald. *The Journals of Zebulon Montgomery Pike.* 2 vols. Norman: University of Oklahoma Press, 1966.

———, ed. *Letters of the Lewis and Clark Expedition with Related Documents, 1783–1854.* 2d ed. 2 vols. Urbana: University of Illinois Press, 1978.

———. *Thomas Jefferson and the Stony Mountains: Exploring the West from Monticello.* Urbana: University of Illinois Press, 1981.

Jacobs, James Ripley. *Tarnished Warrior: Major-General James Wilkinson.* New York: Macmillan, 1938.

James, Edwin. *Account of an Expedition from Pittsburgh to the Rocky Mountains performed in the Years 1819, 1820 . . . Under the Command of Maj. S. H. Long.* London: 1823. Rpt. in Reuben Gold Thwaites, *Early Western Travels.* Vol. 14. Cleveland: A. H. Clark Co., 1905.

Jennings, Marietta. *A Pioneer Merchant of St. Louis, 1810–1820: The Business Career of Christian Wilt.* New York: Columbia University Press, 1939.

Johnson, Charles A. *The Frontier Camp Meeting.* Dallas: Southern Methodist University Press, 1955.

Johnson, W. F. *History of Cooper County, Missouri.* 2 vols. Topeka, Kans.: Historical Publishing Co., 1919.

Jones, Charles T., Jr. *George Champlin Sibley: The Prairie Puritan, 1782–1863.* Independence, Mo.: Jackson County Historical Society, 1970.

Keefe, James F., and Lynn Morrow, eds. *A Connecticut Yankee in the Frontier Ozarks: The Writings of Theodore Pease Russell.* Columbia: University of Missouri Press, 1988.

King, Charles R, ed. *The Life and Correspondence of Rufus King.* 6 vols. New York: G. P. Putnam's Sons, 1897.

Kinnaird, Lawrence, ed. *Spain in the Mississippi Valley, 1765–1794.* 3 vols. Annual Report of the American Historical Association for the Year 1945. Washington, D.C.: Government Printing Office, 1946.

Lamar, Howard R. *Dakota Territory 1861–1889: A Study of Frontier Politics.* New Haven: Yale University Press, 1956.

Lipscomb, Andrew A., and Albert E. Bergh, eds. *The Writings of Thomas Jefferson.* 20 vols. Washington, D.C.: Thomas Jefferson Memorial Association, 1903.

Loomis, Noel M., and Abraham P. Nasatir. *Pedro Vial and the Road to Santa Fe.* Norman: University of Oklahoma Press, 1967.

Lyon, E. Wilson. *Louisiana in French Diplomacy, 1759–1804.* Norman: University of Oklahoma Press, 1934.

Lyon, William. *The Pioneer Editor in Missouri, 1808–1860.* Columbia: University of Missouri Press, 1965.

McCandless, Perry. *A History of Missouri, Volume II: 1820 to 1860.* Columbia: University of Missouri Press, 1972.

McColley, Robert. *Slavery and Jeffersonian Virginia*. Urbana: University of Illinois Press, 1964.

McCurdy, Frances Lea. *Stump, Bar and Pulpit: Speechmaking on the Missouri Frontier*. Columbia: University of Missouri Press, 1969.

McDermott, John Francis, ed. *The Early Histories of St. Louis*. St. Louis: St. Louis Historical Documents Foundation, 1952.

——, ed. *The French in the Mississippi Valley*. Urbana: University of Illinois Press, 1965.

——, ed. *Frenchmen and French Ways in the Mississippi Valley*. Urbana: University of Illinois Press, 1969.

——. *Private Libraries in Creole St. Louis*. Baltimore: Johns Hopkins University Press, 1938.

——, ed. *The Spanish in the Mississippi Valley, 1762–1804*. Urbana: University of Illinois Press, 1965.

Madison, James H., ed. *Heartland: Comparative Histories of the Midwestern States*. Bloomington: Indiana University Press, 1988.

Malone, Dumas, ed. *Dictionary of American Biography*. 44 vols. New York: Charles Scribner's Sons, 1933.

——. *Jefferson and His Time*. 6 vols. Boston: Little, Brown, 1948–1981.

Marshall, Howard W. *Folk Architecture in Little Dixie: A Regional Culture in Missouri*. Columbia: University of Missouri Press, 1981.

Marshall, Thomas M., ed. *The Life and Papers of Frederick Bates*. 2 vols. St. Louis: Missouri Historical Society, 1926.

Melton, Emory. *Delaware Town and the Swan Trading Post, 1822–1831*. Cassville, Mo.: privately printed, n.d.

Melville, Annabelle M. *Louis William DuBourg*. 2 vols. Chicago: Loyola University Press, 1986.

Merkel, Benjamin. *The Antislavery Controversy in Missouri, 1819–1865*. St. Louis: Washington University, 1942.

Merrill, Boynton, Jr. *Jefferson's Nephews: A Frontier Tragedy*. Princeton, N.J.: Princeton University Press, 1976.

Miller, John C. *The Wolf by the Ears: Thomas Jefferson and Slavery*. New York: The Free Press, 1977.

Moore, Glover. *The Missouri Controversy, 1819–1821*. Lexington: University Press of Kentucky, 1953.

Moore, John Hebron. *The Emergence of the Cotton Kingdom in the Old Southwest: Mississippi, 1770–1860*. Baton Rouge: Louisiana State University Press, 1988.

Moore, John Preston. *Revolt in Louisiana: The Spanish Occupation, 1766–1770*. Baton Rouge: Louisiana State University Press, 1976.

Moulton, Gary E., ed. *The Journals of the Lewis and Clark Expedition*. Lincoln: University of Nebraska Press, 1986–.

Musick, James B. *St. Louis as a Fortified Town*. St. Louis: R. F. Miller, 1941.

Nagel, Paul. *Missouri: A Bicentennial History*. New York: W. W. Norton, 1977.

Nasatir, Abraham P., ed. *Before Lewis and Clark: Documents Illustrating the History of Missouri, 1785–1804*. 2 vols. St. Louis: St. Louis Historical Documents Foundation, 1952.

——. *Borderland in Retreat*. Albuquerque: University of New Mexico Press, 1976.

——. *Spanish War Vessels on the Mississippi, 1792–1796*. New Haven: Yale University Press, 1968.

Norall, Frank. *Bourgmont: Explorer of the Missouri, 1698–1725*. Lincoln: University of Nebraska Press, 1988.

O'Brien, Michael, et al. *Grassland, Forest, and Historical Settlement: An Analysis of Dynamics in Northeast Missouri*. Lincoln: University of Nebraska Press, 1984.

Oglesby, Richard E. *Manuel Lisa and the Opening of the Missouri Fur Trade*. Norman: University of Oklahoma Press, 1963.

Palm, Mary Borgia. *Jesuit Missions in the Illinois Country, 1673–1763*. Cleveland: Sisters of Notre Dame, 1933.

Peck, John Mason. *Father Clark or the Pioneer Preacher*. New York: Sheldon, Lamport & Blakeman, 1855.

——. *Forty Years of Pioneer Life*. Philadelphia: American Baptist Publication Society, 1864.

Penick, James L., Jr. *The New Madrid Earthquakes of 1811–1812*. Columbia: University of Missouri Press, 1976.

Peterson, Charles E. *Colonial St. Louis: Building a Creole Capital*. St. Louis: Missouri Historical Society, 1949.

Peterson, Merrill, ed. *Thomas Jefferson: Writings*. New York: The Library of America, 1984.

Phillips, Paul C. *The Fur Trade.* 2 vols. Norman: University of Oklahoma Press, 1961.

Pomeroy, Earl S. *The Territories and the United States, 1861–1890: Studies in Colonial Administration.* Philadelphia: University of Pennsylvania Press, 1947.

Primm, James Neal. *Lion of the Valley: St. Louis, Missouri.* Boulder: Pruett, 1981.

Prucha, Paul Francis. *The Sword of the Republic: The United States Army on the Frontier, 1783–1846.* New York: Macmillan, 1969.

Rissover, Jean, ed. and illustrator. *Missouri History on the Table: 250 Years of Good Cooking and Goood Eating.* Ste. Genevieve, Mo.: Ste. Genevieve 250th Celebration Commission, 1985.

Ronda, James P. *Lewis and Clark Among the Indians.* Lincoln: University of Nebraska Press, 1984.

Rothensteiner, John E. *History of the Archdiocese of St. Louis.* 2 vols. St. Louis: Blackwell Wielandy Co., 1928.

Sauer, Carl O. *The Geography of the Ozark Highland of Missouri.* Chicago: University of Chicago Press, 1920.

Savelle, Max. *George Morgan: Colony Builder.* New York: Columbia University Press, 1932.

Schoolcraft, Henry Rowe. *Journal of a Tour into the Interior of Missouri and Arkansaw . . . in the Year 1818 and 1819.* London: Sir R. Phillips and Co., 1821.

———. *Scenes and Adventures in the Semi-Alpine Region of the Ozark Mountains of Missouri and Arkansas.* Philadelphia: Lippincott, Grambo & Co., 1853.

———. *A View of the Lead Mines of Missouri.* New York: C. Wiley & Co., 1819.

Schultz, Christian. *Travels on an Inland Voyage.* 2 vols. New York: Isaac Riley, 1810.

Sheehan, Bernard W. *Seeds of Extinction: Jeffersonian Philanthropy and the American Indian.* Chapel Hill: University of North Carolina Press, 1973.

Shoemaker, Floyd C. *Missouri and Missourians: Land of Contrasts and People of Achievements.* Chicago: Lewis Publishing Company, 1943.

———. *Missouri's Struggle for Statehood, 1804–1821.* Jefferson City, Mo.: Hugh Stephens Printing Co., 1916.

Smelser, Marshall. *The Democratic Republic, 1801–1815.* New York: Harper and Row, 1968.

Sobel, Mechal. *The World They Made Together: Black and White in Eighteenth-Century Virginia.* Princeton: Princeton University Press, 1987.

Steffen, Jerome O. *William Clark: Jeffersonian Man on the Frontier.* Norman: University of Oklahoma Press, 1977.

Stiles, Henry Reed, ed. *Joutel's Journal of La Salle's Last Voyage, 1684–1687.* Albany, N.Y.: Joseph McDonough, 1906.

Stoddard, Amos. *Sketches, Historical and Descriptive of Upper Louisiana.* Philadelphia: Matthew Carey, 1812.

Taylor, Roger W. *Watershed-I: Swamp Hawk.* Ballwin, Mo.: Kestrel Productions, 1984.

Temple, Wayne C. *Indian Villages of the Illinois Country: Springfield.* Illinois State Museum Scientific Papers. Vol. 2, pt. 2., 1958.

Thomas, Alfred Barnaby. *After Coronado: Spanish Exploration Northeast of New Mexico, 1696–1727.* Norman: University of Oklahoma Press, 1935.

Thomas, Rosemary Hyde. *It's Good to Tell You: French Folk Tales from Missouri.* Columbia: University of Missouri Press, 1981.

Thurman, Melburn D. *Building a House in 18th-Century Ste. Genevieve.* Ste. Genevieve, Mo.: Pendragon's Press, 1984.

Thwaites, Reuben Gold, ed. *Collections of the State Historical Society of Wisconsin.* Vols. 11–20. Madison: State Historical Society of Wisconsin, 1888–1911.

———. *The Jesuit Relations and Allied Documents.* 73 vols. Cleveland: Burrows Brothers, 1896–1901.

Trexler, Harrison A. *Slavery in Missouri, 1804–1865.* Baltimore: Johns Hopkins University Press, 1914.

Tucker, Frank C. *The Methodist Church in Missouri, 1789–1939.* Nashville: Parthenon Press, 1966.

Villiers du Terrage, Baron Marc de. *The Last Ten Years of French Louisiana,* edited by Carl A. Brasseaux and Glenn R. Conrad; translated by Hosea Phillips. Lafayette: University of Southwestern Louisiana Press, 1982.

Wade, Richard C. *The Urban Frontier.* Paperback ed. Chicago: University of Chicago Press, 1964.

Walters, Raymond D. *Albert Gallatin: Jeffersonian Financier and Diplomat.* New York: Macmillan, 1957.

Whitaker, Arthur P. *The Mississippi Question, 1795–1803.* New York: D. Appleton-Century Co., 1934.

————. *The Spanish-American Frontier, 1783–1795*. Boston: Houghton Mifflin Co., 1927.

Wiecek, William M. *The Sources of Antislavery Constitutionalism in America, 1760–1848*. Ithaca, N.Y.: Cornell University Press, 1977.

Williams, Gwyn A. *Madoc: The Making of a Myth*. London: Eyre Methuen, 1979.

ARTICLES

Able, Annie H. "The History of Events Resulting in Indian Consolidation West of the Mississippi." *Annual Report of the American Historical Association*. Vol. I. Washington, D.C.: Government Printing Office, 1906, 235–450.

Abramoske, Donald J. "The Federal Lead Leasing System in Missouri." *MHR* 54 (October 1959): 27–38.

Aiton, Arthur S. "The Diplomacy of the Louisiana Cession." *American Historical Review* 36 (July 1931): 701–20.

Ashton, John. "A History of Hogs and Pork Production in Missouri." *Monthly Bulletin of the Missouri State Board of Agriculture* 20 (January 1923): 3–75.

————. "History of Shorthorns in Missouri Prior to the Civil War." *Monthly Bulletin of the Missouri State Board of Agriculture* 21 (November 1923): 3–87.

Baade, Hans W. "The Law of Slavery in Spanish Louisiana, 1769–1803." In *Louisiana's Legal Heritage*, edited by Edward F. Haas and Robert R. Macdonald, 43–56. Pensacola, Fla.: Perdido Bay Press for the Louisiana State Museum, 1983.

Baker, Vaughn, Amos Simpson, and Mathé Allain. "Le Mari est Seigneur: Martial Laws Governing Women in French Louisiana." In *Louisiana's Legal Heritage*, edited by Edward F. Haas and Robert R. Mcdonald, 7–18. Pensacola, Fla.: Perdido Bay Press for the Louisiana State Museum, 1983.

Bannon, John Francis. "Black Robe Frontiersman: Gabriel Marest, S.J." *BMHS* 10 (April 1954): 351–66.

————. "Jacques Marquette, 1637–1675." *MHR* 64 (October 1969): 81–87.

Barbeau, Marius. "Voyageur Songs of the Missouri." *BMHS* 10 (April 1954): 336–50.

Bloom, Jo Tice. "Daniel Boone: Trailblazer to a Nation." *Gateway Heritage* 5 (Spring 1985): 28–39.

Boyle, Susan. "Did She Generally Decide? Women in Ste. Genevieve, 1750–1805." *William and Mary Quarterly* 44 (October 1987): 775–89.

Bray, Robert T. "Bourgmond's Fort d'Orleans and the Missouri Indians." *MHR* 75 (October 1980): 1–32.

————. "The Missouri Indian Tribe in Archaeology and History." *MHR* 55 (April 1961): 213–25.

Brown, Margaret Kimball. "Allons, Cowboys!" *Journal of the Illinois State Historical Society* 76 (Winter 1983): 273–82.

Burgess, Charles E. "The DeSoto Myth in Missouri." *BMHS* 24 (July 1968): 303–25.

Caldwell, Norman W. "Charles Juchereau de Saint-Denis: A French Pioneer in the Mississippi Valley." *MVHR* 28 (March 1942): 563–80.

Carter, Clarence E. "The Burr-Wilkinson Intrigue in St. Louis." *BMHS* 10 (July 1954): 447–64.

Chambers, William N. "Pistols and Politics: Incidents in the Career of Thomas H. Benton, 1816–1818." *BMHS* 5 (October 1948): 5–17.

Chapman, Carl H. "The Indomitable Osages in Spanish Illinois (Upper Louisiana), 1763–1804." In *The Spanish in the Mississippi Valley*, edited by John Francis McDermott, 287–312. Urbana: University of Illinois Press, 1974.

Chaput, Donald. "The Early Missouri Graduates of West Point: Officers or Merchants?" *MHR* 72 (April 1978): 262–70.

Christelow, Allan. "Proposals for a French Company for Spanish Louisiana, 1763–1764." *MVHR* 27 (March 1941): 603–11.

Christensen, Lawrence O. "Cyprion Clamorgan, the Colored Aristocracy of St. Louis." *BMHS* 31 (October 1974): 3–31.

————. "Missouri: The Heart of the Nation." In *Heartland: Comparative Histories of the Midwestern States*, edited by James H. Madison, 86–106. Bloomington: Indiana University Press, 1988.

Cleland, Hugh C. "John B. C. Lucas, Physiocrat on the Frontier." *The Western Pennsylvania Historical Magazine*, part 1: 36 (March 1953): 1–15; part 2: 36 (June 1953): 87–100; part 3: 36 (September-December 1953): 141–68.

Coles, Harry L., Jr. "Applicability of the Public Land System in Louisiana." *MVHR* 43 (June 1956): 39–58.

Corbett, Katherine T. "Veuve Chouteau: A 250th Anniversary." *Gateway Heritage* 3 (Spring 1983): 42–48.

Cozzens, Arthur B. "The Iron Industry of Missouri." *MHR* 35 (July 1941): 509–38.

Cronon, William, and Richard White. "Indians in the Land." *American Heritage* 37 (August/September 1986): 19–25.

Dart, Henry P., ed. "Oath of Allegiance to Spain." *Louisiana Historical Quarterly* 4 (April 1921): 205–15.

Davis, Ronald L. F. "Community and Conflict in Pioneer Saint Louis, Missouri." *Western Historical Quarterly* 10 (July 1979): 337–55.

De Menil, Alexander. "A Century of Missouri Literature." *MHR* 15 (October 1920): 74–125.

Denman, David. "History of 'La Saline': Salt Manufacturing Site, 1675–1825." *MHR* 78 (April 1979): 307–20.

Denny, James M. "Early Southern Domestic Architecture in Missouri, 1810–1840: The 'Georgianization' of the Trans-Mississippi West." *Pioneer America Society Transactions* 8 (1985): 11–22.

Din, Gilbert. "The Immigration Policy of Governor Esteban Miró in Spanish Louisiana." *Southwestern Historical Quarterly* 73 (October 1969): 155–75.

———. "Protecting the 'Barrera': Spain's Defenses in Louisiana, 1763–1779." *Louisiana History* 19 (Spring 1978): 183–211.

———. "Spain's Immigration Policy in Louisiana and the American Penetration, 1792–1803." *Southwestern Historical Quarterly* 76 (January 1973): 255–76.

"Documents Relating to the Attack Upon St. Louis in 1780." *Missouri Historical Society Collections* 2 (July 1906): 41–54.

Dorsey, Dorothy P. "The Panic of 1819 in Missouri." *MHR* 29 (January 1935): 79–91.

Douglas, Walter B. "The Spanish Domination of Upper Louisiana." In *Proceedings of the State Historical Society of Wisconsin for 1913*, 74–90. Madison: State Historical Society of Wisconsin, 1914.

Drumm, Stella M. "Samuel Hammond." *Missouri Historical Society Collections* 4 (1923): 402–22.

Eccles, W. J. "The Fur Trade and Eighteenth-Century Imperialism." *William and Mary Quarterly* 40 (July 1983): 341–62.

Ekberg, Carl. "Antoine Valentin de Gruy: Early Missouri Explorer." *MHR* 76 (January 1982): 136–50.

Ellenwood, Dewitt, Jr. "Protestantism Enters St. Louis: The Presbyterians." *BMHS* 12 (April 1956): 253–73.

Ellis, Richard N., and Charlie R. Steen, eds. "An Indian Delegation in France." *Journal of the Illinois State Historical Society* 67 (September 1974): 385–405.

Emmons, Ben L. "The Founding of St. Charles and Blanchette Its Founder." *MHR* 18 (July 1924): 507–20.

Faherty, William Barnaby. "The Personality and Influence of Louis William DuBourg, Bishop of 'Louisiana and the Floridas' (1776–1833)." In *Frenchmen and French Ways in the Mississippi Valley*, edited by John Francis McDermott, 43–55. Urbana: University of Illinois Press, 1969.

———. "St. Louis College: First Community School." *BMHS* 24 (January 1968): 122–38.

Fisher, Robert L. "The Treaties of Portage des Sioux." *MVHR* 19 (March 1933): 495–508.

Flanders, Robert. "Caledonia, Ozarks Legacy of the High Scotch-Irish." *Gateway Heritage* 6 (Spring 1986): 34–52.

Foley, William E. "The American Territorial System: Missouri's Experience." *MHR* 65 (July 1971): 403–26.

———. "Antebellum Missouri in Historical Perspective." *MHR* 82 (January 1988): 179–90.

———. "Different Notions of Justice: The Case of the 1808 St. Louis Murder Trials." *Gateway Heritage* 9 (Winter 1988–1989): 2–13.

———. "Justus Post: Portrait of a Frontier Land Speculator." *BMHS* 36 (October 1979): 19–26.

———. "The Laclède-Chouteau Puzzle: John Francis McDermott Supplies Some Missing Pieces." *Gateway Heritage* 4 (Fall 1983): 18–25.

———. "The Lewis and Clark Expedition's Silent Partners: The Chouteau Brothers of St. Louis." *MHR* 77 (January 1983): 131–46.

———. "Slave Freedom Suits Before Dred Scott: The Case of Marie Jean Scypion's Descendants." *MHR* 79 (October 1984): 1–23.

Foley, William E., and C. David Rice. "Pierre Chouteau, Entrepreneur as Indian Agent." *MHR* 72 (July 1978): 365–87.

———. "The Return of the Mandan Chief." *Montana, the Magazine of Western History* 29 (July 1979): 2–15.

———. "'Touch Not a Stone': An 1841 Appeal to Save the Historic Chouteau Mansion." *Gateway Heritage* 4 (Winter 1983–1984): 14–19.

———. "Visiting the President: An Exercise in Jeffersonian Indian Diplomacy." *American West* 16 (November/December 1979): 4–14, 56.

Foreman, Grant, ed. "Notes of Auguste Chouteau on Indian Boundaries of Various Indian Nations." In *Missouri Historical Society's Glimpses of the Past* (October-December 1940): 119–40.

Gardner, James A. "The Business Career of Moses Austin in Missouri, 1798–1821." *MHR* 50 (April 1956): 235–47.

Garraghan, Gilbert J. "First Settlement on the Site of St. Louis." In *Chapters in Frontier History: Research Studies in the Making of the West*, 73–84. Milwaukee, 1934.

———. "Fort Orleans of the Missoury." *MHR* 35 (April 1941): 373–84.

Garrison, George P., ed. "A Memorandum of Moses Austin's Journey, 1796–1797." *American Historical Review* 5 (April 1900): 518–42.

Gerlach, Russel. "Spanish Land Grants in Missouri." *Missouri Geographer* 20 (Fall 1973): 10–11.

Giraud, Marcel. "Etienne Veniard De Bourgmont's 'Exact Description of Louisiana.'" *BMHS* 15 (October 1958): 3–19.

Gracy, David B. "Moses Austin and the Development of the Missouri Lead Industry." *Gateway Heritage* 1 (Spring 1981): 42–48.

Graham, Hugh. "Ste. Genevieve Academy: Missouri's First Secondary School." *Mid-America* 4 (October 1932): 67–79.

Gregg, Kate L. "Building the First American Fort West of the Mississippi." *MHR* 30 (July 1936): 345–64.

———. "The History of Fort Osage." *MHR* 34 (July 1940): 439–88.

———. "The War of 1812 on the Missouri Frontier." *MHR* 33 (October 1938): 3–22.

Guenther, Charles. "An Early St. Louis Poet: Pierre François Regnier." In *The French in the Mississippi Valley*, edited by John Francis McDermott, 59–80. Urbana: University of Illinois Press, 1965.

Hagan, William T. "The Sauk and Fox Treaty of 1804." *MHR* 51 (October 1956): 1–7.

Hall, F. R. "Genet's Western Intrigue, 1793–1794." *Journal of the Illinois Historical Society* 21 (October 1928): 359–81.

Hibbert, Wilfrid. "Major Amos Stoddard: First Governor of Upper Louisiana and Hero of Fort Meigs." *The Historical Society of Northwestern Ohio Quarterly Bulletin* 2 (April 1930): n.p.

Hicks, Frederick C. "Territorial Revenue System of Missouri." *Missouri Historical Society Collections* 1 (1896): 25–40.

Hill, Leslie Gamblin. "A Moral Crusade: The Influence of Protestantism on Frontier Society in Missouri." *MHR* 45 (October 1950): 16–34.

Holt, Glen. "The Heritage of Transportation." In *Heritage of St. Louis*, Veiled Prophet Fair Program and Magazine, 1982.

———. "St. Louis's Transition Decade, 1819–1830." *MHR* 76 (July 1982): 365–81.

Hunter, Lloyd A. "Slavery in St. Louis, 1804–1860." *BMHS* 30 (July 1974): 233–65.

Jackson, Donald. "Old Fort Madison, 1808–1813." *The Palimpsest* 47 (January 1966): 1–62.

Jennings, Francis. "The Discovery of Americans." *William and Mary Quarterly* 41 (July 1984): 436–43.

Jordan, Terry G., and Matti Kaups. "Folk Architecture in Cultural and Ecological Context." *Geographical Review* 77 (January 1987): 52–75.

Keller, Kenneth W. "Alexander McNair and John B. C. Lucas: The Background of Early Missouri Politics." *BMHS* 33 (July 1977): 231–45.

Kinnaird, Lawrence. "American Penetration into Spanish Louisiana." In *New Spain and the Anglo-American West*, edited by George P. Hammond, 1:211–37. Lancaster, Pa.: Lancaster Press, 1932.

———, ed. "The Clark-Leyba Papers." *American Historical Review* 41 (October 1935): 92–112.

———. "The Spanish Expedition Against Fort St. Joseph in 1781: A New Interpretation." *MVHR* 19 (September 1932): 173–91.

Kirkpatrick, R. L. "Professional, Religious, and Social Aspects of St. Louis Life, 1804–1816." *MHR* 44 (July 1950): 373–86.

Klemp, Alberta H. "Early Methodism in the New Madrid Circuit." *MHR* 69 (October 1974): 23–47.

Knudson, Jerry W. "Newspaper Reaction to the Louisiana Purchase: 'This New, Immense, Unbounded World.'" *MHR* 63 (January 1969): 182–213.

Kushner, Howard I. "The Suicide of Meriwether Lewis: A Psychoanalytic Inquiry." *William and Mary Quarterly* 38 (July 1981): 464–81.

Kyte, George W. "A Spy on the Western Waters: The Military Intelligence Mission of General Collot in 1796." *MVHR* 34 (December 1947): 427–42.

Lance, Donald M. "The Origin and Pronunciation of 'Missouri.'" *Missouri Folklore Society Journal* 7 (1985): 1–27.

Liljegren, Ernest R. "Frontier Education in Spanish Louisiana." *MHR* 35 (April 1941): 345–72.

———. "Jacobinism in Spanish Louisiana." *Louisiana Historical Quarterly* 22 (January 1939): 47–97.

Loeb, Isidor. "The Beginnings of Missouri Legislation." *MHR* 1 (October 1906): 53–71.

McDermott, John F. "The Confines of Wilderness." *MHR* 29 (October 1934): 3–12.

———. "Culture and the Missouri Frontier." *MHR* 50 (July 1956): 355–70.

———. "The Exclusive Trade Privileges of Maxent, Laclède and Company." *MHR* 29 (July 1935): 272–78.

———. "Museums in Early St. Louis." *BMHS* 4 (April 1948): 129–38.

———. "The Myth of the 'Imbecile Governor': Captain Fernando de Leyba and the Defense of St. Louis in 1780." In his *The Spanish in the Mississipi Valley, 1762–1804,* 314–405. Urbana: University of Illinois Press, 1974.

———. "Myths and Realities Concerning the Founding of St. Louis." In his *The French in the Mississippi Valley,* 1–15. Urbana: University of Illinois Press, 1965.

———. "Paincourt and Poverty." *Mid-America* 5 (April 1934): 210–12.

———. "Private Schools in St. Louis, 1809–1821." *Mid-America* 11 (April 1940): 96–119.

———. "Travelers on the Western Waters." *Proceedings of the American Antiquarian Society* 77 (1968): 255–80.

McMillan, Margaret, and Monia C. Morris. "Educational Opportunities in Early Missouri." *MHR* 33 (April 1939): 307–25.

Magnaghi, Russell M. "The Belle Fontaine Indian Factory, 1805–1808." *MHR* 75 (July 1981): 396–416.

———. "The Role of Indian Slavery in Colonial St. Louis." *BMHS* 31 (July 1975): 264–72.

March, David. "The Admission of Missouri." *MHR* 65 (July 1971): 427–49.

Marshall, Howard W. "How to Say 'Missouri.'" *Midwestern Journal of Language and Folklore* 12 (Spring 1986): 5–14.

Morrow, Lynn. "New Madrid and Its Hinterland, 1783–1826." *BMHS* 36 (July 1980): 241–50.

———. "Trader William Gilliss and Delaware Migration in Southern Missouri." *MHR* 75 (January 1981): 147–67.

———. "The Yocum Silver Dollar: Image, Realities to Traditions." In *The German-American Experience in Missouri: Essays in Commemoration of the Tricentennial of German Immigration to America, 1683–1983,* edited by Howard W. Marshall and James W. Goodrich, 159–75. Columbia: Missouri Cultural Heritage Center, 1986.

Morrow, Lynn, and Dan Saults. "The Yocum Silver Dollar: Sorting Out the Strands of an Ozarks Frontier Legend." *Gateway Heritage* 5 (Winter 1984–1985): 8–15.

Murphy, Lawrence E. "Beginning of Methodism in Missouri, 1798–1824." *MHR* 21 (April 1927): 370–94.

Nasatir, Abraham P. "The Anglo-Spanish Frontier in the Illinois Country during the American Revolution, 1779–1783." *Journal of the Illinois State Historical Society* 21 (October 1928): 291–358.

———. "The Anglo-Spanish Frontier on the Upper Mississippi, 1786–1796." *Iowa Journal of History and Politics* 29 (April 1931): 155–232.

———. "Ducharme's Invasion of Missouri: An Incident in the Anglo-Spanish Rivalry for the Indian Trade of Missouri." *MHR,* part 1: 24 (October 1929): 3–22; part 2: 24 (January 1930): 238–60; part 3: 24 (April 1930): 420–39.

———. "The Formation of the Missouri Company." *MHR* 25 (October 1930): 10–22.

———. "Jacques Clamorgan, Colonial Promoter of the Northern Border of New Spain." *New Mexico Historical Review* 17 (April 1942): 101–12.

———. "Jacques d' Eglise." In *The Mountain Men and the Fur Trade of the Far West,* edited by Leroy Hafen, 2:123–34. Glendale, Calif.: Arthur H. Clark, 1966.

———. "James Mackay." In *The Mountain Men and the Fur Trade of the Far West*, edited by Leroy Hafen, 4:185–206. Glendale, Calif.: Arthur H. Clark, 1966.

———. "John T. Evans." In *The Mountain Men and the Fur Trade of the Far West*, edited by Leroy Hafen, 3:99–117. Glendale, Calif.: Arthur H. Clark, 1966.

———. "St. Louis During the British Attack of 1780." In *New Spain and the Anglo-American West*, edited by George P. Hammond, 1:239–61. Lancaster, Pa.: Lancaster Press, 1932.

Ogilvie, Leon P. "Governmental Efforts at Reclamation in the Southeast Missouri Lowlands." *MHR* 64 (January 1970): 150–76.

Peterson, Charles. "Early Ste. Genevieve and Its Architecture." *MHR* 35 (January 1941): 207–32.

———. "The Houses of French St. Louis." In *The French in the Mississippi Valley*, edited by John Francis McDermott, 17–40. Urbana: University of Illinois Press, 1965.

Phelps, Dawson A. "The Tragic Death of Meriwether Lewis." *William and Mary Quarterly* 13 (July 1956): 305–18.

Poole, Stafford. "The Founding of Missouri's First College: Saint Mary's of the Barrens, 1815–1818." *MHR* 65 (October 1970): 1–22.

Price, Anna. "The Three Lives of Fort de Chartres: French Outpost on the Mississippi." *Historic Illinois* 3 (June 1980): 1–4.

Price, James. "The Widow Harris Cabin Site: A Place in the Ozarks." *OzarksWatch* 1 (Spring 1988): 6–8.

Read, Allen Walker. "Pronunciation of the Word 'Missouri.'" *American Speech* 8 (December 1933): 22–36.

Rehkopf, Charles F. "The Beginnings of the Episcopal Church in Missouri, 1819–1844." *BMHS* 11 (April 1955): 265–78.

Reichard, Maximilian. "Black and White on the Urban Frontier: The St. Louis Community in Transition, 1800–1830." *BMHS* 33 (October 1976): 3–17.

Richardson, Lemont K. "Private Land Claims in Missouri." *MHR*, part 1: 50 (January 1956): 132–44; part 2: 50 (April 1956): 271–86; part 3: 50 (July 1956): 387–99.

Ronda, James P. "Dreams and Discoveries: Exploring the American West, 1760–1815." *William and Mary Quarterly* 46 (January 1989): 145–62.

Rothensteiner, John E. "Earliest History of Mine La Motte." *MHR* 20 (January 1926): 199–213.

———. "The Missouri Priest." *MHR* 21 (July 1927): 562–69.

Rutman, Darrett. "Assessing the Little Communities of Early America." *William and Mary Quarterly* 43 (April 1986): 163–78.

Schroeder, Walter A. "Spread of Settlement in Howard County, Missouri, 1810–1859." *MHR* 63 (October 1968): 1–37.

Shepherd, William R. "The Cession of Louisiana to Spain." *Political Science Quarterly* 19 (September 1904): 439–58.

———. "Wilkinson and the Beginnings of the Spanish Conspiracy." *AHR* 9 (April 1904): 490–506.

———, ed. "Papers Bearing on James Wilkinson's Relations with Spain, 1787–1789." *AHR* 9 (July 1904): 748–66.

Shoemaker, Floyd. "Cape Girardeau, Most American of Missouri's Original Five Counties." *MHR* 50 (October 1955): 49–61.

———. "Herculaneum Shot Tower." *MHR* 20 (January 1926): 214–16.

Simmons, Lucy. "The Rise and Growth of Protestant Bodies in the Missouri Territory." *MHR* 22 (April 1928): 296–306.

Spencer, Joab. "John Clark, Pioneer Preacher and Founder of Methodism in Missouri." *MHR* 5 (April 1911): 174–77.

Steffen, Jerome O. "William Clark: A New Perspective on Missouri Territorial Politics, 1813–1820." *MHR* 67 (January 1973): 171–97.

Stephens, E. W. "History of Missouri Baptist General Association." *MHR* 7 (January 1913): 76–88.

Strickland, Arvarh E. "Aspects of Slavery in Missouri, 1821." *MHR* 65 (July 1971): 505–26.

Temple, Wayne C. "The Piasa Bird: Fact or Fiction." *Journal of the Illinois State Historical Society* 49 (Fall 1956): 308–27.

Thomas, Rosemary Hyde. "La Guillonnée: A French Holiday Custom in the Mississippi Valley." *Mid-South Folklore* 6 (Winter 1978): 77–84.

Usner, Daniel H., Jr. "The Frontier Exchange Economy of the Lower Mississippi Valley in the Eighteenth Century." *William and Mary Quarterly* 44 (April 1987): 165–92.

Van Ravenswaay, Charles. "The Creole Arts and Crafts of Upper Louisiana." *BMHS* 12 (April 1956): 213–48.
Viles, Jonas. "Old Franklin: A Frontier Town of the Twenties." *MVHR* 9 (March 1923): 269–82.
Violette, Eugene M. "The Black Code in Missouri." *Proceedings of the Mississippi Valley Historical Association* 6 (1912–1913): 287–316.
————. "Spanish Land Claims in Missouri." *Washington University Studies* 8 (April 1921): 167–200.
Vogel, Virgil J. "The Origin and Meaning of 'Missouri.'" *BMHS* 16 (April 1960): 213–22.
Voss, Stuart F. "Town Growth in Central Missouri, 1815–1880: An Urban Chaparral." *MHR*, part 1: 64 (October 1969): 64–80.
Wamble, Hugh. "Negroes and Missouri Protestant Churches." *MHR* 61 (April 1967): 321–47.
Webre, Stephen. "The Problem of Indian Slavery in Spanish Louisiana, 1769–1803." *Louisiana History* 25 (Spring 1984): 117–35.
Wedel, Mildred Mott. "Claude-Charles Dutisné: A Review of His 1719 Journeys." *Great Plains Journal*, part 1: 12 (Fall 1972): 4–25; part 2: 12 (Spring 1973): 146–73.
Whitaker, Arthur. "The Retrocession of Louisiana in Spanish Policy." *AHR* 39 (April 1934): 454–76.
Windell, Marie George. "The Camp Meeting in Missouri." *MHR* 37 (April 1943): 253–70.
————, ed. "The Road West in 1818: The Diary of Henry Vest Bingham." *MHR*, part 1: 40 (October 1945): 21–54.
Wood, Peter H. "La Salle: Discovery of a Lost Explorer." *AHR* 89 (April 1984): 294–323.
Wood, W. Raymond. "The John Evans 1796–97 Map of the Missouri River." *Great Plains Quarterly* 1 (Winter 1981): 39–53.
————. "Mapping the Missouri River Through the Great Plains, 1673–1895." *Great Plains Quarterly* 4 (Winter 1984): 29–42.
————. "Nicolas de Finiels: Mapping the Mississippi and Missouri Rivers, 1797–1798." *MHR* 81 (July 1987): 387–402.
Wyatt-Brown, Bertram. "The Antimission Movement in the Jacksonian South: A Study in Regional Folk Culture." *Journal of Southern History* 36 (November 1970): 501–29.

THESES, DISSERTATIONS, REPORTS, AND UNPUBLISHED PAPERS

Boyle, Susan. "Opportunities and Inequality: Wealth Distribution in Early Ste. Genevieve." Unpublished paper presented at Social Science History Meeting, Washington, D.C., 1983.
Conrad, Glenn R. "The Administrative Controversies over the Illinois Country." Unpublished paper presented at Annual Meeting of the Louisiana Historical Association, Shreveport, March 1986.
Denny, James M. "McKendree Chapel." National Register of Historic Places Inventory— Nomination Form. Jefferson City: Missouri Department of Natural Resources, 1984.
Dugger, Harold. "Reading Interest and the Book Trade in Frontier Missouri." Ph.D. diss., University of Missouri–Columbia, 1951.
Flanders, Robert. "Caledonia: An Ozarks Village, History, Geography, Architecture." Springfield, Mo.: Center for Ozark Studies, 1984.
Folmer, Henri. "French Expansion Toward New Mexico in the Eighteenth Century." M.A. thesis, University of Denver, 1939.
Forderhase, Rudolph Eugene. "Jacksonianism in Missouri from Predilection to Party, 1820–1836." Ph.D. diss., University of Missouri–Columbia, 1968.
Green, Susan. "The Material Culture of a Pre-enclosure Village in Upper Louisiana: Open Fields, Houses, and Cabinetry in Colonial Ste. Genevieve, 1750–1804." M.A. thesis, University of Missouri–Columbia, 1983.
Knox, William F. "The Constitutional and Legal Basis of Public Education in Missouri." Ed.D. diss., University of Missouri–Columbia, 1938.
Melom, Halvor Gordon. "The Economic Development of St. Louis, 1803–1846." Ph.D. diss., University of Missouri–Columbia, 1947.
Overby, Osmund. "House and Home in the New Village of Ste. Genevieve." Paper presented at Ste. Genevieve Seminar, Ste. Genevieve, Mo., October 1985.
Rollings, Willard. "Prairie Hegemony: An Ethnohistorical Study of the Osage from Early Times to 1840." Ph.D. diss., Texas Tech University, 1983.
Ronnebaum, Chelidonia. "Population and Settlement in Missouri, 1804–1820." M.A. thesis, University of Missouri–Columbia, 1936.

Schroeder, Walter. "Settlement of the Historic Ste. Genevieve District, 1790–1819." Paper presented at Ste. Genevieve Seminar, Ste. Genevieve, Mo., October 1985.

Thorne, Tanis Chapman. "People of the River: Mixed-Blood Families on the Lower Missouri." Ph.D. diss., UCLA, 1987.

Tice, Nancy Jo. "The Territorial Delegate, 1794–1820." Ph.D. diss., University of Wisconsin–Madison, 1967.

Westover, John G. "The Evolution of the Missouri Militia, 1804–1819." Ph.D. diss., University of Missouri–Columbia, 1948.

COLLECTIONS AND PAPERS

Library of Congress, Washington, D.C.
    Breckinridge Family Papers.
    Jefferson, Thomas, Papers.
    Madison, James, Papers.
    Monroe, James, Papers.
Lovejoy Library, Southern Illinois University–Edwardsville.
    Finiels, Nicolas de. "Notice sur la Louisiane Supérieure."
    McDermott, John Francis. Mississippi Valley Research Collection.
Missouri Historical Society, St. Louis, Mo.
    Billon Papers.
    Bissell, Daniel, Papers.
    Bourgmont, Sieur de, Papers.
    Carr, William C., Papers.
    Clark Family Papers.
    Chouteau Collections.
    Chouteau, Pierre, Letterbook.
    Church Papers—Baptist.
    Church Papers—Presbyterian.
    Delassus Collection.
    Easton, Rufus, Papers.
    Emmons, Ben, Papers.
    Governors Papers.
    Graham, Richard, Papers.
    Gratiot, Charles, Letterbook.
    Gratiot Papers.
    Hempstead, Stephen, Letterbook.
    Hempstead Papers.
    Journals and Diaries Collection.
    Louisiana Purchase Papers.
    Louisiana Territory Papers.
    Lucas Collection.
    Post, Eliza, Memorandum Books.
    Post, Justus, Letters.
    Ste. Genevieve Papers.
    St. Louis Archives.
    St. Louis History Papers.
    Sibley Papers.
    Stoddard, Amos, Papers.
    Territorial Supreme Court Minute Books.
    Von Phul Family Papers.
    Washington County Papers.
    Wilkinson, James, Papers.
    Wilt, Christian, Letterbook.
Missouri State Archives, Jefferson City, Mo.
    Hunt, Theodore, compiler. Testimony Before the Recorder of Land Titles. St. Louis, 1825. 3 vols.
    Minute Books of the Board of Land Commissioners.
    U.S. v. William Tharp Case File.

National Archives, Washington, D.C.
  Auditor's Reports, 1804–1820.
  Letters of Application and Recommendation during the Administration of Thomas Jefferson.
  Letters Received by the Secretary of War Relative to Indian Affairs, 1800–1816, M–271.
  Letters Sent by the Secretary of War Relative to Indian Affairs, M–15.
New York Historical Society
  Gallatin, Albert, Papers.
St. Louis Mercantile Library, St. Louis, Mo.
  Auguste Chouteau's Narrative of the Founding of St. Louis.
  Bissell Papers.
  Journal of the Proceedings of the Territory of Louisiana, 3 [11] June 1806 to 9 October 1811.
State Historical Society of Missouri, Columbia, Mo.
  Representation and Petition of the Representatives Elected by the Freemen of the Territory of
    Louisiana. Washington City, 1805.
  Ste. Genevieve Archives, microfilm copy.
  Smith, Thomas A., Collections.
State Historical Society of Wisconsin, Madison.
  Draper Manuscripts.
  Boone, Nathan, Interview.
  Cole, Samuel, Testimony.
  Cooper, Benjamin, Testimony.
  Farmer, Barney, Testimony.
  Hempstead, Stephen, Testimony.
  Hyatt, Frederick, Testimony.
  Musick, Elizabeth, Testimony.

NEWSPAPERS
Boston Recorder.
Franklin Missouri Intelligencer.
St. Louis Missouri Gazette.
St. Louis Enquirer.

UNITED STATES GOVERNMENT DOCUMENTS
*American State Papers: Finance, Foreign Relations, Indian Affairs, Military Affairs, Public Lands,
  Miscellaneous.* 38 vols. Washington, D.C.: Gales & Seaton, 1832–1861.
Annals of the Congress of the United States, 1789–1824. 42 vols. Washington, D.C.: Gales & Seaton,
  1834–1836.
Biographical Directory of the American Congress, 1774–1927. Washington, D.C.: U.S. Government
  Printing Office, 1928.
Carter, Clarence E., ed. *The Territorial Papers of the United States.* Vol. 13, *Louisiana-Missouri,
  1803–1806* (1948); vol. 14, *Louisiana-Missouri, 1806–1814* (1949); vol. 15, *Louisiana-Missouri,
  1815–1821* (1954). Washington, D.C.: U.S. Government Printing Office, 1934–1962.
Laws for the Territory of Louisiana. St. Louis, 1808.
*Report of the Committee on Elections on the Memorial of Rufus Easton, contesting the election and
  returns of John Scott, the Delegate from the Territory of Missouri.* Washington, D.C., 1817.
*Report of the Committee on elections, to which was recommitted their report of the 31st ult. on the
  Petition of Rufus Easton, contesting the election of John Scott.* Washington, D.C., 1817.
U.S. Statutes at Large. Washington, D.C., 1850.

INDEX